AF701556

The Dow Jones-Irwin Guide to Financial Modeling

The Dow Jones-Irwin Guide to Financial Modeling

James R. Morris

DOW JONES-IRWIN
Homewood, Illinois 60430

© DOW JONES-IRWIN, 1987

All rights reserved. No part of this publication may be reproduced, stored in a retrieval system, or transmitted, in any form or by any means, electronic, mechanical, photocopying, recording, or otherwise, without the prior written permission of the publisher.

This publication is designed to provide accurate and authoritative information in regard to the subject matter covered. It is sold with the understanding that the publisher is not engaged in rendering legal, accounting, or other professional service. If legal advice or other expert assistance is required, the services of a competent professional person should be sought.

From a Declaration of Principles jointly adopted by a Committee of the American Bar Association and a Committee of Publishers.

ISBN 0-87094-748-6

Library of Congress Catalog Card No. 86-71214

Printed in the United States of America

1 2 3 4 5 6 7 8 9 0 K 4 3 2 1 0 9 8 7

PREFACE

In a business environment that has been growing more uncertain and risky, there is an increasing need for financial planning for business firms. Yet, until recently, organized financial planning efforts for business firms were frequently a very expensive luxury that appeared not to be worth the cost for many firms. For many other firms that most needed the planning, it couldn't be afforded. Nevertheless, the need was there, and an increasing number of business executives have recognized the need.

Now, the technology is available to make financial planning easier, more reliable, and much less expensive. The technological innovation that has made financial planning more attainable is the development and distribution of low-cost computers—personal microcomputers and the systems of desktop computers—and the availability of the programming software that is oriented toward financial planning.

The need for planning and modeling is there, and the technology to carry it out is there. What is missing is the knowledge and skill to develop financial planning models that are complete and correct. It is true that a growing number of financial managers and analysts are developing skill on small computers, and they exhibit a growing proficiency in using the relevant software packages such as Lotus, VisiCalc, Multiplan, IFPS, and others. Few of them, however, bring together these skills with the necessary knowledge about financial planning and modeling.

The purpose of this book is to help bridge these gaps. This

book is intended to present a clear and practical explanation of the ideas and concepts of financial planning and methods and techniques of financial modeling.

In response to the demand for more thorough explanation of financial planning, this book will present useful concepts and ideas about developing financial plans for the business firm. The necessary ingredients for developing an effective plan are discussed in a way that gives the novice planner a framework for handling most financial planning problems.

The more extensive corporate financial planning efforts require the construction of financial models. This book will help the prospective financial modeler to understand the necessary components of financial models by explaining in careful detail how financial models should be structured. The linkages and interrelationships between the various components are explained so the intelligent, conscientious nontechnician can design or at least understand the intricacies of a financial planning model. In addition, because there are numerous types of models, approaches to financial planning, and modeling techniques, this book discusses the various types of models, approaches, and techniques. The intent is to give the reader an understanding of how models can be used in the planning process and to develop an awareness of the types of models available. Familiar with the types of modeling techniques, the reader will be able to choose the appropriate model type or technique to fit the problem, and he or she will be able to assess knowledgeably the usefulness, advantages, and disadvantages of the modeling technique and, indeed, of the modeling effort itself.

The more specific objective of this work is to explain how to build models for financial planning. The essential features of financial models are explained to develop an understanding of how models should be constructed, how the components of the model should be linked together, and how the model structure relates to the financial objectives of the firm. If the reader understands the structure of the model, then he is prepared to develop a valid model on his own, or to understand the working of a model that was developed by someone else.

Armed with greater and deeper knowledge of financial models, the reader is equipped to assess the validity of a model and to evaluate its output. Consequently, the use of financial models need not be regarded as mysterious or suspicious by the informed nonmodeler, who now can use them more effectively.

One of the major roadblocks to successful modeling and planning in the past has been the gap between the computer expert who knew how to program a model, but knew little finance, and the financial expert who knew finance, but was ignorant of computers and modeling. This book is intended to help eliminate this gap by providing the financial personnel with the modeling background, and the computer personnel with the necessary financial knowledge.

Both should be able to develop independently a valid planning model without having to have an interpreter bring them together to pool their knowledge. If they both understand the purposes, structure, and problems of modeling, then each can contribute more effectively to the planning process.

While this book is focused on models that would be used on a computer, it is not focused on any particular software. It does not assume the reader is using IFPS, VisiCalc, or any other particular package. The material is presented in such a way that the reader learns about how to construct models and about the modeling process, regardless of the type of computer software used. Consequently, we don't present computer codes to perform a particular task. Rather, the logic or general equations to perform the task are discussed.

This book is written for the novice in planning and modeling. However, one cannot make a book totally self-contained without making it of encyclopedic length and scope. Some basic knowledge must be assumed. To derive the maximum benefit from this book, the reader should have a knowledge of the concepts of basic finance as would be taught in a university level course in financial management or in some accounting courses. Knowledge of present value, cost of capital, and capital budgeting is assumed. In addition, every effort has been made to avoid excessive or unnecessary mathematics or mathematical notation. In most instances, rather than using notation to denote variables, everyday words are used. Modeling, however, particularly optimization modeling, is inherently quantitative. Consequently, some compressed notation is used in the latter part of the book, and some knowledge of mathematical optimization techniques such as linear programming is helpful.

The book has been written with two different audiences in mind—practitioners and students. The practitioners that will find it useful include the planner who wants to know more about finance and modeling, the financial executive or analyst who needs to develop greater knowledge about planning and modeling, and the computer/information systems analyst who needs more background in planning, finance, and/or modeling.

The intended student audience includes more advanced and specialized classes, either graduate or undergraduate, that deal with financial planning and modeling. This book could be used as a supplement to other standard finance texts at an advanced level, or it could be used as a primary source to be supplemented with technical journal articles such as those cited in this book. This latter use would seem to be ideal for more advanced work. The extensive literature of planning, modeling, and optimization that exists as diverse journal articles needed some source to make it cohesive and provide some perspective. This need is met well by this book.

Finally, to give credit where it is due, I want to thank the friends who helped me complete this book: Estella Breitler for her cheerful efforts in typing the manuscript; Donald L. Stevens and the College of Business Administration of the University of Colorado at Denver for providing the time, support, and resources to complete the manuscript; Craig Kloer, my neighbor, for reading the draft and providing helpful comments; Rich Pettit of the University of Houston for his support and encouragement; colleagues Jean-Claude Bosch, James Suver, and Larry Johnston for providing helpful comments; and most of all, thanks to Judy, Suzanne, and Karen for being a nice family.

James R. Morris

CONTENTS

CHAPTER ONE Introduction: Planning, Modeling, and Computers 1

Reference.

CHAPTER TWO An Overview of Financial Planning 8

2.1 What Is Planning?

2.2 What Is Financial Planning?

2.3 The Input to Financial Planning.

The Goals of Financial Decisions. The Decision Alternatives. The Link between Decisions and Goals. Resources and Constraints. The Planning Horizon and the Amount of Detail.

2.4 What Do We Get Out of It?

References.

CHAPTER THREE The Tools of Financial Planning 29

3.1 Anticipating Seasonal Financing Needs with Cash Receipts and Disbursements.

3.2 Break-Even Analysis.

Degrees of Leverage. Revenues. Production and Costs.

3.3 Growth and Projecting the Needs for Financing.

3.4 Summary.

References.

CHAPTER FOUR Financial Modeling 80

4.1 What Is a Model?

4.2 What Does a Model Do?

4.3 Managerial Benefits of Modeling.
4.4 How to Develop the Model.
The Problem. The Output. The Structural Input. The Data Input.
4.5 Types of Models.
Simulation. Optimization.

CHAPTER FIVE An Introduction to Forecasting **104**
5.1 Quantitative Forecasting Methods.
Time Trend Extrapolation. Smoothing of Time Trends. Decomposition into Seasonal, Trend, and Cyclical Factors. Structural Econometric Forecasting Models. Time Series Models.
5.2 Subjective Forecasting.
5.3 Summary.

CHAPTER SIX Financial Simulation Models **147**
6.1 The Accounting Module.
Equations of the Module. Equilibrium in the Simulation Model.
6.2 The Income Generation Module.
Revenues. Cost Generation.
6.3 The Investment Module.
Adjustment to Sales. Direct Investment Evaluation.
6.4 The Financing Module.
Spontaneous Financing. Discretionary Sources of Financing. A Case Study Analyzing the Financing Decision.
6.5 Summary.
References.

CHAPTER SEVEN Dealing with Uncertainty **267**
7.1 Introduction.
7.2 Scenario Simulation.
7.3 Monte Carlo Simulation.
Simulation of NPV.

7.4 Risk Adjustment.
7.5 Conclusion.
References.

CHAPTER EIGHT Optimization Models for Financial Planning **293**
8.1 The Process of Optimization.
Constrained Optimization. Linear Programming.
8.2 Investment Decisions on a Limited Budget.
An Example of Capital Rationing. Elaborations on the Basic Model. The Transition to a Long-Range Planning Model.
8.3 A Linear Programming Model for the Planning and Management of Current Assets and Liabilities.
Planning Horizon. Decision Alternatives. Objective. The Link between Decisions and Goals. Constraints. The Completed Model. The Solution. Analysis of Results.
Summary.
References.

CHAPTER NINE Monitoring the Financial Plan **373**
References.

INDEX **385**

CHAPTER ONE

Introduction: Planning, Modeling, and Computers

Most intellectual, technological, and commercial advances occur when a number of different ideas or inventions become available and are combined. A familiar example is the introduction of the automobile, which required the invention of the internal combustion engine and Henry Ford's ideas of the assembly line and mass production to make it available to the common man. A similar marriage of ideas and technology is now taking place that will make financial planning far more widespread and effective than in the past. The technological advances have taken place in the areas of computer software and micro, or personal, computers. The ideological advance is that management, of necessity, is beginning to appreciate the value of financial planning and to want to develop and use planning models.

According to John Kenneth Galbraith, in *The New Industrial State,* the advance of technology makes planning an imperative. This advance and the concomitant specialization and division of labor have a number of consequences that necessitate planning. First, the administration of technological enterprises requires organization and specialized personnel. The tasks of the organization must be planned because they "must be performed so that they are right not for the present but for that time in the future when, companion and related work having also been done, the whole job is completed" (p.28).

Second, technology requires the commitment of more capital to the production process and a commitment of more time between investment of capital and the sale of the final product. These commitments mean that funds are tied inflexibly to the performance and success of a particular undertaking, and it is ever more important that the undertaking be successful. "So conditions at the time of completion of the whole task must be foreseen as must developments along the way. And steps must be taken to prevent, offset or otherwise neutralize the effect of adverse developments, and to insure that what is ultimately foreseen eventuates in fact."[1]

While our industrial system, based on an increasingly complex technology, has long required that businesses plan their production, planning has been given slight attention until very recently. There is good reason why planning efforts have been scanty in the past and why these efforts are now intensifying.

For more than 20 years after the end of World War II, the U.S. economic environment was fairly stable and safe for the business firm. During that period, domestic business was fairly well insulated from foreign competition. In this safe environment major planning efforts were less critical. The Full Employment Act of 1946 committed the federal government to the goal of maintaining full employment and stable prices. Moreover, during the postwar years the economy was sufficiently stable that both government and business began to believe that these goals could be attained.

In 1967 Galbraith argued that increasing technological complexity made planning both essential and difficult, and that the state would ease the task by absorbing the risks. Galbraith had the Keynesian faith that the government could deliver on the promise: "It can provide or guarantee a market for the product. And it can underwrite the costs of development so that if they increase beyond expectation the firm will not have to carry them. Or it can pay for and make available the necessary technical knowledge."[2]

In the 20-year postwar period Galbraith's faith was not misplaced. Government policy appeared able to absorb the risks and provide the guarantees necessary to make the business envi-

---

[1]John Kenneth Galbraith, *The New Industrial State* (New York: New American Library, 1967), p. 28.

[2]Ibid., p. 32.

ronment safe. It appeared that whatever government planning was necessary would be aimed at ensuring economic stability. Businesses would not have to commit substantial effort or resources to planning under such conditions.

The economic situation changed, however, becoming less manageable and more hostile. First, the growth of the international economy and accelerating competition from foreign companies limited the government's ability to provide an economic environment that was as safe as before. Second, events beginning in the mid 1970s converged so that the economy became much less stable, and the government's ability to control the economy with monetary and fiscal policy appeared to fade rapidly. The oil embargoes and energy shortages coincided with the beginning of a period of high inflation and high and volatile interest rates. The government was unable to control these factors without causing adverse effects to surface in other sectors of the economy.

More recently, the government has moved further away from guaranteeing the future for many businesses by the process of deregulation. Many industries previously had had their markets protected and stability guaranteed by an intricate framework of protective government regulation. Beginning in the late 1970s, and accelerating in the first half of the 80s, the government has retreated from this protective role and toward a policy of deregulation. Deregulation has forced many industries, including banking, transportation, and communications, to adapt to much stronger competition. Firms slow to make this adjustment have failed. Part of the necessary adaptive process has been the introduction of more careful planning of financial decisions.

In a changed economic environment that cannot or will not be planned and controlled by the government, planning has become far more essential for business firms. To survive in the more competitive and more hostile environment, businesses must plan for the things that can go wrong and protect themselves against the many possible disasters that could emanate from the economy.

Most people, when faced with a very risky task, will want to plan that task with great care. Imagine the person who must climb an 80-foot tower to repair a high-voltage line in a hurricane. Or, consider the soldier crossing a mine field with enemy riflemen also trying to terminate his trek. Faced with the difficulties and risks, either individual is probably more inclined to devise a plan than if the task presented fewer hazards.

Similarly, in the business environment, the greater the risk and uncertainty, and the more formidable the obstacles, the greater the necessity to plan. What we should plan for is uncertainty and risk. That is, we plan for the eventuality that the plan may go wrong. By planning, we are attempting to be prepared for misfortune, or as Galbraith puts it, planning implies "a sensible concern for what might happen in the future and a disposition, by forehanded action, to forestall avoidable misfortune."

Thus, with the economic environment more uncertain and the future of business more risky, not only has planning become more necessary, but managers have become more willing to commit resources to the planning process. The unanticipated inflation, coupled with the periodic recessions that have been the worst since the end of the Great Depression, have left managers shocked and confounded as their best laid plans have gone awry. As a result, managers are now more receptive to—and indeed, are demanding greater use of—financial planning.

The greater willingness to plan cannot necessarily lead to more planning unless the planning effort can lead successfully and efficiently to its objective. Thus, for planning to come of age not only must the times require it, but also the technology must be available to make it cost efficient. The technology for financial planning now has become available so that management that wants to plan should be willing to commit the necessary resources to the effort because this technology, consisting of computer hardware and software has become relatively inexpensive.

The computer hardware advance that will facilitate financial modeling is the development of micro, or personal, computers that are inexpensive, readily available, and easy to use. One would have to live on a remote desert island to be unaware of the computer revolution that is taking place. Open any newspaper and you see the large amount of space devoted to advertising the personal computers. For a small investment, ranging from $1,000 to $5,000, one can purchase a complete computer system that gives as much computing power as was available as recently as 15 years ago only at a cost of many thousands of dollars from a computer that would fill a small room. With the newer machines so easily available, every manager has the capacity to develop rather sophisticated financial plans. The only additional requirements are some of the right software and some knowledge of planning and modeling.

The term *computer software* refers to the programs that enable the user to convey instructions to the electronic devices that constitute the *hardware* and that present the results in convenient forms. The recent software advance that will accelerate the application of financial modeling is the development of very simple, user-oriented languages or systems that are specifically designed to handle financial or accounting problems. These financial planning languages are much more like our everyday language, and less like the more mathematical, more general (and more temperamental) languages such as FORTRAN. For example, Exhibit 1.1 shows the programming in two languages, FORTRAN and IFPS, for calculation and printing of operating income for each of five years. The main point is that with "user-friendly" software such as IFPS the programming conforms to our normal method of describing a problem, including the use of everyday language. One does not have to learn a whole new language with very particular rules of syntax in order to use the machine. Other software such as VisiCalc®, Lotus® 1-2-3®, and Multiplan offer the ability to bypass programming altogether by simply typing numbers onto an "electronic spreadsheet."[3]

Because the financial planning software systems respond to instructions given in English-like terms, they are less formidable and much easier to use for the nonexpert in computers. The result of this development is that many financial managers who previously avoided financial modeling because of the complexity of the computer can now easily develop their own financial models without having to have the model programmed for the computer by someone unfamiliar with finance.

Not only do we now have easy-to-use financial planning soft-

---

[3]VisiCalc and 1-2-3 are registered trademarks of Lotus Development Corporation, and Multiplan is a registered trademark of the Microsoft Corporation.

EXHIBIT 1.1 Programming of Income (FORTRAN versus IFPS)

FORTRAN PROGRAMMING

```
      Dimension Price(5), Units(5), Cost(5), Sales(5), Opcost(5), Opincom(5)
      Data (Price(I), I = 1,5) / 1.50, 1.50, 2.00, 2.00, 2.00 /
      Data (Units(I), I = 1,5) / 100, 150, 200, 250, 300 /
      Data (Cost (I), I = 1,5) / 1.25, 1.25, 1.25, 1.25, 1.25 /
      DO 100 J = 1, 5
      Sales(J) = Price(J) * Units(J)
      Opcost(J) = Cost(J) * Units(J)
      Opincome(J) = Sales(J)-Opcost(J)
 100  continue
      Write (6,200)
      Write (6,210) Sales(J), J = 1,5
      Write (6,220) Opcost(J), J = 1,5
      Write (6,230) Opincom(J), J = 1,5
 200  Format (20X, 'Year 1', 9X, 'Year 2', 9X, 'Year 3,' 9X, 'Year 4,' 9X, 'Year 5', '')
 210  Format (3X, 'Sales', 12X, 5(F10.2, 5X))
 220  Format (3X, 'Operating Costs', 2X, 5(F10.2, 5X))
 230  Format (3X, 'Operating Income', 1X, 5(F10.2, 5X))
      END
```

IFPS PROGRAMMING

```
      Columns Year 1, Year 2, Year 3, Year 4, Year 5
      Price            =    $1.50 for 2, 2.00
      Units            =    100, 150, 200, 250, 300
      Cost             =    1.25
      Sales            =    Price * Units
      Operating Cost   =    Cost * Units
      Operating Income =    Sales-Operating Cost
```

ware, but we also have other statistical and mathematical software that aids in the financial modeling and planning process. For example, the statistical techniques necessary for development of many types of forecasting models were formerly available only on large mainframe computers and were usable only by the resident statistician or econometrician. Now, numerous inexpensive statistical packages are available for microcomputers that can be used very easily by anyone familiar with elementary statistical concepts. In addition, mathematical optimization formerly was another arcane device necessitating large computers used by the mathematical cognoscenti. Even this barrier has been broken, and there are many inexpensive, user-friendly packages of software to solve linear programming problems on the personal computer.

The problem for most people is that they tend to be so specialized in their field of expertise that they cannot competently venture outside that field. The computer expert doesn't know finance, or modeling for that matter, and the financial expert knows nothing about computers or modeling. What is needed is the knowledge to bridge these gaps. The chapters to follow in this book will help to provide that necessary knowledge.

Chapter Two discusses planning so as to broaden the reader's perspective about planning and what it is. Chapter Three presents examples that demonstrate some of the standard tools of financial planning and analysis such as those found in most textbooks on managerial finance. Chapter Four explains what we mean by a model and presents and discusses the ingredients that go into almost any financial planning model. Because forecasting is such an important part of any planning and modeling effort, it is necessary to have some passing familiarity with the techniques of forecasting. That is what Chapter Five provides—a brief survey of forecasting techniques. Chapter Six is the centerpiece of this book—it explains how we can go about constructing a model for analyzing financial planning problems of business firms. Obviously, not all types of models can be explained in one chapter. We present a general model and discuss how that model could be modified to handle different types of planning problems. Chapter Seven presents a brief survey of the different ways we can take our uncertainty about the future into account in our modeling efforts. Chapter Eight explains how to develop linear programming models, and finally, Chapter Nine concludes the book with a brief discussion of the importance of monitoring the progress of a financial plan.

REFERENCE

GALBRAITH, JOHN KENNETH *The New Industrial State.* New York: New American Library, 1967.

CHAPTER TWO

An Overview of Financial Planning

The purpose of this chapter is to provide some perspective regarding the purpose of financial planning, and to explain what the ingredients of a thorough financial planning effort should be.

2.1 WHAT IS PLANNING?

Most managers engage in some aspect of planning. After all, the first step in business is the establishment of the enterprise—a step that is the result of the entrepreneur's dream about the wealth that could accrue from providing some good or service to others. That initial dream about what could happen is part of the process of business planning. From its establishment throughout the firm's existence the manager is thinking about the future, wondering what will happen tomorrow, asking what will be the results of current decisions, and perhaps even dreaming of new enterprises.

Not every effort to know the future is planning, however. For example, forecasting is passive in that it involves the projection of future events but involves little consideration of the actions that can be taken to affect the future. While forecasting is a necessary input to business planning, planning is much more than forecasting. Planning combines elements of forecasting with the specifications of decisions, actions, and intended results. A broad definition of planning is the specification of future decisions and actions to reach a stated goal. Very simply put, planning is deciding what you are going to do to get where you want to go.

It is useful to think of a traveler planning a trip. The traveler first sets the primary objective by deciding where to go. He may also have subgoals or constraints regarding when he wants to reach his goal and how much he wants to spend. The travel plan specifies the route, which signposts to look for that will guide him on the route, where to stop, and where to turn.

If there is no uncertainty about future events on the trip, planning is relatively simple, involving a single specification of the route. The best route is chosen in advance with the assurance that it is the correct one, no detours will be necessary, and the traveler will not get lost. No alternative routes or actions need to be chosen because under conditions of certainty no random events can interfere with the completion of the trip.

However, the traveler invariably has some uncertainty about the trip. Random events may interfere with the plan: A landslide may block the route, a storm can close the airport, the plane may crash. The smart traveler takes the uncertainty into account by planning alternative routes to the goal if obstructions are encountered; in considering whether the plane may crash, the traveler carefully assesses whether the benefits of flying are worth the risks. With uncertainty, even though any given plan may not be met, it is especially important for the traveler to make plans that anticipate possible difficulties so as to reduce the resulting inconvenience and delay.

Similarly, the greater the uncertainty in the business environment, the greater the necessity for planning. Perhaps one would think that with greater uncertainty about future events planning would be less useful, because "the best laid plans of mice and men often go awry," and there would be little use for planning if the plans are destined to go awry. However, if the plans are truly best laid, they make allowance for things going awry. Or, as Murphy's Law says, "Everything that can go wrong, will," and the best laid plans should take that unfortunate truth into account.

Whether planning is complex and detailed, or very broad and simple, it should specify the objectives and the actions that lead to the objectives.

The concept and process of planning is pointless unless one decides first what is to be achieved. Deciding on a destination seems so obvious that it hardly needs to be discussed. Yet, the setting of goals is so fundamental to business planning that it does need extra stress. One plans in order to achieve a goal successfully; but without first stating the goal, there is no way to decide along the way which actions should be taken, nor can one judge whether the actions have been successful. Thus, the first step in planning a trip or in planning a business venture is deciding on the goal or the objective.

Once the primary objective is set it is necessary to specify some criteria for judging the progress toward that objective. The traveler uses signposts along the road to tell whether he is on the correct route and how far it is to his destination. The business planner must develop some standards with which he can compare the firm's performance. For example, with the primary objective of maximizing the market value of the firm, a set of measures of financial performance such as asset turnover, profit margin, and return on assets can help measure progress toward the objective. If these standards are properly specified, they can be used as subgoals or intermediate objectives toward which management's decisions can be directed. Thus, in day-to-day management each decision need not necessarily be considered with the objective of maximizing the firm's value. Rather, the operational decision is made based on a more mundane standard, such as attaining a target profit margin. Of course, it is crucial that reaching these subgoals be consistent with attaining the primary objective.

Usually, defining the link between the decision and the objective is the primary source of complexity and difficulty in business planning. If you know that a particular decision will lead unambiguously to the objective, there is very little problem in either planning or decision making. However, the effect a decision will have on progress toward the objective is usually unclear. There are often very complex and poorly understood relationships between a given management action and the objective. For example, suppose the goal is to maximize the value of the firm's stock, and management is considering issuing bonds to finance a capital investment. To consider these actions, the planner needs to know how they will affect the value of the stock; yet, these relationships are complex, and what is even worse, not fully understood. One task of the planner is to utilize the theory of finance to shed some light on the links between the investment and financing decisions and the value of the stock, and then trace through these complex relations to determine the best decision.

2.2 WHAT IS FINANCIAL PLANNING?

From the financial point of view the firm is represented by the two sides of its balance sheet; that is, it is described by its assets and its liabilities. This same dichotomy can be used to describe the broad range of decisions and problems that fall under the heading of finance: Finance is concerned with problems and decisions relating to the firm's assets and liabilities. Investment decisions identify which assets should be purchased, and financing decisions concern the source of the funds necessary to purchase the assets. Almost all management decisions that we regard as financial fall under one of these categories: investment (assets) or financing (liabilities).

Consequently, the questions addressed in financial planning generally concern investment and financing problems. Financial planning is concerned with setting the objectives for future investment and financing decisions, judging the effect of various decisions on progress toward the objectives, and based on these judgments, deciding which investment or financing alternative should be undertaken.

The range of problems addressed under the heading of financial planning is enormous. They range from the very detailed specifications of working capital decisions over a planning horizon as short as a day or a week, to very broad plans about a business strategy over the next decade.

For example, a commercial bank must decide how to satisfy the reserve requirements of the Federal Reserve Bank at weekly intervals. The bank has a range of choices about which days of the week will show reserve surpluses and which will show deficits, just so long as its daily average meets the requirements; it has a range of choices of how it can invest any excess funds and how it can obtain funds to cover any deficits. All these decisions involve borrowing and lending on a daily or even hourly basis. In this case the financial plan has a very short horizon, and it may involve very detailed analyses of a small number of specialized asset and liability accounts.

An example at the other end of the spectrum is the development of a very broad, long-range plan for strategic investment and expansion. One type of broad strategic analysis considers what lines of business the firm should be involved in and whether divisions should be divested. Such an analysis tends to have a very long planning horizon, and it does not develop the fine detail in terms of specific assets and liabilities. Rather, it emphasizes business strategy in the broadest sense. This type of strategic planning fits the description by Brealey and Myers (1984) of strategic investments that may not directly have attractive values. Rather, they constitute the purchase of options that allow the firm to undertake attractive investments in the future because the firm positions itself strategically now.

In the quintessential financial planning problem, the firm's sales and production forecast is taken as given, and the investment and financing plan necessary to support the sales must be developed. An example of such a problem will be presented in Chapter Six.

2.3 THE INPUT TO FINANCIAL PLANNING

Obviously, there are many different needs and applications for financial planning. Given this wide variety of problems, what general statements can be made about the necessary ingredients, or input, for the financial planning process? There are a number of inputs that all financial plans should have. To give us some insight into these ingredients, let us return to the travel plan analogy discussed earlier.

What are the necessary ingredients for a thorough plan for travel? Some of these ingredients have already been discussed, but it is informative to elaborate on them. First, the *destination* must be specified. Second, the various possible *alternative routes* and methods of transportation should be enumerated. Without a careful and complete listing of the possibilities, some of the most attractive routes might be overlooked. Third, each route should be evaluated as to whether it actually *leads to the destination,* and the costs, advantages, and disadvantages of each route should be determined. Fourth, the *resources* available for making the trip must be considered. The amount of money and time available, suitable clothing and luggage, and the availability and condition of a car all are resources that can affect the decision about the trip. Each of these resources is limited, imposing limitations, or *constraints,* on what can be done on the trip. There are other constraints, too. It may be desirable to see particular sights along the way, so that would constrain the route selected. Visiting certain countries might be prohibited by legal restrictions. Finally, the traveler must decide what kind of *detail* is wanted in the plan, and how specific the time schedule should be. The plan could be made very broad, simply specifying the countries to be visited and the approximate dates. Or, one could make an extremely detailed plan, scheduling the activity for each hour of each day. The advantages of more detailed planning must be weighed against the extra time and effort in making the detailed plan. Furthermore, the traveler may not really want to be tied to the strict requirements of an hourly schedule.

These ingredients of a travel plan may not be exhaustive; there may be others, but this is a good start. These ingredients can be listed in summary as:

a. The destination or goal.
b. The alternative routes or modes of transport.
c. The relation between the route and destination.
d. The resources and constraints.
e. The level of detail.

Obviously, not every travel plan would consider each item on the list in an explicit manner. The trip may be so routine and simple that an elaborate plan is unnecessary. Some travelers may not even require an explicit listing; they may develop the plan in their head without bothering to write it down. Still, many of the ingredients will be considered, even if only perfunctorily.

A financial plan that is thorough will have the same basic ingredients. The ingredients form the input to the planning process, and most financial plans should begin with the enumeration of the necessary input. Whatever the financial planning problem, whether it involves detailed analysis or a very broad consideration of strategy, the financial planning process is intended to aid in making future decisions to reach the firm's goal. The factors or ingredients that form the major input categories to the plan include:

a. The goal.
b. The decision alternatives.
c. The link between the decisions and the goal.
d. The resources for implementing the decisions and constraints inhibiting goal attainment.
e. The planning horizon and the desired amount of planning detail.

These elements may be specified explicitly, or the planner may have only an intuitive or even subconscious idea of some or all of them. Nevertheless, they should be specified to develop a complete financial plan. There are considerable benefits to be derived from going through the exercise of carefully and explicitly specifying the elements in this list.

The Goals of Financial Decisions

With respect to investment and financing decisions, there is general agreement among economists that the proper objective is to maximize the value of the firm's equity shares. That is, in considering decision alternatives, management should choose the one that makes the market price of the stock as high as possible. A number of arguments support this position. First, management serves as the fiduciary agent of the stockholders and has the responsibility to act in the best interests of the stockholders and to carry out their wishes. The market price of the stock serves as a barometer of stockholder preferences. If stockholders and investors like management's decisions, they will purchase the stock, driving up its price. Conversely, if they don't like management decisions, they will sell, driving down the price. Second, maximization of share prices makes all stockholders wealthier, which is one of the reasons they buy shares in the company. As stated by Haley and Schall (1979):

> [E]ach shareholder prefers the firm policy that maximizes the value of the firm's shares because the maximum share value provides the widest choice of income stream opportunities. With a higher share value, the shareholder can acquire anything that could be acquired if shares are worth less and can acquire even more. Therefore, policies which generate higher share values are preferred by all shareholders. (p. 474)

Third, from a broader point of view, it has been shown that decisions that maximize share value are decisions that use the firm's resources efficiently and result in a more efficient allocation of resources for society as a whole.

Of course, management and stockholders may have other objectives, ranging from offering stable employment to the work force to protecting the environment from pollution. In some instances the alternative goal is consistent with share value maximization, and for others it can be viewed as a constraint. That is, management would make decisions that would maximize share prices subject to the constraint that the alternative goal also be met.

The Decision Alternatives

The purpose of financial planning is to specify the future actions and decisions that will lead to the goal of making the value of the firm's equity shares as large as possible. The second necessary ingredient of the financial planning process is a complete list of the possible decisions and actions.

It may seem rather obvious that the possible decision alternatives should be considered as an input to the financial planning process. Yet, this obvious step is frequently overlooked. The mistake many managers make in planning is to ask, "What will happen if I make *this* decision?" They do not fully consider the many different possible decisions and ask which one is best. Consequently, many decision alternatives are overlooked that could be superior to the one examined.

The planner should develop a list of decision alternatives that is as comprehensive as possible. The list should include all possible actions, ranging from doing nothing to many actions that, at first, seem infeasible or even, perhaps, counterproductive. Many possibilities can be quickly eliminated, but it is well at least to engage in the brainstorming exercise of listing them prior to eliminating them.

The Link between Decisions and Goals

To decide what actions will maximize value, one must know how a chosen action will affect share value. That is, the link between the action and value must be identified. The necessary link is a model of valuation that tells us what the hypothetical value of the firm is, based on the prospective decision. This is where the theory of finance makes its contribution—the theory of finance provides us with a framework, or way of thinking about financial problems, that explains how these decisions affect the market value of the firm and the stock.

This book will not present a complete survey of the theories of valuation.[1] However, central ideas will be discussed, and the idea of value will always be in the background of our discussions of planning.

The central idea of valuation is that the value of an asset is the risk-adjusted present value of the cash flow generated by that asset. The task in valuing an asset is to forecast the future cash flows and to determine the discount rate that properly adjusts for the risk or uncertainty of those cash flows. For equity securities, the value of the stock would be the present value of the stream of dividends that will be paid to the stockholders over the life of the firm, adjusted for the uncertainty of the dividends. It is useful to focus on the ability of the firm to pay dividends, rather than to try to forecast specific dividends, because there may be a wide range of dividend policies that could be followed. Consequently, the value can be stated as the present value, adjusted for risk, of the cash flow that is *available* to pay dividends to the stockholders. There are numerous methods for adjusting present value for risk or uncertainty. One approach widely espoused is to adjust the discount rate to take account of the systematic, nondiversifiable risk of the cash flows. This approach is based on the capital asset pricing model

---

[1]Ideas and models of valuation are presented by Fama and Miller (1972), Haley and Schall (1979), Weston and Copeland (1986), and Jacob and Pettit (1984); a very practical reference is Pratt (1981).

(CAPM) first developed by Sharpe (1964), Lintner (1964), and Mossin (1966); it will be explained in greater detail as it is needed to understand the problems of financial planning.

In terms of the problems of financial planning, one must relate the decision problem at hand to the value of the firm and the stock. The basic approach in almost all cases is to focus on the risk-adjusted present value of the cash flows as the thing to be maximized. One does not necessarily have to determine what the value of stock would be for different decision alternatives. Rather, the objective for the problem at hand can be stated in operational terms that are consistent with the stock value maximization. For example, in capital budgeting, the investment project is chosen so as to maximize net present value; and in deciding on the best mix of debt and equity, the mix that minimizes the weighted average cost of capital is chosen. In each case the objective is stated in narrower, more specific terms that have been shown to be consistent with share price maximization.

Resources and Constraints

Because the purpose of financial planning is to decide on future actions to reach a goal, it is essential that the plan take account of those factors that are (or will be) available to assist in attaining the goal. In addition, there are inevitably many factors that limit the actions the firm can undertake or that limit its ability to attain the goal. We could regard the positive factors as resources and the negative ones as constraints. The dichotomy is not always clear, however. Almost all resources are also constraints, in that the resources are usually limited, and the limitation is itself a constraint.

Resources and constraints consist of those that exist right now and describe the company's current situation, and those that are anticipated to affect the company in the future. Both present and future resources and constraints are factors that can be classified as:

a. Company-specific.
b. Industry-specific.
c. Related to the economy as a whole.
d. Influenced by the legal and political environment.

From whatever source, these factors are important input to the planning process that should be considered explicitly in evaluating the desirability and feasibility of some plan of action. The starting point is the firm's current situation, the base from which the company's future will develop. Thus, the financial planning effort should begin with a careful assessment of present resources and constraints and should develop the plan on the basis of assumptions and forecasts of future resources and constraints.

Company-Specific Resources and Constraints. The firm's present condition forms the base from which it will develop and build in the future. The present condition is described by the balance sheet, showing assets and liabilities, and by its production technology, sources and nature of the supply of raw materials, products, labor, and management.

Balance Sheet. The firm's assets are part of the resources that will be available to implement a plan, and they also are a constraint on successful attainment of the goals. For example, liquid assets are potentially available to finance planned expenditures, but because the liquid assets are of limited amounts, a limit or constraint is imposed on expenditures financed from this source. The fixed assets are a resource representing investment in capacity to produce output in the future, but future potential production is limited by this existing capacity unless more capital investment is undertaken.

The firm's liabilities represent obligations to make promised payments in the future and are constraints on future actions. For example, the necessity to make interest and principal payments on debt means that funds must be used to service debt that otherwise could be used to fund the firm's planned expenditures.

Production Technology. The firm's ability to generate output and profits is determined initially by the capacity of its plant and equipment, which is a resource for implementing its plans. Conversely, its future opportunities are constrained by the nature of its technology and its capacity. The production technology determines what inputs must be used, their relative amounts, and the level of output attainable. The firm's production equipment, plant, and so on, determine the costs and profit margins. Even the variability of the firm's income, and thus the business risk of the firm, is heavily influenced by its production methods and technology. The relative mix of fixed and variable cost methods of production determine the operating leverage, the break-even point, and the variability of the operating income.

Sources of Supply. Established sources of raw materials and good relationships with suppliers are resources for the future. Interruption of these supplies may be a major source of risk for future plans, and the limitations on these supplies constrain the rate of production. Obviously the costs of materials are an important factor in the firm's current and future profitability.

Labor and Management. The people in an organization have always been an important resource, and they can also be a source of the problems and difficulties for the firm. As our economy becomes more oriented toward service and information, personnel will increasingly become the major resource for reaching the firm's goals, and also a primary constraint. In evaluating any financial plan, the reliability and productivity of the firm's labor supply must be considered. Similarly, the strength, ambition, and creativity of management are major factors in determining whether the firm can carry out its plans and whether the firm can respond effectively to a changing environment and the surprises that can undo the plans.

Products. The nature of the firm's products, the uniqueness of its products, and any special product advantages such as patents are important factors in the plans for the future. The financial planning effort must evaluate the firm's product mix and the future prospects for the products and relate them both to its industry and market.

Industry-Specific Constraints. The ability of the company to attain its goals is highly dependent on the industry environment within which it operates and the future prospects for that industry. In most cases the industry context presents limitations and constraints to the attainment of goals, rather than resources that assist the firm. To the extent that opportunities are regarded as a resource, however, the opportunities for growth in the industry may be considered a resource.

Many of the factors that should be considered in developing the financial plan are related either to demand for the firm's product or to the structure of the industry.

Demand. Probably the most important input to any planning effort is the forecast of future demand for the product. In fact, for most financial planning efforts the sales forecast is the variable said to "drive the model" and is the factor on which almost all other forecasts depend. Usually, one of the first steps in generating a forecast of company sales is to prepare a forecast of industry sales. Thus, industry sales constrain the company's actions, because the company is subject to the growth and vagaries of its entire industry.

In addition to a basic forecast of industry sales, there are numerous other more specific factors under the heading of demand that may be of major importance as input to the financial planning effort. These factors, which affect the sales forecast, include pricing, advertising by the company and the industry, growth of market, product life cycle, and the nature of the customers.

Demand for the product depends on the price charged for the product. A major input to analysis of the company's and industry's future is an estimate of the demand function for the product; that is, an estimate of how demand changes as the price is changed. For example, any analysis of the firm's pricing policy must take account of the demand function.

The pricing policy of other firms in the industry will also serve as an important constraint on the company's decisions and will affect the financial plans.

The future demand for the product and the growth in the demand will depend on prices, the economy, and sociological and demographic trends. All of these factors may have to be considered in developing a sales forecast and will definitely play a part in more detailed analyses that are concerned with such things as pricing and marketing policies.

Industry Structure. The structure of the industry will influence sales by the company and will constrain many of the company's actions. Company sales may be expressed as the product of the total industry sales and the company's share of the market. In turn, the share of the market depends on the number of firms in the industry, their competitiveness, and the degree of concentration in the industry. In very competitive industries with many firms, the sales of a particular company will constitute a small market share, and that firm will be constrained in its ability to change prices and to change its share of the market. Just the opposite is true for more concentrated, less competitive industries.

Competition and industry structure will be influenced by whether patents and licenses protect the various products and production methods. In addition, the nature of the production process, which may exhibit decreasing, constant, or increasing returns to scale, will affect industry concentration and competition.

Finally, marketing and distribution practices in the industry will be important factors that constrain the ability of the company to attain its goals.

Constraints Imposed by the Economy. A financial plan is forward looking and almost always uses a forecast—of the firm's sales or production or some other company variable. One cannot ignore the crucial dependence of the forecast of the company's fortunes on what happens in the economy as a whole. Every company is to some degree dependent on the vicissitudes of national and even international economic conditions. Indeed, it is now well accepted that the best measure of a firm's risk is the extent to which the firm's fortunes are systematically related to the economy as a whole. Thus, one of the most important inputs to any financial planning effort is a forecast of general economic conditions. In addition, more specific regional forecasts may be necessary, and it is important to relate the general conditions to the forecast for the industry and company. In many instances, it is impractical to forecast. Rather, one simply makes assumptions about economic conditions, so that the financial plan is based on these assumed conditions.

Economic conditions are a constraint on the attainment of a

firm's goals in the same sense that industry sales forecasts are. The firm exists within the context of the economy and seldom can escape it. If a recession occurs, the company would be influenced by those recessionary conditions, and the actions available to the company may be constrained, or the results of those actions available may be dependent on economic conditions.

Of course, different companies and different industries vary in how much they are influenced by economic conditions. Some industries, such as automobiles, housing, and machine tools, are particularly vulnerable to the economic cycle, while others, such as utilities and grocery chains, while still influenced, are not quite so sensitive to the cycle. In still other sectors, such as banking, a single, specialized economic variable, such as interest rates, may be of prime importance in developing a company forecast.

In summary, the financial plan will depend on a forecast of, or set of assumptions about, the future economic conditions. Just as important as the forecast itself is the link between the national (or regional) economy and the industry and company forecast.

Constraints Imposed by the Legal and Political Environment. The rules and regulations promulgated by government and the demands of political reality seldom could be considered as resources that assist the firm in attaining its goals. More often, these factors impose constraints and limitations on the actions the firm can undertake, and they may influence the results of actions taken by the firm. In developing a financial plan, it is important to recognize these constraints and take explicit account of them. In addition, it may be important to attempt to forecast future legal and political conditions—one of the most difficult forecasting tasks.

One purpose of financial planning is to plan for the unexpected and to be prepared to respond to surprises. The company should be prepared to respond to society's demands for such things as pollution control, equal opportunity, and product liability. In addition, it should consider the effects on the company of major political upheaval such as wars, foreign revolutions, expropriations, and devaluations. If a company depends on international trade, it would be particularly short-sighted not to anticipate the effects of devaluation, and plans should be made to meet such events.

The Planning Horizon and the Amount of Detail

This last item on the list of ingredients of a thorough financial planning effort refers to the appropriate length of the planning horizon and the appropriate amount of detail to be generated for the financial plan. Before developing the financial plan, the analyst must decide how many months or years should be considered in the plan. This length of time over which the plan will apply is called the *planning horizon*. In addition, the analyst must decide how detailed to make the plan. The appropriate length of the planning horizon and the desired amount of detail are important decisions that are part of the initial input to the planning process.

In developing a financial plan, one could consider a plan with a planning horizon of almost any length. The plan could extend over one day, one month, one year, five years, or any number of periods. The choice of the planning horizon can affect the results and usefulness of the plan and obviously influence the amount of effort and cost necessary to develop the plan and the amount of detail incorporated in the plan. Therefore, it is important to give serious thought to the planning horizon and to view it as an important ingredient of the process.

Factors that should be considered in deciding on the planning horizon are the nature of the planning problem, the amount of output detail desired from the plan, the horizon of reasonable forecasts, and the period over which the planning horizon makes a difference.

The nature of the planning problem obviously influences the planning horizon. If one is concerned with the long-run effects of a very broad strategic decision, then a long planning horizon obviously is appropriate. In analyzing the effects of a research and development program involving new product development over the next 10 years, a long planning horizon is called for, and it makes little sense to limit the analysis to, say, one year. If the problem is to determine the financing requirements over the firm's seasonal production cycle, a one-year planning horizon would usually be appropriate because the cycle would tend to repeat itself each year, and seasonal financing would not normally be arranged for more than one year.

One would want to make the planning horizon sufficiently long to show the full effects of the decisions considered and the cycle or trend involved. If the problem involves the firm's annual seasonal production cycle, a six-month planning horizon would be too short to show the effects of the cycle or the results of the decisions being considered.

The nature of the problem will also influence how the planning horizon is divided into subperiods, the time intervals that make up the planning horizon. That is, a one-year planning horizon could be divided into 12 monthly subperiods or, say, four quarterly subperiods. The length of the subperiod would determine how frequently prospective decisions and forecasted results could be changed. With quarterly subperiods, results could be calculated for each quarter, and prospective decisions could be changed quarterly, but not more frequently. If a broad, long-term strategic policy is under consideration, where the basic decisions would not be varied more often than annually, then one probably would not be interested in developing a plan that generated weekly results. Conversely, if the problem is one of managing the marketable security portfolio where daily decisions may be important, it would make sense to use daily, or perhaps weekly, subperiods, and it would be pointless to consider a five-year planning horizon composed of annual subperiods.

The length of the planning horizon and the number of subperiods influence the amount of detail considered in the financial plan. If many subperiods make the planning horizon, and decisions and results are considered for each subperiod, an excessive amount of detail could be produced. In determining the length of the planning horizon and the subperiods, one must consider how much detail is useful. One frequently finds that the additional detail is a disadvantage. Too much detail tends to overwhelm the user so that one loses track of how results relate to decisions and objectives. It is too easy, particularly with computers, to generate so much detail that it cannot be evaluated. In addition, generating and evaluating detail is costly in terms of effort and time, so that the information and detail must be balanced against the cost and effort involved.

It is useful to distinguish between "cross-sectional" detail and "time series" detail. Cross-sectional detail refers to the amount of data, variables, and decisions considered for a given point in time. Financial statements broken down into many account categories for a given point in time, say June 1985, generate a large amount of cross-sectional detail. Time series detail refers to data, variables, and decisions considered at different points in time. A forecast of net income for each month of a 10-year planning horizon would include much time series detail, but because only one variable (net income) is considered for each subperiod (one month) there would be little cross-sectional detail.

The amount of detail usually should be minimized and kept to a level sufficient to help the analyst understand the problem. Thus, if the problem involves a long planning horizon, one may control the size of the problem by minimizing the amount of cross-sectional detail (consider few accounts for each subperiod) and limit the amount of time series detail by dividing the planning horizon into fewer (longer) subperiods. Many short-run problems, such as working capital management, have short planning horizons and require a great deal of cross-sectional detail (consider many different investment and financing accounts). Here, the amount of detail may be controlled by shortening the planning horizon and lengthening the subperiods as much as possible so as to minimize the time series detail but allow a larger amount of cross-sectional detail.

The length of the planning horizon should be limited to the horizon of reasonable forecasts. If the financial plan depends on forecasts (of sales, interest rates, gross national product, or the like), it does not make much sense to extend the analysis beyond the time over which one can make reasonable forecasts. For example, sales forecasts for specific months make sense for one year into the future, but it may be nonsense to try to distinguish between June and July sales five years hence. Consequently, developing a forecast of month-by-month financing needs may be appropriate for the next year or so, but inappropriate over a five-year planning horizon. On the other hand, estimates of long-run growth trends may be quite reasonable, and would be useful for broad, general financial planning, and a very long planning horizon would be appropriate. For example, an electric utility may need to plan its construction to meet growth in energy demand over the next 25 years. It can't forecast month-by-month demand 25 years hence, but it can make useful forecasts of long-run growth based on demographic trends. In this case, a 25-year planning horizon divided into annual subperiods may be appropriate.

Finally, as pointed out by Orgler (1970, p. 48), one useful way to decide on the planning horizon is to simply extend it out to the point where further extensions do not change your conclusions or decisions. For example, using a planning horizon of one year, develop the financial plan showing results of decisions, and determine the best decision. Then, extend the planning horizon to two years, determining the results and the best decision. If extending the horizon the extra year does not change the decisions or conclusions, then the one-year horizon is adequate.

2.4 WHAT DO WE GET OUT OF IT?

The financial planning process can be expensive in terms of money, time, and effort. Is it worth it? What benefits are we going to get out of this process? Obviously, the process will usually result in some output that constitutes the financial plan. This is the explicit benefit, but there are many implicit and intangible benefits that may be more valuable than the explicit output.

The explicit benefits are those derived from the documents that make up the financial plan. The basic purpose of planning is to assist in decision making by determining the likely future effects of alternative decisions and helping to choose the best decision. The typical financial plan generates a set of future (pro forma) financial statements that are intended to show how the firm would look as a result of the given decision. This allows the planner to anticipate the results of the decisions. With this output, the best decision should be discernible. Thus, financial planning generates financial statements, allows for anticipating the results, and assists in determining the best decision.

Many benefits from the planning process are intangible and implicit in the process itself. First, the process forces the planner to systematize his thoughts about objectives, decisions, assumptions, and the interactions among parts of the firm and between variables. As pointed out by Ackoff (1970):

> The value of planning to managers lies more in their participation in the process than in their consumption of its product. . . . Such participation stimulates the development of a deeper understanding of the business and its environment, and it forces the systematic formulation and evaluation of alternatives that would not otherwise be considered. (p. 137)

In addition, the plan provides consistency between different parts of the firm in terms of assumptions, forecasts, decisions, and results. Finally, a well-documented plan allows the planner to review and analyze the plan after it has been implemented in order to determine where triumphs and mistakes occurred.

REFERENCES

ACKOFF, R. L. *A Concept of Corporate Planning.* New York: John Wiley & Sons, 1970.

BREALEY, R., and S. MYERS. *Principles of Corporate Finance.* 2nd ed. New York: McGraw-Hill, 1984.

DALE, E. *Long Range Planning,* London: British Institute of Management, 1967.

DRUCKER, P. F., "Long Range Planning: Challenge to Management Science." *Management Science* 5 (1959), pp. 238–49.

EWING, D. W., ed. *Long Range Planning for Management.* New York: Harper & Row, 1958.

FAMA, E., and M. MILLER. *The Theory of Finance.* New York: Holt, Rinehart & Winston, 1972.

HALEY, C., and L. SCHALL. *The Theory of Financial Decisions.* 2nd ed. New York: McGraw-Hill, 1979.

JACOB, N., and R. PETTIT. *Investments.* Homewood, Ill.: Richard D. Irwin, 1984.

LINTNER, J. "Security Prices, Risk, and Maximal Gains from Diversification." *Journal of Finance,* December 1965, pp. 587–616.

MOSSIN, J. "Equilibrium in a Capital Asset Market." *Econometrica,* October 1966, pp. 768–83.

ORGLER, Y. *Cash Management: Methods and Models.* Belmont, Calif.: Wadsworth, 1970.

PRATT, S. *Valuing a Business: The Analysis and Appraisal of Closely Held Companies.* Homewood, Ill.: Dow Jones-Irwin, 1981.

SHARPE, W. F. "Capital Asset Prices: A Theory of Market Equilibrium under Conditions of Risk." *Journal of Finance,* September 1964, pp. 425–42.

STEINER, G. A. *Top Management Planning,* New York: Macmillan, 1969.

WESTON, J. F., and T. COPELAND. *Managerial Finance.* 8th ed. Hinsdale, Ill.: Dryden Press, 1986.

CHAPTER THREE

The Tools of Financial Planning

This chapter explains some of the standard tools used in financial planning. These tools are introduced through a series of financial planning examples. The examples show how the ingredients of financial planning relate to the tools, and they serve as a basis for discussion of the ideas, issues, and difficulties of financial planning.

The standard tools of the financial planner include cash budgeting, break-even analysis, sources and uses of funds, portfolio analysis, and forecasting of financial statements. All of these tools, and more, are suited to various aspects of the tasks of financial planning. None of these tools really requires the technology of the computer and its software, and they don't require the development of complex computer models. Indeed, such tools were developed and used long before anyone dreamed of applying advanced technology to the tasks of financial planning.

Before immersing oneself in the technological tools and techniques of planning and modeling that are the topic of this book, the reader should become familiar with the basic tools. These tools are introduced in this chapter through a series of financial planning examples. These examples not only introduce some of the techniques, but they also help to show how the ingredients of financial planning, which were discussed in the last chapter, relate to solving financial planning problems. The examples presented in this chapter serve as a basis for discussion of the issues, ideas, and difficulties of financial planning.

3.1 ANTICIPATING SEASONAL FINANCING NEEDS WITH CASH RECEIPTS AND DISBURSEMENTS

A common problem faced by a financial manager is that there is a lag between disbursements for expenses of production and receipts from sales. This is particularly true for a firm that has a seasonal sales cycle. The lag between receipts and disbursements results in a need for seasonal financing. The financial planning problem is to anticipate the financing needs, determine the amount of financing required, and find the best way to meet this requirement.

The following example is typical. It demonstrates the seasonal financing needs by developing a statement of cash receipts and disbursements. This statement (cash budget) is applicable to a wide variety of problems, both short term and long term, but it is especially useful for considering short-term (quarterly, monthly, or even weekly or daily) cash flows.

EXAMPLE: THE MOGUL CORPORATION

Mogul Corporation manufactures skis that are sold on credit to retail outlets. The sales are seasonal as retailers stock up on skis in anticipation of winter sales. The production cycle, the seasonal sales pattern, and the credit terms granted to the retailers all influence the firm's financing requirements. The question is: What will be the firm's financing requirements for the coming season, given the anticipated sales?

The starting point for analyzing the firm's financing requirements is to develop a pro forma statement of cash receipts and disbursements. This will require a set of assumptions and forecasts about the company's resources and constraints and the future condition of the economy. The major assumptions are

EXHIBIT 3.1 Assumptions Used for Developing Cash Budget for Mogul Corporation

a. To meet the demand, Mogul Corporation manufactures skis one month ahead of anticipated sales.
b. Purchases of materials (line 7) are 50 percent of sales and occur two months prior to sales. Purchases are made on trade credit and are paid one month after the purchase. Thus, July purchase disbursements of $4,000 are 50 percent of August sales.
c. Wages and salary payments (line 8) are 20 percent of sales and are paid in the month the skis are manufactured. Thus, July wages of $1,600 are 20 percent of August sales because the skis sold in August are manufactured in July.
d. Rent (line 9) for the building is $2,000 per month.
e. An outstanding loan required interest payments (line 10) of $600 per month, and quarterly principal payments (line 11) of $1,500 in March, June, September, and December.
f. Quarterly payment of estimated income taxes (line 12) of $1,000 must be made in April, June, September, and December.
g. Miscellaneous other expenses (line 13) will amount to $500 per month.
h. All receipts are from sales. Ten percent of each month's sales are typically on a cash basis (line 2) and 90 percent are on credit.
i. Forty percent of sales are collected the first month after the sale (line 3), 30 percent are collected the second month (line 4), 15 percent are collected three months after the sale (line 5), and 5 percent are bad debts and are never collected.

shown in Exhibit 3.1, and the forecast of sales for the coming year is shown in line 1 in Exhibit 3.2, where the fiscal year is assumed to start in July. Sales are at a seasonal low in June and July, then start increasing rapidly to reach a peak in November, then they decline over the winter and spring months. The sales forecast is the primary input that "drives" the calculation of the firm's financing needs that will be the output of this exercise. Obviously, any change (or inaccuracy) in the sales forecast would lead to a change (or error) in the forecast of the financing needs. Based on the forecast and assumptions, Exhibit 3.2 is the cash receipts and disbursements statement showing the cash flows and required financing over a one-year planning horizon that is divided into monthly subperiods. This statement is only a first approximation and is not yet complete because it does not

EXHIBIT 3.2

MOGUL CORPORATION
Cash Receipts and Disbursements
July 1986–June 1987

	July	*Aug*	*Sept*	*Oct*	*Nov*	*Dec*	*Jan*	*Feb*	*Mar*	*Apr*	*May*	*June*	*Annual Total*
1. Sales	$3,000	$8,000	$18,000	$40,000	$60,000	$35,000	$20,000	$15,000	$ 5,000	$ 3,000	$ 2,000	$ 1,000	
Receipts													
2. Cash sales (10%)	300	800	1,800	4,000	6,000	3,500	2,000	1,500	500	300	200	100	
Credit sales													
3. First month (40%)	400	1,200	3,200	7,200	16,000	24,000	14,000	8,000	6,000	2,000	1,200	800	
4. Second month (30%)	600	300	900	2,400	5,400	12,000	18,000	10,500	6,000	4,500	1,500	900	
5. Third month (15%)	450	300	150	450	1,200	2,700	6,000	9,000	5,250	3,000	2,250	750	
6. Total receipts	1,750	2,600	6,050	14,050	28,600	42,200	40,000	29,000	17,750	9,800	5,150	2,550	199,500
Disbursements													
7. Purchases	4,000	9,000	20,000	30,000	17,500	10,000	7,500	2,500	1,500	1,000	500	1,500	

8. Wages and salaries	1,600	3,600	8,000	12,000	7,000	4,000	3,000	1,000	600	400	200	600	
9. Rent	2,000	2,000	2,000	2,000	2,000	2,000	2,000	2,000	2,000	2,000	2,000	2,000	
10. Interest	600	600	600	600	600	600	600	600	600	600	600	600	
11. Debt principal	—	—	1,500	—	—	1,500	—	—	1,500	—	—	1,500	
12. Taxes	—	—	1,000	—	—	1,000	—	—	—	1,000	—	1,000	
13. Miscellaneous	500	500	500	500	500	500	500	500	500	500	500	500	
14. Total disbursements	8,700	15,700	33,600	45,100	27,600	19,600	13,600	6,600	6,700	5,500	3,800	7,700	194,200
15. Net Cash Flow plus	<6,950>	<13,100>	<27,550>	<31,050>	1,000	22,600	26,400	22,400	11,050	4,300	1,350	<5,150>	5,300
16. Beginning cash balance without financing	5,000	<1,950>	<15,050>	<42,600>	<73,650>	<72,650>	<50,050>	<23,650>	<1,250>	9,800	14,100	15,450	
17. Cumulative cash less	<1,950>	<15,050>	<42,600>	<73,650>	<72,650>	<50,050>	<23,650>	<1,250>	9,800	14,100	15,450	10,300	
18. Desired cash	5,000	5,000	5,000	5,000	5,000	5,000	5,000	5,000	5,000	5,000	5,000	5,000	
19. Required financing	6,950	20,050	47,600	78,650	77,650	55,050	28,650	6,250	—	—	—	—	
20. Excess cash	—	—	—	—	—	—	—	—	4,800	9,100	10,450	5,300	

Note: Figures enclosed in angle brackets < > are negative.

show interest expenses related to financing the deficit. This is because we need to work through the budget first, to know how much needs to be borrowed prior to calculating the financing costs. We will take these financing costs into account when we explicitly consider the form of financing. Similarly, any earnings on investment of excess cash are not yet considered in this preliminary statement. At this stage, the purpose is to develop a preliminary estimate of our financing need without yet taking account of these added details.

Notice that noncash expenses such as depreciation are not reflected in the cash budget. In addition, there is no bad debt expense because bad debts are reflected by sales never collected. Also, it was assumed that the past months and future months (not shown) follow the same monthly sales pattern as shown, in order to show the disbursements for June that depend on sales forecasted beyond June, and the receipts on credit accounts that depend on sales prior to July.

In Exhibit 3.2 the net cash flow (line 15) is equal to total receipts (line 6) minus total disbursements (line 14). Net cash flow plus the cash balance at the beginning of the month yields the month-end cash balance. In the exhibit the cash balance is calculated as if no additional funds are obtained. Thus, cumulative cash (line 17) shows what the cash balance would be at the end of the month if no funds were borrowed (or invested). The cumulative cash balance of ⟨$1,950⟩ at the end of July indicates that a cash deficit of $1,950 must be financed to restore the balance to zero, since it is meaningless to have negative cash. In addition, because the firm desires a cash balance of $5,000, the total required financing (line 19) for July is $6,950.

The cumulative cash item carries the deficit (or surplus) from month to month in a cumulative manner. That is, the deficit in July is $1,950, in August it is $13,100, and the total of these two amounts is $15,050. This cumulative deficit plus the $5,000 desired cash balance means that a total of $20,050 must be financed in August—$6,950 left over from July, plus an additional loan of $13,100 to cover the August deficit.

This cumulative required financing is shown as required financing (line 19). The required financing increases from July through October to a peak of $78,650. This $78,650 represents the total amount of financing that will be necessary over the one-year cycle. Note that the required financing declines after October because the firm receives a positive net cash flow. This positive net cash flow allows some of the financing to be repaid so the required financing declines. In November the net cash flow is $1,000, which potentially can be used to repay the loan, so the required financing declines. By March there has been sufficient cash inflow to allow any loans to be repaid and to build up the cash balance. Thus, by the end of March, the required financing is zero, and there is excess cash of $4,800, indicating that the cash balance would be $4,800 in excess of the $5,000 desired cash balance.

Exhibits 3.3 and 3.4 show the time profile of the firm's required funding. Exhibit 3.3 shows the month-by-month funding needs and funds available. The additional required financing represents the marginal deficit for each month that must be funded either through borrowing or through drawing down the cash balance (as in June). The funds available represents the funds that can be used to repay debt, build up the cash balance, or invest in securities.

Exhibit 3.4 shows the cumulative required financing or excess cash. The required financing builds up to $78,650 in October and then declines because it is presumed the $1,000 cash inflow in November is used to repay the debt.

EXHIBIT 3.3

EXHIBIT 3.4

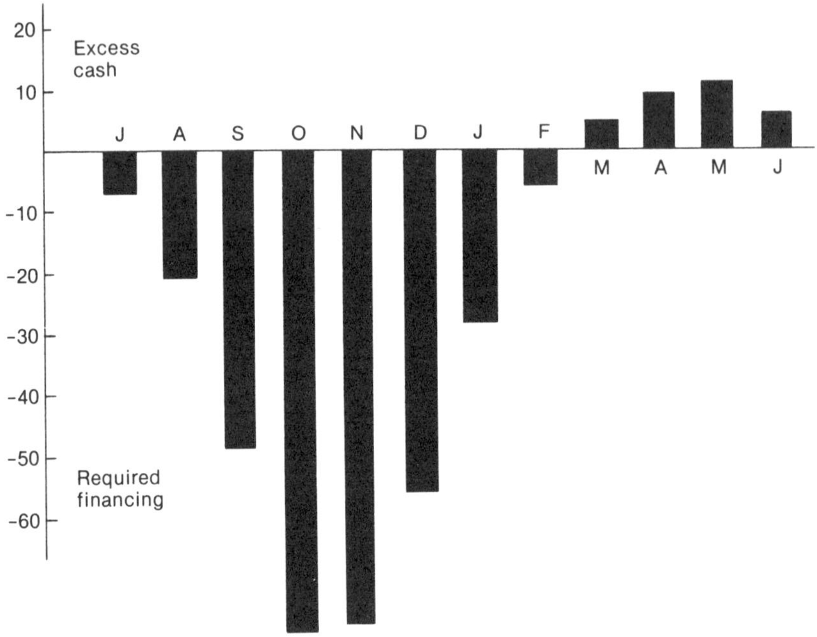

Note that the rapid increase in required financing is the result of expenses leading (occurring in advance of) sales and receipts lagging (occurring after) sales. The lead of expenses and lag of receipts tends to magnify the deficits and make them last longer. One question management should consider is what actions can be taken to narrow the time gap between the disbursements and receipts. That is, in terms of the ingredients of financial planning, the decision alternatives that address the problem must be specified.

In approaching such a planning problem it is important to choose correctly the length of the planning horizon (one year in this example) and the length of the subperiods (months in this case). If the analyst had looked only at the annual figures, the total annual receipts would be $199,500, the total disbursements would be $194,200, and the annual net cash flow would be $5,300. It is not immediately apparent from these figures that the required financing would total $78,650. By neglecting to consider the monthly cash flows, the analyst would be completely unprepared to meet the firm's financing needs. The various factors influencing the proper length of the planning horizon will be discussed subsequently.

It was noted previously that planning involves more than forecasting and that planning is the specification of future decisions and actions to reach a stated goal. In terms of this definition, the cash budgeting problem just analyzed was not really planning, rather it was forecasting. It generated a forecast of future required financing based on a forecast of sales and a set of assumptions about how customers pay their accounts, and how the firm would produce and pay for the goods it sold.

For this problem, planning would extend beyond this simple forecast of financing needs to explore alternative policies and decisions so as to determine the best way to reach the firm's goal. This requires that the goal and the various decisions alternative be specified and analyzed.

It is generally agreed that with respect to financial decisions the proper objective is to make the market value of the firm as large as possible. This very broad objective is made operational by specifying a set of goals that lead to value maximization. For present purposes, assume the goal is to make decisions to maximize the present value of the net cash flow available to equity over the planning horizon. Assume the discount rate for calculating present value is the firm's cost of equity capital, which is estimated to be 20 percent and is assumed not to vary any meaningful amount with different decision alternatives.

In the context of this example, the net cash flow available to equity would be the amount of cash flow available that could potentially be paid to the firm's owners after all expenses and after servicing any debt associated with financing the seasonal cash deficits.

To analyze any decision alternatives one must begin by considering the effect of the present policy on the goal. This requires the determination of the present value of the net cash flows from the present policy, which will provide a base for comparison for any alternative decisions considered. Exhibit 3.5 is a revised cash budget based on Exhibit 3.2, with total receipts from Exhibit 3.2 shown as the first line of Exhibit 3.5, with the line number 6 on the left indicating that this matches line 6 of

EXHIBIT 3.5 Mogul Corporation: Cash Budget (revised to include debt service)

		July	Aug	Sept	Oct	Nov	Dec	Jan	Feb	Mar	Apr	May	June
6.	Total receipts	$1,750	$ 2,600	$ 6,050	$14,050	$28,600	$42,200	$40,000	$29,000	$17,750	$ 9,800	$ 5,150	$ 2,550
14.	Total other disbursements	8,700	15,700	33,600	45,100	27,600	19,600	13,600	6,600	6,700	5,500	3,800	7,700
a.	Incremental interest	0	58	168	399	661	658	475	259	74	0	—	—
c.	Net cash flow plus	<6,950>	<13,158>	<27,718>	<31,449>	339	21,942	25,925	22,141	10,976	4,300	1,350	<5,150>
d.	Funds borrowed	6,950	13,158	27,718	31,449	<339>	<21,942>	<25,925>	<22,141>	<8,928>	0	0	0
e.	Net increase in cash	—	—	—	—	—	—	—	—	2,048	4,300	1,350	<5,150>
f.	Beginning cash	5,000	5,000	5,000	5,000	5,000	5,000	5,000	5,000	5,000	7,048	11,348	12,698
g.	Ending cash	5,000	5,000	5,000	5,000	5,000	5,000	5,000	5,000	7,048	11,348	12,698	7,548
h.	Loan balance	$6,950	$20,108	$47,826	$79,275	$78,936	$56,994	$31,069	$ 8,928	$ 0	$ 0	$ 0	$ 0

i. Present value of net increase in cash: $2,312.

Note: Figures enclosed in angle brackets < > are negative.

Exhibit 3.2; similarly, the second line of Exhibit 3.5 reproduces line 14 of Exhibit 3.2. However, now we explicitly take account of the costs of financing, and Exhibit 3.5 is based on the assumption that any required financing is financed by funds borrowed at 10 percent annual interest, with interest paid monthly, and the debt is repaid from any excess cash held above the desired level of $5,000. Thus, line a shows the interest that would be paid for funds borrowed. The $58 interest paid in August is one month's interest on the $6,950 borrowed in July ($6,950 × 0.10/12 = $58). Funds borrowed is shown in line d, with negative values beginning in November indicating debt repayment. The net increase in cash, shown on line e, represents the cash available from operations after paying interest and principal on the funds borrowed, and is the amount that potentially could be paid to the firm's owners after all expenses and debt servicing without decreasing the cash balance or requiring other financing. The present value of the net increase in cash, amounting to $2,312 on line i, represents the contribution of this 12-month period's operations to the value of the equity of the firm, and it serves as the value basis for evaluating alternative policies.

There are numerous alternative policies and decisions that should be evaluated to determine the one that is most likely to help the firm reach its objective. These alternatives include changing credit terms to affect the lag between sales and collections, changing the production schedule and purchasing and payment policies so as to affect the lead of disbursements over sales, and considering various ways to fund the financing requirements. Not all decision alternatives will be analyzed here. Rather, just one policy alternative is considered as an example to demonstrate the approach.

The policy change to be evaluated in this case involves an effort to speed up collection of receivables. Assume that increased collection efforts will persuade customers to speed up their payments so the firm would narrow the gap between sales and collections. Ten percent of sales would be cash, and 90 percent would be credit sales. Additional costs of collection would be 2 percent of sales per month, and 70 percent of sales would be collected one month after sales, 15 percent would be collected in the second month, and there would still be a 5 percent bad debt rate. The required financing will be funded with a revolving line of credit at 10 percent annual interest, with interest paid monthly, and the debt is assumed to be repaid out of the positive net cash flows that will begin in November.

Exhibit 3.6 shows the receipts and disbursements for this alternative. The line numbers correspond to those of Exhibit 3.2, with line 14 showing the total disbursements from Exhibit 3.2. Line a shows the incremental interest that must be paid for the funds borrowed, analogous to line a in Exhibit 3.5; and line b shows the additional 2 percent collection costs associated with the increased collection efforts. The net increase in cash (line e) corresponds to line e of Exhibit 3.5 and represents the cash flow available to equity associated with this policy. The present value of the net increase in cash of $207 is to be compared with the $2,312 shown on line i of Exhibit 3.5. This policy will result in a smaller contribution to the value of equity than the present policy evaluated in Exhibit 3.5. Thus, even though the more rigorous collection efforts accelerate the collections, the present value of receiving these funds sooner is not sufficient to offset the cost of the collection effort, and the old policy should be retained.

This example shows the usefulness of the cash receipts and disbursements statement. It helps to focus attention on the potential financing needs over the planning horizon being considered and shows when financing will be necessary, how *much* is necessary, and when it can be repaid.

The cash budget can be used to analyze many types of financial planning problems, regardless of the length of the planning horizon. It is particularly suited to the short planning horizon that is broken up into short periods such as days, weeks, or months, as in the foregoing example. In cases where there is a seasonal pattern to the funds flows, the cash budget is an ideal tool.

3.2 BREAK–EVEN ANALYSIS

One of the standard questions of financial analysis is: What is the break-even point, and how likely is it that the firm will be able to operate above that point? Break-even analysis is the tool that helps us to answer these questions that frequently arise in financial planning and investment analysis.

EXHIBIT 3.6 Mogul Corporation: Cash Receipts and Disbursements (evaluating more rigorous collection procedures, July 1986–June 1987)

	July	*Aug*	*Sept*	*Oct*	*Nov*	*Dec*	*Jan*	*Feb*	*Mar*	*Apr*	*May*	*June*
1. Sales	$3,000	$ 8,000	$18,000	$40,000	$60,000	$35,000	$20,000	$15,000	$ 5,000	$ 3,000	$ 2,000	$1,000
Receipts												
2. Cash sales (10%)	300	800	1,800	4,000	6,000	3,500	2,000	1,500	500	300	200	100
Credit collections												
3. First month (70%)	700	2,100	5,600	12,600	28,000	42,000	24,500	14,000	10,500	3,500	2,100	1,400
4. Second month (15%)	300	150	450	1,200	2,700	6,000	9,000	5,250	3,000	2,250	750	450
6. Total receipts	1,300	3,050	7,850	17,800	36,700	51,500	35,500	20,750	14,000	6,050	3,050	1,950
Disbursements												
14. Other disbursements	8,700	15,700	33,600	45,100	27,600	19,600	13,600	6,600	6,700	5,500	3,800	7,700
a. Incremental interest	0	62	169	388	626	565	310	133	19	0	0	3
b. Collection costs	60	160	360	800	1,200	700	400	300	100	60	40	20
c. Net cash flow plus	<7,460>	<12,872>	<26,279>	<28,488>	7,274	30,635	21,190	13,717	7,181	490	<790>	<5,773>
d Funds borrowed	7,460	12,872	26,279	28,488	<7,274>	<30,635>	<21,190>	<13,717>	<2,283>	—	—	1,175
e. Net increase in cash plus									4,898	490	<790>	<4,598>
f. Beginning cash	5,000	5,000	5,000	5,000	5,000	5,000	5,000	5,000	5,000	9,898	10,388	9,598
g. Ending cash	5,000	5,000	5,000	5,000	5,000	5,000	5,000	5,000	9,898	10,388	9,598	5,000
h. Loan balance	$7,460	$20,332	$46,611	$75,099	$67,825	$37,190	$16,000	$ 2,283	$ 0			$1.175

i. Present value of net increase in cash: $207

Note: Figures enclosed in angle brackets < > are negative.

The break-even point is defined as the level of output for which revenue just covers the costs. For production processes that involve just variable costs, so long as the sale price exceeds the variable cost per unit, the firm will be profitable at all output levels. However, if there are costs that are fixed so that they do not vary with the level of output, there is some minimum level of output necessary before revenue covers both fixed and variable costs.

In break-even analysis, costs are classified as fixed or variable. Fixed costs are costs that do not vary (in the short run) with the number of units of product produced or sold. Variable costs are costs that are related to the volume of production or sales, so that the variable costs increase as sales increase. Examples of fixed costs are salary expenses for personnel that are employed regardless of the level of production, rental and lease expenses that depend on time but not on sales volume, and, of course, noncash expenses such as depreciation and amortization. Examples of variable costs include sales commissions, labor costs related to manufacturing process that depend on the volume of output, and cost of materials used in production.

It should be emphasized that the dichotomy of costs into fixed and variable depends on the time horizon of the analysis. In the long run all costs are variable, but in the short run many costs are fixed and independent of sales volume. The shorter the horizon, the more costs are fixed.

EXAMPLE: THE LACKLAND CORPORATION

A short example is sufficient to introduce the basics of break-even analysis. Assume that the Lackland Corporation incurs fixed costs of $1.5 million per year that consist of costs of management salaries, rent, insurance, property taxes, and depreciation. Its variable costs, including materials, direct labor, and sales commissions amount to $7 per unit sold, where the sales price per unit is $10.

Exhibit 3.7 shows a graph of revenue and costs, with the number of units sold shown on the horizontal axis and revenue and costs shown on the vertical axis. Revenue is shown by the line starting at the origin and sloping upward. The slope indicates the rate at which revenue increases as the number of units sold is increased. Fixed cost is shown by the horizontal line intersecting the vertical axis at $1.5 million. The fact that the fixed cost line is horizontal indicates that these costs remain at $1.5 million regardless of the number of units sold.

Variable costs are shown as the line originating at $1.5 million and sloping upward, where the slope indicates the rate at which these costs increase as the number of units sold increases. The variable costs are measured by the distance between the fixed cost line and the line labeled total cost.

Total costs are the sum of fixed and variable costs, and are shown as the distance between the horizontal axis and the total cost line. At levels of sales below 500,000 units, total costs exceed

EXHIBIT 3.7

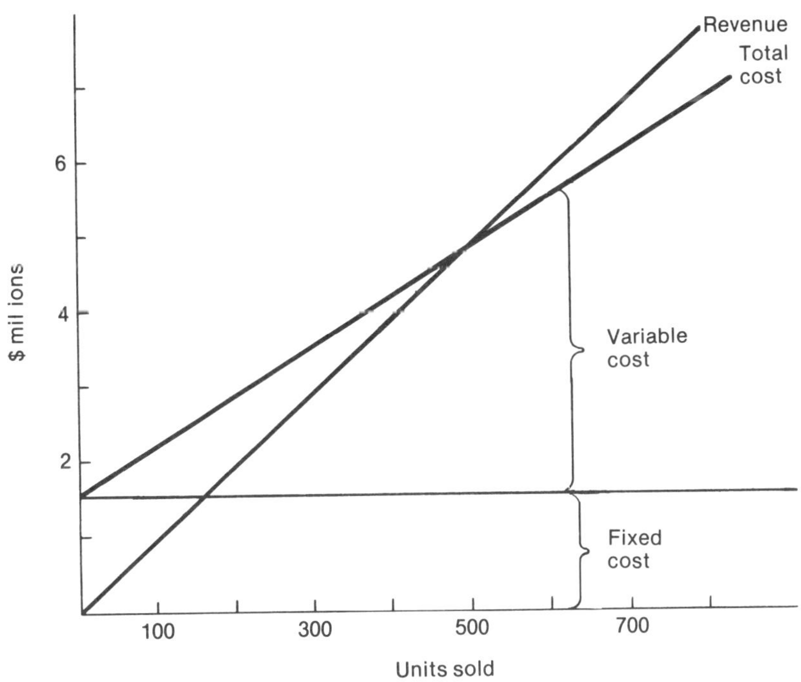

revenue, and at higher levels of sales, revenue exceeds costs and a profit is earned. At 500,000 units sold, revenue is just equal to total cost, so the firm is just breaking even with zero profit. Hence, we call 500,000 units sold the break-even point.

The break-even point is imposed by the existence of fixed costs of $1.5 million, in this example. Without fixed costs the operation would be profitable at all sales levels so long as the sales price exceeds the cost per unit. With fixed costs, the sales level has to be high enough so the "contribution margin" per unit (sales price minus variable cost per unit) makes up for the fixed costs. Here the contribution margin is $3 per unit, and the fixed costs are $1.5 million, so that 500,000 units must be sold before the contribution margin covers the fixed costs; that is, $1,500,000/$3 per unit = 500,000 units. Not surprisingly, this is just how one calculates the break-even point—calculate the number of units that must be sold in order for the total contribution margin to cover the fixed costs:

$$\begin{aligned} \textit{Break-even volume} &= \textit{Fixed costs/(Price per unit} \\ &\quad - \textit{Cost per unit)} \qquad (3.1) \\ Q^* &= \$1{,}500{,}000/(10-7) \\ Q^* &= 500{,}000 \text{ units,} \end{aligned}$$

or $5 million of sales when the product is sold at $10 per unit, where Q^* denotes the break-even level expressed in units.

There are a number of useful extensions of break-even analysis. These include defining the break-even point in terms of net income or cash flow, sensitivity analysis that considers what income will be at various sales levels, and the analysis of operating leverage and financial leverage.

In the example just presented, the costs were defined as fixed and variable, but it was not clear which costs were included in these categories, and it was not clear whether the break-even level was defined in terms of earnings before interest and taxes (EBIT), net income (NI), or cash flows. Any such analysis should clarify which definition of income is being used to calculate the break-even point. Consider Exhibit 3.8, which displays the income statement for our example firm in two formats. The first format is the standard as would be seen in an annual report. The costs are categorized as to the general pur-

EXHIBIT 3.8 Income Statements (two formats)

LACKLAND CORPORATION
Standard Income Statement
($000)

Sales	$12,000
Costs and expenses:	
Cost of goods sold	8,500
Selling, general, and administrative expenses	1,400
Interest expense	300
Income tax expenses	700
Net income (NI)	$ 1,100

LACKLAND CORPORATION
Revised Income Statement
($000)

Sales	$12,000
Less: Variable operating costs (70% of sales)	8,400
Fixed costs: Cash operating expense	600
Earnings before depreciation, interest, and taxes (EBDIT)	3,000
Fixed cost: Depreciation expense	900
Earnings before interest and taxes (EBIT)	2,100
Interest expense	300
Earnings before tax (EBT)	1,800
Income tax expense	700
Net income (NI)	$ 1,100

pose of the expense, but they are not classified as fixed or variable. Both costs of goods sold and selling, general, and administrative expenses include both fixed and variable components, with depreciation expense being included in costs of goods sold. All costs and expenses are shown with no intermediate calculation of income.

In the revised format, the expenses are classified as fixed or variable, and the income is shown at intermediate levels such as EBDIT and EBIT before reaching the bottom line, which is net income. This revised format is useful for analyzing the effects of fixed and variable costs; the distinctions between EBDIT (earnings before depreciation, interest, and tax), EBIT, and NI are useful for analyzing cash flows and distinguishing between income for the firm as whole, and income to equity.

First, consider the cash flow to the firm generated by operations. Assume that variable operating costs are actual cash outlays, as is that part of the fixed costs that does not include depreciation expense. The operating income (EBDIT) represents the cash generated by operations, prior to considering interest or taxes. Thus, EBDIT shows the before-tax cash earnings, independent of how the firm is financed or how taxes are affected by depreciation. In the context of break-even analysis, one can ask, "What minimum level of sales is necessary for the firm to reach EBDIT–break-even—that is, break-even defined in terms of operating cash flow?" In this case, variable costs are 70 percent of sales (denoted by v) and fixed costs are \$600,000. The cash-flow break-even level of sales is calculated as

$$\begin{aligned} \textit{Cash break-even sales} &= \frac{\textit{Fixed cash operating expense}}{1 - v} \qquad (3.2) \\ &= \frac{600{,}000}{1 - 0.70} \\ &= \$2{,}000{,}000 \end{aligned}$$

or 200,000 units at a sales price of \$10 per unit. Note that in this example, the fixed costs are divided by the contribution margin expressed as a decimal (0.30), yielding the *dollar* level of sales necessary to break even. In the first example, the denominator was the contribution margin expressed as a dollar amount, so the break-even point was the number of *units* necessary for income to be zero.

Furthermore, in the first example, break even was implicitly assumed to be defined in terms of EBIT because the fixed costs were given as \$1.5 million, which included depreciation expense of \$900,000, versus the cash fixed costs of \$600,000, which excludes depreciation expense in this latter example. Thus, the firm must reach a sales level of \$5 million before EBIT is zero, but at a sales level of \$2 million, its cash flow (EBDIT) would reach zero, but at sales of \$2 million, EBIT would be ⟨\$900,000⟩ because of the depreciation expense, which involves no cash outflow from the firm.

Breaking even also may be defined in terms of net income. That is, what minimum level of sales is necessary before net income reaches zero? The principle is the same: determine the sales level such that the total contribution margin covers the fixed costs. Now, the fixed costs included interest expense plus all previous fixed costs. In the present example assume there are no variable costs below the level of operating costs on the income statement and the fixed costs amount to \$1.8 million (\$600,000 fixed cash operating costs, \$900,000 depreciation expense, and \$300,000 interest expense). With a proportional variable cost of 0.70 and a per-unit variable cost of \$7, the dollar volume of sales required to break even is

$$Sales^* = \frac{\$1{,}800{,}000}{1 - 0.70} = \$6{,}000{,}000,$$

or, in terms of units,

$$Q^* = \frac{1{,}800{,}000}{\$10 - \$7} = 600{,}000 \text{ units},$$

when the sale price per unit is \$10.

Note that income taxes play no role in the calculation of net income break-even level so long as income taxes are strictly proportional to taxable income, and are zero when taxable income is zero.

The last variation of break even that we will discuss takes into account the return required on the firm's equity capital. This approach treats the required return on the equity capital employed by the firm as a fixed cost that must be covered by the firm's operations, and it shows the level of sales that would be necessary to cover all costs, including this required return on equity capital. In our present example, assume the Lackland Corporation has equity capital of \$8 million, and the stockholders require a return on equity of 15 percent. This means that Lackland requires net income of \$1.2 million (.15 × \$8,000,000) in order to be able to meet the return objectives of the stockholders. Treating this required net income as a fixed cost, the dollar level of sales necessary to break even is

$$\text{Sales} = \frac{\{(\textit{Fixed cash operating expense} + \textit{Depreciation expense} + \textit{Interest expense})\,(1 - T) + \textit{Required net income})\}}{(1 - v)\,(1 - T)}$$

For Lackland, for which $v = .7$ and the tax rate is $T = .39$, we have

$$\text{Sales} = \frac{\{(600{,}000 + 900{,}000 + 300{,}000)\,(1 - .39) + 1{,}200{,}000\}}{(1 - .7)\,(1 - .39)}$$

$$= \$12{,}557{,}377.$$

Thus, even though Lackland would require sales of only $6 million to break even in terms of net income, it requires almost double that amount to provide an adequate return to the firm's stockholders. In analyzing its prospects, this company should not neglect this version of break-even analysis because it would be short-sighted to focus on actions that provide positive income but do not generate an adequate return on invested capital.

In the financial planning context the analyst is interested not only in the break-even point, but also in the likelihood that the firm's sales will exceed the break-even point, in the firm's cash flows and earnings at various level of sales, and in the sensitivity of the firm's earnings to variations in the level of sales. The analysis of fixed and variable costs helps to consider each of those concerns.

One can easily determine the expected income generated by a given level of sales according to the definition of income:

$$\textit{EBDIT} = \textit{Sales} \cdot (1 - v) - \textit{Fixed cash operating expense},$$

where v is the variable cost expressed as a proportion of sales; and

$$\textit{EBIT} = \textit{Sales} \cdot (1 - v) - \textit{Fixed cash operating expense} - \textit{Depreciation expenses},$$

and

$$\textit{NI} = [\textit{Sales} \cdot (1 - v) - \textit{Fixed cash operating expense} - \textit{Depreciation expense} - \textit{Interest}] \cdot (1 - T),$$

where T is the corporate income tax rate.

EXHIBIT 3.9 Earnings at Different Sales Levels

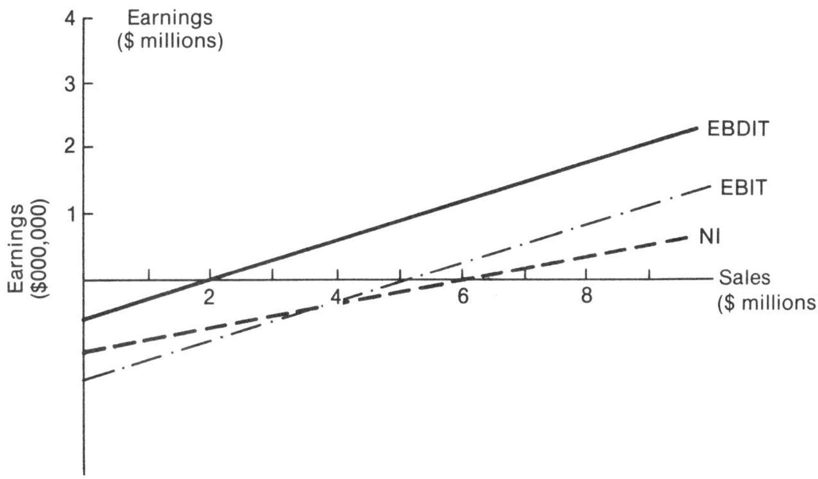

With accurate estimates of the cost factors, the level of sales can be varied to provide an estimate of income at each level of sales, as shown in Exhibit 3.9. Note that the graph of net income has less slope than that of either EBDIT or EBIT. This is the effect of the income tax: as sales increase, NI increases less than EBIT because of proportional corporate income tax.

Degrees of Leverage

Planning is a forward-looking exercise, and future revenues and costs are uncertain. With uncertain sales, one useful form of analysis is to explore the sensitivity of income to variation in the level of sales. One way to do this is to consider the elasticity of earnings with respect to sales, or to measure the degree of operating and financial leverage. The sales elasticity of earnings measures the percentage variation in the firm's earnings that results from a 1 percent change in sales. For example, if at a given level of sales a 1 percent increase in sales would result in a 2 percent increase in EBIT, then we say the sales elasticity of EBIT is 2.

Earnings are elastic relative to sales (elasticity greater than 1) because of the presence of fixed costs. If all costs were directly proportional to sales, then earnings would vary directly with sales on a one-for-one basis. However, when some costs are fixed, independent of sales, increases in sales can occur without concomitant increases in all the costs, so that earnings can increase proportionally more than sales. The use of fixed-cost methods of operation (e.g., the use of machinery rather than labor) is referred to as using *operating leverage,* and we measure the degree of operating leverage (DOL), with the calculation of the sales elasticity of EBIT. It can be shown that this elasticity or degree of operating leverage can be calculated (at a given level of sales) as

$$DOL = \frac{Sales - Variable\ costs}{EBIT} = \frac{Sales \cdot (1 - v)}{Sales \cdot (1 - v) - Fixed\ operating\ costs} \tag{3.3}$$

For example, at a sales level of \$12 million, our example firm has

$$DOL = \frac{12{,}000{,}000\ (1 - 0.70)}{2{,}100{,}000} = 1.7.$$

Thus, at this sales level, a 1 percent change in sales will result in a 1.7 percent change in EBIT because of the operating leverage resulting from fixed cost methods of operation.

By substituting variable-cost methods for fixed-cost methods, thereby increasing v to, say, 0.90, and decreasing the annual fixed costs to, say, \$200,000, the firm would have

$$DOL = \frac{12{,}000{,}000\ (1 - 0.90)}{1{,}200{,}000 - 200{,}000} = 1.2,$$

so that a 1 percent change in sales would result in a 1.2 percent change in EBIT, rather than the 1.7 percent change shown previously.

The firm may face another fixed cost besides the fixed costs of producing its product. Interest expense is a fixed cost that is paid for debt financing, and debt financing provides leverage to the equity owners. Thus, the ideas about break-even points, leverage, and elasticity that apply to operating leverage also apply to the use of the fixed-cost source of financing, debt.

In the absence of debt financing, any variation in EBIT is translated directly into an equal proportional variation in net income. Because of the necessity to meet the obligation to make a fixed interest payment, any variation in EBIT will be leveraged (or magnified) into a more than proportional change in net income. This effect is referred to as *financial leverage* and is measured by the elasticity of net income with respect to EBIT, or the degree of financial leverage (DFL), expressed by the equation

$$DFL = \frac{EBIT}{EBIT - I} \tag{3.4}$$

where I denotes the interest payment. For our examples, at a sales level of \$12 million, the degree of financial leverage is

$$DFL = \frac{2{,}100{,}000}{2{,}100{,}000 - 300{,}000} = 1.17,$$

meaning that at that sales level, a 1 percent change in EBIT would be translated into a 1.17 percent change in after-tax net income.

The equity owners of the firm are subject to both operating leverage and financial leverage. Variations in sales are translated into magnified variations in net income by the combined effects of fixed-cost production methods and fixed-cost financing methods. This effect is summarized and measured as the *degree of combined leverage* (DCL), which can be calculated as

$$\begin{aligned} DCL &= DOL \cdot DFL \\ &= \frac{Sales - Variable\ costs}{EBIT} \cdot \frac{EBIT}{EBIT \quad I} \\ &= \frac{Sales - Variable\ costs}{EBIT - I} \end{aligned} \tag{3.5}$$

at a given level of sales. For our example, at a sales level of \$12 million, the degree of combined leverage is

$$DCL = \frac{12{,}000{,}000 - 8{,}400{,}000}{2{,}100{,}000 - 300{,}000} = 2.$$

or, expressed as the product of DOL and DFL,

$$\begin{aligned} DCL &= DOL \times DFL \\ &= 1.71 \times 1.17 = 2. \end{aligned}$$

This means that at a sales level of $12 million a 1 percent change in sales would be translated into a 2 percent change in net income and earnings per share available for the stockholders.

The ideas of sales elasticity and degree of operating leverage are of use to the planner in contemplating the effects of the structure of the firm on the firm's future performance. It should be remembered, however, that both these measures depend on the level of sales. Generally, as the level of sales considered is increased (above the break-even point) the degree of leverage will decline.

This elementary analysis assumed that costs and revenues are linearly related to the number of units sold. That is, the graphs of revenues and costs as shown in Exhibit 3.7 are straight lines, as opposed to curved lines. This assumption is a useful approximation for many situations and is well suited to introducing the concepts. In real life, the relationships may be more complex, and indeed, the concept of break-even point itself may be more complicated than is apparent from the standard one-period example. In the Lockheed L-1011 example to follow, the cost and revenue relationships are not necessarily linear (straight lines), and even the concept of break-even point can be redefined to take account of the multiperiod nature of the problem. In that case, breaking even is defined in terms of the level of sales for which the *present value* of the stream of income over the life of the project is zero.

EXAMPLE: LOCKHEED L–1011

In the early 1970s Lockheed Aircraft Company developed a wide-bodied airliner, the Lockheed L-1011 TriStar. A controversy arose because Lockheed appealed to the U.S. Congress for loan guarantees to help it complete the L-1011 program. Lockheed contended that the program and the airplane were both economically viable and were worthy of support. Opponents contended that the program was economically unsound and should not be supported by the government. Some of the basic questions in planning such a project and in discussing its merits are: How many aircraft could be sold? How much profit could the firm expect from the project? and What is the net present value of the project? Some of these issues are clarified with break-even analysis, and the following example demonstrates the application of break-even analysis to investment planning. The example to follow is based on cost estimates and analysis presented by Reinhardt (1973) and its point of view is that of an analysis made prior to the development of the project.

Based on analysis of publically available data, the revenues and costs associated with the L-1011 are assumed to be as follows.

Revenues

The total market for aircraft of this size is forecasted to be, at most, 775 units to be absorbed over the next 10 years. Lockheed hopes to capture about 35 to 40 percent of the market, or to sell a total of 270 to 310 units. These aircraft would be delivered at a rate of three per month, starting in 42 months.

Each L-1011 will be sold at a price of $15.5 million. Payment will be received at the date of delivery.

Production and Costs

Manufacture of the aircraft consists of three phases. First is the research, development, testing, and evaluation phase; second is the initial investment and tooling phase, in which production facilities are constructed; and third is the manufacturing phase.

The first two phases involve costs that are nonrecurring and fixed in that they do not depend on the number of aircraft units manufactured. These fixed costs are estimated to be between $800 million and $1 billion. We will assume they will be in the middle of this range, at $900 million. These costs would be incurred over a period of 42 months that it takes to develop, toolup, and begin production. For present purposes, it is assumed these costs are incurred at an even rate over the 42-month period, or at a rate of $21.4 million per month.[1]

The manufacturing phase involves recurring costs that vary with the number of units produced. Because of the beneficial

---

[1]Development costs in advanced technology typically start out small, build up to a peak in the middle of the development period, and then taper off as the production date approaches. This pattern is not used here in order to simplify the analysis.

effects of learning, the average cost per unit declines as more units are produced. The best estimate of the relation between the number of units produced and the costs has resulted in the cost function shown in Exhibit 3.10, where the variable costs are expressed (in millions of dollars) as

$$\textit{Total variable cost} = 100\ (\textit{Units produced})^{0.63}, \qquad (3.6)$$

where the exponent, 0.63, is a parameter that represents the rate at which costs increase with the number of units produced. An exponent between 0 and 1 means that costs increase at a decreasing rate as production increases. The total cost of producing aircraft is the total of the fixed (nonrecurring) cost and variable (recurring) cost, and is expressed (in millions of dollars) as

$$\textit{Total cost} = 900 + 100\ (\textit{Units produced})^{0.63}. \qquad (3.7)$$

Because the total cost increases at a decreasing rate as the number of units produced increases, the average cost per unit declines as the number of units is increased.

Exhibit 3.10 shows total costs and revenues. Revenues increase linearly at a rate of \$15.5 million per unit sold. Total costs start out at about \$1 billion for the first unit sold and increase at a decreasing rate as more units are sold. For levels of output less than about 286 units, total costs (fixed plus variable) exceed total revenue, and the firm would operate at a loss.[2] At a level of 286 units there is a small profit, so the break-even point—in terms of earnings before interest and taxes (EBIT)—is about 286 units. (Obviously, it makes no sense to produce less than a full aircraft, so it is meaningless to say the break-even point is 285½ aircraft.) With total production of 286 aircraft, we have

$$\begin{array}{lrr} \textit{Total revenue} & = \qquad 15.5 \cdot (286) = & \$4{,}433 \text{ million} \\ \textit{Total cost} & = 900 + 100\ (286)^{0.63} = & \underline{4{,}428} \text{ million} \\ \textit{EBIT} & & \$ \quad 5 \text{ million} \end{array}$$

[2]This break-even point differs very slightly from that derived by Reinhardt. The present analysis is based on Reinhardt's equation (4), which is identical to the present equation (3.7). The present analysis is expressed in terms of units produced, whereas Reinhardt's equations are expressed in terms of time.

EXHIBIT 3.10

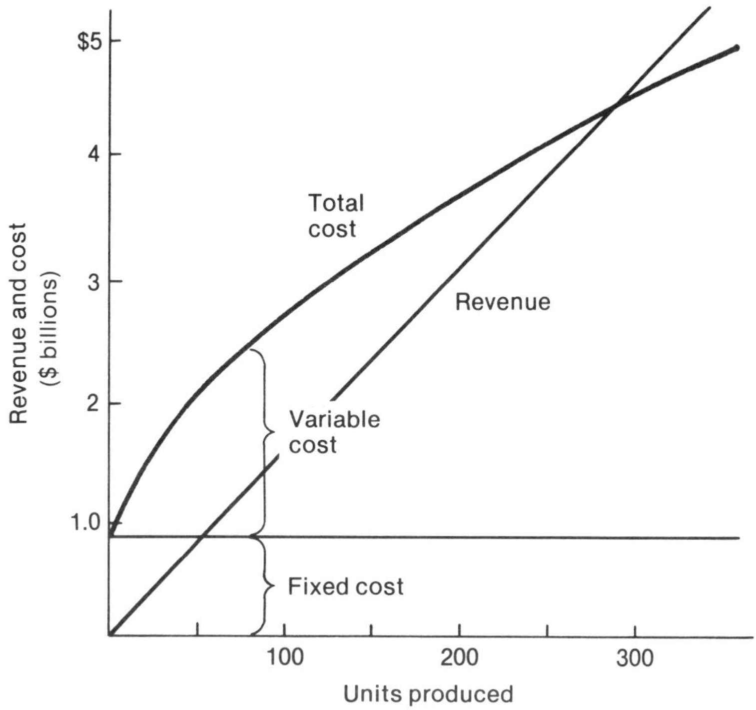

At an output of 286 aircraft, the average cost per unit will be $15.48 million, as compared to an average sale price of $15.50 million per unit. At this break-even level of total output, with a production rate of three units per month, aircraft must be produced for 95 months, or almost eight years, before the project reaches its EBIT break-even point, and note this is *after* the 42-month period of development and does not take into account the time value of money.

Not only will it take a long time to break even, but the profit potential appears to be small relative to the amount of money invested. If sales reach the maximum of 310 units, or 40 percent of the forecasted market, EBIT will be only about $193 million. Some questions for management are, How likely is it that Lockheed can sell between 286 and 310 aircraft? And, Is it likely that their share of the market might exceed 40 percent? If sales turn

EXHIBIT 3.11

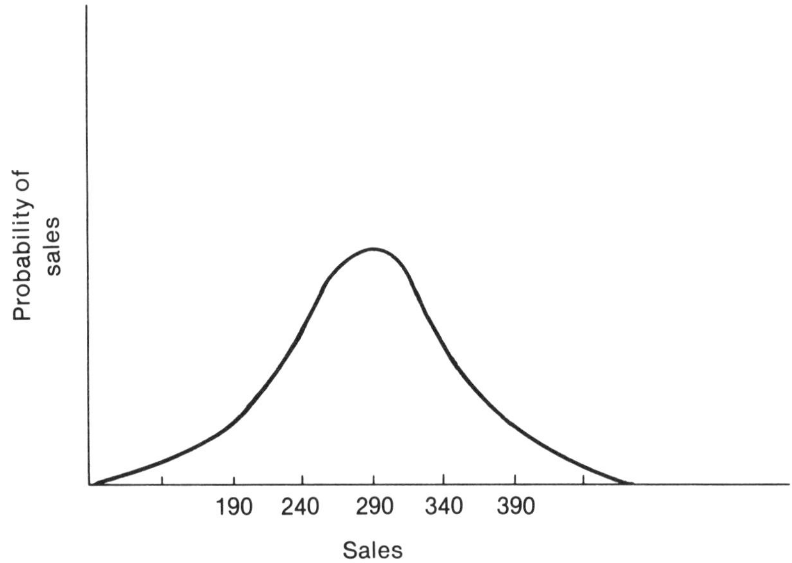

out to be on the low end of the forecasted market share of 35 percent, or 270 aircraft, the project will never break even.

One way to gain some insight into these questions is to consider explicitly the uncertainty of future sales and costs and to analyze the risks. For example, future sales are quite uncertain, so just assume, hypothetically, that sales is a random variable that is normally distributed with average, or mean, value of 290 units, with standard deviation of $\sigma = 50$ units. With these parameters the probability distribution would look as shown in Exhibit 3.11.

For a normal distribution, it is useful to remember that there is: (*a*) a 50 percent chance that the random variable will be less than the mean value, so that there is one chance in two that sales will be less than 290 units (which is just four units above break-even); and (*b*) a 65 percent chance that the random variable will occur in the range within one standard deviation of the mean, so that there are about two chances out of three that the sales will be between 240 units (290 − 50) and 340 units (290 + 50).

If costs are certain to be determined according to expression (3.7), with no randomness, but sales are random as assumed, EBIT over the life of the project will be a random variable with mean \$36 million and standard deviation of \$50 million. Thus, without costs being uncertain, there is a 50 percent chance that EBIT will be less than \$36 million, and about two chances out of three EBIT will be between −\$14 million and \$86 million, and there is a 24 percent chance the project will lose money.[3]

The manager should be alerted to these probabilities so that the benefits of the project can be weighed against the risks.

There are many different ways to define break-even. We have discussed break-even in terms of EBIT. Other break-even points could be defined in terms of cash flow (sales level at which cash flow is zero), profit before tax, net income after tax, and even in terms of net present value (NPV).

Net present value is the discounted present value of the cash inflows from an investment project less the present value of the cash outflows (cost). For the L-1011 project, it is particularly important to consider the time value of money because of the long time period of production. After all, it was already noted that without discounting it would take almost eight years to break even in terms of EBIT.

Reinhardt provides an analysis of net present value of the L-1011 project, using an estimate of Lockheed's weighted average cost of capital of 10 percent (which is probably on the low side). Exhibit 3.12 shows the profile of project NPV for different levels of output. When the time value of money and the long time period of production are considered, the attractiveness of the project rapidly disappears. According to Reinhardt's calculations, it would take a total output of about 510 aircraft for NPV to reach zero. At any output less than 510 units, the NPV would be negative. That is, the present value of the cash outflows would exceed the present value of the cash receipts from the project. The 510 units required to reach NPV break-even is about 66 percent of the total projected market for wide-bodied

---

[3]EBIT of zero is 0.720σ below the mean $[(0-36)/50 = -0.72]$, and from a normal probability table, the probability that the random variable will be less than 0.72σ below the mean is 23.6 percent.

EXHIBIT 3.12

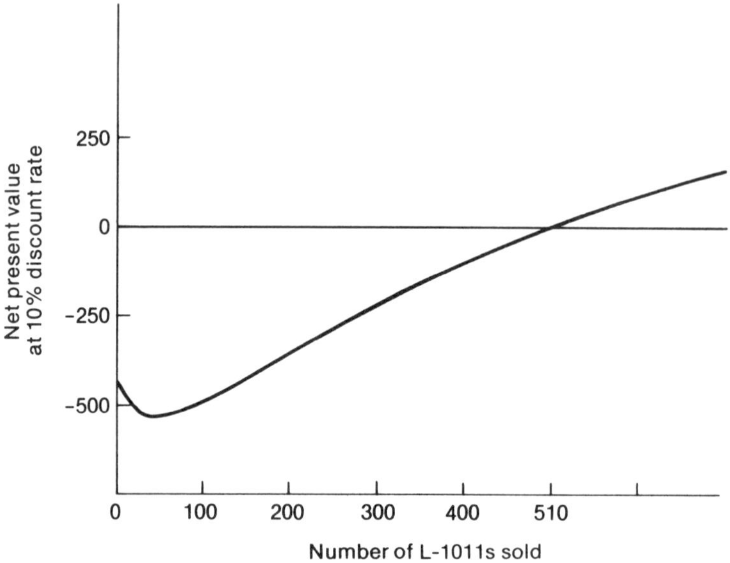

aircraft, and one would have to consider how likely it is that the L-1011 will capture this market share. If our previous estimates of the probability distribution of aircraft sales is even remotely correct, it would be extremely unlikely that 510 units could be sold because this is 4.4 standard deviations above the mean, an extreme point with less than 3 chances in 100,000 of occurring.

This example demonstrates some aspects of the use of break-even analysis in planning and evaluating an investment project. There are many other aspects that should be pursued. These include considering how changing the price of the aircraft would affect demand, profit, and NPV; whether we can get better estimates of the probabilistic aspects of the future; and the effect on the attractiveness of the project of the uncertainty of the costs. In addition, there are strategic aspects to be considered. The project may not pay off by itself, but it may be attractive because it maintains Lockheed in the commercial aircraft market and provides necessary diversification away from the purely military aspects of the business. One policy question would be, How much should Lockheed give up (how big a loss should it take) to obtain this diversification?

3.3 GROWTH AND PROJECTING THE NEEDS FOR FINANCING

One of the more difficult phases in the life cycle of a firm is the period of rapid growth. It would seem that growth would be a blessing, yet there are countless stories of firms that failed because they were unable to plan and manage their growth. The major difficulty is that as a firm grows, its needs for funds to finance expansion rapidly outrun its ability to generate funds from its operations. Faced with the opportunity to expand, but lacking the internal financing, these firms turn to debt as the source of financing, and frequently they find themselves with debt servicing obligations that exceed their ability to pay. Failure is eventually brought about because the needs of expansion have overwhelmed the firm's resources for expansion.

The difficulties and dangers of too rapid expansion can be mitigated by planning that anticipates the firm's financing requirements and management policy that controls growth at a pace consistent with the firm's ability to finance it. The following example will discuss simple techniques for determining the firm's financing needs, for determining the firm's feasible growth rate, and for analyzing the proposed financing plans.

EXAMPLE: THE COMBEX CORPORATION

The Combex Corporation designs and sells a specialized line of computer hardware and software that is sold to the oil and chemical industries. Its products are patented and there are no direct competitors. It has experienced very rapid growth in recent years and anticipates that this growth will continue for at least the next five years. The recent rapid growth has put a strain on the company's finances, and there is concern about the effects of growth on the firm's financial position in the future. The tasks at hand are to analyze the likely effect of growth on the firm, determine the needs for future financing, and to project the firm's financial position for future periods.

Exhibits 3.13 and 3.14 show Combex's income statement and balance sheet for the year just completed, 1985, and selected financial ratios are shown in Exhibit 3.15. The ratios show that

EXHIBIT 3.13

COMBEX CORPORATION
Income Statement
Year Ended December 31, 1985
(in thousands)

		Percent of Sales
Sales	$4,500.0	100%
Cost of goods sold	3,375.0	75
Selling, general, and administrative expenses	540.0	12
Depreciation expense	58.2	1.3
Earnings before interest and taxes	526.8	11.7
Interest expense	117.3	2.6
Earnings before tax	409.5	9.1
Income tax expense	168.3	3.7
Net income	$ 241.2	5.4%

EXHIBIT 3.14

COMBEX CORPORATION
Balance Sheet
December 31, 1985
(in thousands)

Assets			*Percent of Total Assets*	
Cash and securities		$ 120		5.6%
Trade receivables		760		35.7
Inventories		620		29.1
Total current assets		$1,500		70.4
Plant and equipment	$970		45.5%	
Less: Depreciation allowance	340		16.0	
Net fixed assets		630		29.5
Total assets		$2,130		100.0
Liabilities and Stockholders' Equity				
Trade accounts payable		$ 318		14.9
Other current liabilities		208		9.8
Notes payable		257		12.1
Taxes payable		22		1.0
Total current liabilities		805		37.8
Long-term debt		581		27.3
Common stock $1 par	$100			
Earned surplus	644			
Total stockholders' equity		744		34.9
Total liabilities and stockholders' equity		$2,130		100.0%

EXHIBIT 3.15

COMBEX CORPORATION
Selected Financial Ratios
1985

Liquidity		
Current ratio	$\frac{\text{Current assets}}{\text{Current liabilities}}$	1.86
Activity		
Average collection period	$\frac{\text{Receivables}}{\text{Sales}/360}$	60.8 days
Inventory turnover	$\frac{\text{Cost of goods sold}}{\text{Inventory}}$	5.4×
Average inventory period	$\frac{\text{Inventory}}{\text{Cost of goods sold}/360}$	66.1 days
Fixed asset turnover	$\frac{\text{Sales}}{\text{Net fixed assets}}$	7.1×
Total asset turnover	$\frac{\text{Sales}}{\text{Total assets}}$	2.1×
Leverage		
Debt ratio	$\frac{\text{Total debt}}{\text{Total assets}}$	0.65
Debt-to-equity	$\frac{\text{Total debt}}{\text{Total equity}}$	1.86
Times interest earned	$\frac{\text{EBIT}}{\text{Interest}}$	4.5
Profitability		
Net profit margin	$\frac{\text{Net income}}{\text{Sales}}$	5.4%
Return on assets	$\frac{\text{EBIT}}{\text{Total assets}}$	24.7%
Return on equity	$\frac{\text{Net income}}{\text{Total equity}}$	32.4%

Combex is able to generate a very high return on investment for its stockholders; one reason for this is the very heavy use of financial leverage that has helped finance their recent growth. While the use of debt financing has not yet caused any difficulty, the managers and creditors of Combex are concerned that any decline in sales could lead to the firm having difficulty meeting its debt obligations. One aspect of this fear is that if debt is used to finance future growth, the firm will become increasingly vulnerable to adversity. Consequently, both the management and the creditors would like to get a better idea of what financing will be required for future growth, what form that financing could take, and how different financing schemes would affect the firm, the stockholders, and the creditors.

The first task is to project the needs for financing that are imposed by its growth. If it is assumed that the amount of assets required to support the sales is more or less a constant proportion of sales (*Total assets/Sales*), then the assets required to support forecasted future sales in period t are

$$\textit{Required total assets}_t = \left(\frac{\textit{Total assets}}{\textit{Sales}}\right) \textit{Sales}_t. \qquad (3.8)$$

For Combex, assume that the total asset-to-sales ratio will be maintained at about 0.48, so that with a sales forecast of \$5.4 million for 1986, the required assets are

$$\begin{aligned}\textit{Required total assets} &= (0.48)\ \$5{,}400{,}000 \\ &= \$2{,}592{,}000.\end{aligned}$$

The investment in assets required to support the increase in sales from year $t - 1$ to year t is

$$\textit{Required investment}_t = \left(\frac{\textit{Total assets}}{\textit{Sales}}\right) \cdot \left(\textit{Sales}_t - \textit{Sales}_{t-1}\right),$$

and the investment required during 1986 will be

$$\begin{aligned}\textit{Required investment} &= (0.48)(\$5{,}400{,}000 - \$4{,}500{,}000) \\ &= \$432{,}000.\end{aligned}$$

Obviously, any investment in new assets must be financed from some source. For present purposes, the sources can be classified as spontaneous financing, internal equity financing, and external financing.

Spontaneous financing refers to the increases in liabilities, particularly current liabilities, that are related directly to the production and sales cycle. Liability accounts such as accounts payable, wages payable, and various liability accrual accounts normally increase along with production and sales, so they help finance part of the required increase in assets. In addition, these liabilities will normally increase in step with sales, so there is a constant ratio of these spontaneous sources of financing to sales.

In this case assume that the spontaneous components of current liabilities are the trade accounts payable, other liabilities, and income taxes payable, and that the total of these accounts is expected to remain equal to about 12 percent of sales for the foreseeable future. The spontaneous financing from these sources in period t will be

$$\mathit{Spontaneous\ financing} = \frac{\mathit{Spontaneous\ current\ liabilities}}{\mathit{Sales}} \cdot \left(\mathit{Sales}_t - \mathit{Sales}_{t-1}\right),$$

which for Combex in 1986 will amount to

$$\begin{aligned}\mathit{Spontaneous\ financing} &= (0.12)\ (\$5{,}400{,}000 - \$4{,}500{,}000)\\ &= \$108{,}000\end{aligned}$$

Another source of financing to meet the needs of expansion is internal equity financing, that is, retained earnings. The firm's dividend policy will determine how much of each period's earnings is available to help finance expansion and how much will be paid to the stockholders. With a given amount of financing required, the greater the dividend paid, the smaller will be the internal financing, and the greater the amount of external financing that is required. For the present example, assume the policy is to pay out 60 percent of earnings as dividends, so the internal financing is

$$\mathit{Internal\ equity\ financing} = \mathit{Net\ income} \cdot (1 - \mathit{Payout\ ratio}),$$

which, for 1986, would be

$$\begin{aligned}\mathit{Internal\ equity\ financing} &= \$297{,}000\ (1 - 0.60)\\ &= \$118{,}800,\end{aligned}$$

or, stated in terms of the net profit margin, which is expected to average about 5.5 percent, is

$$
\begin{aligned}
\textit{Internal equity financing} &= \textit{Sales} \cdot \left(\frac{\textit{Net income}}{\textit{Sales}}\right) \cdot (1 - \textit{Payout ratio}) \\
&= \$5{,}400{,}000\ (0.055)\ (1 - 0.60) \\
&= \$118{,}800.
\end{aligned}
$$

After considering spontaneous financing and internal financing, the remainder of the funds for expansion must come from external sources—borrowing or issuing equity securities. The required external financing is

$$
\begin{aligned}
\textit{Required external financing} &= \textit{Required investment} \\
&\quad - \textit{Spontaneous financing} \\
&\quad - \textit{Internal equity financing},
\end{aligned}
$$

which can be expressed as

$$
\begin{aligned}
&\textit{Required external financing} = \\
&\left[\left(\frac{\textit{Total assets}}{\textit{Sales}}\right) - \left(\frac{\textit{Spontaneous current liabilities}}{\textit{Sales}}\right)\right]\left(\textit{Sales}_t - \textit{Sales}_{t-1}\right) \\
&\quad - \textit{Sales}_t \left(\frac{\textit{Net income}}{\textit{Sales}}\right)\left(1 - \textit{Payout ratio}\right)
\end{aligned}
$$

which, for 1986, would be

$$
\begin{aligned}
\textit{Required external financing} &= (0.48 - 0.12)\ (\$5{,}400{,}000 - \$4{,}500{,}000) \\
&\quad - \$5{,}400{,}000\ (0.055)\ (1 - 0.60) \\
&= \$205{,}200.
\end{aligned}
$$

Extending this analysis through 1990, assuming that sales increase at 20 percent per year and the ratios remain unchanged, the required external financings are \$246,240, \$295,488, \$354,586, and \$425,502, respectively.

Note the kinds of trade-offs that can be considered with this analysis. Any increase in the turnover of total assets (sales/total assets) can make a substantial difference in the amount of external financing that is required. For example, if the asset turnover ratio can be increased from the present level, about 2.08, to 3, the required external financing could be cut from \$205,200 to \$70,200. Alternatively, with the other ratios unchanged, if the payout ratio is reduced to zero, the firm can meet all but \$27,000 of its growth financing needs from spontaneous and internal equity financing.

Another question that can be considered with this framework is: What growth rate in sales can be supported without having to resort to outside financing? It can be shown that this growth rate, g^*, can be calculated as

$$g^* = \frac{\left(\dfrac{\textit{Net income}}{\textit{Sales}}\right) \cdot \left(1 - \textit{Payout ratio}\right)}{\left(\dfrac{\textit{Total assets}}{\textit{Sales}}\right) - \left(\dfrac{\textit{Spontaneous CL}}{\textit{Sales}}\right) - \left(\dfrac{\textit{Net income}}{\textit{Sales}}\right) \cdot \left(1 - \textit{Payout ratio}\right)}$$

$$= \frac{(0.055)\,(1 - 0.60)}{0.48 - 0.12 - (0.055)\,(1 - 0.60)}$$

$$= 0.065,$$

or about 6.5 percent growth in sales per year. If the firm's annual growth in sales exceeds 6.5 percent, outside financing (either debt or equity) will be required and the higher the growth rate, the more external funds will be required, but at any rate below 6.5 percent, Combex will be able to meet its needs with spontaneous financing and internal equity financing.

Confining the financing of growth to spontaneous current liabilities and internal equity may constrain the firm's growth unnecessarily. If management is willing to utilize debt financing, in addition to these other sources, then greater growth may be possible without exceeding the limits of prudence. One could ask how much growth the firm could finance without increasing the proportional amount of debt in the firm's permanent capital structure. Higgins (1984) provides a formula similar to the one for g^* above that represents the highest sustainable rate of growth, g^{**}, in sales that the firm can generate and finance without changing the financing mix of debt and equity. Higgins' formula is

$$g^{**} = \frac{\left(\dfrac{\textit{Net income}}{\textit{Sales}}\right)\left(1 - \text{Payout ratio}\right)\left(1 + \dfrac{\textit{Debt}}{\text{Equity}}\right)}{\left(\dfrac{\textit{Total assets}}{\textit{Sales}}\right) - \left(\dfrac{\textit{Net income}}{\textit{Sales}}\right)\cdot\left(1 - \textit{Payout ratio}\right)\left(1 + \dfrac{\textit{Debt}}{\textit{Equity}}\right)}$$

which for Combex, with a debt-to-equity ratio of 1.86, yields

$$g^{**} = \frac{(0.55)\,(1 - 0.60)\,(1 + 1.86)}{0.48 - (0.55)\,(1-0.60)\,(1 + 1.86)} = 0.15.$$

Thus, Combex could sustain sales growth of 15 percent per year with the assumed profit margin, payout ratio, and asset turnover by financing the expansion in such a way that the firm's total debt (including spontaneous financing) to total equity is maintained at its current level of 1.86 to 1.

This use of various ratios to determine required future financing and to clarify the sources of financing is helpful and provides insight. However, it is very general and glosses over the specifics of the situation. For example, to the extent that all these ratios used in the formulas do not stay constant over the forecast periods, this analysis will provide incorrect answers. To gain greater insight, and perhaps greater accuracy, it is useful to develop more detailed analysis of investment and financing with pro forma financial statements.

To develop pro forma statements for future planning periods, many assumptions must be made. Exhibit 3.16 lists the major assumptions that have been made to develop estimates of future account balances and future financing requirements. Based on these assumptions, the forecasted statements for 1986–90 are shown on Exhibits 3.17 and 3.18. These forecasted pro forma statements allow one to develop rough estimates of future required investment and required external financing, as shown in Exhibit 3.19. However, these statements are only first approximations because the external financing sources are not yet specified. Without specifying the method of meeting this

EXHIBIT 3.16 Assumptions Used for Pro Forma Statements

Income statement

1. Sales increase at 20 percent annually.
2. Cost of goods sold is 75 percent of sales.
3. Selling, general, and administrative expenses are 12 percent of sales.
4. Depreciation expense is 6 percent of gross plant and equipment.
5. Interest expense is 14 percent of outstanding debt.
6. Income taxes are $26,000 + 0.46 (taxable income − $100,000).
7. Dividends are 60 percent of net income.

Balance sheet

1. Cash and securities are 3 percent of sales.
2. Receivables are 17 percent of sales.
3. Inventories are 14 percent of sales.
4. Gross plant and equipment is 22 percent of sales.
5. Accounts payable are 7 percent of sales.
6. Other liabilities are 4 percent of sales.
7. Taxes payable are 17 percent of income tax expense.

Investment and financing

1. Required investment is the required change in total assets.
2. Spontaneous financing is the increase in current liabilities, excluding notes payable.
3. Internal equity financing is equal to retained earnings.
4. Required external financing is equal to required investment less spontaneous financing and internal equity.
5. No additional notes payable, long-term debt, or common stock is assumed to be issued prior to calculating required external financing.

financing requirement, the pro forma statements are not correct (that is why they are first approximations). The net income is incorrect because it does not reflect interest expenses associated with any additional borrowing, and the liabilities are not correct on the balance sheet because the specifics of additional borrowing or issue of common stock are not yet shown. Rather, the amount of new funds that would have to be raised is included as the variable, total financing, shown on the balance sheet.

To develop correct statements, specific financing methods must be assumed, and the implications of these methods must be reflected in the statements. The management of Combex is considering two alternative financing plans to meet the firm's

EXHIBIT 3.17 Combex Corporation Pro Forma Income Statements with 20 Percent Growth and Financing Unspecified

	1985	*1986*	*1987*	*1988*	*1989*	*1990*
Sales	$4,500,000	$5,400,000	$6,480,000	$7,776,000	$9,331,200	$11,197,440
Cost of goods sold	3,375,000	4,050,000	4,860,000	5,832,000	6,998,400	8,398,080
Selling, general, and administrative expenses	540,000	648,000	777,600	933,120	1,119,744	1,343,693
Depreciation expense	58,200	71,280	85,536	102,643	123,172	147,806
Earnings before interest and taxes	526,800	630,720	756,864	908,237	1,089,884	1,307,861
Interest expense	117,320	117,320	117,320	117,320	117,320	117,320
Earnings before income tax	409,480	513,400	639,544	790,917	972,564	1,190,541
Income tax expense	168,361	216,164	274,190	343,822	427,380	527,649
Net income	241,119	297,236	365,354	447,095	545,185	662,892
Dividends	$144,672	$178,342	$219,212	$268,257	$327,111	$397,735
Retained earnings	96,448	118,894	146,142	178,838	218,074	265,157

EXHIBIT 3.18 Combex Corporation Pro Forma Balance Sheets with 20 Percent Growth and Financing Unspecified

Assets	*1985*	*1986*	*1987*	*1988*	*1989*	*1990*
Cash and securities	$ 120,000	$ 162,000	$ 194,400	$ 233,280	$ 279,936	$ 335,923
Trade receivables	760,000	918,000	1,101,600	1,321,920	1,586,304	1,903,565
Inventories	620,000	756,000	907,200	1,088,640	1,306,368	1,567,642
Total current assets	1,500,000	1,836,000	2,203,200	2,643,840	3,172,608	3,807,130
Fixed assets	970,000	1,188,000	1,425,600	1,710,720	2,052,864	2,463,437
Depreciation allowance	340,000	411,280	496,816	599,459	722,631	870,437
Net plant	630,000	776,720	928,784	1,111,261	1,330,233	1,593,000
Total assets	$2,130,000	$2,612,720	$3,131,984	$3,755,101	$4,502,841	$5,400,129
Liabilities and Stockholders' Equity						
Notes payable	$ 257,000	$ 257,000	$ 257,000	$ 257,000	$ 257,000	$ 257,000
Trade accounts payable	318,000	378,000	453,600	544,320	653,184	783,821
Other liabilities	208,000	216,000	259,200	311,040	373,248	447,898
Taxes payable	22,000	36,748	46,612	58,450	72,655	89,700
Total current liabilities	805,000	887,748	1,016,412	1,170,810	1,356,087	1,578,419
Total financing	0	281,078	525,536	815,417	1,159,807	1,569,606
Long-term debt	581,000	581,000	581,000	581,000	581,000	581,000
Common stock	100,000	100,000	100,000	100,000	100,000	100,000
Earned surplus	644,000	762,894	909,036	1,087,874	1,305,948	1,571,105
Total stockholders' equity	744,000	862,894	1,009,036	1,187,874	1,405,948	1,671,105
Total liabilities and stockholders' equity	$2,130,000	$2,612,720	$3,131,984	$3,755,101	$4,502,841	$5,400,129

EXHIBIT 3.19 Combex Corporation Pro Forma Financing and Financial Ratios with 20 Percent Growth and Financing Unspecified

	Investment and Financing					
	1985	*1986*	*1987*	*1988*	*1989*	*1990*
Required investment	$ 0	$482,720	$519,264	$623,117	$747,740	$897,288
Spontaneous financing	0	82,748	128,664	154,397	185,277	222,332
Internal equity financing	0	118,894	146,142	178,838	218,074	265,157
Required external financing	0	281,078	244,458	289,881	344,389	409,799
Profit margin	0.054	0.055	0.056	0.057	0.058	0.059
Return on assets	0.247	0.241	0.242	0.242	0.242	0.242
Return on equity	0.324	0.344	0.362	0.376	0.388	0.397
Debt to total capital	0.651	0.670	0.678	0.684	0.688	0.691
Assets to sales	0.473	0.484	0.483	0.483	0.483	0.482
Current liabilities to sales	0.179	0.164	0.157	0.151	0.145	0.141
Growth rate	0.200	0.200	0.200	0.200	0.200	0.200
Payout ratio	0.600	0.600	0.600	0.600	0.600	0.600

growth needs. Plan A uses equity financing, and Plan B uses debt financing.

Plan A calls for financing all the firm's external needs by issuing new common stock; the results of this alternative are shown in Exhibit 3.20A. Before issuing new stock there are 100,000 shares outstanding. It is assumed that new shares will be issued at a price (net to the company) of $15 per share, and the number of new shares required to be issued each year ranges from 18,739 in 1986 to 27,320 in 1990. Using the equity financing alternative, interest expenses are constant over the planning horizon, and earnings per share grow at an average annual rate of 6 percent from $2.41 in 1985 to $3.24 in 1990. The ratio of debt to total capital is 65 percent in 1985, and with equity financing it declines to 40 percent by 1990.

Plan B calls for financing the firm's external requirements by issuing long-term debt. It is assumed that the required funds can be borrowed at an interest rate of 14 percent. The results of this alternative are shown in Exhibit 3.20B. The additional amount borrowed each year is equal to required external financing, shown on line 4 of the exhibit; and because the debt grows over time, the interest expense also increases. However, because the return on investment exceeds the cost of borrowed funds, and because no new shares of stock are issued, the earnings per share grow from $2.41 in 1985 to $5.71 by 1990 (as compared to $3.24 in 1990 under the equity alternative). In addition, the ratio of debt to total capital increases from 65 percent in 1985 to 71 percent in 1990.

Projecting the firm's financial position on the basis of two financing alternatives is just part of financial planning. There may be many other decision alternatives that should be considered, but in this example only these two alternatives will be considered. Once all the relevant decision alternatives are specified and their financial results are described, they should be compared to determine which one is the best decision. As has already been discussed, a basic aspect of evaluating decision alternatives is to specify the objective or goal of the decision. Thus, to evaluate any of the alternatives, we must describe specifically how we are to compare the forecasted results.

Assume our objective is to choose the alternative that would make the value per share of stock as large as possible. To evalu-

EXHIBIT 3.20A Combex Corporation: Pro Forma Results of Equity Financing

	1985	*1986*	*1987*	*1988*	*1989*	*1990*
Investment and Financing						
Required investment	$0	$ 482,720	$ 519,264	$ 623,117	$ 747,740	$ 897,288
Spontaneous financing	0	82,748	128,664	154,397	185,277	222,332
Internal equity financing	0	118,894	146,142	178,838	218,074	265,157
Required external financing	0	281,078	244,458	289,881	344,389	409,799
Share issue price	—	15	15	15	15	15
Shares issued	—	18,739	16,297	19,325	22,959	27,320
Liabilities and Stockholders' Equity						
Total current liabilities	$ 805,000	$ 887,748	$1,016,412	$1,170,810	$1,356,087	$1,578,419
Long-term debt	581,000	581,000	581,000	581,000	581,000	581,000
Common stock	100,000	381,078	625,536	915,417	1,259,807	1,669,606
Earned surplus	644,000	762,894	909,036	1,087,874	1,305,948	1,571,105
Stockholders' equity	744,000	1,143,972	1,534,572	2,003,291	2,565,754	3,240,710
Total liabilities and stockholders' equity	$2,130,000	$2,612,720	$3,131,984	$3,755,101	$4,502,841	$5,400,129

Income						
Earnings before interest and taxes	S 526,800	$ 630,720	$ 756,864	$ 908,237	$1,089,884	$1,307,861
Interest expense	117,320	117,320	117,320	117,320	117,320	117,320
Earnings before income tax	409,480	513,400	639,544	790,917	972,564	1,190,541
Income tax expense	168,361	216,164	274,190	343,822	427,380	527,649
Net income	241,119	297,236	365,354	447,095	545,185	662,892
Dividends	144,672	178,342	219,212	268,257	327,111	397,735
Retained earnings	$ 96,448	$118,894	$146,142	$178,838	$218,074	$265,157
Shares outstanding	100,000	118,739	135,036	154,361	177,320	204,640
Earnings per share	S2.41	$2.50	$2.71	$2.90	$3.07	$3.24
Dividends per share	S1.45	$1.50	$1.62	$1.74	$1.84	$1.94
Return on equity	32%	26%	24%	22%	21%	21%
Debt to total capital	65%	56%	51%	47%	43%	40%

EXHIBIT 3.20B Combex Corporation: Pro Forma Results of Debt Financing

	1985	*1986*	*1987*	*1988*	*1989*	*1990*
Investment and Financing						
Required investment	$0	$ 482,720	$ 519,264	$ 623,117	$ 747,740	$ 897,288
Spontaneous financing	0	82,748	125,587	151,594	181,895	218,245
Internal equity financing	0	118,894	137,642	162,596	192,490	228,282
Required external financing	0	281,078	256,035	308,927	373,356	450,761
Share issue price	—	15	15	15	15	15
Shares issued	—	0	0	0	0	0
Liabilities and Stockholders' Equity						
Total current liabilities	$ 805,000	$ 887,748	$1,013,335	$1,164,929	$1,346,824	$1,565,069
Long-term debt	581,000	862,078	1,118,113	1,427,040	1,800,395	2,251,157
Common stock	100,000	100,000	100,000	100,000	100,000	100,000
Earned surplus	644,000	762,894	900,536	1,063,132	1,255,621	1,483,904
Stockholders' equity	744,000	862,894	1,000,536	1,163,132	1,355,621	1,583,904
Total liabilities and stockholders' equity	$2,130,000	$2,612,720	$3,131,984	$3,755,101	$4,502,841	$5,400,129

Income						
Earnings before interest and taxes	$ 526,800	$ 630,720	$ 756,864	$ 908,237	$1,089,884	$1,307,861
Interest expense	117,320	117,320	156,671	192,516	235,766	288,035
Earnings before income tax	409,480	513,400	600,193	715,721	854,119	1,019,826
Income tax expense	168,361	216,164	256,089	309,232	372,895	449,120
Net income	241,119	297,236	344,104	406,489	481,224	570,706
Dividends	144,672	178,342	206,463	243,894	288,734	342,424
Retained earnings	$ 96,448	$118,894	$137,642	$162,596	$192,490	$ 228,282
Shares outstanding	100,000	100,000	100,000	100,000	100,000	100,000
Earnings per share	$2.41	$2.97	$3.44	$4.06	$4.81	$5.71
Dividends per share	$1.45	$1.78	$2.06	$2.44	$2.89	$3.42
Return on equity	32%	34%	34%	35%	36%	36%
Debt to total capital	65%	67%	68%	69%	70%	71%

ate the decision alternatives, the link between the decisions and this value must be specified in an operational manner. That is, we must be able to determine what the value of the stock is for each alternative, and this requires that we specify a valuation model for the stock.

Assume that the value per share of the stock is determined according to the following formula:

$$\text{Price per share} = \sum_{t=1}^{\infty} \textit{Dividend}_t \, [1/(1 + k)^t],$$

where $\textit{Dividend}_t$ is the dividend per share forecasted to be paid in period t in the future, and k is the investor's discount rate, representing the minimum expected return required by investors for investments with the level of risk inherent in each of the decision alternatives. Assume it has been determined that with Plan A the investor's required return is $k = 0.20$, and that with Plan B, $k = 0.28$, which is higher because of the increased risk associated with the high level of financial leverage that results from the debt financing alternative.

Next, assume that growth in dividends will taper off to 4 percent per year after 1990 for both alternatives. It can be shown[4] that with these assumptions the value of the stock can be calculated as

$$\text{Price per share} = \sum_{t=1}^{5} \textit{Dividend}_t \, [1/(1+k)^t] + [\textit{Dividend}_6 \, / (k - g)]/(1 + k)^5,$$

where $\textit{Dividend}_6$ is the dividend forecasted for period 6 in the future, or 1991 in this example, and g is the rate of annual growth in dividends.

For these two decision alternatives, assume the forecasts for $\textit{Dividend}_6$ are \$2.02 and \$3.56 per share respectively, and that these values will grow at 4 percent annually for an indefinite

---

[4]The constant growth dividend valuation model is explained in standard finance texts such as Weston and Copeland (1986, chap. 23).

period into the future. The values of the stock for the two alternatives are:

Plan A

$$\text{Price per share} = 1.50\,(1/1.20) + 1.62\,(1/1.20^2) + 1.74\,(1/1.20^3) + 1.84\,(1/1.20^4) + 1.94\,(1/1.20^5) + [2.02/(0.20 - 0.04)]\,(1/1.20^5)$$

$$= 1.50\,(0.833) + 1.62\,(0.694) + 1.74\,(0.579) + 1.84\,(0.482) + 1.94\,(0.402) + [12.625]\,(0.402)$$

$$= \$10.12;$$

Plan B

$$\text{Price per share} = 1.78\,(1/1.28) + 2.06\,(1/1.28^2) + 2.44\,(1/1.28^3) + 2.89\,(1/1.28^4) + 3.42\,(1/1.28^5) + [3.56/0.28 - 0.04)]\,(1/1.28^5)$$

$$= \$14.52.$$

From this valuation it would be concluded that the debt-financing alternative would be more likely to lead to the value maximizing objective than the equity alternative. While the debt-financing alternative is more risky, this risk is taken into account by the higher discount rate of 28 percent; even with this higher required return, the flow of dividends to the stockholders is sufficiently large using the debt alternative to result in higher value to the stockholders. Thus, if these are the only two alternatives available and our assumptions are acceptable, the debt financing should be chosen.

Having worked through the pro forma statements and appraised the value of the stock, one must go back and evaluate the assumptions and the forecasted results. For example, under Plan A it was assumed the firm's stock could be sold for $15 per share. However, the appraised value of the stock calculated above shows the value as $10.12 per share. Is this valuation plausible? Are its underlying assumptions correct? Or is the $15 sale price unrealistic? If the $15 is incorrect, then one should go back and recalculate the pro forma figures on the basis of another assumed sale price. This would change the number of shares sold, the dividends per share, and the appraised value. To develop a forecast that is consistent with rational investors in an efficient stock market, this calculation process would have to be repeated until the appraised value was consistent with the assumed sale price of the stock.

3.4 SUMMARY

The purpose of this chapter has been to introduce some of the standard tools and analytical methods of financial planning. These included an analysis of financing requirements with a statement of receipts and disbursements, analysis of break-even points that relies on distinguishing between fixed and variable costs, and projecting financing requirements by relating investment and financing to the growth in sales. It was noted, in the Lockheed example, that break-even may need to be formulated in terms of present value when we are faced with a long planning horizon. A useful set of concepts that are related to break-even are the concepts of degrees of leverage. The degree of operating leverage measures the change in EBIT resulting from a change in sales, and the degree of financial leverage measures the change in net income resulting from a change in EBIT. The degree of combined leverage measures their joint effect—the elasticity of net income with respect to changes in sales. In relating financing requirements to the firm's growth, we discussed using financial ratios to obtain rough estimates of required financing and sustainable growth. Pro forma financial statements were developed to get a more accurate picture of the influence of future growth on the financial position of the firm.

None of these techniques really requires the technology of computers or financial software, yet each can be used more easily with the assistance of the financial modeling software that is easily accessible on computers.

The remainder of the book is concerned with the methods for constructing models for financial planning. The next chapter begins by introducing the idea of a financial model and discussing the process of modeling.

REFERENCES

HIGGINS, R. C. *Analysis for Financial Management.* Homewood, Ill.: Richard D. Irwin, 1984.

REINHARDT, U. E. "Break-Even Analysis for Lockheed's TriStar: An Application of Financial Theory." *Journal of Finance* 28, no. 4 (September 1973), pp. 821–38.

WESTON, J., and T. COPELAND. *Managerial Finance.* 8th ed. Hinsdale, Ill.: Dryden Press, 1986.

CHAPTER FOUR

Financial Modeling

In Chapter Three, numerous examples were presented that demonstrated different problems and approaches to financial planning. Many of these financial planning problems required that we determine which particular decision was best, and how the choice of that decision would affect the firm. In most cases, this determination required that we develop some sort of model of the firm and evaluate its response in different circumstances. In most cases one does not think of financial relationships as being a model. Nevertheless, the relationships that underlay the financial calculations were models. This chapter explains what a model is and discusses how a model is constructed and used.

4.1 WHAT IS A MODEL?

Webster defines a model as "a small copy or imitation of an existing object; or, a preliminary representation of something, serving as a plan from which the final object is to be constructed." Everyone is familiar with model airplanes and recognizes that they are intended to imitate real airplanes. But, how they are supposed to imitate the real thing depends on their intended use. For a child, it is necessary only that the model have the shape of an airplane, and is not important that the model is simply a block of wood and does not truly duplicate the real thing. But the aircraft manufacturer may construct a very detailed model that resembles the full-sized prototype in enough important respects that the performance potential of the real plane can be tested. Note that even in this case, the model does not need to include every detail of the real plane to be useful for testing. Only the essential features are necessary to test certain aspects of performance. If a feature of the real plane is irrelevant to the particular performance to be tested, that feature can be omitted from the model.

It is easy enough to understand what a model airplane is and how it imitates the real airplane. However, it is somewhat more difficult to understand what a financial model is and how it is supposed to imitate the real thing. In business finance the real object to be modeled is the set of interrelationships and linkages between the firm's environment, the decisions and actions, and the firm's objectives. None of these is really tangible like an airplane. For example, the question may be: What is the effect of an increase in interest rates on the earnings and value of the firm? Interest rates, earnings, and value are all considerably more abstract than an airplane, and it would be difficult to construct a tangible model of them and have it show their relationships. However, it is possible that these relationships could be expressed verbally or mathematically with enough essential detail to trace out the potential effects.

A financial model is a set of verbal or mathematical statements that expresses the system of relations and links between the firm's environment, its decisions and actions, and its objectives.

The following example of a very simple model of a firm's sales can help one to analyze the effects of the firm's pricing decision by showing the links between the price, units sold, and total revenue.

Model of Total Revenue

$$\textit{Total revenue}_t = (\textit{Units sold}_t) \cdot (\textit{Price per unit}_t) \quad (4.1)$$

$$\textit{Units sold}_t = 500 - 30 \cdot (\textit{Price per unit}_t) \quad (4.2)$$

This model consists of two *equations,* (4.1) and (4.2). There are three *variables* in the model, *Total revenue*$_t$, *Units sold*$_t$, and *Price per unit*$_t$, where the subscript t denotes the time period. Management can decide what price to charge for the product, so *Price per unit* is called the *decision variable.* The question is, what price should be set so that the firm can best attain its objective. *Units sold* is a variable that management cannot set, but it can be influenced by the value set for the decision variable.

Equation (4.2) portrays the link between the *Price per unit* and *Units sold.* This is what economists call a demand function because it shows the number of units demanded at different prices. Over the range of prices to be considered, each $1 increase in the *Price per unit* causes demand for the product to decline by 30 units. Thus, if the *Price per unit* is $5, *Units sold* will be 350 units, but if the *Price per unit* is increased to $6, *Units sold* declines to 320 units. Equation (4.2), the demand function, represents the link between the firm and its competitive environment. In terms of constraints discussed previously, the demand function summarizes the effects of the industry and the economy. The competitive structure of the industry, the nature of consumer demand for the product, and the general condition of the economy all influence the way product demand responds to the price of the product. These factors all constrain management's ability to set any price it wants in order to attain its goal.

Equation (4.1) shows how price and demand combine to determine *Total revenue.* This expression is essentially a definition. If we assume that goal of management is to maximize *Total revenue,* then this expression is what is called the *objective function*—the term that is to be optimized. In this case, the decision variable, *Price per unit,* is supposed to be chosen so as to make the objective, *Total revenue,* as large as possible.

Exhibit 4.1 shows how *Total revenue* varies as the *Price per unit* is changed. At a *Price per unit* of $8.33, 250 units would be sold, for total revenue of $2,083. At any higher price, demand would decline sufficiently to offset the advantage of the higher price. The optimal decision—the one that maximizes *Total revenue*—would be to charge a price per unit of $8.33.

This model is made up not just of equations and variables; there are also *parameters.* The parameters are the numbers (constants) in the equations that operate (in this case, multiply or add) on the variables to yield the value of the equations. In (4.2) the parameters are 500 and 30. These parameters in the

EXHIBIT 4.1 Total Revenue as a Function of Price per Unit

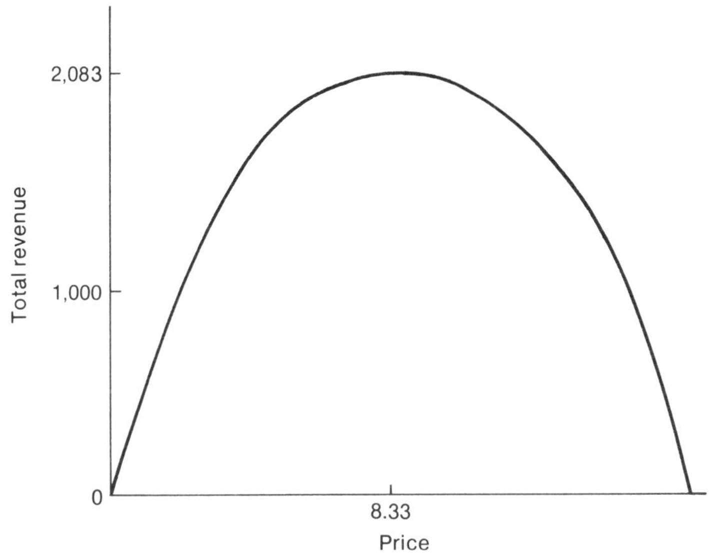

demand function are intended to represent the way demand changes as price is changed. In the same equation, if these parameters are changed, then of course, the number of *Units sold* will be different. The parameters in any model are usually just estimates, made by the modeler, of how one variable responds to another. They usually represent estimates of economic behavior or technological relationships.

The general form of the equation shows how it looks without specifying particular values for parameters. In the case of demand function (4.2) the general form is

$$\textit{Units sold} = a + b \cdot \textit{Price per unit}, \qquad (4.3)$$

where a and b are generalized constant parameters. This general form of the demand function is based on the modeler's estimate (guess?) or derivation of the general relationship.

Two tasks of financial model building are (1) to determine the general form of the relationships and (2) to estimate the parameter values. To make (4.3) usable, the values of parameters a and b must be estimated. In some cases the modeler may just guess the values, but more correctly, and preferably more often, the parameter estimates will be based on a study of data. This is where forecasting and econometrics comes into the modeling process.

Another element that was explicit in Models (4.1)–(4.2) was time. The variable *Units sold*$_t$ referred to sales during period t, and the definition of the length of period t is an important part of the model. *Units sold* must be defined in terms of sales per period, and if the length of the period is one year, the parameters in (4.2) would be very different from those appropriate if the period was one month.

The way the Model (4.1)–(4.2) was written, it was not clear what the planning horizon was. The model may apply over a number of periods, with an equation assigned to each period in the planning horizon. If the same equations with the same parameters apply identically to each of, say, 10 periods, the model could be written in general form as

$$\begin{aligned} \textit{Total revenue}_t &= (\textit{Units sold}_t) \cdot (\textit{Price per unit}_t) \\ \textit{Units sold}_t &= a - b \quad (\textit{Price per unit}_t) \end{aligned}$$

for $t = 1, \ldots, 10$, where $t = 1, \ldots, 10$ means that the expression is repeated for each t from 1 through 10. Alternatively, if the parameters were different for each period t, this could be denoted with a subscript on the parameters as a_t, b_t for $t = 1, \ldots, 10$. This would mean that there would be different parameters a and b in the demand function for each of the 10 periods in the planning horizon.

The two-equation model of total revenue that we have discussed was very simple, but it has been instructive. It was shown that a financial model is made up of equations, variables, and parameters. Some of the variables may represent the prospective decisions and are called decision variables; there may be an equation that shows the relation between these decision variables and the goal or objective, and we refer to this expression as the objective function. There may be other expressions that represent the relations between variables, and perhaps expressions that portray the constraints and limitations on the firm's decisions. The model usually will have parameters that must be estimated from data. The model provides a mechanism for making a link between the decision and the objective. The equations in the model help make the link and portray the influence of resources and constraints on the firm's ability to attain the goals set for the financial planning process.

4.2 WHAT DOES A MODEL DO?

With the relationships between variables expressed as a set of equations that comprise the financial model, one can assess the effect of a decision by tracing through all the complex financial relationships before actually implementing the decision. In this sense the financial model is a small copy of the firm and serves as a plan on which the final action is to be based. The financial model serves the purpose of allowing one to try out the decision first on a copy of the firm, rather than subject the firm itself to experimentation.

A financial model of the firm is helpful and sometimes essential because of the complexity of the relationships between the firm's financial variables. For some problems one may be able to discern the general direction of the result of a decision, but because of the complex relationships, it may be nearly impossible to assess the magnitude of the effect without the help of a model. In other cases it may not even be feasible to assess the direction of an effect without such a model.

A properly structured model can portray the links between management decisions and the firm's objectives in as much detail as is necessary to analyze a decision alternative. For some problems it may be necessary to develop a very detailed model; for others too much detail may be confusing and unnecessary.

To analyze short-run, day-to-day operating decisions, a very detailed model can show how individual operating decisions affect the position of the firm. For example, the investment manager may want to know the effect on this month's interest income of buying and selling particular securities. A short-run investment portfolio model could show the results of investment decisions about individual securities. Such a model could be sufficiently detailed to account for individual security transactions, enabling the manager to track the results of investment decisions over several months.

A model intended for analysis of decisions concerned with broader policy that affects the firm over a longer planning horizon would show only the broadest detail about the firm. For example, a long-term planning model might be used to analyze the effects of introducing a new product for which it would take many months before the sales could reach their potential. The financial effects could be analyzed by considering just the most aggregated balance sheet and income statement accounts. Thus, detail such as individual security transactions would be unnecessary and would serve only to confuse the broader issues being considered. In addition, even more aggregated account balances would not have to be considered over short intervals such as weeks. Rather, the model could show the firm's financial position, say, every six months or even each year.

4.3 MANAGERIAL BENEFITS OF MODELING

Financial models serve the needs of management first, by enabling management to try out its decisions on this small copy of the firm without subjecting the firm itself to management by trial and error; and second, by forcing the modeler and managers to systematize their thought.

Financial models can show the linkages between the firm's operating environment, management decisions, and the potential results of the decisions. The model itself allows management to test ideas and decisions before they are actually implemented. This allows management to analyze more carefully and to explore how their decisions relate to their overall objectives. In addition, the modeling process itself is beneficial to management because it tends to force the planner to consider systematically the interrelationships between parts of the firm and those between environment, decisions, and results.

The process of building the model forces one to think more carefully about the complex relationships between decisions and the financial variables that constitute the firm. If managers actively participate in the process of building the model, this process itself can be beneficial by forcing managers to trace through the various interrelated effects of their decisions to understand the loops and feedback effects that their decisions involve.

In deciding what type of model to use, and in designing the model itself, one is forced to clarify the distinction between operating and strategic decisions. Usually the type of model used differs according to whether one is analyzing an operating or strategic decision. The operating decision usually involves a shorter planning horizon and is evaluated relative to the firm's subgoals, so that a more detailed model is appropriate. On the other hand, the strategic problem requires consideration of the most basic objectives of the firm and usually has longer-term consequences, so that a less detailed model will help focus attention on the correct decisions and variables. If the managers are involved in the modeling process, in deciding what detail should be included and excluded in the model, their thoughts are focused on how their decisions relate to operational subgoals versus strategic objectives.

Finally, this whole process helps managers to wrestle with the most basic questions about the firm's objectives and with the issue of how progress toward the objectives should be measured. This is especially true with simulation models. So much output can be generated in the modeling process that one is forced to summarize the results. In deciding how results can be presented, one must consider what the objectives are and whether the data relate to the objectives.

In addition to the benefits derived from management participation in the modeling process, management obviously gains from judicious use of well-designed models.

The financial planning model provides the framework for systematically tracing out the results of a decision. That is, it provides the computational mechanism for determining what the results of a decision may be and thus eases the manager's task of computing those results. Relieved of this mundane task, managers are released to consider the broader issues of setting and evaluating policy and defining policy alternatives. Thus, the use of models helps managers to use their talents more effectively for the broader issues that should concern them.

4.4 HOW TO DEVELOP THE MODEL

There are as many different ways to make a financial model as there are potential model builders. Any given problem can be approached from many different directions, so there is seldom just a single correct model suited to a given problem. With such a variety of approaches possible, how and where does one begin to develop a financial model? It is helpful to approach the problem by considering a set of questions that organize and structure the modeling effort. These questions relate to the problem, the output, and the input.

The Problem

What Is the Problem? This is the most fundamental question in approaching the modeling effort. The model must be suited to the decision problem, so one should make a thorough assessment of the nature of the financial planning problem and let that dictate the type of model to be built. This assessment should be as broad as possible so all facets of the problem are explored. The model must be at least as broad as the problem. That is, the model must be suited to the analysis of all important facets of the problem and all reasonable decisions. If the model is too narrow and limited, it may not allow the planner to consider some important decision alternatives, and some possibly useful solutions will be ignored. Thus, the initial definition of the problem should be broad enough so the subsequently developed model is sufficiently general to allow a full analysis.

What Questions Must Be Answered? For most problems there are questions, which, if answered, would eliminate the problem or provide a solution. The model builder should enumerate these questions as completely as possible. The list of questions can be helpful in defining the model. To the extent that it is possible to develop a model that will answer these crucial questions, they can help dictate how the model is to be structured. For example, the important questions that require answers will influence what kind of data and answers one would want to get out of the model.

What Is the Time Horizon of the Problem? Financial planning problems are almost always concerned with time. In model building there are usually various aspects of time that are important determinants of the structure of the model. If the problem being considered is inherently of a long-run nature, or has long-run consequences, then the planning horizon should be long. If the problem involves decisions that are made frequently over short time intervals, then the length of the subperiods constituting the planning horizon should be consistent with the decision timing.

How Important Is the Problem? The importance of the problems for the goals of the firm and for its survival should be considered in deciding how much time, effort, and expense should be committed to model development. If a very complex, expensive modeling effort is necessary to provide solutions to unimportant problems, the modeling effort may be unjustified. If the problems can be handled with a scaled-down model, then, by all means, scale down. In any case, these issues should be considered before embarking on a model development effort that could involve great cost and little benefit.

The Output

What Kind of Information Is Needed? After considering the planning/modeling problem facing the firm, and broadly defining what questions need answering, the planner should decide more specifically what information must be generated as output from the model. All too often a model is developed that generates mountains of information, but very little that actually helps the planner make a better decision. This is, in part, because the model is designed before deciding what output needs to be generated. For example, the problem may involve evaluation of an investment project. If the model generates just future pro forma financial statements, that may be insufficient for a valid investment analysis. If the investment analysis requires calculation of expected net present value and an assessment of the risk of the investment, the model should be developed with this in mind.

How Will the Information Be Evaluated? One should decide ahead of time how the output can be evaluated. For example, if the problem involves the comparison of alternative financing decisions, it must be decided how one could conclude that one alternative is better than another. The model should be developed so that the output it generates is suitable for making such an evaluation. Many models generate standard financial statements, and so many statements—with so much detail—are produced that the user is still unable to evaluate alternative decisions correctly. This mistake should be avoided by designing the model so it will produce output that is relevant to the problem and can be evaluated. In this regard, it is important to relate the information to the firm's objectives. In other words, the correct decision is the one that will lead to the objective, and you can't evaluate the decision unless you have information that shows the effect of the decision on the objective.

What Kind of Detail Is Necessary? In deciding what output is necessary for making a planning decision, it is important to specify the level of detail needed for evaluating progress toward the planning objective. In modeling, too much detail is more often a problem than is too little detail. The planner/modeler should ask: What is the smallest amount of detail necessary to enable me to make a decision? If I consider increased amounts of detail, at what point will more detail and more information lead to the same decision as less information? The model must be structured so that the detail it generates is no less than the smallest amount necessary—that's the lower limit. The upper limit of detail is defined by the amount beyond which further detail does not change a decision.

Who Will Use the Information? The type of output from the modeling process and the format of the output should be tailored to the audience that will use the output. It may be appropriate to generate a large volume of finely detailed data if it will be used by the planning analyst. As one goes up the level of the organizational structure, however, the user of the data may be much less concerned with great detail and more concerned with a broad picture of the firm. Output should be consolidated and summarized so it can be quickly and easily grasped by the executive who takes a broader view of the plans for the firm's future.

The Structural Input

After the planner has broadly defined the problem and decided what kind of output is necessary from the model, the model itself is developed and solved with two kinds of input. We first concern ourselves with the input that determines the structure of the model; in a later section, we will turn to the data input that determines the solution to the model.

The structural input is related to the broad set of ideas and questions that are the reason for the modeling process. These ideas and questions that underlie the structural input are some of the factors discussed previously as the ingredients of the financial planning process: the goal, decisions, linkages, constraints, and planning horizon. The structural input to the model determines the number and form of the equations, the number and type of variables in the equations, and the form of the objective function. In this context, only the general form of the equations and objective function is decided; the specific equations are determined by the parameters that are based on the data input.

What Are the Decision Alternatives? One purpose of the financial model is to facilitate the choice among decision alternatives. In most financial models some of the variables represent the decisions that must be made. Thus, a fundamental input to the model is an enumeration of the decision variables that go into the model. For example, the planning problem may require decisions about the level of capital investment in each of the next four quarters, the amount of short-term borrowing in each quarter, and the amount of dividends to be paid in each quarter. The decision variables might be listed abstractly by letting

X_t = Amount invested in quarter t, for t = 1, 2, 3, 4;
W_t = Amount borrowed in quarter t, for t = 1,2,3,4; and
d_t – Dividends paid in quarter t, for t = 1,2,3,4.

The solution process will determine (or set) the values of these decision variables.

One purpose of modeling the problem will be to determine the best values of these variables, X_t, W_t, and d_t. One way to model the problem is to set a value for the decision variable ahead of time and test it in the model to determine the result—this is simulation. Another approach would be to have the model choose the best value of the decision variables—this is optimization.

What Are the Constraints? The constraints are limitations on the range of choice of the decision variables. These constraints may arise from limitations in the amount of resources available to implement the financial plan; from technological relationships that limit choices; from the industry, the economy, or the law; or finally, they may be limitations that are true by definition. Most of the equations in a financial model represent, or are related to, constraints.

An example of a resource constraint is a limit on capital expenditures: the most we can spend on capital investment over the next four quarters may be $10 million. Using the notation shown above, this constraint is written as

$$X_1 + X_2 + X_3 + X_4 < 10{,}000{,}000,$$

and is one of the equations (an inequality in this case) that make up the model. This expression places a limitation on the amount of capital expenditures that can be chosen.

Technology often places constraints on the actions chosen by management. For example, management might like to produce more product from a plant, but there are limitations on how much could be produced at the plant because of the technology of the manufacturing process. Suppose a production function describes the maximum amount of output (Y) that can be produced with a specified amount of labor (L) and capital equipment (K), according to the expression

$$Y = 100\ L^{0.33}\ K^{0.67},$$

and the number of units of capital equipment available is 40, and the maximum amount of labor available is 58 units. The maximum output that can be produced can be expressed in the model in a number of different ways. One way would be to show in the model the constraints on capital and labor, and show output according to the production function:

$$\begin{aligned} Y &= 100\ L^{0.33}\ K^{0.67} \\ L &\le 58 \\ K &\le 40. \end{aligned}$$

Note that in these expressions the numbers 100, 0.33, 0.67, 58, and 40 are all parameters that are data input to the model. It is the concept of the constraint and the general form of the expressions that is the structural input to the model. Depending on the problem and the approach, the decision variables could be either the amount produced, Y, or the amounts of labor, L, and capital, K, to be used.

As was discussed in Chapter 2, many constraints can be placed on the firm's actions by competitive conditions in the industry, by economic conditions, and by the legal and political environment. It may be necessary to include expressions reflecting these constraints in the financial model.

An example of a legal constraint is the regulatory requirement for a member bank to maintain reserves with the Federal Reserve Bank conforming to the currently required reserve ratio. The bank's planning model would include an expression that shows the bank's reserves as a function of the relevant decision variables, which could include reserve deposits with the Fed, discount borrowing from the Fed, and reserves borrowed from other banks (Fed funds). The model would have a constraint requiring that the average daily reserves be no less than the required reserves.

A major part of most financial models is a set of equations that are definitions. In particular, models oriented toward accounting have many such equations. These definitional equations can be viewed as constraints because they constrain the model to conform to these definitions. They maintain consistency within the model, they aggregate groups of accounts into broader categories, and they link account balances from one period to the next. Very general examples of such definitional equations are:

$$\textit{Total assets} = \textit{Current assets} + \textit{Fixed assets} \quad (4.5)$$

$$\textit{Net worth} = \textit{Common stock} + \textit{Paid-in capital} + \textit{Earned surplus} \quad (4.6)$$

$$\textit{Marketable securities}_t = \textit{Marketable securities}_{t-1} - \textit{Securities matured}_t - \textit{Securities sold}_t + \textit{Securities purchased}_t. \quad (4.7)$$

Expressions (4.5) and (4.6) aggregate accounts according to standard accounting definitions, and (4.7) maintains consistency from one period to the next.

Expressions (4.5)–(4.7) do not show explicitly how the decision variables enter the expressions. It is certainly possible to expand these expressions to show the effects of the decision variables, but it is frequently easier to show these definitional equations in this very general form, and have other, subsidiary expressions that are more detailed and show the decision variables. For example, there could be a whole set of expressions that deal with current asset decisions and fixed asset decisions that feed into (4.5). The accounting equations are a crucial part of most financial models, and they are discussed in much greater detail in Chapter Six.

What Is the Goal? Not every model will explicitly show a goal or objective function as a function of the decision variables. It is certainly helpful to consider whether one is necessary and appropriate before building the model, however. We would want to structure the model, specify the variables, and develop the equations so that the result can be related to the goal.

What Are the Linkages between the Decisions and the Goal? Of course, one purpose of modeling is to determine how planning decisions will affect the firm's goals. The purpose served by an objective function in a model is to show how this linkage occurs. If an explicit objective function is to be used, the model should be structured so it generates output that will fit into the objective function.

For example, assume the decision variables are X_t, W_t, and d_t, as previously defined. Assuming a linear relationship between the decision variables and the objective, these decision variables would enter the objective function in general form as

$$\sum_{t=1}^{4} (a_t X_t + b_t W_t + c_t d_t),$$

where the coefficients a_t, b_t, and c_t are the parameters that measure the effect of the decision variable on the value of the objective function. The model would have to be constructed so it would generate output that would be compatible with calculation of the coefficients *a, b,* and *c.*

What Is the Planning Horizon? The length of the planning horizon and the number of subperiods constituting the horizon are important structural inputs to the model. The horizon and subperiods will influence the number of equations, number of variables in the model, and the volume of output from the model. Many of the considerations of planning horizon have been discussed already as they related to the ingredients to financial planning and the amount of detail in the plan. Suffice it to say that as the number of subperiods is increased, the number of variables, the number of equations, and the complexity of the model will be increased. It is crucial that the model builder carefully evaluate these factors before actually specifying the model.

Careful consideration of the questions relating to the problem, the output, and the structural input should provide the modeler with a start on developing the model in its general form. In its general form the model would consist of a set of equations (and/or inequalities), a set of decision variables that are the arguments in the equations, generalized parameters that enter the equations as constants or coefficients of the decision variables, and possibly an objective function. At this stage, most of the parameters are still shown only in general form (such as a, b, c). The data input must be utilized to give specific values to the parameters so the model can be solved.

The Data Input

Having defined the problem and the required output of the model, and having specified the structural input to the model, one should be able to develop a model in general terms, without the parameters of the model having been given specific numerical values. To make the model usable, these parameters must be specified. This is the role of the data input—to give specific values to the parameters that are not shown as having particular numerical values in the generalized model. That is, the data input enables us to fill in the blanks in the general model so that everything except the values of the decision variables is specified.

The data input can be classified into three broad categories: data that describe the current state of the system, data describing the relationships between variables, and forecasts of future conditions.

The Current State of the System. Financial planning can be thought of as anticipating decisions and consequences over a number of periods of time in order to reach an objective. That is, it plots the time path of the firm. Obviously, where the firm goes in the future depends on where it starts—the firm's current condition and current conditions of the firm's environment will be important determinants of where it goes in the future. Therefore, the financial plan and the financial model must take account of the current condition of the firm and its environment. This is what is meant by the current state of the system—the condition or situation from which the firm begins its planned trip into the future. The current state of the system is related to many of the resources and constraints that were discussed as input to the financial planning process.

Internal Data: The Firm. The firm's current condition consists of its endowment of resources, its productive capacity, and its obligations and commitments. The financial statements are the main source of data that describe these factors. Particularly for accounting models that generate future pro forma financial statements, the current statements are the most important data input describing the initial condition from which the future will evolve.

The model may require additional input data to describe the firm's current condition. These may include facts about production technology, sources of supply, labor and management, and the firm's products.

Whatever input data is necessary, there must be congruence between the model and the data. The level of input detail demanded by the model must be matched to the detail available in the accounting statements that provide the input data. A short-run working capital model may require a great deal of detail about the initial conditions. If that detail exceeds what is available from the firm's accounting system, then the model should be revised so it is matched to the available data.

External Data: The Economic Environment. The current conditions that prevail in the firm's operating environment are also important determinants of the actions the firm can take and where it can go in the future. Most of the factors that describe current conditions relate to economic conditions. These include data such as current interest rates, stock prices, and prices of goods and labor.

Relations between Variables. Variables in the financial model may be related to each other in a way that is not completely known to the modeler, but the modeler estimates the relationship from available data. Past observed data may be used to estimate the parameters of the relationship, and the estimated parameters are the input to the model. For example, accounts receivable may be assumed to be related to past sales according to the distributed lag relationship,

$$\begin{aligned} \text{Accounts receivable}_t = a + b_1\, Sales_{t\text{-}1} + b_2\, Sales_{t\text{-}2} \\ + b_3\, Sales_{t\text{-}3}, \end{aligned} \tag{4.8}$$

where parameters a, b_1, b_2, and b_3 are unknown. Using past observations of accounts receivable and sales, these parameters can be estimated with least squares regression techniques. The past observations are necessary for parameter estimation, but are not used directly in the model. The parameter estimates of a_1, b_1, b_2, and b_3 are data that are input of the model.

For most financial planning and modeling, the relation between variables that is of interest is the relation that will prevail in the future. Obviously, this relation is unknown, and a relation such as (4.8), with estimates based on past observations, is only a guess about the future relationship. The form of the relationship may be different from that actually assumed, and it may change in the future. Other variables that are omitted may influence the relationship, and there will inevitably be random events that cause the future values to depart from those predicted by the equation. The modeler should be constantly aware that the relations in the model may be erroneous and that the model itself may be incorrect.

Forecasts of Future Conditions. One purpose of planning and modeling is to help the firm deal with the uncertainty of the future. A most important part of dealing with the future is to forecast what future conditions will be like, and forecasts are obviously a major input to the modeling process.

Expression (4.8) was intended to portray the future relationship between accounts receivable and sales. In a model concerned with the future level of accounts receivable, this relation requires that future sales be forecast. Thus, in using (4.8) in the model there are really three types of input. First, there was the structural input that led the modeler to specify the general form of the relation shown in (4.8). Second, there are the estimates of the parameters a, b_1, b_2, and b_3 that are based on past observations of accounts receivable and sales. Third, there are the forecasts of future sales that are necessary to generate forecasts of future accounts receivable.

The forecast input is basic to solving the model and developing a financial plan. One important issue in the planning process is how sensitive to forecast errors and variations are the financial plan and the attainment of the firm's goals? The modeler should always maintain a healthy skepticism of the accuracy of the forecasts and consider how forecast errors affect the financial plan. Forecasting techniques will be discussed in Chapter 5 so the modeler will be equipped to consider and evaluate alternative forecasting methods.

If one has asked and answered the questions relating to the nature of the planning problem, the output required, and the available and necessary input, much of the modeling effort will have been completed. In the next section the types of models will be discussed, and in Chapter 6, a typical model will be presented and discussed.

4.5 TYPES OF MODELS

There are two general approaches to financial modeling: simulation and optimization. Simulation models show the result of a decision or action that is specified by the user, while optimization models solve for the decision that is best. Simulation is more widely used and understood, but optimization models can be very useful. Both approaches will be discussed in this book so the prospective user will be able to choose the approach that best suits his needs.

Simulation

Simulation is best understood as a technique that allows the user to answer the question "What will happen if . . .?" Simulation is the process of imitating the firm or organization so that the consequences of alternative decisions, actions, and strategies can be analyzed. Simulation allows management to ask about the consequences of undertaking a particular decision, and the hypothetical results are shown so that management can evaluate the consequences prior to implementing a decision.

The simulation model is the link between the prospective decision and the hypothetical results. The model consists of a set of mathematical expressions that reflect the relationships and links between the firm's environment and the organization, between units of the organization, and between action and result. Thus, the simulation model provides the necessary bridge between the input and output of the simulation process.

The input to the model normally would consist of the specification of conditions at the beginning of the process (the "state of the system"), the decisions or actions that are to be considered, and the forecasts of future conditions. Exhibit 4.2 shows the state of the system (environment) as being described by (*a*) conditions external to the firm such as economic conditions, and (*b*) conditions internal to the firm, such as its capacity, resources, and financial condition. The state of the system constitutes the initial condition of the firm and its environment and is used as input to the simulation model.

There are a multitude of possible alternative decisions in each category of production, pricing, investment, and financing. A set of decisions is prescribed as input to the simulation model. The model uses these inputs in order to generate the output, showing the consequences of the decisions. These consequences are, in turn, part of the description of the state of the system for a subsequent period.

The simulation approach does not try to tell the user which decision is best. Rather, it allows the user to specify a decision, and the model traces through the relationships so the results can be evaluated by the user. The simulation answers the planner's question, "What will happen if I make this decision?" The consequences of alternative decisions and strategies can be examined with a simulation model, but the assessment of which strategy is best is left to the user. For example, suppose the decision being considered is whether to finance a new investment project with equity by issuing new common stock, or to

EXHIBIT 4.2

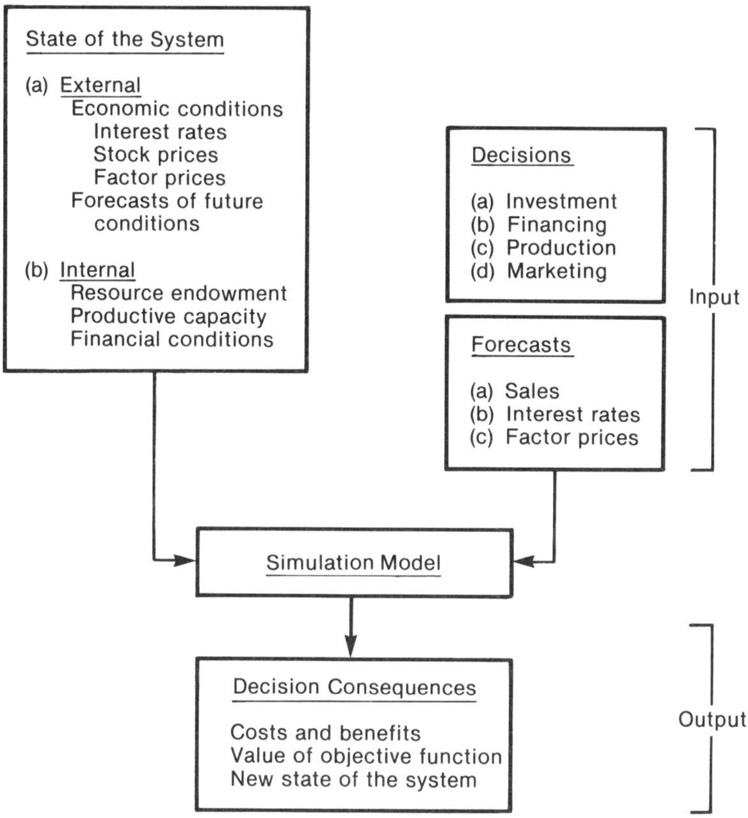

finance it with debt by borrowing from the bank. The typical simulation would trace through the consequences of each of these alternatives and would present the user with sets of financial statements so he can evaluate the results of the decisions in terms of the financial status of the firm.

Advantages of the simulation approach are that the simulation model may be more easily developed and solved than an optimization model, managers may more easily understand what the simulation model does, and the output, in the form of standard financial statements, is understood and accepted by management. In addition, as compared to an optimization model that tells management which decision is best, managers may have more confidence in, and provide more support for, a decision that they made themselves after being shown the prospective consequences generated by the simulation model.

One problem with some simulations is that they can generate so much output, in the form of pro forma financial statements, that the user is swamped with output and cannot evaluate the results. All too frequently, the user is inundated with such a volume of detailed results that he is confused and still cannot tell which decision is best. For example, in the debt-versus-equity financing problem mentioned above, output consisting of an income statement and balance sheet for each period over a number of periods, for each decision alternative, can be so overwhelming and confusing that it is not at all helpful to the decision maker.

Oftentimes, users of simulation models develop detailed models that are capable of generating detailed financial statements, but the user neglects to specify how these simulated financial statements were to be compared to determine the best decisions. If many different decision variables are to be considered and many different financial factors are to be compared, it is difficult to compare financial statements and pick out one as the best. For example, one decision alternative may result in a more liquid current position, but with greater long-term debt. The user still must decide how to evaluate the trade-off between liquidity and greater leverage. What is necessary to help evaluate such trade-offs is a specification of the goal that is the object of the decision evaluation process. That is, the user needs to specify an objective function that will measure the relative desirability of the results of the various decisions that are being considered.

Of course, the user of the simulation model can always choose to develop an objective function to be used in conjunction with the simulation results. In this case, the simulated results can be generated, and the user can inspect the simulated values of the objective function and choose the best decision. The difficulty with this approach is that there still may be so many different decision alternatives that it is inefficient to inspect the results of them all, even when they are summarized by an objective function. For example, suppose a planning problem involves just 10 different decision variables—the amount of cash balance to carry, the level of inventory, investment in fixed plant, and so forth—and suppose each of these decision variables can take on any of 15 different values. The number of different decision combinations would be $15^{10} = 5.767 \times 10^{11}$. It would certainly take a long time for the planner to examine the result of each possible decision combination. What is needed is an efficient way to search through all decision combinations to find the best one. This is the task performed by optimization models—such a model can quickly determine which of the many possible combinations of decisions best meets the specified objective.

Optimization

An optimization model determines which decision alternative leads to a desired objective. Whereas a simulation model simply shows the consequences of a decision specified by the user, the optimization model solves for the best decision.

The optimization model usually consists of an equation that expresses the objective or goal of the decision, and a set of equations and inequalities that represent constraints. The constraints are usually closely related to the sets of equations that constitute the simulation model—the equations that reflect the relationships and links between the firm's environment and the organization, between the units of the organization, and between action and result. Thus, one can think of an optimization model as being like a simulation model to which is added an expression representing the goal of the decision that we call the objective function.

The objective function of an optimization model is an equation that portrays the influence of the decision variables on the objective. The objective is the thing that the user wants to make as large as possible (maximize) or as small as possible (minimize). For example, the user may want to make decisions so as to maximize the market value of the firm's common stock. The objective function would be a mathematical expression that shows the effect on the market value of the stock of the decision variables being considered in the model.

The decision variables would be the variables in the model

that represent choices available to the decision maker. For example, the decision variables might include the amount to be borrowed to finance an inventory, the number of shares of stock to be sold, and the level of investment in inventory. Thus, this objective function would show the influences of the amount borrowed, the number of new shares, and the level of inventory on the market value of the firm's stock. The purpose of the optimization model would be to find the values of these three decision variables that would make the value of the stock as large as possible.

The constraints in an optimization model are sets of equations (or inequalities) that express the limitations that prohibit one from choosing the decision variables so as to make the objective arbitrarily large (in the case of a maximization problem). Some of the constraints may express subgoals and other objectives that the user wants to attain in addition to the primary goal specified by the objective function, and other constraint equations would be identical to the equations of a simulation model. Examples of constraint equations associated with the inventory financing problem could include, among others,

a. A limitation on the number of common stock shares that could be sold.
b. A limitation on the amount borrowed so the borrowing would not exceed the firm's line of credit.
c. A requirement that the inventory be no less than next month's anticipated sales, but no greater than three times these anticipated sales.

Two advantages of the optimization approach are, first, that it forces the user to clarify and clearly state the objectives in order to specify the objective function and, second, that it relieves the user of the confusing task of searching through simulated results to evaluate numerous decision alternatives. Chapter Eight will explain optimization in more detail.

CHAPTER FIVE

An Introduction to Forecasting

A crucial ingredient to financial modeling and planning is the forecast about future conditions that will serve as input to the model. The forecast will serve as a basis for developing the strategy for the future. At the same time, because we can seldom forecast completely accurately, one of the functions of the financial model is to develop contingency plans for those frequent occasions when our forecasts are incorrect.

An important first step in the education of the financial modeler and planner is to learn about alternative forecasting techniques. First, it would be helpful to be able to generate your own forecasts that are accurate and reliable. Second, and perhaps more important, even if you do not turn out to be an accomplished forecaster yourself, it is important to be aware of the different approaches to forecasting and to know how to judge the accuracy of a forecast.

The purpose of this chapter is to introduce you to various forecasting techniques that might be used in conjunction with financial models. In the space of one short chapter it is not practical to introduce all techniques or to make the reader completely competent in these forecasting techniques. It takes a careful study of the specialized tools of forecasting to develop this required expertise. Here, we can only build some initial understanding and familiarity. The reader who needs more complete understanding is directed to the references at the end of the chapter—particularly the works by Wheelwright and Makridakis (1977), Gross and Peterson (1983), and Pindyck and Rubinfeld (1976). The reader who is not interested in forecasting but is concerned only with modeling need not be delayed by this chapter, and is encouraged to go on to Chapter Six.

There are many different methods and techniques for generating the forecasts that would be necessary in a financial model. The technique that is best will depend on factors such as the time horizon over which we will be making the forecast, the level of detail and required accuracy of the forecast, the costs of being wrong, the type of data available to the forecaster, and the competence of the forecaster. All these factors, and more, need to be evaluated to determine which technique is appropriate. There may be a highly sophisticated technique available, but its use may be costly, it may not have the belief or confidence of the people in the organization, or it may produce forecasts more detailed than is appropriate for the task. It may make more sense to use less sophisticated forecasting methods for some applications and reserve the more sophisticated techniques for special situations. The main point is that the forecasting technique should be chosen so it is suited to the task and its benefits are not outweighed by its costs. This chapter is intended to give the reader a feel for different methods so this type of evaluation can be made.

The various methods of forecasting can be classed very generally as qualitative or quantitative. We will discuss both, but this chapter will be focused on the quantitative methods—not because they are inherently superior, but because they are more easily taught and evaluated. It is very difficult to discuss and teach the methods by which a knowledgeable businessperson generates subjective forecasts based on good judgment and detailed knowledge of an industry.

5.1 QUANTITATIVE FORECASTING METHODS

There are many different kinds of quantitative techniques for forecasting economic and business variables. The techniques that will be discussed here include time trend extrapolation, moving averages, exponential smoothing, time series decomposition, linear regression and econometric models, and time series analysis.

Quantitative methods of forecasting have the advantage that they are consistent, can be replicated and tested, and are amenable to careful evaluation of their results. This does not mean that they necessarily generate better forecasts than more subjective methods, only that we can teach, analyze, and test them more easily.

In the following sections we will discuss some of the methods of forecasting and demonstrate them with some examples. The examples focus on sales forecasting. Obviously, other variables—such as costs, interest rates, and prices—also need to be forecasted. Sales are used as an example; the techniques could equally well apply to other variables, although there are cases where one technique may be better suited to one forecasted variable than another.

Time Trend Extrapolation

We can discuss some of the methods of extrapolating time trends of variables by considering the quarterly sales reported by the Salisbury Equipment Corporation from the first quarter of 1981 (1981.I) through the second quarter of 1985 (1985.II), as shown in Exhibit 5.1. Exhibit 5.2 shows the sales as a graph over the same period. Based on this data we want to forecast the company's sales for quarters 1985.III through 1986.IV.

Percentage Change. One of the simplest approaches is to forecast the rate of change expected in future periods based on average rates of change in the variable that have been observed in the past. The rate of change in quarterly sales is shown in columns 4 and 6 of Exhibit 5.1; the arithmetic average of these growth rates is 1.11 percent per quarter, or roughly 4.5 percent per year.

If we base our forecast for 1985.III on this arithmetic average growth rate in sales, a first approximation forecast would be to say that the sales are expected to be

$$\begin{aligned} Sales_{85.\mathrm{III}} &= Sales_{85.\mathrm{II}} \cdot (1.011) \\ &= 1092.5 \cdot (1.011) \\ &= 1104.5 \end{aligned}$$

EXHIBIT 5.1 Salisbury Equipment Corporation: Sales and Percent Change in Sales by Quarters, 1981–1985

Year	*Quarter*	*Sales ($000)*	*Percent Change*
1981	I	$ 906.7	
	II	903.3	−0.38%
	III	913.2	1.10
	IV	935.0	2.39
1982	I	913.0	−2.35
	II	921.6	0.94
	III	951.2	3.21
	IV	961.1	1.04
1983	I	967.5	0.67
	II	$ 986.7	1.98%
	III	998.9	1.24
	IV	1,017.3	1.84
1984	I	993.6	−2.33
	II	1,015.7	2.22
	III	1,044.3	2.82
	IV	1,052.7	0.80
1985	I	1,064.9	1.16
	II	1,092.5	2.59
	Average growth rate		1.11%

and then $1,116.7, $1,128.9, $1,141.4, $1,153.9, and $1,166.6 for 1985.IV through 1986.IV, respectively.

The simple arithmetic average may not be a good estimator of the growth rate (percentage change) in some cases, and a different kind of average growth rate, the geometric average, may provide a better estimate. The geometric average growth rate corresponds to the average compound rate of growth for the variable. For example, with quarterly sales growing from $906.7 in 1981.I to $1,092.5 in 1985.II, we can ask what the average quarterly compound growth rate in sales was over that period. If g denotes the average compound growth rate over the 17 periods, then

$$Sales_{81.\mathrm{I}}\,(1 + g)^{17} = Sales_{85.\mathrm{II}}.$$

Solving for the growth rate g, we have

$$\begin{aligned} g &= (Sales_{85.\mathrm{II}}/Sales_{81.\mathrm{I}})^{1/17} - 1 \\ &= (1092.5/906.7)^{1/17} - 1 \\ &\doteq 0.011. \end{aligned}$$

In general, for growth over n periods, where *Start* and *End* denote the values of the variables at the start and end of the growth periods, the geometric average growth rate is calculated as

$$g = (End/Start)^{1/n} - 1.$$

where $(\cdot)^{1/n}$ means the nth root. The geometric average is generally regarded as a better indicator of the true growth rate because the average is not distorted by a few large increases or decreases in the intervening periods.

Regardless of whether the arithmetic or geometric average is used, the percentage change (or average growth) method offers the advantage of being simple to apply and understand, and is probably the most widely used method for extrapolating recent observations into the future to generate forecasts. For short-term forecasts that don't require a high degree of accuracy or sophistication this may be the best approach. For longer-term forecasts such extrapolation may be misleading because there may be little basis to assume that past growth trends will continue at the same rate in the future. On the other hand, even for short-run forecasts this method can be misleading because any extrapolation of a general trend, by its very nature, takes no account of seasonal or cyclical departures from the general trend. Thus, while the approach can be useful and is easy to apply, the forecaster should be aware of its potential shortcomings.

Time Trend with Linear Regression. The projection of a time trend is very closely related to the percentage change approach to forecasting, offering many of the same advantages and disadvantages. The time trend approach is simply an attempt to isolate the basic underlying trend that the series of observations are apparently following. This can be done either by subjectively drawing a line through points representing the data or by using a more precise method such as fitting the line using a least squares linear regression technique.

The Constant-Change Model. In the latter case, with one independent variable, *Time,* and a dependent variable, *Sales,* the linear regression relationship could be expressed with a mathematical model (equation) of the general form

$$Sales_t = a + b \cdot Time + e_t,$$

where $Sales_t$ denotes the sales during period t, *Time* represents the number of periods. The constants a and b are called *parameters* or *regression coefficients,* and e_t is a random error term

EXHIBIT 5.2 Salisbury Equipment Corporation: Time Trend of Sales per Quarter, 1981.I–1985.IV

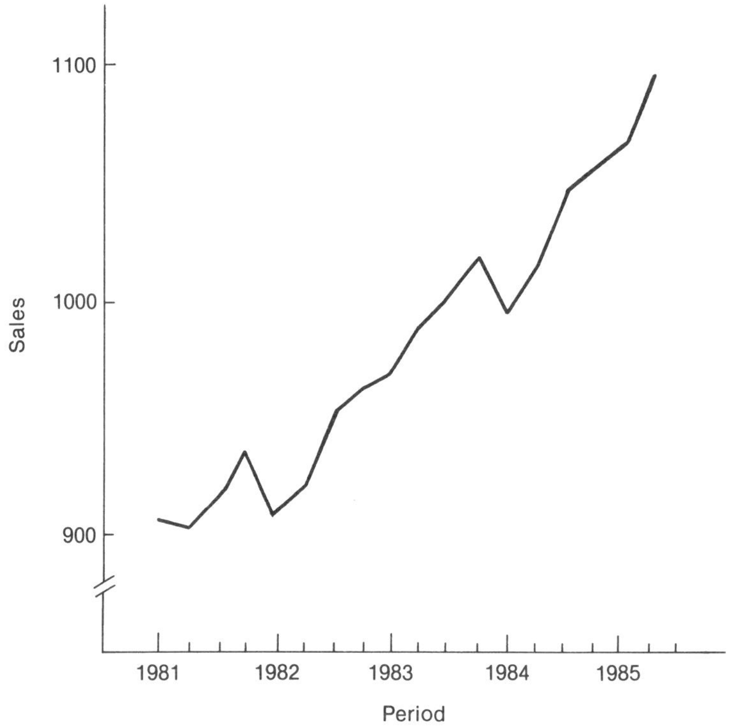

(also called a *deviation* or *residual* term) that is included because sales will not be perfectly related to time.

The task of least squares regression is to estimate the values of the parameters a and b so the resulting equation fits the data by defining the one line for which the sum of the squared error (deviation) terms has the least possible value. For example, consider the points representing the quarterly sales of the Salisbury Corporation, shown as Exhibit 5.3. The observed sales levels are shown as the points on the graph. If a straight line is drawn through the points, it will not pass through all of them: some will be above and some will be below the line. For example, for period 5 (1982.I) the point is below the line, as shown by the arrow, so the observed value deviates from the line. This deviation from the line can be regarded as a random error term, e_t, where the subscript t refers to the observation for period t—in this case observation $t=5$, and the error is denoted by e_5. Of course, there are many ways we could draw a line through the data to represent the trend—perhaps a horizontal line or a vertical line. The least squares regression line is the line that minimizes the sum of the squared deviations (e^2_t) of the observed values from the line, and is generally regarded as one of the best ways to describe the data.

For this set of data, the parameters that satisfy the least squares criterion are $a = 877.11$ and $b = 10.83$, resulting in the equation

$$Sales_t = 877.11 + 10.83\ (Time), \tag{5.2}$$

where *Time* is the number of quarters elapsed since 1979.IV.[1] For 1982.I, for example, five quarters after 1979.IV, we can calculate the *Sales* that would be predicted for that quarter *if* sales followed the trend represented by the line, by substituting 5 for the (*Time*) variable in Equation (5.2):

$$Sales_5 = 877.11 - 10.83(5) = \$931.26.$$

Note, however, that the actual sales in that quarter were \$913.0, a value that deviates from that predicted by the regression equation by $913.0 - 931.26 = -18.26$. This -18.26 is the error (deviation or residual) of the fifth observation, so we say $e_5 = -18.26$. Exhibit 5.4 shows the error terms or residuals for all observations over the 20-quarter period. Column 2 shows the actual sales values, column 3 the values that would be predicted based on the relation (5.2), and column 4 the deviations of the observed values from the predicted values. If each residual term is squared, we get 20 positive terms that we refer to as the squared residuals. Least squares regression is the statistical technique that determines the relationship (the line through the data as shown in Exhibit 5.3) that minimizes the sum (over all 20 observations in this case) of the squared residuals.

If we accept Equation (5.2) as a valid representation of the relation between sales and time, and we believe it will continue

---

[1]The personal computer software used for this regression was Micro Statistics Package (MSP) by Keller and Marsh, 1414 Smith Court, San Luis Obispo, CA 93401. MSP is an inexpensive software for general statistical problems. It is simple to use, but does not have the sophistication or flexibility of more expensive and harder to learn packages.

EXHIBIT 5.3 Salisbury Equipment Corporation: Least Squares Regression Line

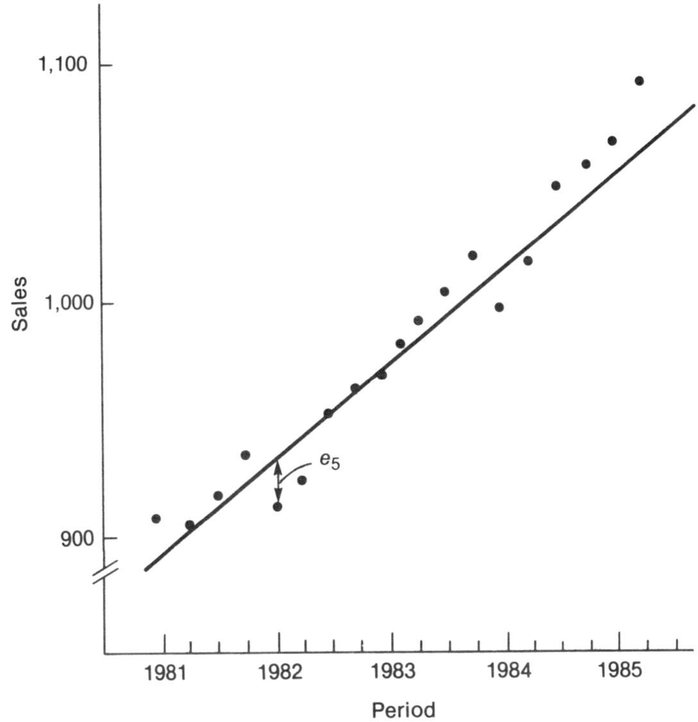

in the future, we can use it as a basis for forecasting future sales. For example, our last sales observation was for 1985.II, which we designated as period 18. To forecast sales for periods 19, 20, 21, 22, 23, and 24 we substitute these values for (*Time*) into (5.2) to obtain forecasts of

$$Sales_{19} = 877.11 + 10.83(19) = 1{,}082.88$$

for 1985.III and 1093.71, 1,104.54, 1,115.37, 1,126.20, and 1,137.03 for quarters 1985.IV through 1986.IV.

The particular time trend equation (model) used in this example has several potential shortcomings. First, the form of the equation implies that we believe that the increase in sales would be a constant amount each quarter regardless of the volume of sales. This means that the rate of increase as a percentage of

EXHIBIT 5.4 Salisbury Equipment Corporation: Actual Sales, Predicted Sales, and Residual Error Terms

Period	*Actual Sales ($000)*	*Predicted Sales ($000)*	*Residual Error, e_t*
1	$ 906.7	$ 887.94	18.76
2	903.3	898.76	4.53
3	913.2	909.59	3.60
4	935.0	920.41	14.58
5	913.0	931.26	−18.26
6	921.6	942.06	−20.46
7	951.2	952.89	−1.69
8	961.1	963.71	−2.61
9	967.5	974.54	−7.04
10	986.7	985.36	1.33
11	998.9	996.19	2.70
12	1,017.3	1,007.01	10.28
13	993.6	1,017.84	−24.24
14	1,015.7	1,028.67	−12.97
15	1,044.3	1,039.49	4.80
16	1,052.7	1,050.32	2.37
17	1,064.9	1,061.14	3.75
18	1,092.5	1,071.97	20.52

sales would be decreasing over time as the level of sales increased. That is, the rate of growth in sales is decreasing as time passes. Second, as would be true of almost any forecast based on past data, the results will be highly dependent on the particular period chosen from which to estimate the trend parameters. If we had chosen to estimate the trend based on data starting at, say, 1984.I, we would get quite different results, predicting a larger quarterly increase. Third, there may be little justification for assuming that the past observed pattern of quarterly sales increases will continue in the future. Finally, the future level of sales may not really be dependent on time, as Equation (5.2) implies; there may be other variables that influence sales from which we could obtain a much more accurate forecast. There are many other types of forecasting models that we could use that would take care of some of these shortcomings of this *constant* change model.

The Constant-Growth Model. A *constant-growth* model of the time trend of sales is an alternative that shows the periodic increase in sales as a constant proportion, or percentage, of sales. That is, assume we write the relation between sales in period t and period $t-1$ as

$$Sales_t = Sales_{t-1}(1 + g),$$

or

$$Sales_t = Sales_0(1 + g)^t, \qquad (5.3)$$

where g is the rate of growth and $Sales_0$ denotes a base period from which sales are growing. The linear regression that we can use to estimate the relation between *Sales* and *Time* would be written as

$$\log(Sales_t) = a + b \cdot Time, \qquad (5.4)$$

where the dependent variable is measured as the logarithm of sales. The coefficient, b, of the *Time* variable can be interpreted as the average continuous rate of growth of sales, or as $\log(1 + g)$.[2]

For the Salisbury Corporation's quarterly sales, the regression of the form (5.4) generates the estimate that

$$\log(Sales_t) = 6.78 + 0.011\ (Time), \qquad (5.5)$$

which estimates an average quarterly rate of continuous growth in sales of 1.1 percent. This growth trend estimate of 1.1 percent per quarter is close to the average compound growth rate determined earlier, and would lead to the same forecast as that estimate.

This constant-growth approach, when appropriate, may answer the criticism against the constant-*change* assumption. In this model the change will be proportional to the level of sales. We don't know beforehand which approach is most valid, and we need a way to assess which equation best represents the relation between the dependent variable (*Sales*) and the independent variable (*Time*).

---

[2]The continuous growth model would be of the form $Sales_t = Sales_0 \cdot \exp(g \cdot t)$, and with a regression of the form (5.4) we have $\ln(Sales_t) = \ln(Sales_0) + \ln[\exp(g \cdot t)]$, which reduces to $\ln(Sales_t) = a + bt$, where $a = \ln(Sales_0)$ and $b = g$. In the discrete time version of (5.3), the coefficients are $a = \log(Sales_0)$ and $b = \log(1+g) \cdot t$, so the estimate of the average periodic growth rate is $g = \text{antilog}(b) - 1$.

Assessing the Regression Results. One way to evaluate how well the regression equation fits the data is to determine how much of the variation in the dependent variable is accounted for by its relationship with the independent variable. The *coefficient of determination,* denoted by R^2 and frequently referred to as "R-squared," is one of the statistics generated by a typical regression program that measures the "fit of the regression." R^2 measures the proportion of the total variance in the independent variable that is accounted for by its relationship with the independent variable. If $R^2 = 1$, all (100 percent) of the variance in the dependent variable is accounted for by its relation to the independent variable *Time,* so the regression provides a perfect fit of the data. If $R^2 = 0$, there is no relationship. In regressions using time series data it is common to find R^2 as high as 0.95 (95 percent) or 0.99 (99 percent), simply because most economic variables follow a time trend. For the two regressions relating Salisbury's *Sales* to *Time,* over the period 1981.I to 1985.II, the constant-change model (5.2) had an $R^2 = 0.954$ and the constant growth model (5.5) had $R^2 = 0.958$. This means that the constant-growth model fit the data just slightly better than the constant-change model.

Another way to evaluate the results is to use a measure of the average error or deviation of the data from those predicted by the regression equation. The first measure we will discuss is the *mean square error* (MSE). The mean square error is an average of the squared error terms (e^2_t). For example, Exhibit 5.5 shows the residual error terms for both the constant-change and constant-growth models in columns 2 and 4, respectively. Columns 3 and 5 show the error terms squared, e^2_t, for each model for each of the 18 observations. The average error terms are shown at the bottom and are quite small—close to zero (not zero because of rounding)—because the calculation of the regression line causes the average error term to be zero. The averages of the squared error terms are also shown at the bottom and are 152.46 and 134.72 for the two models. The mean square error provides one measure of the accuracy of the model. The model with the smaller mean square error is the one that has the smaller sum of squared errors and a better fit with the data. The last item in Exhibit 5.5 is the root mean square error, simply the square root of MSE, which restates the average squared error in

EXHIBIT 5.5 Salisbury Equipment Corporation: Calculation of Mean Square Errors for Constant-Change and Constant-Growth Models

	Constant-Change Model		*Constant-Growth Model*	
Period	*Residual Error, e_t*	*Squared Error, e^2_t*	*Residual Error, e_t*	*Squared Error, e^2_t*
1	18.76	351.94	15.74	247.73
2	4.53	20.52	2.48	6.17
3	3.60	12.96	2.42	5.86
4	14.58	212.58	14.15	200.15
5	−18.26	333.43	−18.04	325.37
6	−20.46	418.61	−19.74	389.50
7	− 1.69	2.86	− 0.55	0.30
8	− 2.61	6.81	− 1.17	1.38
9	− 7.04	49.56	− 5.42	29.36
10	1.33	1.77	3.02	9.12
11	2.70	7.29	4.34	18.84
12	10.28	105.68	11.74	137.82
13	−24.24	578.58	−23.08	532.79
14	−12.97	168.22	−12.23	149.51
15	4.80	23.04	5.00	25.03
16	2.37	5.62	1.91	3.64
17	3.75	14.06	2.48	6.17
18	20.52	421.07	18.33	336.13
Average error:	0.0037		0.0777	
Mean square error (MSE):		152.46		134.72
Root mean square error ($\sqrt{MSE}$):		12.35		11.61

the same units as the sales. Thus, we say the root mean square error was slightly smaller for the constant-growth model, and the constant-growth model provides a slightly better fit with the data.

The ideas of average error, mean square error, and root mean square error could subsequently be carried over to a forecast, where we talk of the average forecast error, mean square forecast error, and root mean square forecast error. In these cases we compare a forecast with the actual occurrence and calculate the errors to compare the accuracy of different forecasting techniques.

One drawback of using a time trend approach to forecasting, whether it is linear regression or simple average percentage change, is that we will usually get different answers and forecasts when we use different periods for the beginning and end of our study. For example, when we estimate the time trend starting in 1975 we get regression coefficients quite different from those we get when we start our study period in 1981.

Smoothing of Time Trends

Moving Averages. It is always a problem to know how much past data should be taken into account in developing the forecast. Conditions may have changed sufficiently over time that data many periods in the past may be irrelevant, and the more recent events may be more important in developing our forecast. The use of moving averages is one method that places more emphasis on recent events, so it may be a more appropriate method when relationships are changing over time.

With the simplest moving-average approach, an average is computed each period based on the most recently observed values of the variable to be forecast. This average is then used as the forecast for next period. Then next period, a new moving average is computed that adds the newest observation and drops the oldest observation, and this new average is used as a subsequent forecast.

For example, consider the sales data for the Tudor Corporation that is shown from the first quarter of 1982 (1982.I) until the last quarter of 1986 (1986.IV) in column 2 of Exhibit 5.6. The Tudor Corporation is in a very cyclical business, but its sales have not been following any particular trend, as is evident in the graph of sales shown as Exhibit 5.7. Suppose we use a four-period moving average as a forecast of the next period's sales. Starting in 1982.IV, the forecast for 1983.I would be calculated as

$$\begin{aligned} \textit{Forecast sales}_{83.\mathrm{I}} &= [\mathrm{Sales}_{82.\mathrm{I}} + \textit{Sales}_{82.\mathrm{II}} + \textit{Sales}_{82.\mathrm{III}} + \\ &\qquad \textit{Sales}_{82.\mathrm{IV}}]/4 \qquad (5.6) \\ &= (607 + 743 + 675 + 493)/4 \\ &= 629.5, \end{aligned}$$

which, in this case, exceeds the actual level of 562. In each succeeding period the new moving average is calculated with the newest sales data, dropping the oldest period in this four-period

EXHIBIT 5.6 Tudor Corporation: Moving Average Forecasts of Sales ($000)

			Four-Period Moving Average		Six-Period Moving Average	
Year	*Quarter*	*Sales (Actual)*	*Forecast*	*Error*	*Forecast*	*Error*
1982	I	$607				
	II	743				
	III	675				
	IV	493				
1983	I	562	629.5	−67.5		
	II	809	618.3	190.7		
	III	821	634.8	186.2	648.2	172.8
	IV	512	671.3	−105.3	683.8	−171.8
1984	I	535	676.0	−141.	645.3	−110.3
	II	732	669.3	62.7	622.0	110
	III	618	650.0	− 32.	661.8	− 43.8
	IV	417	599.3	−182.3	671.2	−254.2
1985	I	565	575.5	− 10.5	605.8	− 40.8
	II	672	583.0	89.	563.2	108.8
	III	501	568.0	− 67.	589.8	− 88.8
	IV	451	538.8	− 87.8	584.2	−133.2
1986	I	598	547.3	50.7	537.3	60.7
	II	784	555.5	228.5	534.0	250.
	III	753	583.5	169.5	595.2	157.8
	IV	825	646.5	178.5	626.5	198.5
Average error:				28.9		15.4
Mean square forecast error (MSE):				17,522		22,842.5
Root mean square forecast error ($\sqrt{MSE}$):				132.4		151.1

moving average. These forecasts are shown as column 3 in Exhibit 5.6, and is also shown as the dotted line in Exhibit 5.7.

The moving average is a method for smoothing the data to eliminate the influence of random fluctuations that occur period-to-period. The greater the number of past periods included in the average, the greater the smoothing effect. For example, column 5 of Exhibit 5.6 shows the forecast that would result from a six-period moving average, and the same data are shown as the dashed line on Exhibit 5.7. By using more periods in the moving average, the effect of any single period's random fluctuation is dampened, resulting in a less variable period-to-period forecast.

Naturally, we cannot rely on making completely accurate

EXHIBIT 5.7 Tudor Corporation: Moving Average Forecasts of Sales

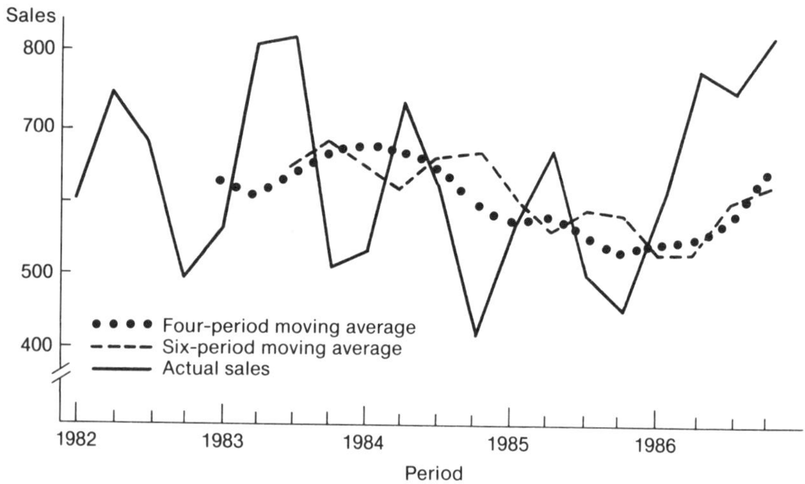

forecasts, particularly when we make simple calculations using only past data. Our forecasts will always have errors, and what we would like is that the errors be as small as possible and will not be systematically too high or too low. Columns 4 and 6 of Exhibit 5.6 show the errors made in our forecasts, calculated as

$$Sales_t - Forecast\ sales_t$$

for each period for which a forecast has been made. If we simply average these forecast errors we would, ideally, get an average of zero, indicating that whatever "over-forecasts" we made would be counterbalanced by "under-forecasts"; that is, we have made forecasts that are not biased either upward or downward. The average errors for the two moving averages are shown at the bottoms of columns 4 and 6. In both cases, the average errors are positive, indicating that on the average the actual sales exceed our forecast, and our forecast is biased downward—that is, our forecasts are too low.

Another way to evaluate the forecasts is with the mean square forecast error (MSE), or its square root, the root mean square forecast error ($\sqrt{\text{MSE}}$), which are also shown at the bottom of columns 4 and 6. These measures do not show whether our forecast is biased downward or upward, but they are good measures for comparing the accuracy of the forecasts. Because the

MSE squares the error terms, it eliminates any effect of the forecast being positive or negative. However, it magnifies the effect of large errors relative to small errors, so that a forecasting approach that results in larger errors will show a much larger MSE or $\sqrt{\text{MSE}}$. In this case, the four-period moving average does perform slightly better than the six-period average although the difference is not great. That is, while its average error is larger, (28.9 versus 15.4), it makes fewer very large errors, so it has smaller $\sqrt{\text{MSE}}$ (132.4 versus 151.1).

In its simplest form the moving average does not take account of the time trend in the data. Consequently, it is most appropriate for forecasting a variable for which there is no apparent trend, but for which there are random fluctuations around a constant average. In the case of the Tudor Corporation, the quarterly sales don't show an apparent trend, so the approach is acceptable. However, for Salisbury Corporation's sales there is a distinct trend, and the simple moving average would be inappropriate because the moving average would consistently generate a forecast that was below the trend. There are more sophisticated moving average methods that take account of the trend, but they will not be discussed in this chapter. The reader is directed to the forecasting texts cited at the end of this chapter.

One difficulty with using the moving average is to determine the best number of periods to use in computing the average. There is no definitive way to determine this except to try different lags to see which one generates the best forecast. In certain instances, the nature of the time pattern of the variable to be forecast will dictate a particular lag. For example, the Tudor Corporation's sales followed an annual cycle, typically hitting a peak in the second or third quarter and a trough in the fourth quarter. This pattern would suggest using an average over four periods, or maybe eight or twelve periods, so it reflects the overall annual cycle. In contrast, a five-period moving average would tend to put too much weight on an extra period that could systematically increase the forecast error.

While a simple moving average can offer the advantage of taking into account the more recent events, one drawback is that it gives equal weight to all observations included in the average and gives zero weight to data from periods not included in the average. A technique that solves these problems is exponential smoothing.

Exponential Smoothing. This is a forecasting approach analogous to a moving average that puts greater weight on the most recently observed events and modifies each new forecast according to how much error there is in our earlier forecasts. If we let a denote a proportional weight between 0 and 1, the exponentially smoothed forecast of a variable such as sales could be written as

$$\begin{aligned} \textit{Forecast sales}_{t+1} &= a\ \textit{Sales}_t + a(1-a)\textit{Sales}_{t-1} \\ &+ a(1-a)^2\textit{Sales}_{t-2} + \ldots, \end{aligned} \tag{5.7}$$

where the + . . . at the end of the expression means we keep adding terms of the form $a(1-a)^j \cdot \textit{Sales}_{t-j}$. With the smoothing constant a between 0 and 1, the terms $a(1-a)^j$ get smaller and smaller as we consider sales further in the past. Thus, the forecast of sales is simply a weighted average of *all* past values of *sales,* with greater weight being placed on the most recent observations. For actually making the forecast, we don't really need to use all the past data because it can be shown that (5.7) can be written as

$$\textit{Forecast sales}_{t+1} = a \cdot \textit{Sales}_t + (1-a)\ \textit{Forecast sales}_t, \tag{5.8}$$

where the last term is the forecast of sales for this period (t) that was forecast last period ($t-1$). Thus, with the exponential smoothing approach, the forecast for next period is a weighted average of this period's observed value ($\textit{Sales}_t$) and last period's forecast of this period's sales ($\textit{Forecast Sales}_t$), where the weights are a and $(1-a)$, respectively.

Another interesting interpretation of the exponential smoothing expression is that (5.8) can also be written as

$$\begin{aligned} \textit{Forecast sales}_{t+1} &= \textit{Forecast sales}_t + \\ &a(\textit{Sales}_t - \textit{Forecast sales}_t) \end{aligned} \tag{5.9}$$

Note that the term ($\textit{Sales}_t - \textit{Forecast sales}_t$) is the error made in the forecast for this period's sales. If our forecast that was made last period turns out to have been correct, we just use the same forecast again. But, if our forecast was incorrect, we adjust our forecast for next period by some proportion, a, of the error in the forecast.

To see how this technique is applied, assume the smoothing constant is $a = 0.10$, and assume that our initial forecast of

Tudor's sales for 1983.I is $630, and the actual sales for that quarter turn out to be $562. Then our forecast for 1983.II, according to (5.8), is

$$\begin{aligned} \textit{Forecast sales}_{83.\text{II}} &= (0.10)\ 562 + (1 - 0.10)630 \\ &= 623.2, \end{aligned}$$

or, according to (5.9), we have

$$\begin{aligned} \textit{Forecast sales}_{83.\text{II}} &= 630 + 0.10\ (562 - 630) \\ &= 630 - 6.8 = 623.2, \end{aligned}$$

where the latter approach adjusts the forecast downward because actual sales this period turned out to be below what we previously forecast would occur this period.

Exhibit 5.8 shows the forecast for Tudor's sales for the periods 1983.I through 1986.IV using exponential smoothing with a smoothing weight of $a = 0.10$. The average error, the mean square error, and the root mean square error of the forecast are shown at the bottom. In this particular example, the root mean square error is between those obtained with the moving averages, so this forecast is not quite as accurate as the four-period moving average, but is slightly better than the six-period moving average, but the small average error shows that it has less bias than the other two forecasts. By changing the smoothing constant we might be able to improve the forecasting accuracy, but the determination of the best value of a frequently ends up being a trial and error process.

Decomposition into Seasonal, Trend, and Cyclical Factors

In the previous section we discussed the identification of the time trend of a variable and its use in generating a forecast. Obviously, the data may have other influences besides a trend. Economic data are frequently subject to variations due to seasonal and cyclical factors in addition to the trend. The decomposition approach is a method for identifying these different factors and using them to generate our forecast.

For example, Exhibit 5.9 shows the pattern of sales for a company that has seasonal, cyclical, and trend factors. The underlying time trend is shown as the straight line that slopes upward. The firm's sales are subject to systematic ups and

EXHIBIT 5.8 Tudor Corporation: Sales and Sales Forecast Based on Exponential Smoothing ($000)

Year	*Quarter*	*Sales (Actual)*	*Forecast (a = 0.10)*	*Error*
1982	I	$607		
	II	743		
	III	675		
	IV	493		
1983	I	562	$630	$ 68
	II	809	623.2	−185.8
	III	821	641.8	−179.2
	IV	512	659.7	147.7
1984	I	535	644.9	109.9
	II	732	633.9	− 98.1
	III	618	643.7	25.7
	IV	417	641.1	224.1
1985	I	565	619.3	54.3
	II	672	613.9	− 58.1
	III	501	672.0	171.0
	IV	451	654.9	203.9
1986	I	598	634.5	36.5
	II	784	598.0	−186.0
	III	753	616.6	−136.4
	IV	825	630.2	−194.8
	Average error			0.16
	Mean square error (MSE)			20,947.9
	Root mean square error ($\sqrt{MSE}$)			144.7

downs of the economic cycle on top of their long-term trend. This cyclical pattern is shown by the dashed curve around the trend. There also is a seasonal influence because the firm's sales are relatively slow in the winter months, pick up in the spring, slow down again in the summer, and pick up again in the fall. This seasonal pattern is shown as the solid wavy line imposed on the cycle. Finally, in spite of these various patterns, there is a component of the firm's sales that is simply unsystematic, or random, and that can't be accounted for by the trend, the cycle, or the seasonal influences. The actual sales that were observed for this company are shown as the dots on the graph that cluster around these various lines. The fact that the dots don't fall exactly on the lines is due to the unsystematic, random components.

What decomposition tries to do is to use the actual data to

EXHIBIT 5.9 Seasonal, Trend, and Cyclical Components of Sales

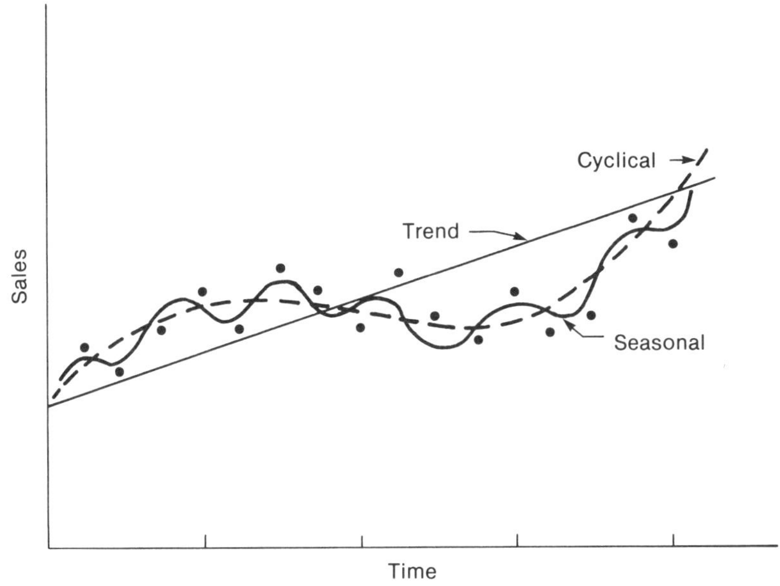

identify the systematic components of trend, cycle, and season so that we can get a better forecast based on these components. Because of the random component of the variables, we would expect that we would seldom be able to make completely accurate forecasts. The best we can do is to say what level of sales we would expect based on the systematic influences of trend, cycle, and season.

The first step in this decomposition is to separate out the seasonal influence by determining *seasonal adjustment factors.* There are several different approaches of varying degrees of sophistication that could be used. The simplest is to determine how each season's sales behave relative to an annual average. For example, consider Exhibits 5.10 and 5.11, which show the monthly sales figures for the Warwick Corporation from January 1982 through December 1985. It is evident from the figures that there is a pattern in the monthly sales. January, February, and March tend to be low; there is an increase in April, May, and June; a decline in July and August; then a high level of sales in the last four months of the year. The question is: How much do these monthly figures consistently vary from month to month? This is answered by determining the ratio of a given month's sales to a moving average of monthly sales.

The monthly seasonal adjustment factor is calculated as

$$\textit{Seasonal adjustment factor} = \frac{\textit{Sales for month}}{\textit{Centered 12-month average sales}} \quad (5.10)$$

For example, the centered moving average for January 1983 is the average of two 12-month averages: the first is the average of monthly sales from July 1982 to June 1983, the second from August 1982 to July 1983. These two averages are 524.8 and 525.9, respectively.

The centered 12-month average is the average of these two averages:

$$\begin{aligned}\textit{Centered 12-month average for January} &= (524.8 + 525.9)/2 \\ &= 525.35.\end{aligned}$$

The seasonal adjustment factor for January 1983 is calculated as

$$\begin{aligned}\begin{matrix}\textit{January seasonal} \\ \textit{adjustment factor}\end{matrix} &= \frac{\textit{Sales for January 1983}}{\textit{Centered 12-month average for January}} \\ &= \frac{105}{525.35} = 0.20.\end{aligned}$$

For each month a seasonal adjustment factor is calculated using the observed sales for that month as the numerator and the *centered 12-month average* that is centered on that month. The average for February 1983 is the average of: (1) the average over 12 months' sales from August 1982 to July 1983, and (2) the average over 12 months' sales from September 1982 to August 1983. Exhibit 5.12 shows the calculation of the adjustment factors for each month of 1983.

These factors can be used to deseasonalize the observed sales to determine whether there are other patterns in the data, such as trend or cyclical influences. For example, let us apply these seasonal factors to 1985 data to deseasonalize or eliminate the monthly fluctuations. This is done by dividing the observed values by the seasonal adjustment factor:

EXHIBIT 5.10 Warwick Corporation: Monthly Sales, 1982–1985

	1982	*1983*	*1984*	*1985*
January	$ 101	$ 105	$ 110	$ 115
February	255	266	276	288
March	461	479	499	519
April	519	540	562	585
May	567	590	614	639
June	620	646	672	699
July	311	324	337	351
August	260	271	282	293
September	575	598	622	648
October	629	655	681	709
November	894	930	968	1,008
December	1,003	1,044	1,086	1,130

$$\textit{Seasonally adjusted monthly sales} = \frac{\textit{Sales}}{\textit{Monthly seasonal adjustment factor}} \tag{5.11}$$

For January 1985 this is

$$\textit{Seasonally adjusted January sales} = \frac{115}{0.20} = 575.$$

This operation has eliminated the normal January decline in sales and shows what the typical sales would be. By multiplying by 12 we would obtain the January 1985 sales stated at a seasonally adjusted *annual* rate of $12 \times 575 = 6{,}900$. Exhibit 5.13 shows the seasonally adjusted figures for each month of 1985.

By making this seasonal adjustment we have filtered out the confusion of the monthly fluctuations and can discern the trend, which in this case is shown by the smooth increase in seasonally adjusted sales. The parameters of this trend could be determined by fitting a regression line to the seasonally adjusted data. For the case with growth in sales, the best model would be the regression

$$\log(\textit{Sales}) = a + b\,(\textit{Time}),$$

which, with 1985 data, yields the estimate $b = 0.0032$, which implies an estimated monthly growth rate of 0.32 percent, or about 3.9 percent annually. The trendline fits the data with an

EXHIBIT 5.11 Warwick Corporation: Monthly Sales, 1982–1985

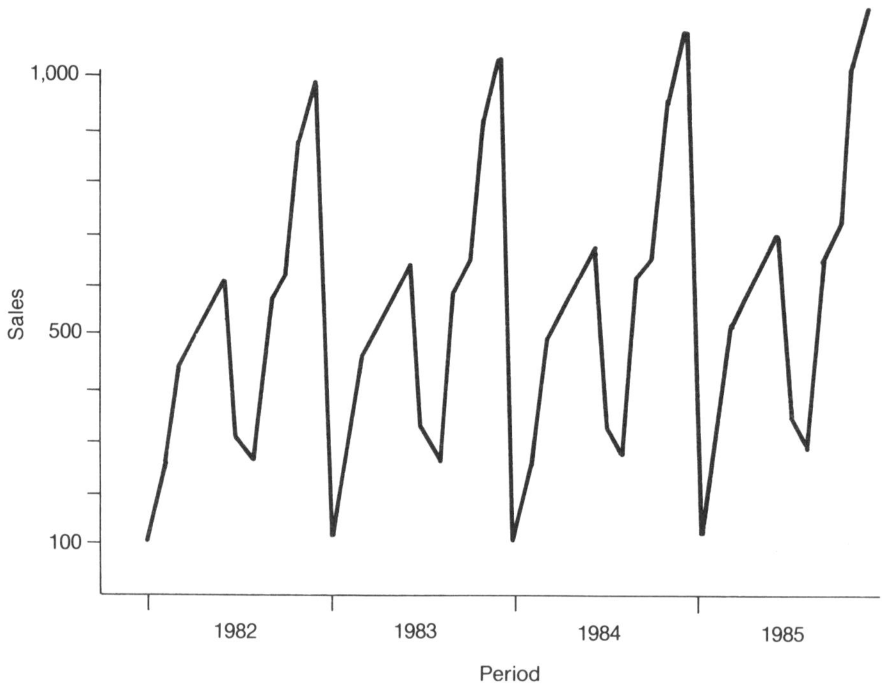

R^2 of 0.99—an almost perfect fit. Thus, in this particular example, there is great month-to-month variation in sales, but when this effect is removed, we see that sales are following a quite smooth growth curve from one year to the next.

With knowledge of the seasonal influences and the growth trend, and the assumptions that these will continue in the future, we can make a forecast for 1986. We can just extend the 0.32 percent monthly growth trend of seasonally adjusted sales, and then apply the seasonal adjustment to obtain a forecast of actual sales. For example, with seasonally adjusted sales of 594.74 for December 1985, we forecast seasonally adjusted sales for January 1986 of

$$594.74 \times 1.0032 = 596.64,$$

and, putting the seasonal factor back into the forecast, we get for January 1986

EXHIBIT 5.12 Warwick Corporation: Calculation of Seasonal Adjustment Factors

(1) Month	*(2) Sales*	*(3) Centered 12-Month Average*	*(4) Monthly Seasonal Adjustment Factor**
January 1983	$ 105	$515.35	0.2
February	266	534.7	0.5
March	479	536.12	0.9
April	540	538.16	1.0
May	590	540.75	1.1
June	646	543.96	1.2
July	324	545.88	0.6
August	271	546.5	0.5
September	598	547.75	1.1
October	655	549.5	1.2
November	930	547.25	1.7
December	1,044	545.16	1.9

*Column (2) divided by Column (3).

$$Sales = 596.64 \times 0.20 = 119.33,$$

where 0.20 is the seasonal factor for January from Exhibit 5.12. Alternatively, we can just take the actual January 1985 sales and project annual growth of 3.9 percent to obtain the same forecast.

The example of the Warwick Corporation does not exhibit any cyclical influence, but only seasonal and trend factors. If we remove the seasonal factors and then discern a trend, but we still have considerable variation in our data around the trend, some of it may be attributable to a cyclical component. The cyclical component may represent the systematic relation between the sales of our firm and the business cycle of the economy in general.

Because the business cycle is not really cyclical in the sense of being predictably periodic in its ups and downs, we cannot easily filter out the cyclical component to identify it. One approach to determining the relation to the cycle is to use a least squares regression. After having removed the seasonal components from the observed data, we can regress the deseasonalized

EXHIBIT 5.13 Warwick Corporation: Seasonally Adjusted Sales for 1985

Month	*1985 Sales*	*Seasonal Adjustment Factor*	*Seasonally Adjusted Monthly Sales*	*Seasonally Adjusted Annual Sales*
January	$ 115	0.2	$575	$6,900
February	288	0.5	576	6,912
March	519	0.9	576.6	6,920
April	585	1.01	579.2	6,950
May	639	1.1	580.9	6,971
June	699	1.2	582.5	6,990
July	351	0.6	585	7,020
August	293	0.5	586	7,032
September	648	1.1	589.1	7,069
October	710	1.2	591.7	7,100
November	1,007	1.7	592.4	7,108
December	1,130	1.9	594.7	7,137

sales against a variable that measures the business cycle, perhaps in addition to a time trend variable. The next section elaborates on this procedure.

Structural Econometric Forecasting Models

In many cases we can develop a useful forecasting model based on the relation between the forecast variable and other measures of economic activity. For example, the sales of our company may be strongly influenced by the general level of economic activity and the business cycle. With data from the past we can estimate the parameters of this relationship and utilize these estimates in generating a forecast of the future.

Typically, we use statistical regression analysis to estimate these relationships, and we refer to this approach as econometric forecasting. In developing an econometric forecasting model we may hypothesize that, for example, our company's sales are influenced by two economic variables, *Variable 1* and *Variable 2,* and we have determined that the relation can be written as

$$Sales_t = a + b_1(Variable\ 1) + b_2(Variable\ 2), \quad (5.12)$$

where a, b_1, and b_2 are the parameters that we need to estimate.

With past data on *Sales, Variable 1,* and *Variable 2,* we use linear regression techniques to estimate these parameters. Then, for a forecast of future *Sales,* we use a forecast of *Variable 1* and *Variable 2* and our parameter estimates plugged into expression (5.12) to generate our estimate of future *Sales.*

Obviously, such an approach requires that we make a forecast of future values of the independent variables, *Variable 1* and *Variable 2.* This may be a disadvantage when these independent variables are just as difficult to forecast as our company's sales, or when their forecasts are just as uncertain. On the other hand, we may be able to obtain forecasts of general economic variables such as gross national product, personal income, or business investment from other forecasting sources such as Data Resources, the Wharton Econometric Forecasting Unit, or Chase Econometrics, and use these forecasts, imperfect as they are, in developing our own forecast.

To see how we might develop an econometric forecasting model, consider the Salisbury Equipment Corporation,[3] which manufactures and sells equipment for which sales have seasonal, trend, and cyclical components. Salisbury's business is cyclical because it manufactures components used in industrial machinery used by other manufacturers, and its sales appear to be related to general economic conditions as measured by real gross national product and by the level of interest rates—higher interest rates tend to depress demand because manufacturers delay capital investment when rates are high. Salisbury's sales also have been following a slow upward trend over time. Because the economy is growing, the demand for the product grows with the long-term growth of gross national product; the demand has grown also because Salisbury's product is being used in the electronics industry, which has been growing quite rapidly. Salisbury's sales also follow a seasonal pattern, with sales rising in the spring and summer months, and then declining during the fall and winter.

An econometric model involves formulating a hypothesis about the relationships between variables and then using data to investigate these relations. On the basis of the hypothesized

---

[3]This example was developed with the help of Mark Hirschey.

relations between Salisbury's sales and the independent variables—time, gross national product, and interest rates—we formulate the model of quarterly sales as

$$\begin{aligned} Sales_t = a &+ b_1\,(Time_t) + b_2\,(GNP_t) \\ &+ b_3\,(T\text{-}Bill\ rate_t), \end{aligned} \tag{5.13}$$

where t denotes the quarter, *Time* is a time trend variable, GNP_t is the real (adjusted for inflation) gross national product in quarter t, expressed at a seasonally adjusted annual rate, and T-$bill\ rate_t$ is the interest rate on 90-day U.S. Treasury bills during quarter t. We will base our forecast on seasonally adjusted annual data, so the $Sales_t$ will also have the seasonal components removed and will be expressed at a seasonally adjusted annual rate. After making our seasonally adjusted annual forecast, we can restore the seasonal effects to the forecast by multiplying each quarter's seasonally adjusted annual forecast by the seasonal adjustment factor.

Exhibit 5.14 shows quarterly data from 1975.I through 1985.II for the variables *GNP, T-bill rate,* and Salisbury's *Sales*—all expressed as seasonally adjusted annual rates.

The estimation and evaluation of the model (5.13) is in two stages. First, using data from 1975.I through 1982.IV, the least squares linear regression of the form (5.13) was run[4] to estimate parameters a, b_1, b_2, and b_3. Second, the estimated equation is used to predict *Sales* for quarters 1983.I through 1985.II, for which we know the actual sales and can evaluate the accuracy of our forecasts.

The least squares procedure yields the estimated regression

$$\begin{aligned} Sales_t = {} & \underset{(1.634)}{224.54} + \underset{(1.766)}{2.038}\,(Time_t) + \underset{(4.532)}{0.502}\,(GNP_t) - \underset{(-4.198)}{8.979}\,(T\text{-}Bill\ rate_t), \end{aligned} \tag{5.14}$$

where the numbers 224.54, 2.038, 0.502, and -8.979 are our estimates of parameters a, b_1, b_2, and b_3, respectively; the numbers in parentheses are the t-statistics, which measure the statistical significance of the coefficients; the coefficient of variation of the

[4]The personal computer software used for the regression was Regression Analysis of Time Series (RATS) by VAR Econometrics, 134 Prospect Avenue South, Minneapolis, MN 55419. RATS cost $200 in 1985. RATS offers great flexibility and many options for the statistically inclined, although it is not as well documented nor as easy to use as some other statistical software.

EXHIBIT 5.14 Salisbury Equipment Corporation: Real GNP, Treasury Bill Rates, and Quarterly Sales Data, Seasonally Adjusted at Annual Rates

Year	*Quarter*	*Gross National Product ($billions)*	*Treasury Bill Rate (percent)*	*Sales ($millions)*
1975	I	$1,206.3	5.750%	$ 777.73
	II	1,221.0	5.393	791.62
	III	1,248.4	6.330	799.99
	IV	1,259.7	5.627	814.76
1976	I	1,287.2	4.917	837.22
	II	1,295.8	5.157	840.74
	III	1,303.3	5.150	847.57
	IV	1,315.4	4.673	858.59
1977	I	1,341.3	4.630	875.18
	II	1,363.3	4.840	886.17
	III	1,385.8	5.497	892.60
	IV	1,388.4	6.110	977.15
1978	I	1,400.0	6.393	809.61
	II	1,437.0	6.477	918.31
	III	1,448.8	7.313	916.26
	IV	1,468.4	8.570	916.93
1979	I	1,472.6	9.383	913.99
	II	1,469.2	9.377	912.60
	III	1,486.6	9.673	922.57
	IV	1,489.3	11.84	904.71
1980	I	1,496.4	13.35	897.52
	II	1,461.4	9.617	915.71
	III	1,464.2	9.153	922.27
	IV	1,477.9	13.61	891.65
1981	I	1,510.1	14.39	906.66
	II	1,512.5	14.90	903.33
	III	1,525.8	15.05	913.17
	IV	1,506.9	11.75	934.99
1982	I	1,485.8	12.81	913.01
	II	1,489.3	12.42	921.58
	III	1,485.7	9.317	951.21
	IV	1,480.7	7.913	961.12
1983	I	1,490.1	8.107	967.50
	II	1,525.2	8.397	986.72
	III	1,553.3	9.127	998.89
	IV	1,572.5	8.800	1,017.2
1984	I	1,610.9	9.44	993.6
	II	1,638.8	9.94	1,015.7
	III	1,645.2	10.4	1,044.3
	IV	1,662.4	8.16	1,052.7
1985	I	1,663.5	7.56	1,064.9
	II	1,671.3	7.01	1,092.5
	III	1,688.9	7.1	1,102.2

regression over this 32-quarter sample period was $R^2 = 0.81$, indicating that 81 percent of the variation in sales was accounted for by its linear relationship with these hypothesized independent variables, and 19 percent was unaccounted for by this relation.

The t-statistics allow us to evaluate the likelihood that the true coefficients (as opposed to those we have estimated) are really significantly different (in the statistical sense) from zero. If the t-statistics are small, then it is possible that the true coefficients are zero, and we have obtained our estimates by chance occurrence. On the other hand, if the t-statistics are large, it is unlikely that we would obtain these estimates if the true coefficients were zero. In this case, with a sample size of 32 quarters and three independent variables, a t of 1.7 is statistically significant, allowing us to conclude that the true coefficients are not zero. Generally speaking, for samples smaller than this one, a t-statistic of 2 or greater indicates statistically significant coefficient estimates.

To evaluate this relation for forecasting purposes, we can test it against the actual sales from 1983.I until 1985.III, periods for which we have past data against which we can compare. For example, suppose we are standing at the beginning of 1983, and our forecast of the gross national product for the first quarter is ($GNP_{83.I}$ = \$1,490.1 billion, at a seasonally adjusted annual rate, and we forecast the average *T-Bill rate* during the quarter will be 8.107 percent. Substituting these forecasts in the estimated regression Equation (5.14), we get our *Sales* forecast for 1983.I as

$$\begin{aligned} Sales_{83.I} &= 224.54 + 2.038(33) + 0.502(1490.1) - 8.979(8.107) \\ &= 967.03, \end{aligned}$$

where 33 is the value of variable *Time*, the number of quarters elapsed since 1974.IV, since 1975.I was quarter 1 in our sample.

For each quarter subsequent to 1982.IV for which we have data, we can generate a forecast of *Sales* based on this regression relationship. These forecasts up through 1985.III are shown in Exhibit 5.15, based on the actual values of *GNP* and *T-Bill rate* for those periods. The *Sales* actually attained by Salisbury are shown in column 4 and the *Forecasted Sales* are shown in column 5.

EXHIBIT 5.15 Salisbury Equipment Corporation: Sales Forecast Based on Econometric Model, 1983.I through 1985.III

(1) Quarter	(2) Actual GNP ($billions)	(3) Actual Treasury Bill Rate (%)	(4) Actual Sales ($millions)	(5) Forecasted Sales ($millions)	(6) Error of Forecast	(7) Squared Error
1983 I	$1,490.1	8.107	$ 967.51	$ 967.03	0.48	0.23
II	1,525.2	8.397	986.72	984.08	2.64	6.97
III	1,553.32	9.127	998.89	993.68	5.21	27.14
IV	1,572.5	8.80	1,017.26	1,008.29	8.97	80.46
1984 I	1,610.9	9.44	993.60	1,023.86	−30.26	915.67
II	1,638.8	9.94	1,015.7	1,035.41	−19.71	388.48
III	1,645.2	10.4	1,044.3	1,036.53	7.77	60.37
IV	1,662.4	8.16	1,052.7	1,067.32	−14.62	213.74
1985 I	1,663.5	7.56	1,064.9	1,075.29	−10.39	107.95
II	1,671.3	7.01	1,092.5	1,086.19	6.31	39.82
III	1,688.9	7.1	1,102.2	1,096.25	5.95	35.4
Mean (average) forecast error:					+ 2.93	
Mean square forecast error (MSE):						170.56
Root mean square forecast error ($\sqrt{MSE}$):						13.06

We can assess these forecasts by considering their errors, which are calculated by subtracting forecast sales from actual *Sales,* and are shown in column 6 of the exhibit. A negative forecast error means that the actual *Sales* were below the forecasted *Sales,* and our forecast was too high. The average or mean forecast error was +2.93, which is small, but indicates that the forecast is biased—if it was unbiased, our mean forecast error should be zero.

Column (7) of the exhibit shows the squared error. The squaring eliminates the influence of the sign of the errors and places greater emphasis on large errors. The mean square error (MSE), the simple average of these squared errors, is 170.56—a number that would be compared with the results of another forecasting method.

For example, if we use the time-trend model of sales for Salisbury of the form

$$Sales_t = a + b\,(Time_t), \tag{5.15}$$

with data for 1975.I to 1982.IV, we get the estimated equation

$$Sales_t = 820.53 + 4.147(Time_t), \tag{5.16}$$

where $Time_t$ is the number of quarters elapsed since 1974.IV. This regression had $R^2 = 0.60$, and the coefficient of the *Time* variable was statistically significant. We would forecast sales for 1983.I as

$$\begin{aligned} Sales_{83.I} &= 820.53 + 4.147(33) \\ &= 957.38. \end{aligned}$$

This model was used to forecast sales from 1983.I to 1985.III, and the mean forecast error was 52.5 as compared with 2.93 with the econometric model, and the root mean square error was 60.3 versus 13.06 for the econometric model. While the econometric model seems to be biased downward, it is certainly much more accurate than this simple time trend model.

With additional investigation and testing we might be able to improve upon the econometric model also. One would have to weigh the costs of additional forecasting accuracy against the benefits. While additional accuracy is almost always desired, the costs of research, data gathering and so on, may exceed the benefits of the forecast.

Assessing Forecast Accuracy. One of the major advantages of quantitative forecasting techniques, particularly regression and time series analysis, is that they enable the forecaster to judge the margin of error in the forecast. This is especially useful in financial modeling. After all, one of the main uses of the financial model is to work out the joint consequences of events that are forecasted and the decisions that may be made. But because our forecasts are almost never entirely correct, we need to know how far wrong we might be and what the consequences will be when we make inaccurate forecasts. It is essential to have some idea of the range of accuracy of our forecasts, and some of the quantitative forecasting models can provide this.

Forecasting models that use least squares regression generate output that can help us establish confidence intervals for our forecasts. These confidence intervals are based on a statistic called the standard error of the forecast, which takes into account the various errors we may have made in estimating the coefficients of the regression.

Consider the relation between a dependent variable, denoted by Y, and an independent variable, denoted by X, expressed as

$$Y_t = a + b \cdot X_t + e_t. \tag{5.17}$$

Suppose we gather data and estimate the value of parameters a and b, and then use the estimated relation to forecast Y next period. Because of the random disturbance term, e_t, our forecast will tend to be wrong, even if our specification of the relation (5.17) is correct and our parameter estimates are correct.

Furthermore, we inevitably will have some error in our estimates of the parameters a and b, and these errors will cause some inaccuracy in our forecast. That is, the estimates of a and b are just that—only estimates. We don't really know the true, underlying values of these parameters, and we are destined never really to know. Thus, our parameter estimates of a and b are probably wrong.

However, assuming that the basic form of model, as shown by (5.17), is correct, we can develop confidence intervals for our forecast based on the number of observations. If our estimated regression relation is highly accurate, then we can be quite confident that the future actual value of Y will close to the value we forecast; in that case we would say the confidence interval is very narrow—that we can be confident that the actual value will be within a narrow band around the forecasted value. On the other hand, if our estimates are inaccurate, we would have to recognize the fact that the true value of Y could occur much further away from the forecasted value—in that case we say the actual value will be within a much wider confidence interval.

The confidence interval is a band around our forecast within which we can expect the true value of the predicted variable to occur a specified percentage of the time. Consider Exhibit 5.17, that shows the regression line we have estimated from observed values of X and Y. A confidence interval at, say, the 95 percent level, is a band above and below the regression line that shows the range within which, 95 percent of the time, we would expect Y actually to occur, when, based on a value of X, we forecast the corresponding value of Y to be right on the regression line. If the band is very narrow, we are quite confident the predicted value will be close to the actual value; if the band is wide; our confidence is low.

EXHIBIT 5.17 Confidence Interval for Forecast of Dependent Variable Y

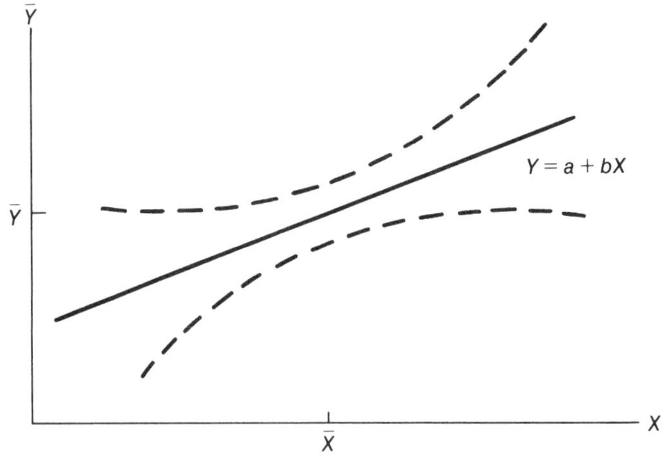

Note that the confidence band around the regression line curves away from the line at the upper and lower ends. The idea is that as we move away from the center of the data used to estimate the regression, we can be less and less confident that the estimated regression is correct, and we have to accept the likelihood that our forecast is less accurate. In this case, the points marked $\bar{X}$ and $\bar{Y}$ are the averages of the observed values of X and Y that were used to estimate the regression parameters. At increasing distances from $\bar{X}$, the confidence band widens.

What this means is that if we have an estimated relation, for example, between *Time* and *Sales,* based on data from years 1975 through 1982, then our confidence that the relation is valid diminishes for years far from our sample period. The relation may be valid in 1984 and we may have a narrow confidence interval then, but for 1998 our confidence interval would have to be quite wide. Similarly, if we estimated a relation between *Sales, Time, Gross national product,* and *T-Bill rates,* the estimated relation may be valid for values of the independent variables close to those used in the estimation, but for more distant values, we can have considerably less confidence in our forecasts.

For the case with one independent variable, X, the confidence interval for our forecast is based on the standard error of the forecast—denoted by SE_f—which is calculated from the formula

$$SE_f = \sigma_e \left[1 + \frac{1}{n} + \frac{(X_f - \overline{X})^2}{\Sigma(X_i - \overline{X})^2}\right], \tag{5.18}$$

where σ_e is the standard error of the regression (standard deviation of the error terms distributed about the regression line), n is the size of the sample used to estimate the regression parameters, X_f is the *forecast* of the independent variable that is used as the basis for forecasting the dependent variable, $\overline{X}$ is the average of the observed values of the independent variables used in estimating the regression, and $\Sigma(X_i - X)^2$ is the sum of squared differences between the observed values of the independent variable and its average value, $\overline{X}$.[5]

Applying this formula to the forecast of Salisbury's *Sales* based on the *Time* trend (5.16), the sample size was $n = 32$ quarters (1975.I to 1982.IV), the independent variable was *Time* with quarters numbered from 1 to 32, the sample average independent variable was $\overline{X}$ = average *Time* = 16.5, and $\Sigma(X - \overline{X})^2 = 1{,}605$. The standard error of the regression was $\sigma_e = 32.19$. Suppose we want to use the time trend relation (5.16) to forecast *Sales* for 1985.II, which would be period 42 in our numbering scheme, or $X_f = 42$. The forecast would be

$$\begin{aligned} Sales_{85.\text{II}} &= 820.53 + 4.147(42) \\ &= 994.70, \end{aligned}$$

and the standard error of the forecast is

$$\begin{aligned} SE_f &= 32.19 \left[1 + \frac{1}{32} + \frac{(42 - 16.5)^2}{1605}\right] \\ &= 46.24 \end{aligned}$$

The 95 percent confidence interval for this 1985.II forecast would be

$$994.7 \pm 1.64(46.24)$$

---

[5]For multiple regression with more than one independent variable, the concepts of the confidence interval still apply, but the mathematics is more complex, and the reader should consult an econometrics text such as Pindyck and Rubinfeld (1976).

or

$$994.7 \pm 75.83,$$

where the factor 1.64 is obtained from a standard normal distribution table, indicating the distance (measured in standard deviations) above the average (mean) such that there is a 5 percent probability of being further from the average. The confidence interval shown above means that we can be 95 percent sure that the actual value of *Sales* in 1985.II will be in the range indicated—that is, between 994.7 − 75.83 and 994.7 + 75.83; that is, between 918 and 1,071. This is a fairly wide confidence interval, so we are rather unsure that our forecast of 994.7 is correct. The confidence interval for a prediction for 1983.I would be much narrower because it is closer to our sample period, and a forecast for 1995 would have a very wide confidence interval because it is far from our sample period.

While we do not develop statistics deeply enough here to make you into a finished statistician or forecaster, it is important to be exposed to the techniques and ideas. It is particularly important that the financial modeler and planner be exposed to the concept of confidence intervals. In making the financial plan it is essential to recognize that the forecast that you or anyone else makes will almost never be correct. The relevant question is, How far wrong can it be? Related to that question are: What are the consequences when the forecast is wrong? What is the likely range for the actual value? How can I plan for reality being different from the forecast? All these questions can be approached with the concept of a confidence interval.

Time Series Models

One of the more powerful techniques for generating forecasts is time series analysis that identifies the periodic patterns in observed historical data and develops the forecast on the basis of the characteristics of these patterns. Time series analysis is quite technical in its detail, and a thorough explanation is beyond the scope of this book. The method will only be introduced here. The interested reader is directed to the references at the end of the chapter, particularly Chapters 13–17 of Pindyck and Rubinfeld (1976), Nelson (1973), and Box and Jenkins (1976).

Time series analysis, also known as Box Jenkins analysis or ARIMA is a forecasting methodology that can be used for short-term forecasting of time series variables such as sales, interest rates, or prices. It differs from a structural econometric approach in that it usually does not attempt to explain *why* a variable behaves as it does—it does not deal with causality.[6] It simply tries to identify the patterns that can be detected in a series of observations over time and use that information to generate forecasts. In its focus on the patterns in the time series it has some similarities to the seasonal adjustment methods we discussed, but it is a more general method and, unfortunately, much more technical.

What time series analysis does is analyze a series of observations of a variable over time, and on the basis of the correlations between observations at different points in time (i.e., autocorrelations: the correlation of the value of a variable in a given period with the value of the same variable in an earlier period) it estimates the parameters of the process that generates these observations. Then, these parameter estimates are used to forecast future values of this variable.

Consider an example presented in the tutorial for Micro TSP, which estimates the time series parameters for quarterly automobile sales.[7] Exhibit 5.18 shows a graph of quarterly auto sales at annual rates for the period 1960.I to 1978.IV. The striking feature is the extreme volatility of auto sales from one quarter to the next. It seems to ask too much of any forecasting method to deal with this type of extreme volatility. Yet, it is just this type of randomness that Box-Jenkins time series analysis attempts to handle.

Time series analysis identifies a series of variables over time, such as auto sales, as being generated from processes called Autoregressive (AR), Moving Average (MA), or mixtures that

[6]Time series analysis can be combined with structural econometric models, potentially resulting in forecasting models that are more powerful than either alone.

[7]Micro TSP is statistical software for regression and forecasting published by Quantitative Micro Software, available through McGraw-Hill Book Company, 1221 Avenue of the Americas, New York, NY 10124. The TSP software cost $595 in 1986. TSP is a well-documented, easy-to-use package that offers many powerful features, including time series analysis.

EXHIBIT 5.18 U.S. Auto Sales by Quarters, at Annual Rates (1960–1978)

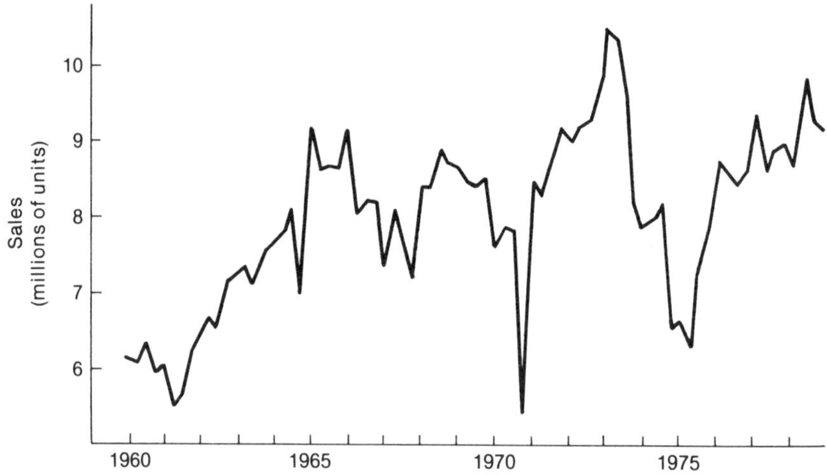

are called Autoregressive–Moving Average (ARMA), or even Autoregressive Integrated Moving Average (ARIMA). If the values over time of a variable are generated by one of these processes, we can use the observed values to estimate the parameters that govern the process. This approach analyzes the correlations of the variable with itself across periods to *suggest* the type of process: AR, MA, ARMA, or ARIMA. Armed with an indication of the type of process, a planner can estimate parameters and test the estimated relation to see whether it generates acceptable forecasts.

Autoregressive Processes. In an autoregressive (AR) process, the value of a variable at time *t* depends on the past observed values of that variable. For example, suppose automobile sales fluctuate randomly from period to period because they conform to an autoregressive process of the form

$$Sales_t = b_0 + b_1 \cdot Sales_{t-1} + b_2 \cdot Sales_{t-2} + e_t, \quad (5.19)$$

where coefficients b_0, b_1, and b_2 are parameters (whose values we don't know but will try to estimate) and e_t is a random error term. This is an autoregressive process because it is like a linear regression that involves regressing period t's value of the dependent variable against past values of the same variable.

If we can estimate the values of parameters b_0, b_1, and b_2, we can use this information to help predict any period's sales from those of the two preceding periods. For example, suppose we have estimated these parameters to be $b_0 = 1.98$, $b_1 = 0.593$, and $b_2 = 0.245$, and automobile sales were observed to be 9.37 and 9.27 million units in 1978.III and 1978.IV, respectively. Then, the forecast for the next quarter, 1979.I, would be

$$\begin{aligned} Sales_{t+1} &= 1.98 + 0.593(9.27) + 0.245\,(9.37) \\ &= 9.78 \text{ million units.} \end{aligned} \tag{5.20}$$

This time series analysis will provide statistics that allow us to estimate a confidence interval to show how far off the actual value might be from our forecast.

Moving Average Processes. In a moving average (MA) process, the value of a variable depends on an average of past random-error terms. For example, suppose that auto sales fluctuate randomly over time, being generated by a process of the form

$$Sales_t = d_0 + e_t + d_1 e_{t-1} + d_2 e_{t-2}, \tag{5.21}$$

where the e terms are random-error or disturbance terms that occurred this period, t, and the last two periods.

Using the Box-Jenkins methods we can estimate the parameters d_0, d_1, and d_2 to be used to forecast next period's variable. Suppose an analysis of the data provides parameter estimates that are $d_0 = 8.06$, $d_1 = 0.632$ and $d_2 = 0.679$, and the error terms (residual error terms around estimated regression) were $e_{78.III} = 0.507$, and $e_{78.IV} = 0.028$; then the forecast for next period would be

$$\begin{aligned} Sales_{79.I} &= 8.06 + 0 + 0.632\,(0.507) + 0.679\,(0.028) \\ &= 8.399 \text{ million units,} \end{aligned} \tag{5.22}$$

where the zero is the expected value of the error term next period. As in the case of structural econometric models, we would be able to determine a confidence interval for our forecast from the statistics generated by the program.

Autoregressive–Moving Average Processes. The two different types of processes we have just discussed can be combined to be autoregressive–moving average (ARMA) processes, where the random variable, such as sales, is generated according to

$$Sales_t = a_0 + b_1 \cdot Sales_{t-1} + b_2 \cdot Sales_{t-2} + d_1 e_{t-1} + d_2 e_{t-2} + e_t, \tag{5.23}$$

so the actual value turns out to be related to *Sales* in previous periods and random error terms that occurred in previous periods, plus a random error term that occurs in period t. To use this relation for forecasting, we would estimate parameters a_0, b_1 b_2, d_1, and d_2 from past data. These parameter estimates are then combined with the current and past observed values of *Sales* and error terms to generate a forecast for next period.

The discussion to this point has considered only one- and two-period lags in the AR terms (e.g., $Sales_{t-1}$ and $Sales_{t-2}$) and the MA terms (e.g., e_{t-1} and e_{t-2}). This was only to demonstrate the idea. The Box-Jenkins time series methodology is more general than that—it considers different types of lag structures in the AR and MA terms. A major part of the methodology, some of which is computational and some of which is guesswork, is to determine the lag structure of these terms. That is, a major part of the model building is to decide whether we should use two-period lags, five-period lags, or what. The starting point is to examine the correlations of the variable (such as *Sales*) across periods; that is, how sales in period t are correlated with sales in periods $t-1$, $t-2$, $t-3$, and so on. The correlations between the value of a variable and its own previous values are called autocorrelations, and they help the user decide how to structure the model.

For example, suppose that an examination of the autocorrelations reveals that quarterly sales have a one- and two-period lag structure for the AR terms, and a four- and eight-period lag structure for the MA terms. The resulting ARMA model is estimated to be

$$Sales_t = 8.37 + 0.559\ Sales_{t-1} + 0.305\ Sales_{t-2} - 0.095\ e_{t-4} - 0.26\ e_{t-8} + e_t, \tag{5.24}$$

where the error terms refer to random disturbances that occurred four and eight quarters ago.

Applying this estimated relation to obtain a forecast for 1979.I through 1979.IV, the TSP software generates the forecast of 8.956 million units for 1979.I and 8.855, 8.816, and 8.746 million units for 1979.II to 1979.IV. Note that this method has the potential capability to forecast turning points in the series from the past pattern of autocorrelations. In this case, *Sales* are forecasted to drop from 9.27 million units in 1978.IV to 8.956 million in 1979.I, and continue dropping for the next three quarters.

Even though the time series approach will forecast some turning points, it tends to smooth out the series, so it seldom forecasts ups and downs as extreme as can really occur, and in addition, it will miss many turning points. However, in this regard it is superior to time trend and the simpler smoothing methods for forecasting and usually is better than pure structural econometric models for short-term forecasts because these other methods seldom do an adequate job of predicting turning points. For longer-term forecasting, the structural econometric methods are usually superior.

It is possible to get the best of both by combining them. For example, the TSP auto sales forecast is improved by relating auto sales to the time trend and Treasury Bill rates and using the ARMA model to account for the random error terms. The form of this forecast model is

$$\begin{aligned} Sales_t = a_0 &+ a_1\,(Time) + a_2\,(T\text{-}Bill\ rate_t) + a_2\,(T\text{-}Bill\ rate_{t-1}) \\ &+ a_4\,(T\text{-}Bill\ rate_{t-4}) + b_1\,(Sales_{t-1}) + b_2\,(Sales_{t-2}) \\ &+ d_1\,(e_{t-4}) + e_t. \end{aligned} \tag{5.25}$$

This model improves the fit of the regression to the data and could potentially improve our forecast. One possible difficulty in applying such a forecasting model is that for future periods it requires that we forecast *T-Bill rates,* which are at least as hard to forecast as auto sales. There is an advantage to using a model, either a time series or a structural econometric model, that uses lagged variables because we can base our forecast for next period on independent variables that we can observe this period.

There are other variations of the ARIMA techniques that we could profitably explore, but that would take us too far afield from the main purpose of this chapter, which is simply to gain some exposure to the various techniques for building forecasting models. Each of the techniques we have discussed could and often does occupy a whole book by itself. So, if you plan on going deeper into the forecasting realm, you should consult the more detailed references given at the end of the chapter.

5.2 SUBJECTIVE FORECASTING

Most forecasts are based on the subjective opinions of managers or others like economists, who develop a "feel" for their industry and through experience and exposure can make judgments about what might happen in the future. This is a most important source of forecasts, and we should not underestimate its role or its potential contribution to the financial planning process.

The advantage of the subjective forecast is that the person close to the situation usually has a good idea of what is going on and may be aware of developments that a quantitative forecaster does not recognize. The salesman knows who will turn in an order, and can fairly easily forecast orders for the next few months, yet the quantitative forecaster might have to gather and process data before being able to generate a forecast that is not nearly as reliable. Consequently, one of the easiest and least expensive sources of forecasts is to ask the people involved.

On the other hand, one disadvantage of subjective forecasts is that they tend to be biased. In the forecasting context, bias refers to the fact that the forecasts are consistently too high or too low. It may turn out that our sales force may be consistently overly optimistic, or even too pessimistic. Another disadvantage of subjective forecasts is that we seldom know what assumptions were used to generate them, and this knowledge is helpful, often even essential, to working through the implications of the forecast with a model.

These problems can be handled. With respect to bias, if the forecaster is made aware (diplomatically, of course) of the bias, he may be able to correct the bias. If forecasters are asked about their assumptions regarding key ingredients of their forecasts, we may be able to add a consistent link between these assumptions and the forecasts.

One method that has been used to utilize experts' opinion and still maintain some objectivity is the *Delphi Technique.* The Delphi Technique is simply an adaptive survey method for gathering forecasts from diverse forecasters. The method requires that we solicit independent forecasts from a number of different experts, none of whom presumably knows what the others are forecasting. Their forecasts are tabulated and the participants are informed about the average of these independent forecasts and, perhaps, the spread or range of the forecasts. After receiving this information they are each asked if they want to revise their forecasts. After a couple of iterations, these independent forecasts tend to converge toward a common value. This technique prevents a strong opinion maker from swaying the opinions of others, and the use of a group forecast tends to eliminate the undue influence of some forecasts that are far from the average.

Other sources of subjective opinion are the opinion surveys published by agencies such as the University of Michigan Survey Research Center, which surveys opinion relating to consumer confidence and spending. Surveys are frequently conducted and results published by *Fortune, Business Week,* and other business periodicals. All these and more could be used as input to more detailed forecasts for the company.

5.3 SUMMARY

This chapter has given a brief survey of various methods for constructing forecasting models that could generate input for the financial planning model. Such a forecast is usually the starting point for financial planning.

The methods considered included extrapolation of time trends with linear regression; techniques for smoothing the observations, such as weighted averages and exponential smoothing; decomposition into seasonal and trend components; structural econometric forecasting models; and time series analysis.

Each method can be helpful, but none will produce a perfectly reliable, accurate forecast. They are just tools and we should not expect them to perform miracles. Forecasting models can help indicate the direction events might take, with some measure of the magnitude of change, and we should be satisfied if they produce unbiased, sensible forecasts. Most will provide information about the possible range of outcomes around the forecasted value. This is extremely useful information in the planning context because it gives the planner an idea of the extremes to be included in any contingency plans.

REFERENCES

BLAZEY, T. W. "Putting Forecasts to Work in the Firm." *Business Economics,* January 1976.

BOX, G. E. P., and G. M. JENKINS. *Time Series Analysis, Forecasting and Control.* San Francisco: Holden-Day, 1976.

BROWN, R. G. *Smoothing, Forecasting and Prediction of Discrete Time Series.* Englewood Cliffs, N.J.: Prentice-Hall, 1963.

CHAMBERS, J. C.; S. K. MULLICK; and D. SMITH. "How to Choose the Right Forecasting Technique." *Harvard Business Review,* July–August 1971, pp. 45–74.

DALRYMPLE, D. J. "Sales Forecasting Methods and Accuracy." *Business Horizons,* December 1975.

GERSTENFELD, A. "Technological Forecasting." *Journal of Business,* January 1971, pp. 10–18.

GROSS, CHARLES W., and ROBIN T. PETERSON. *Business Forecasting.* 2nd ed. Boston: Houghton Mifflin, 1983.

JOHNSTON, G. F. "Putting Forecasts to Work in the Corporate Planning Function." *Business Economics,* January 1976.

KMENTA, J. *Elements of Econometrics.* New York: Macmillan, 1971.

MAKRIDAKIS, S., and S. WHEELWRIGHT. *Forecasting: Methods and Applications.* 2nd ed. New York: John Wiley & Sons, 1983.

NELSON, C. R. *Applied Time Series Analysis For Managerial Forecasting.* San Francisco: Holden-Day, 1973.

PAPPAS, J. L.; E. F. BRIGHAM; and M. HIRSCHEY. *Managerial Economics.* 4th ed. Hinsdale, Ill.: Dryden Press, 1983.

PINDYCK, R. S., and D. L. RUBINFELD. *Econometric Models and Economic Forecasts.* New York: McGraw-Hill, 1976.

SOBELS, R. S. "A Manager's Primer on Forecasting." *Harvard Business Review,* May–June 1973, pp. 1–9.

WHEELWRIGHT, S. C., and S. MAKRIDAKIS. *Forecasting Methods for Management.* 2nd ed. New York: John Wiley & Sons, 1973.

CHAPTER SIX

Financial Simulation Models

We have discussed financial planning and financial models in very general terms; it is now time to be more specific and discuss financial models in more detail. This chapter will present a general, generic simulation model of a firm. The specific equations of the model are presented and discussed so the reader will have a thorough understanding of the structure of such a model.

There are at least as many different types of financial simulation models as there are uses for them.[1] The most common or typical financial simulation model is what will be called an accounting model, which consists of a set of mathematical expressions that are used to generate pro forma financial statements so the effect of alternative decision strategies can be evaluated. The mathematical equations specify the relationships, or links, between the economic variables, environmental variables, decision variables, and the financial state of the firm. After these relationships are properly specified, the input, consisting of chosen values of the environmental, economic, and decision variables, is fed through the model to generate output consisting of a description of the firm in terms of its financial statements.

[1]The references at the end of the chapter include many different discussions of simulation models. Some of the more comprehensive discussions of models and model building include Bryant (1982), Francis (1983), Gershefski (1968, 1969), Meyer (1977), Naylor (1973, 1979), Schrieber (1970), and Warren and Shelton (1971).

The first model developed here is what will be termed "sales driven accounting model." It will be oriented to solving the problem of determining the investment and financing necessary to meet a sales forecast. The sales forecast is the primary input that drives the model in the sense that once the sales forecast is made and fed into the model, the required investment and financing follow as output.

The equations of the model can be considered as being structured in modules, or blocks of equations, with a module for each of the following tasks:

I. Accounting.
II. Income generation.
III. Investment.
IV. Financing.

Exhibit 6.1 diagrams the flow between the modules. The income generation module utilizes the economic forecasts, decision specifications, and parameter estimates to generate estimates of revenues and costs that are input to the accounting module, which, in turn, generates trial values for the various accounts of the financial statements. Those trial values are used by the investment and financing modules to calculate the amount of new investment in assets necessary to support the forecast level of sales and the amount and form of new financing necessary to purchase these assets. The new investment and financing is input back to the accounting module to generate the pro forma financial statements consistent with the sales forecast. These financial statements represent the output of the model, from which management can evaluate the forecast and their prospective decisions.

Each of these modules will be explained and an example model presented. The accounting module will be discussed first because it is of central importance in the model.

6.1 THE ACCOUNTING MODULE

Equations of the Module

The skeleton of most financial simulation models is a set of equations that are accounting definitions. These definitional

EXHIBIT 6.1 Structure and Flow of a Financial Simulation Model

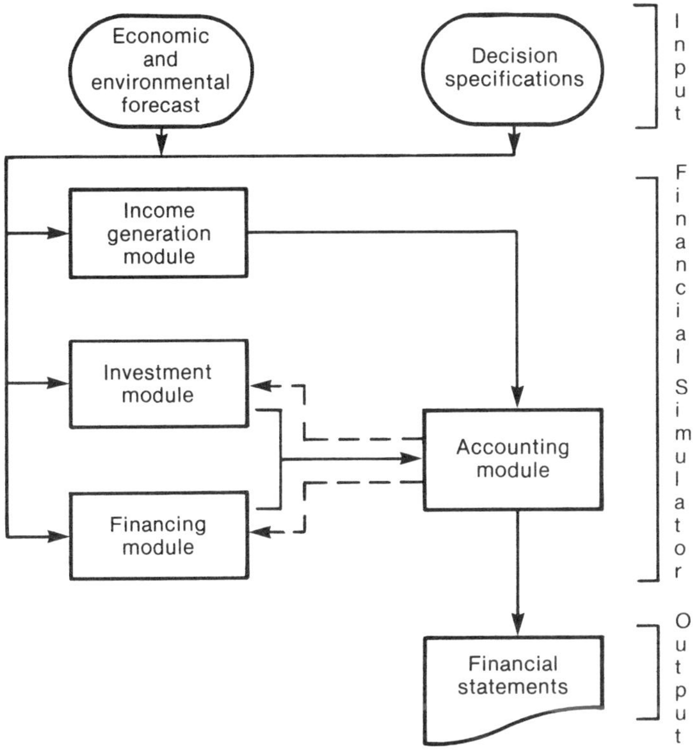

equations maintain accounting consistency, aggregate the detailed accounts into their broad groups, and link the account balances from one period to the next. These equations generate the financial statements for the firm: the income statement, the balance sheet, and a statement of sources and uses of funds.

Exhibits 6.2A, B, and C show, in generalized form, examples of the types of equations necessary to generate the major account categories for the income statement (Exhibit 6.2A), the balance sheet (Exhibit 6.2B), and the sources and uses of cash (Exhibit 6.2C). In these exhibits variables that must be provided as data or generated elsewhere in the simulation system are enclosed in parentheses, and subscript t denotes period t. In the income statement sector, Exhibit 6.2A, each equation defines a revenue or expense account in terms of input variables or in

EXHIBIT 6.2A Income Statement Accounting Equations for a Simulation Model

A.1	$Total\ revenue_t = (Units\ sold_t) \cdot (Price\ per\ unit_t)$
A.2	$Operating\ costs_t = (Units\ sold_t) \cdot (Cost\ per\ unit_t)$
A.3	$EBDIT_t = Total\ revenue_t - Operating\ costs_t$
A.4	$Depreciation_t = Fixed\ assets_{t-1} \cdot (Depreciation\ rate_t)$
A.5	$EBIT_t = EBDIT_t - Depreciation_t$
A.6	$Interest\ expense_t = Notes\ payable_{t-1} \cdot (Note\ rate_t) + Long\text{-}term\ debt_{t-1} \cdot (Long\text{-}term\ rate_t)$
A.7	$Taxable\ income_t = EBIT_t - Interest\ expense_t$
A.8	$Income\ tax_t = Taxable\ income_t \cdot (Tax\ rate_t)$
A.9	$Net\ income_t = Taxable\ income_t - Income\ tax_t$
A.10	$Dividend_t = Net\ income_t \cdot (Dividend\ payout\ ratio)$
A.11	$Addition\ to\ retained\ earnings_t = Net\ income_t - Dividends_t$

terms of other preceding accounts. The balance sheet sector, Exhibit 6.2B, consists of an equation for each account category in the balance sheet, in addition to equations that total the accounts. The sources and uses sector, Exhibit 6.2C, consists of expressions that calculate the flow of cash based on the income statement and changes in the balance sheet accounts.

Of course, every model will differ because of the different type and detail of the input data available and the output data desired. Any given set of expressions can usually be collapsed into a single, less detailed, more general expression, or detail can be added by expanding the number of expressions and variables. However, the system of equations in Exhibits 6.2A, B, and C is representative of the types of expressions necessary.

The detail generated by the model and, thus, the extent to which sections of the model are expanded by adding more variables and equations or sections are shrunk by aggregating variables and decreasing the number of equations, is dependent on the requirements of the user. The user who is more concerned with the effects of sales or production decisions may elaborate and expand into minute detail the equations simulating revenue (A.1) or operating costs (A.2), and at the same time eliminate much of the unnecessary detail represented by the remainder of the model. On the other hand, the financial officer may prefer to take the revenue and costs as given and emphasize in greater detail the financial implications of security investments, capital investments, and financing decisions. This could involve expan-

EXHIBIT 6.2B Balance Sheet Accounting Equations for a Simulation Model

Assets

B.1 $Cash_t = Cash_{t-1} + Net\ cash\ inflow_t$

B.2 $Marketable\ securities_t = Marketable\ securities_{t-1} - (Securities\ matured_t) - (Securities\ sold_t) + (Securities\ purchased_t)$

B.3 $Receivables_t = Receivables_{t-1} + (Increase\ in\ receivables_t)$

B.4 $Inventories_t = Inventories_{t-1} + [(Units\ produced_t) - (Units\ sold_t)] \cdot (Cost\ per\ unit_t)$

B.5 $Current\ assets_t = Cash_t + Marketable\ securities_t + Receivables_t + Inventories_t$

B.6 $Gross\ fixed\ assets_t = Gross\ fixed\ assets_{t-1} + (Fixed\ asset\ investment_t)$

B.7 $Accumulated\ depreciation_t = Accumulated\ depreciation_{t-1} + Depreciation_t$

B.8 $Fixed\ assets_t = Gross\ fixed\ assets_t - Accumulated\ depreciation_t$

B.9 $Total\ assets_t = Current\ assets_t + Fixed\ assets_t$

Liabilities

B.10 $Accounts\ payable_t = Accounts\ payable_{t-1} - (Payments\ on\ account_t) + (Credit\ purchases_t)$

B.11 $Notes\ payable_t = Notes\ payable_{t-1} - (Payment\ on\ notes_t) + (Notes\ signed_t)$

B.12 $Current\ liabilities_t = Accounts\ payable_t + Notes\ payable_t$

B.13 $Long\text{-}term\ debt_t = Long\text{-}term\ debt_{t-1} - (Long\text{-}term\ debt\ repaid_t) + (Long\text{-}term\ debt\ issued_t)$

B.14 $Common\ stock_t = Common\ stock_{t-1} + (Common\ stock\ issued_t)$

B.15 $Retained\ earnings_t = Retained\ earnings_{t-1} + Addition\ to\ retained\ earnings_t$

B.16 $Total\ liabilities\ and\ net\ worth_t = Current\ liabilities_t + Long\text{-}term\ debt_t + Common\ stock_t + Retained\ earnings_t$

sion of the number of equations and variables relating to these decisions, such as those relating to interest expense (A.6), dividends (A.10), working capital (B.1), (B.2), (B.3), and (B.4), plant (B.6) and capital accounts (B.13), (B.14), and (B.15).

The financial simulation consists of a set of equations that must be fulfilled for each period t over the planning horizon. Thus, each equation in Exhibit 6.2 is subscripted with t to denote period t. In most such models, the solution proceeds sequentially, with the first simulated period being solved based upon the initial conditions of the firm. Then, the solution from the first period is used as input for the solution for the second period, and so on, to the end of the planning horizon.

Each sector (income, balance sheet, and sources and uses) of this set of equations is related to the other sectors, and they must be solved as a coherent whole. That is not to say that they

EXHIBIT 6.2C Sources and Uses of Cash Equations for a Simulation Model

C.1 *Cash flow from operations$_t$ = Net income$_t$ + Depreciation$_t$ − Dividends$_t$*

C.2 *Increase in current liabilities$_t$ = (Credit purchases$_t$) − (Payments on account$_t$) + (Notes signed$_t$) − (Payments on notes$_t$)*

C.3 *Increase in permanent capital$_t$ = (Long-term debt issued$_t$) − (Long-term debt repaid$_t$) + (Common stock issued$_t$)*

C.4 *Sources of cash$_t$ = Cash flow from operations$_t$ + Securities matured$_t$ + Securities sold$_t$ + Increase in current liabilities$_t$ + Increase in permanent capital$_t$*

C.5 *Increase in noncash current assets$_t$ = Increase in receivables$_t$ + Inventories$_t$ − Inventories$_{t-1}$*

C.6 *Uses of cash$_t$ = Increase in noncash current assets$_t$ + Securities purchased$_t$ + Fixed asset investment$_t$*

C.7 *Net cash inflow$_t$ = Sources of cash$_t$ − Uses of cash$_t$*

are necessarily simultaneous equations in a mathematical sense—they may be, but it is not necessary. The equations can be structured so the total set can be solved sequentially rather than simultaneously, but certainly they are interrelated.

In this case, sequential solution refers not just to the time sequence from the earliest period to the last, but also to the order in which the equations are solved for a given period. Here, the first input variable, the driver of the model, is usually the sales forecast that is generated exogenously. The results of this sales input are generated by simply working through the list of equations in descending order. Simultaneity is avoided by letting a preceding variable for period t be a function of a succeeding variable for period $t - 1$, instead of a succeeding variable for the same period, t. For example, expression (A.6) calculates interest expense for period t and is dependent on the amount of debt outstanding at the end of period $t - 1$. The amount of debt outstanding at t is as yet unknown, and the equations would be simultaneous if (A.6) required the debt balance at t instead of $t - 1$.

The first block or sector of equations shown as Exhibit 6.2A is the income sector that takes the forecast of sales as input and generates a corresponding forecast of expenses and income. That is, the income statement is simulated in steps shown diagramatically in Exhibit 6.3.

The income statement equations consist of both definitions

EXHIBIT 6.3 Income Statement Generation

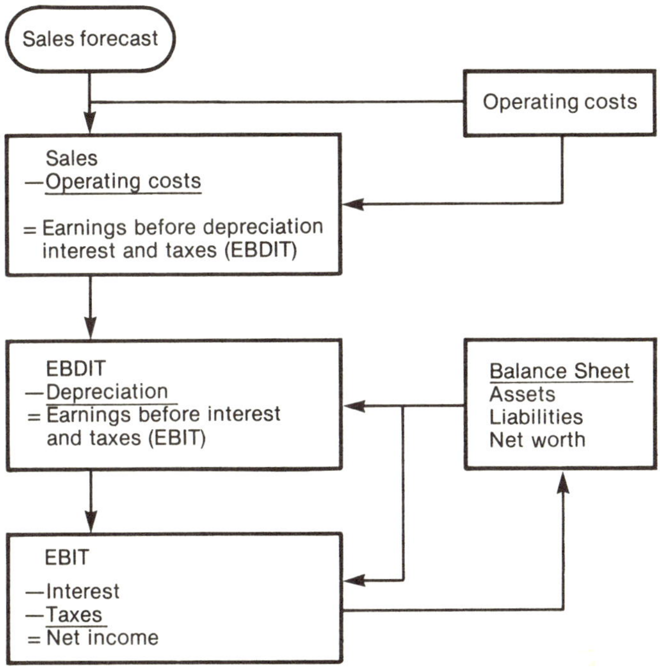

and functional equations. The definitions are those expressions that simply calculate the value of a new variable based on values of previously determined variables, and the expressions are true by definition. For example, *Earnings before depreciation, interest, and taxes* (EBDIT) is defined as *Total revenue* minus *Operating costs,* and this expression requires no parameter estimation or decision specification. Expressions (A.3), (A,5), (A.7), (A.9), and (A.11) are all definitions. Functional equations are those expressions that require the specification of some exogenous parameter or decision variable as are indicated in parentheses; they are not necessarily true by definition. For example, *Total revenue* is the most basic input and will be related to the *Price per unit* and the number of *Units sold,* where both these variables must be forecast or specified as decision variables. *Operating costs* are dependent on the numerous decisions made and the technology of the firm, and the value of the operating cost variable must be based on a forecast or an estimate of the technological relationships of the firm. The development of the functional, nondefinitional relationships will be explained in the section on income generation.

The steps in constructing the simulated income statement cannot be completed independently of input from other sectors of the model. In this example, the expenses and income in period t are related to asset and liability balances at the beginning of the period (end of previous period). The most obvious example is Equation (A.4), which calculates *Depreciation* expense during period t as a proportion of *Gross fixed assets* at the beginning of the period (time $t - 1$). Similarly, *Interest expense* (A.6) for period t is proportional to the amount of debt at the beginning of the period. Both gross fixed assets and the amount of debt would have been generated by the balance sheet equations (B.6), (B.11), and (B.13) on a previous iteration in the sequential run of the simulation model. In a more detailed model, revenue and operating costs would be related to assets and liabilities. For example, in (A.2) the *Units sold* and the *Cost per unit* that determine *Operating costs* would be dependent on balance sheet values at the beginning of the period.

Income data for period t is used to calculate cash flows in the sources and uses sector (Exhibit 6.2C), then to be fed into Exhibit 6.2B to determine asset and liability balances at the end of period t. The general form of the balance sheet expressions is that the balance at the end of the period is equal to the beginning balance plus any additions during the period. For example, in (B.1) the cash balance at the end of period t is equal to beginning cash (Cash_{t-1}) plus *Net cash inflow* during period t that was generated in the sources and uses sector.

Additions to the account balances may be expressed in numerous forms and levels of detail. Expression (B.2) shows the ending balance for *Marketable securities* in terms of the beginning balance plus all possible changes that can occur during the period. These changes are decomposed into sales and purchases of securities and maturing securities. The sales and purchases are usually determined exogenously to this part of the model, perhaps being specified as a decision variable to be manipulated in the simulation, and the *Securities matured* are generated by more detailed auxiliary equations that account for securities.

As an example of a more aggregative expression requiring less detailed input, Expression (B.3) shows *receivables* at the end of the period as equal to the beginning balance plus the *increase in receivables,* which aggregates all receivables transactions into a single figure that may be either positive or negative. Obviously, an expression of this latter type would require much less detailed input data. Which of these two levels of aggregation is to be used in defining the model would depend on the amount of detail desired by the user of the model.

Because the essence of financial simulation is to track the financial status of the firm through time, it is important that the results in one period be properly reflected as input for the next period. This function is served, in part, by the balance sheet equations that use balances at the end of period $t-1$ as the initial conditions, or beginning balances, for period t. Thus, whatever happens in period $t - 1$ affects the results for the next period, t.

The type of simulation model represented in Exhibit 6.2 is driven by the forecast of the flow of revenue, from which the income statement is generated for each period t. The main link between this flow of income and the stock of assets and liabilities is the sources and uses sector represented in Exhibit 6.2C. The sources and uses sector in conjunction with other expressions such as will be shown later as Exhibit 6.8, is the mechanism for maintaining equilibrium in the firm's financial system, and virtually all financial models must have some such mechanism that balances the system. In this case, equilibrium is assured by Expressions (B.1) and (C.7), which force the ending cash balance to reflect the beginning cash balance and all cash inflows and outflows during the period. Thus, the Expressions (C.1) through (C.7), accumulate all possible transactions that provide or use cash, so that these are properly reflected in the ending cash balance (B.1). Because this model is balanced via cash flows, it could be termed a cash flow simulation model.

Equilibrium in the Simulation Model

One of the primary uses of a financial simulation model is to determine the level of additional future investment and/or financing that might be necessary to meet the firm's objectives.

The role of the investment and financing modules is to specify these required levels of investment and financing. It is especially important that the investment and financing be consistent with each other and with the overall financial structure of the firm. That is, the investment and financing must be specified in a way that the firm is in equilibrium in the sense that assets equal liabilities and that sources of funds equal uses. This section will discuss this intrafirm equilibrium or balancing process in the simulation model, and the specifics of the investment and financing modules will be discussed later.

The simulation model can maintain equilibrium either in terms of balancing the flow of funds or by equilibrating the stock balances. The cash flow equations just discussed are one type of flow balancing, but balance in the inflows and outflows could be maintained by variations of expressions of the form

$$\textit{Total uses}_t = \textit{Total sources}_t$$

or

$$\textit{Net change in cash balance}_t = \textit{Net cash inflow}_t.$$

Stock balancing is accomplished by various expressions of the form

$$\textit{Total assets}_t = \textit{Total liabilities}_t$$

or

$$\textit{Total assets}_t = \textit{Total liabilities}_{t-1} + \textit{New financing}_t.$$

While provision is made in the accounting equations for sources to equal uses, or for assets to equal liabilities, the model must be told specifically how to reach this equilibrium. In many financial simulation models this is accomplished with a "plug variable" that is used to force equality between sources and uses or between assets and liabilities. The role of the investment and financing modules is, in part, to specify the amount and composition of these plug variables.

For example, with a given sales forecast the investment module may calculate that additional investment in fixed assets is required, amounting to $100 million. Of the $100 million required investment, $25 million will be generated internally; but, without additional adjustment, the model shows assets exceeding liabilities and net worth by $75 million. To balance the model, in the financing module a variable called *Required External Financing* is a plug variable used to balance the assets and liabilities. It would be up to the user of such a model to determine the source of this financing, and, in subsequent simulation runs, explore the implications of this financing plan.

For the simulation model focusing on the investment and financing necessary to support a sales forecast, the logical steps to reach equilibrium are shown in Exhibit 6.4. Based on a sales forecast, the investment module determines the composition and level of assets necessary to generate the sales. If these required assets differ from the existing level of assets, the amount of new investment is determined, and level of new financing necessary to acquire the investment is calculated in the financing module. In this case, the total new financing is calculated as the difference between total assets (with the new investment) and the level of liabilities and net worth that would exist without the new financing. The amount of the new financing is essentially a plug variable that balances assets and liabilities.

A simulation model cannot make decisions; it can only compute and indicate the results. Consequently, if new financing is required, the user must tell the model the composition of the new financing: whether it is debt or equity or whatever. Frequently, the thing that the user wants to explore is the best form of the financing, so the composition of the financing will be specified for a run of the simulation, then varied for a number of different iterations of the simulation. Thus, the user can see the pro forma financial results for a number of different financing schemes.

The preceding example demonstrates the type of model that balances the stocks of assets and liabilities to determine the amount of new financing required to support a sales forecast and, thus, reach its equilibrium. At appropriate points in the computational sequence, the accounting statement equations typified by Exhibit 6.2 are used to generate financial statements either for intermediate testing (e.g., Do assets equal liabilities?) or for generation of output for user evaluation. The same accounting equations would be used if the model was oriented toward balancing sources and uses of cash, rather than assets and liabilities.

EXHIBIT 6.4 Flowchart to Simulate Required Investment and Financing Based on a Sales Forecast

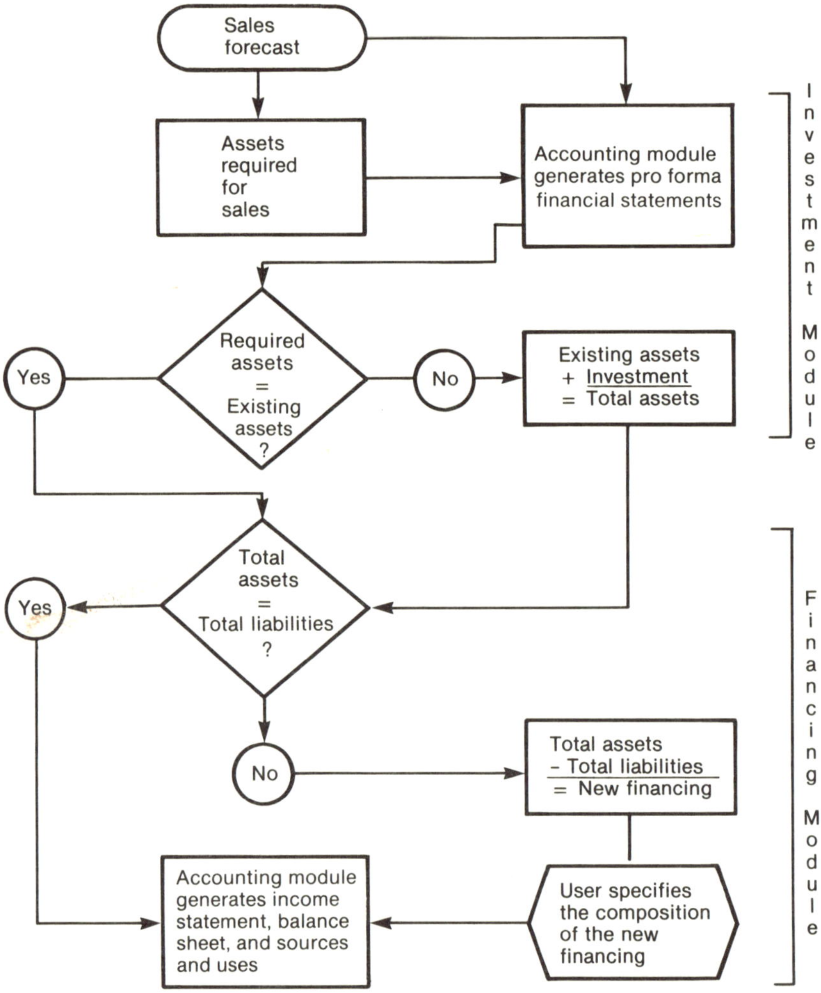

An example of the type of model that focuses on cash flows to balance the system is portrayed in Exhibit 6.5, and the specific equations used to implement this logic are presented later in Exhibit 6.8. In this example the short-term working capital operations are being simulated. Based on the sales forecast and

EXHIBIT 6.5 Flowchart to Simulate Required Short-Term Investment or Borrowing Based on a Sales Forecast

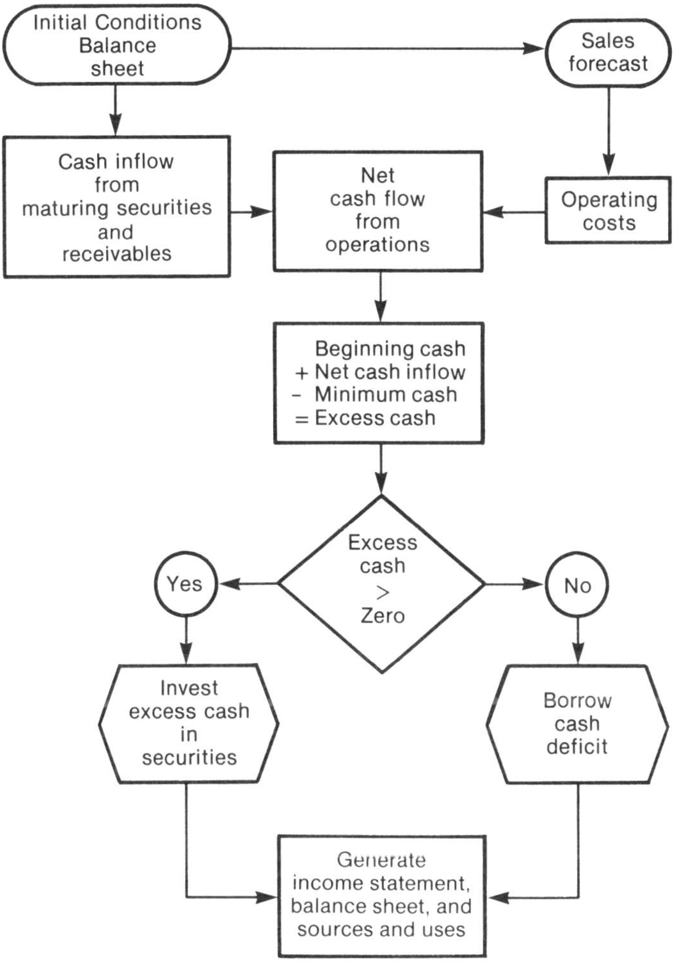

the schedule of maturing securities, the net cash flow from operations is calculated; the ending cash balance is then compared with the firm's minimum required cash balance as determined by management. The model checks for excess cash or for a cash deficit. If ending cash exceeds the minimum, the investment module has the excess invested in securities, and if ending cash is below the minimum, the financing module borrows to finance the deficit. The plug variable in this case is the amount of security purchases or the amount of borrowing necessary to bring the ending cash balance up to the management designated minimum level.

While a cash flow balancing model is ideally suited to the problems of simulating working capital decisions, one should not assume that the same thing cannot be accomplished with a stock balancing model. Furthermore, the cash balancing model can be used for long-term investment and financing simulations just as easily as can the stock balancing approach. These two approaches are interchangeable because, in a properly specified model, actions that balance the cash flows will also balance the stock of assets and liabilities. Nevertheless, in a more aggregative model, especially one that is specified in terms of longer time periods, the stock adjustment approach is easier to develop. In a more detailed model, especially one with shorter time periods, the flow adjustment approach is frequently more useful.

Given this perspective on the balancing role of the investment and financing modules, the next sections consider each module in detail.

6.2 THE INCOME GENERATION MODULE

The income generation module is the sector that generates variables and parameters related to revenues and costs that are, in turn, used in the accounting module. To generate these intermediate inputs to the accounting module, the income sector utilizes forecasts of future economic conditions and forecasts of firm relationships and decisions. These forecasts are input data to the system of equations comprising the income generation module.

Of course, every model will approach the task of forecasting revenue and cost data differently. The amount of detail in the model will depend on the purpose of the modeling effort. The discussion in this section will concentrate on the task of completing the model shown in Exhibits 6.2A, B, C. In addition, alternative approaches will be discussed briefly. The discussion in this section will focus on what needs to be forecasted and how the forecasts are to be used in the model. It will be assumed that

EXHIBIT 6.6 Variables to Be Provided by the Income Generator

Variable	*Expression Where Used*
Units produced	B.4
Units sold	A.1, A.2, B.4
Price per unit	A.1
Cost per unit	A.2, B.4
Depreciation rate	A.4
Note rate	A.6
Long-term rate	A.6
Tax rate	A.8

the necessary forecasts are readily available. We will not be concerned, at this stage, with the technical aspects of forecasting.

Exhibit 6.6 lists the variables and parameters shown in Exhibit 6.2 that relate to revenues and costs that must be developed in the income generator and passed to the accounting sector. Each variable or parameter on the list will be discussed, and alternative methods of generating its value will be considered.

Revenues

For many financial planning models the sales forecast is the most important input that drives the model, and this is certainly true in the model presented here. There are many different approaches to developing a sales forecast; a few will be discussed here.

In the present model the variables related to revenue that must be forecast are *Units sold* and *Price per unit*. The sales model shown as Expressions (4.1) and (4.2) in Chapter 4 is one alternative approach to generating a forecast of future total revenue. Shown in general form, these expressions are

$$Total\ revenue_t = Units\ sold_t \cdot Price\ per\ unit_t \qquad (6.1)$$

$$Units\ sold_t = a_t - b_t \cdot Price\ per\ unit_t. \qquad (6.2)$$

In this model, *Price per unit* is a decision variable that can be set by management in each period t over the planning horizon. The demand function (6.2) reflects the competitive conditions in the industry in each period t by allowing the parameters a_t and b_t to vary with the period.

The forecasting task of the modeler is to forecast the values of the parameters a_t and b_t for each period in the planning horizon. Past data on price and volume could be used to estimate historical parameters of the demand function. The forecast of future parameters would use these historical estimates as a basis, then modify them to produce the forecast of future conditions. For example, suppose a study of past data resulted in estimates of $a_0 = 500$ and $b_0 = -30$, where subscript zero denotes the base period. Based on forecasts of future industry conditions, the forecast for demand is reflected in the parameter forecast over the five-year planning horizon as follows:

Five-Year Forecast of Demand Parameters

Period, t:	1	2	3	4	5
a_t	550	650	653	700	735
b_t	30	40	45	50	55

This particular parameter forecast shows growth in demand over the planning horizon with the demand curve shifting outward, as indicated by the increase of the constant term, a_t, over time. At the same time, the demand curve is becoming more elastic, as indicated by the increase of the slope coefficient, b_t, over time.

A second approach to forecasting demand and unit sales would be to use a direct forecast of *Units sold* and *Price per unit,* rather than utilizing a demand function such as Expression (6.2). *Price per unit* might be extrapolated over time on the basis of a forecast of future inflation and of conditions in the economy and industry. *Units sold* could be forecasted by combining a forecast of unit sales for the industry and a forecast of the company's share of the industry sales.

There are numerous approaches to forecasting sales. The forecast doesn't necessarily have to be formulated in terms of units and price as is done in this model, although the forecast and the model have to be compatible. A common approach is to use a direct forecast of sales revenue. There are many different methods, including the various time series procedures and structural econometric techniques that were introduced in Chapter 5.

Cost Generation

The variables relating to costs shown in Exhibit 6.6 are *Units produced, Cost per unit, Depreciation rate, Note rate, Long-term rate, Tax rate,* and *Dividend payout ratio.* The income generation module will utilize basic data and forecasts to provide a forecast of these variables to be utilized in the accounting module. Naturally, there are many ways to forecast these variables, and there are numerous alternative ways to structure the model to reflect costs. Just a few will be discussed here.

Production Costs. One of the simplest methods to forecast cost is to use a "percentage-of-sales" approach. As commonly applied, the costs are calculated as a percentage of total dollar sales. This percentage cost figure becomes the basis for forecasts of future costs, given the sales forecast. As applied to the present model that is specified in terms of *Cost per unit, Units produced,* and *Units sold,* the percentage-of-sales approach has been modified just slightly. The cost per unit could be expressed as a proportion of the price per unit:

$$\textit{Cost per unit} = c_t \cdot \textit{Price per unit}, \tag{6.3}$$

where c_t is the cost per unit expressed as a proportion of the sales price per unit forecast for period t in the planning horizon. Allowing c_t to vary with t permits one to show changes in costs and profit margins from one period to the next.

The parameter c_t can be estimated from past observations of the *Cost per unit* as a proportion of the *Price per unit.* An average of past costs could be used as an estimate of the future value if the user concludes that is appropriate. Alternatively, a trend in costs may be apparent from past data, and that trend could be taken into account in forecasting future values of c_t.

The percentage-of-sales approach is attractive because of its simplicity, but it may not be a very accurate representation of the behavior of costs. Alternative approaches to cost forecasting may be more accurate or more useful, depending on the needs of the user and the nature of the model. Very aggregative models that are not concerned about the details of costs would use an approach that focuses on total costs, whereas, a more detailed model may require forecasts for different categories of costs.

One approach to developing aggregative forecasts of costs that is a simple extension of the percentage-of-sales approach is a linear regression model of the form

$$Cost_t = a + c \cdot Sales_t. \tag{6.4}$$

Observations of past *Cost* and *Sales* are used to estimate parameters a and c. The estimated parameters are used in conjunction with forecasts of future *Sales* to provide a forecast of future *Cost.*

The linear regression model (6.4) is similar to the unit cost model (6.3) except that it is expressed in terms of total costs and it allows for a fixed cost component. That is, if costs are strictly proportional to sales, then the constant term, a, will be zero, and the coefficient, c, is similar to the unit cost coefficient in (6.3). In (6.4) the presence of the constant term, a, provides a more general model, allowing for costs that are unrelated to variations in sales. Consider Exhibit 6.7 that shows the observations for past *Sales* on the horizontal axis and *Costs* on the vertical axis. Each dot on the graph represents a single observation of *Sales* and *Costs* for a period t in the past. The exhibit includes the least squares regression line that fits the observations, with constant a representing the intercept on the vertical axis and the coefficient c representing the slope of the line. One can interpret the intercept, a, as an estimate of the fixed costs and the slope coefficient, c, as an estimate of the variable costs as a proportion of *Sales.*

The regression model shown above is useful, but it may be inappropriate for some applications. When sales follow a trend over time, (6.4) simply shows *Costs* as following the same trend. If *Sales* and *Costs* do not follow a trend, (6.4) may be misleading, particularly if *Sales* are cyclical. One alternative model that removes the trend component and provides a model that is useful even when sales decline is a first-difference regression model of the form

$$\Delta\ Cost_t = a + c \cdot \Delta\ Sales_t, \tag{6.5}$$

EXHIBIT 6.7

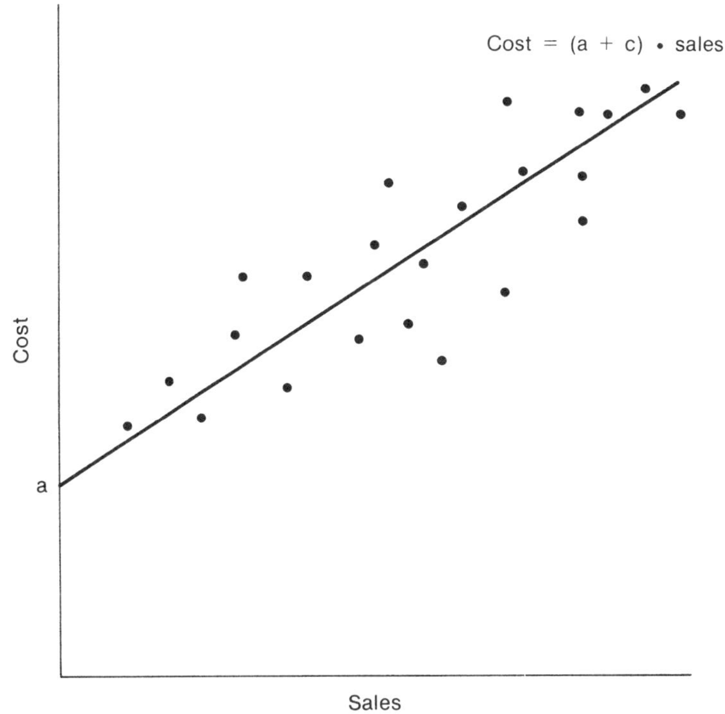

where

$$\Delta\ Cost_t \equiv Cost_t - Cost_{t-1},\ \text{and}\ \Delta\ Sales_t \equiv Sales_t - Sales_{t-1};$$

these are the observed changes (first differences) in *Costs* and *Sales* from one period to the next.

The first-difference model (6.5) requires that one forecast future changes in *sales* and use that forecast in (6.5) to forecast the change in *Costs*. The forecast for *Costs* in future period t would then be

$$Cost_t = Cost_{t-1} + \Delta\ Cost_t, \qquad (6.5)$$

where, for example, $Cost_{t-1}$ would be the observed total costs in period zero (denoted by $t=0$), where the forecast period is the first period (denoted by $t=1$). This first-difference model allows for a more accurate estimate of costs when sales are not following a smooth time trend.

The Lockheed L-1011 case, discussed in Chapter 3, provides an example of another kind of cost relation that may be appropriate for estimation of future costs. In that example, it was assumed that there was a learning curve effect in aircraft construction; that is, the average variable cost per unit was very high for the first units produced and declined rapidly as more units were produced and the firm became more proficient in production. The cost function was shown as

$$\textit{Total variable cost} = a \cdot \textit{Units produced}^{b}, \tag{6.6}$$

where a and b are the parameters that must be estimated. The parameter b affects the rate at which *total variable cost* increases and average costs decrease as more units are produced. With $0 < b < 1$, average costs decrease as more units are produced. In the L-1011 example, b was estimated to be 0.63. These parameters would be estimated from past data with the regression model

$$\log(\textit{Total variable cost}_t) = A + b \log(\textit{Units produced}_t),$$

where $A \equiv \log(a)$ and coefficient b is the estimate of the exponent in (6.6). For forecasting purposes in the model, *Units produced* would be the basic variable to be forecasted, and *Total variable cost* would be forecasted from that.

There have been numerous studies of costs in the field of commercial banking that provide examples of more detailed cost functions, showing costs as a function of various outputs of the banking process. These cost functions are similar in form to the L-1011 cost function (6.6), except that they are expressed in terms of numerous categories of activities carried on by a bank.[2] For example, Longbrake (1973) shows the cost function (abbreviated here) as

$$\textit{Direct demand deposit costs} = a \cdot (\textit{Number of accounts})^{b} \cdot (\textit{Average account size})^{c} \cdot (\textit{Average number of debits})^{d} \cdot (\textit{Average number of deposits})^{e} \cdot (\textit{Average number of checks})^{f} \cdot (\textit{Number of offices})^{g} \cdot (\textit{Average annual wage rate})^{h} \cdot (\textit{Demand deposits/Total deposits})^{i}. \tag{6.7}$$

---

[2]See Bell and Murphy (1968), Longbrake (1973), and Murphy (1973).

For an individual bank, the parameters a through i could be estimated from observations over a number of periods, although the actual studies were carried out with cross-sectional observations from many banks for a given year.

As applied in the planning-forecasting context, a cost function such as (6.7) generates forecasts of costs from forecasts of the independent variables—*number of accounts, average account size,* and so forth—and on estimates of the parameters (a, b, c, d, and so forth). The cost function would be developed on the basis of an analysis of the factors that affected costs (such as the independent variables shown in the bank example). Just as (6.7) applies only to demand deposit costs for a bank, a cost function can be developed for specific activities or divisions of a firm, and a forecast of total firm costs is built up from forecasts of the individual activity or divisional costs.

For a very detailed model, particularly one with a short planning horizon, it may be desirable to develop much more detailed cost forecasts for the model. The cost may be broken down into as fine a categorization as necessary. However, remember that as the model becomes more detailed it gets more complex, perhaps without becoming more useful.

For developing more cost categories, the general principles are the same as for less detail—the cost forecasts are developed from a basic forecast of the driving variable (e.g., sales) and on a relation assumed to exist between the basic forecast and the cost category. The cost will be related to the basic forecast by way of some functional relationship, such as (6.4), that requires the estimation of some parameters, such as a and b.

Some models make a distinction between production and sales, represented in the present model by *Units produced* and *Units sold,* respectively. This distinction may be appropriate for short-term planning models that reflect the cycle of purchasing, production, sales, and collection. For most long-term models, however, such a distinction would be irrelevant.

In the short-run model that does reflect the production cycle, this production versus sales distinction may not only be important, it may even be the *raison d'être* for the modeling process. The nature of the business and the production process will require that production precede the sale of the product, resulting in a buildup of inventories, and requiring extra financing. Therefore, one would want an accurate assessment of the relationship between production and sales.

The relationship between production and sales would be influenced by the production process and management's inventory policy. These factors would determine the time lag between production and sales. There are numerous ways to model this relationship, most of which would show a functional relation between sales and production. For example, if the firm normally produced its output one month ahead of the date it anticipated selling the product, with monthly subperiods we would have

$$\textit{Units produced}_t = \textit{Units sold}_{t+1}, \tag{6.8}$$

where *Units sold* is the basic forecast variable.

Of course, the relation may be far more complex. Rather than assume a precise time lag between production and sales, it may be useful to use econometric techniques, such as least squares regression, to estimate the parameters of the relationship. For example, with observations of past production and past sales, one could estimate the parameters of the regression equation

$$\begin{aligned}\textit{Units produced}_t = {} & a + b_0 \cdot \textit{Units sold}_t + b_1 \cdot \textit{Units sold}_{t+1} \\ & + b_2 \cdot \textit{Units sold}_{t+2} + b_3 \cdot \textit{Units} \\ & \textit{sold}_{t+3},\end{aligned} \tag{6.9}$$

where, in this example, it is hypothesized that production is influenced by the forecast of sales for three periods into the future. One could analyze the data for different lag structures and adopt the estimates that provide the best fit of the equation to the data. For short-term seasonal models with, say, monthly periods, it may be determined that a different equation would apply to each month over the seasonal cycle.

In using a relation such as (6.9) in the planning model, the estimates of the parameters a, b_0, b_1, and b_2, and b_3 are based on past data, but the model uses a forecast of future sales over the planning horizon to generate the forecast of production. When production differs from sales, inventories and costs will both be affected. For purposes of simplicity, this aspect is not fully developed in the accounting module presented here. If these aspects are important in the planning process, however, the model should be specified so as to reflect the full effects of production on costs, cash flows, and inventories. In the basic planning model shown in Exhibit 6.2 these effects are shown in general by the inventory accounting (B.4) and current asset accounting (C.5), which in turn affect cash flows.

Depreciation. In this model the parameter *Depreciation rate* is used in (A.4) to calculate depreciation expense. *Depreciation rate,* as it is used here, is an average that applies to all depreciable assets. It would be estimated by utilizing the recent observed ratio between *Depreciation* expense and *Fixed assets.* For forecasting future depreciation expense any anticipated changes in the tax law and any changes in the type or age of the depreciable assets would be taken into account.

In a more detailed model, the various categories of assets would be considered separately so as to provide a better tracking of depreciation expense. If the model is so detailed as to track individual assets, then each asset could be depreciated each year of the planning horizon, just as it would be in the firm's accounting system. For very broad strategy planning with a long planning horizon, this level of detail would be unnecessary, but for investment analysis, where the tax effects of depreciation play a particularly important role, accurate, period-by-period calculation of depreciation may be essential.

Interest Expense. The parameters *Note rate* and *Long-term rate* are the average interest rates on short-term and long-term debt, respectively. In the case of past data, they would be calculated as the ratio of interest expense to total debt outstanding for the category of debt being considered. For a future-oriented planning model, this ratio would have to be based on the forecast of the future course of interest rates, the mix of debt, and the timing of new debt issues. For very broad policy simulations the use of an average rate could be acceptable, but, if the planning model is concerned with the effects of specific financing plans, a more detailed modeling of interest expenses is in order.

Two approaches to more detailed modeling of interest expense are, first, to expand the average interest rate approach, and, second, to track the interest expense of specific new debt issues. For either method, there are many different variations.

The average interest rate method can yield an acceptable estimate of future interest expenses by estimating the future average rate as a moving average of forecasted future rates. For example, let the estimated average interest rate that applies to period t in the future as

$$Average\ rate_t = \sum_{j=1}^{t} a_{t-j} \cdot Rate_{t-j}, \tag{6.10}$$

where $Rate_{t-j}$ is the interest rate for period $t - j$, and the coefficient a_{t-j} is a weight ($0 < a_{t-j} \leq 1$) representing the proportion of debt outstanding in period t that was issued during period $t - j$. In this case, suppose $t = 3$, three periods in the future, and for $j = 3$, $a_{t-j} = a_0 = 0.30$ refers to the proportion of debt outstanding at time 3 that was issued (already outstanding) at time 0 (the present period); for $j = 2$, $a_{t-j} = a_1 = 0.50$ is the proportion of debt outstanding at $t = 3$ that was issued at time 1; for $j = 1$, $a_{t-j} = a_2 = 0.20$. The proportions would change as time passed, so for (say) t_4, a_0 might be 0.25, representing the decline, by time 4, in the relative amount of debt that was outstanding at time 0. The model can contain a subroutine that tracks the amounts of debt issued each period and calculates the coefficients a_{t-j}, if that much detail is desired.

For additional accuracy where it is important to determine the effects of alternative financing schemes, individual debt issues can be tracked in the model. For example, the model could show interest expense forecasted for period t in the future as

$$Interest\ expense_t = \sum_{j=1}^{t} Rate_{t-j} \cdot \left[Debt\ issued_{t-j} - \sum_{i=j-1}^{t-1} Debt\ repaid_{t-j,t-i} \right], \tag{6.11}$$

where $Debt\ repaid_{t-j,\,t-i}$ denotes repayment during period $t - i$ of debt that was issued during period $t - j$. In this way individual debt issues are accounted for in the model. In more detailed models, there may be different types and maturities of debt that must be tracked. The model can be developed in as much detail as is necessary to fulfill its purpose.

Tax Expense. The parameter *Tax rate* used in the present simulation model is obviously the average tax rate paid by the firm. The easiest way to estimate it is to use the average of past observed ratios of income tax to taxable income. This would be sufficiently accurate for long-range planning that was not intended to focus on the intricacies of the tax law and was not concerned directly with income tax planning. In addition, the larger the firm, the greater its income, and the more complex and varied is its income, the more appropriate it is to focus on the average tax rate.

On the other hand, if taxes are an important aspect of the firm's planning, or if the planning horizon is short, then it may be necessary to model in greater detail. Some of the aspects that may be reflected in the model are the specific progressive rate structure of income tax rates, the distinctions between income tax expense for public reporting purposes, and income taxes paid to the government, and the numerous special features of the tax law such as investment tax credits, capital gains, loss carry-backs and carry-forwards, and so forth. Except for the progressive rate schedule, these complexities will not be covered here.

The specific structure of income tax rates varies as government policy does, and the firm's taxable income may vary so that it falls into different tax brackets in different planning periods. It is easy to build a routine in the planning model that reflects the appropriate tax rate schedule. For example, for a schedule for corporate income taxes with rates of 15, 18, 30, 40, and 46, one could calculate corporate income taxes as follows:

$$\begin{aligned}
\textit{Income tax} = \; & 0.15 \cdot \text{maximum } (0, \text{taxable income}) \\
& + 0.03 \cdot \text{maximum } (0, \text{taxable income} - 25{,}000) \\
& + 0.12 \cdot \text{maximum } (0, \text{taxable income} - 50{,}000) \\
& + 0.10 \cdot \text{maximum } (0, \text{taxable income} - 75{,}000) \\
& + 0.06 \cdot \text{maximum } (0, \text{taxable income} - 100{,}000). \qquad (6.12)
\end{aligned}$$

This assumes positive taxable income; a routine that would handle loss carry-backs and carry-forwards would be more complex.

6.3 THE INVESTMENT MODULE

The purpose of the investment module is to simulate the firm's investment in assets. The investment module specifies the investment schedule so that the cash inflows and outflows related to the investment can be used in the other sectors of the simulation model to generate the output necessary to evaluate the firm's financial plans.

The investment module could be used in two alternative ways. First, investment in new assets may respond passively to the sales forecast. Second, investment may be the driver of the model, with investment plans input directly for the purpose of evaluating specific investments. The first approach is the one considered in previous discussions of the investment required to support a sales forecast, where sales is the driving variable of the model and investment is simply a result of the sales and production plan. This will be referred to as the "adjustment-to-sales" approach. The second approach is directly concerned with evaluating proposed investment projects, with sales and production being part of the secondary data describing the investment. This will be referred to as "direct investment evaluation."

Adjustment to Sales

The adjustment-to-sales approach treats investment as a passive variable that responds to the forecast of sales, which is the driver of the model. Obviously, in such a model the forecast of the asset balances is usually based directly on the sales forecast.

The relationship between sales and assets would, of course, depend on which particular asset category was being considered. Different assets would depend on different variables, and there are many alternative approaches to forecasting asset investment and asset balances to be used in the simulation models. In Exhibit 6.2B, the assets that require forecasting are cash, marketable securities, inventories, and fixed assets. Each category will be discussed after a general consideration of the technique of relating assets to sales.

The simplest investment model has the total stock of each category of assets proportional to the sales forecasted for that period, and investment is calculated as the change in required assets from one period to the next (see Gershefski [1968], Warren & Shelton [1971], and Naylor [1979]). For example, assume the income generation module specifies $Sales_t$ and the required stock of a given category of assets is calculated according to the relation

$$Assets_t = a \cdot Sales_t \tag{6.31}$$

where a is the parameter representing the required ratio of assets to sales. The parameter a is specified exogenously to the model. It may be obtained by estimating it from historical data regarding sales and asset levels, or it may be based on anticipated technological relationships or on policy decisions that are being analyzed with the simulation.

The investment required by the percent-of-sales model (6.31) is

$$\begin{aligned} Asset\ investment_t &= Assets_t - Assets_{t-1} \\ &= a(Sales_t - Sales_{t-1}). \end{aligned} \tag{6.32}$$

The relation between required assets and sales would seldom be strictly proportional over a wide range of sales, and estimates of required assets could be derived by techniques ranging from linear regression using historical data to estimation based on production functions. For example, the simplest approach to estimating the relation of assets to sales would be a time series linear regression of the form

$$Assets_t = a_0 + a_1 \cdot Sales_t, \tag{6.33}$$

where past data would provide the estimates of parameters a_0 and a_1.

More complex relations are frequently used in macroeconomic models of capital investment (see Duesenberry, Fromm, Klein & Kuh [1965], and Evans [1969]), and these models may possibly be adapted to make forecasts of firm investment. Examples of such relations include

$$Assets_t = a_0 + a_1 \cdot Sales_{t-1} + a_2 \cdot Assets_{t-1},$$

or,

$$Asset\ investment_t = a_0 + a_1 \cdot Sales_{t-1} + a_2 \cdot Assets_{t-1} + a_3 \cdot Capacity\ utilized_{t-1}. \quad (6.34)$$

Of course, many more complex lagged relationships may prove to be useful. The various approaches to modeling asset balances and investment are clarified as we make the discussion more specific to different types of assets.

The percent-of-sales approach is particularly appropriate for working capital because the primary motive for holding balances of current assets is to meet the needs of sales. Of course, the best example is inventory, which is held solely to meet the requirements of future sales. However, this statement itself points out one of the difficulties of modeling working capital investment: whether working capital balances in the model should be related to current sales, past sales, or future sales. Other questions include whether working capital investment should be strictly proportional to sales, and what degree of detail should be built into the working capital sector.

If the purpose of the simulation is to analyze the effects of broad strategic decisions over a long planning horizon, then the details of working capital are unimportant. Only the general details of working capital would have to be modeled to pursue the implications of long-run policies. Thus, for longer run planning purposes it would usually be satisfactory to let the balances in the current asset accounts be directly proportional to sales, as was shown in Expression (6.31). With a long planning horizon comprised of long subperiods, any seasonal variation in current assets disappears, as does the cycle of investment from inventory to receivables to cash. Consequently, the longer the horizon the less the need to distinguish between the component accounts of working capital.

As the planning horizon and the planning periods are shortened, greater detail is needed in modeling current asset investment. Indeed, one of the most useful applications of financial simulation models is to explore short-run decisions that affect seasonal current asset balances, so it is necessary to build much more detailed accounting for current assets by increasing the number of accounts and variables, and more carefully linking current assets to the sales forecast. The following sections will discuss each different account category in terms of alternative ways it can be modeled.

Cash. There are numerous ways to model the cash balances. The approach used would depend on the type of model, the length of the subperiods and planning horizon, and, of course, the purpose of the modeling effort.

If the subperiods and the planning horizon are long, and the purpose of the planning model is to address very broad planning issues, then one would not be as concerned with the specific detail of the balances of liquid assets. In such a case it would usually be appropriate to combine cash and marketable securities in a single account, and use the percent-of-sales approach for modeling the desired balance of liquid assets. Cash normally is held to meet the transaction requirements that are generated by the firm's production and sales, so that the percent-of-sales approach fits the situation, and the cash balance held at the end of period t could be modeled as

$$Cash_t = c \cdot Sales_t, \tag{6.35}$$

where parameter c is obtained from historical data or is based on the anticipated policy for the planning period.

An alternative approach that would be appropriate under the same circumstances would be to relate the balance of liquid assets to the stock of total assets. That is, total assets would depend on sales, and cash would be a constant proportion of total assets:

$$Cash_t = c \cdot Total\ assets_t. \tag{6.36}$$

However, one must be aware of the way that *Total assets* are computed in the model to avoid the problem of simultaneity. That is, if the balance in *Cash* must be known to calculate *Total assets,* then the model has simultaneous equations if the amount of *Total assets* must also be known to calculate the *Cash* balance.

The approach to modeling the cash balance would also depend on whether the planning model is a "stock balancing" or a "flow balancing" model.

In the standard stock balancing model that is driven by the

sales forecast, the sales forecast leads to the required asset balances, and the liability balances are adjusted to equal total assets. That is, a plug variable on the liability side of the balance sheet is chosen so as to balance the system. In this case, it is permissible to have the cash balance adjust to the forecast of sales or total assets independently from the balancing mechanism for the system that forces liabilities to equal assets.

On the other hand, if the model is of the flow balancing variety, it cannot be assumed that the liquid assets would automatically be a constant proportion of either sales or total assets. This is because in the typical flow balancing model the mechanism for maintaining equilibrium is the adjustment of the cash and liquid asset accounts. The equation that balances the system is of the general form

$$\textit{Net change in cash balances}_t = \textit{Net cash inflow}_t.$$

A flow balancing model where *Cash* is the balancing account for the system is well suited to a planning problem where the planning horizon and the subperiods are short and greater detail about cash and marketable security accounts is needed.

The model represented by Exhibits 6.2 is a flow balancing model with cash being the balancing account. In that model the cash balance is calculated as

$$\textit{Cash}_t = \textit{Cash}_{t-1} + \textit{Net cash inflow}_t, \qquad \text{(B.1)}$$

where the *Net cash inflow* is calculated in the sources and uses section as

$$\textit{Net cash inflow}_t = \textit{Sources of cash}_t - \textit{Uses of cash}_t. \qquad \text{(C.7)}$$

By elaborating on the inputs to these expressions we can explore alternative ways to model the cash account.

For the cash flow balancing model to function properly, the model must be equipped with some decision rules that tell it how to balance the system in a way that realistically reflects management's policies. In the absence of such instructions, there is nothing to prevent the cash balance getting excessively large or small, or even negative to balance the system. The kinds of decision rules necessary are instructions stating the desired balance of cash and stating what should be done when the actual balance departs from the desired balance. The logic of these instructions previously was shown as a flow diagram in Exhibit 6.5. The expressions necessary to carry out this logic are shown in Exhibit 6.8.

In developing the expressions in Exhibit 6.8, the assumptions and policies are

a. The firm will maintain its cash balance at a level assigned to the variable *Desired cash.*
b. Any cash in excess of *Desired cash* that would build up from the firm's operations would be invested in marketable securities.
c. If operations generate a cash outflow so that the cash balance would be less than *Desired cash,* the cash balance is restored to the desired level by first, selling marketable securities, and second by borrowing.
d. If security sales are necessary, the amount of *Securities sold* is limited to the amount of securities in the portfolio at the beginning of the period, *Marketable securities*$_{t-1}$.
e. If *Cash deficit* exceeds the amount that can be obtained by selling securities, then the remainder of *Cash deficit* is financed by borrowing an amount equal to *Long-term debt issued.*

The expressions in Exhibit 6.8 provide the model with a mechanism for managing the cash account, but they do not determine the *Desired cash* level. That must be based on the firm's policy, which takes account of the firm's needs for cash balances to meet emergencies, and, perhaps, the compensating balances required by the bank.

One use of a short-run planning model is to simulate the firm's cash inflows and outflows to determine the appropriate level of cash to hold. By specifying a *Desired cash* balance and then allowing the inflows and outflows to be chosen randomly from a probability distribution that is valid for this firm, the costs and benefits associated with different cash policies can be explored. If too little cash is maintained, the firm will have to liquidate securities or borrow too frequently and its transaction costs will be excessive. If too much cash is maintained, the

EXHIBIT 6.8 Cash Balance Adjustment Sector

Trial sources of cash$_t$ = *Cash flow from operations*$_t$ + *Securities matured*$_t$ + *Increase in current liabilities*$_t$
Trial uses of cash$_t$ = *Increase in noncash current assets*$_t$ + *Fixed asset investment*$_t$
Trial cash balance$_t$ = *Cash*$_{t-1}$ + *Trial sources of cash*$_t$ − *Trial uses of cash*$_t$
Trial excess cash$_t$ = *Trial cash balance*$_t$ − *Desired cash*$_t$
Excess cash$_t$ = Maximum [0, *Trial excess cash*$_t$]
Cash deficit$_t$ = 0 − Minimum [0, *Trial excess cash*$_t$]
Securities purchased$_t$ = *Excess cash*$_t$
Securities sold$_t$ = Minimum [*Cash deficit*$_t$, *Marketable securities*$_{t-1}$]
Long-term debt issued$_t$ = Maximum [0, *Cash deficit*$_t$ − *Securities sold*$_t$]
Net cash inflow$_t$ = *Trial sources of cash*$_t$ − *Trial uses of cash*$_t$ − *Securities purchased*$_t$ + *Securities sold*$_t$ + *Long-term debt issued*$_t$
Cash$_t$ = *Cash*$_{t-1}$ + *Net cash inflow*$_t$

transactions are avoided, but the firm foregoes the income it could have earned if the funds were invested.[3]

Another approach to determining the appropriate cash balance has been to borrow from the techniques of inventory theory to derive decision rules regarding the inventory of cash. For example, Miller and Orr (1966) present a model for managing cash balances that allows the cash balance to wander randomly between an upper limit, h, and a lower limit, l, and when the cash balance hits either the upper or lower limit, actions are taken to restore the balance to a restoration level, z. The limits and the restoration point are determined by a formula that considers the parameters of the probability distribution that describes the random daily cash flows, the transaction cost of restoring the cash balance, and the interest rate that represents the opportunity cost of holding funds as cash.[4] With the Miller and Orr (h,z,l) policy, the cash balance would follow the pattern shown in Exhibit 6.9, where securities are purchased when the cash balance hits the upper limit to restore the balance to z, and securities are sold (or funds borrowed) when the lower limit, l, is breached.

[3]The issues relating to cash management are discussed in Smith (1979) and Orgler (1970).

[4]The Miller and Orr formula is $z = (3b\sigma^2/4i)^{1/3}$ and, $h = 3z$, $l = 0$, where b is the fixed dollar cost of a transaction, i is the interest rate per day, and σ^2 is the variance of the random, normally distributed daily cash flows.

EXHIBIT 6.9 Cash Balances Using the Miller and Orr Model

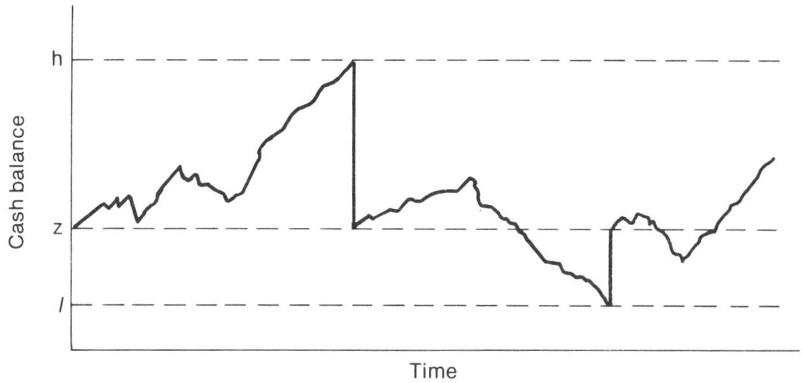

EXHIBIT 6.10 Expressions to Be Added to Exhibit 6.2C to Implement Miller and Orr Policy

$$\textit{Unmanaged cash}_t = \textit{Cash}_{t-1} + \textit{Net cash inflow excluding securities transactions}_t$$

$$\textit{Securities purchased}_t \begin{cases} = \textit{Unmanaged cash}_t - z \text{ if } \textit{Unmanaged cash}_t \geq h \\ = 0 \text{ otherwise} \end{cases}$$

$$\textit{Securities sold}_t \begin{cases} = z - \textit{Unmanaged cash}_t \text{ if } \textit{Unmanaged cash}_t \leq l \\ = 0 \text{ otherwise} \end{cases}$$

$$\textit{Cash}_t = \textit{Unmanaged cash}_t - \textit{Securities purchased}_t + \textit{Securities sold}_t$$

where

$$\begin{aligned} &\textit{Net cash inflow excluding securities transactions}_t = \\ &\quad \textit{Net cash flow from operations}_t + \textit{Increase in current liabilities}_t \\ &\quad + \textit{Increase in permanent capital}_t - \textit{Fixed asset investment}_t \\ &\quad - \textit{Increase in receivables and inventories}_t \\ &\quad + \textit{Securities matured}_t \end{aligned}$$

The Miller and Orr cash management decision rules could be built into a short-run planning model such as Exhibit 6.2 with the expressions shown in Exhibit 6.10. In this case, the modeler would determine the limits (h,z,l) from a study of the firm's operating cash flows.

Marketable Securities. As was stated earlier, if the planning horizon and the subperiods making up the horizon are long, there is little need to distinguish between cash and marketable securities; they can be combined in a liquid asset category for purposes of analyzing a plan, and a straightforward percent-of-sales approach could be used. On the other hand, if the planning horizon is short and the purpose of the model is to consider the effects of short-run investment strategies, then more detailed modeling of marketable securities would be appropriate.

For the longer run model, the percent-of-sales approach would simply specify marketable securities as

$$\textit{Marketable securities}_t = \textit{ms} \cdot \textit{Sales}_t, \tag{6.37}$$

where *ms* is a single parameter based either on historical relationships or on anticipated policy. Alternatively, securities could be specified as a percent of assets as in

$$\textit{Marketable securities}_t = m \cdot \textit{Total assets}_t, \tag{6.38}$$

but care must be taken to avoid simultaneity.

For the shorter run model focusing on working capital management, the details of the securities accounts would be of concern, and more detailed modeling would be required. Expression B.2 of Exhibit 6.2B represents a good starting point to model marketable securities transactions, which are shown as:

$$\begin{aligned}\textit{Marketable securities}_t = {} & \textit{Marketable securities}_{t-1} \\ & - \textit{Securities matured}_t \\ & - \textit{Securities sold}_t \\ & + \textit{Securities purchased}_t.\end{aligned}$$

One only has to expand on the components of this expression to have a complete model of marketable securities.[5] Exhibit 6.11 shows expressions that would be developed to model security transactions over a short planning horizon.

To express such a securities planning model some notation must be introduced—with apologies to the more nonmathematical readers. Two subscripts will be used: the first subscript will denote the period in which a security matures; the second will

---

[5]A model of short-term security transactions in the context of a linear programming model for working capital management is presented in Orgler (1970), and a similar example will be presented in Chapter 8.

EXHIBIT 6.11 A Short-Term Securities Planning Model

$$\textit{Securities purchased}_t = \sum_{j=t+1}^{h} a_{jt} \cdot \textit{Securities purchased}_{jt} \tag{1}$$

$$\textit{Securities sold}_t = \sum_{j=t+1}^{h} a_{jt} \cdot \textit{Securities sold}_{jt} \tag{2}$$

$$\textit{Securities held}_{jt} = \textit{Securities held}_{j,\,t-1} + \textit{Securities purchased}_{jt} - \textit{Securities sold}_{jt} \text{ for } j = t+1, \ldots, h \tag{3}$$

$$\textit{Securities matured}_t = \textit{Securities held}_{t,t-1} \tag{4}$$

$$\textit{Marketable securities}_t = \sum_{j=t+1}^{h} a_{jt} \cdot \textit{Securities held}_{jt} \tag{5}$$

$$\textit{Security cash flow}_t = \textit{Securities matured}_t + \textit{Securities sold}_t - \textit{Securities purchased}_t \tag{6}$$

$$\textit{Security basis}_{jt} = \sum_{n=0}^{t} a_{jn} \cdot \textit{Securities bought}_{jn} - \sum_{n=1}^{t} a_{jn} \cdot \textit{Securities sold}_{jn} \quad \text{for } j = t+1, \ldots, h \tag{7}$$

$$\textit{Security income}_t = \textit{Securities matured}_t - \textit{Security basis}_{t,\,t-1} + \sum_{j=t-1}^{h} [a_{jt} \cdot \textit{Securities sold}_{jt} - \textit{Portion sold}_{jt} \cdot \textit{Security basis}_{jt}] \tag{8}$$

denote the current period, when the action is taken. For example, *Securities purchased*$_{jt}$ refers to purchases in period t that will mature in period j, and *Securities sold*$_{jt}$ denotes sale at time t of securities maturing in period j. The index h denotes securities that mature at or beyond the planning horizon.

For this model it is assumed that the securities of concern are short-term discount securities, such as Treasury bills, that are bought at a discount from face value, and the increase in value from purchase until sale or maturity is interest income, and is shown as *Security income*$_t$. The values of the variables *Securities purchased*$_{jt}$, *Securities sold*$_{jt}$, *Securities held*$_{jt}$, and *Securities matured*$_t$ are all stated in terms of face, or maturity, value. To convert from face value to market value, we define the coefficient $a_{jt} \equiv 1/(1+r_{jt})$ as the present value factor that converts the face (maturity) value of securities to the discounted value at time t, with r_{jt} representing the interest rate for $j - t$ periods prevailing at date t. For example, $a_{5,3}$ • *Securities pur-*

chased$_{5,3}$ would be the amount spent in period 3 to purchase securities that mature in period 5 because *Securities purchased*$_{5,3}$ is their time-5 maturity value, which multiplied by $a_{5,3}$ yields the market value as of period 3. The values of r_{jt} would be provided as input to the model by a forecast of future interest rates over the planning period.

The variables *Securities purchased*$_t$, *Securities sold*$_t$, and *Marketable securities*$_t$ all are totals for all maturities, and are stated in terms of market values at time t. *Security cash flow*$_t$ represents the net inflow or outflow from security transactions during period t. *Security basis*$_{jt}$ represents the purchase price of securities that mature in period j, so that *Security income*$_t$ can be calculated as the difference between the purchase price of the security and its maturity or sale value. In Expression (7) of Exhibit 6.11 subscript $n = 0$ refers to securities held at the beginning of the planning horizon, time t_0. In Expression (8) *Portion sold*$_{jt}$ refers to the proportion of securities that mature in period j that are sold in period t and is equal to *Securities sold*$_{jt}$/*Securities held*$_{j,t-1}$ · *Security income*$_t$ would usually be included in the firm's income statement as Other Income (which is not shown in Exhibit 6.2A).

Accounts Receivable. In Exhibit 6.2, receivables are shown in Expression (B.3) as

$$Receivables_t = Receivables_{t-1} + Increase\ in\ receivables_t$$

as an example of an aggregative stock adjustment approach that shows little detail about receivables. The user of the model would either have to specify the *Increase in receivables* as an input to the model, or the *Increase in receivables* could be determined in a separate sector of the model that, perhaps, could relate the *Increase in receivables* to the sales forecast.

Accounts receivable are generated by sales, so obviously the *Increase in receivables* and the level of *Receivables* outstanding at the end of a period are going to be related to the past sequence of sales, and will be influenced by company policy and economic events exogenous to the firm. The problem here is how these relationships should be modeled and how much detail should be included.

For a model with a long horizon and planning periods of a year or more, receivables at the end of the year would depend on sales that year, and only in unusual cases would they depend at all on sales prior to that year. Consequently, receivables can be expressed as a simple proportion of sales:

$$Receivables_t = a \cdot Sales_t, \tag{6.40}$$

where a is the parameter that can be estimated directly from past observations of receivables and sales. The parameter a can be varied in the simulation to reflect changes in company credit policies or the effects of exogenous economic events.

As the length of the periods is shortened the amount of detail can be increased with the accounts receivable shown as dependent on the sequence of past observed sales. A "distributed lag" relationship of a form such as

$$Receivables_t = a_0 \cdot Sales_t + a_1 \cdot Sales_{t-1} + a_2 \cdot Sales_{t-2} \tag{6.41}$$

may be appropriate, where parameters a_0, a_1, and a_2 are estimated from past data or, perhaps, based on credit policy and anticipated payment practices. For example, assume the model has a planning horizon of one year and subperiods of one month, that credit sales are 80 percent of total sales, and 60 percent of the credit sales are collected in the first month after the sales occur, 30 percent are collected in the second month, and 10 percent are collected in the third month. Assuming there is no uncertainty in the process, the receivables collected would be

$$\begin{aligned} Receivables\ collected_t &= 0.60(0.80)\ Sales_{t-1} + 0.30(0.80) \\ &\quad Sales_{t-2} + 0.10(0.80)\ Sales_{t-3} \\ &= 0.48\ Sales_{t-1} + 0.24\ Sales_{t-2} + \\ &\quad 0.08\ Sales_{t-3}, \end{aligned} \tag{6.42}$$

and the balance at the end of period t would be

$$\begin{aligned} Receivables_t &= 0.80\ Sales_t + 0.40(0.80)\ Sales_{t-1} + \\ &\qquad 0.10(0.80)\ Sales_{t-2} \\ &= 0.80\ Sales_t + 0.32\ Sales_{t-1} + 0.08\ Sales_{t-2}, \end{aligned} \tag{6.43}$$

where the parameter estimates are $a_0 = 0.80$, $a_1 = 0.32$, and $a_2 = .08$. Obviously, with these percent-of-sales models, the primary input is the sales forecast. For the distributed lag example, the *Receivables* forecast at any future date t would be generated by the forecast of *Sales* at dates $t - 1$ and t. Suppose the sales forecasts for the next 12 months are as shown in Exhibit 6.12; with the parameters a as shown, the *Receivables* balance in each month will be as shown in the second line. For example, *Receivables* in the eighth month would be

$$\begin{aligned} Receivables_8 &= 0.8\ Sales_8 + 0.32\ Sales_7 + 0.08\ Sales_6 \\ &= 0.8\ (350) + 0.32\ (400) + 0.08\ (350) \\ &= \$436. \end{aligned}$$

To the extent that receivables and/or collections are affected by economic conditions, estimates may be improved by adding appropriate economic variables to the estimated predictive equation. Just remember that while such elaborations may generate better estimates using past data, to use them in the simulation of future periods, the future values of the economic variables must also be forecasted. The economic forecast may be more elusive than forecasting receivables.

Of course, there are numerous other ways in which receivables can be modeled. An alternative example is:

$$\begin{aligned} Receivables_t = Receivables_{t-1} &- Receivables\ collected_t \\ &+ Credit\ extended_t, \end{aligned} \tag{6.44}$$

where the variables *Receivables collected*$_t$ and *Credit extended*$_t$ are each estimated separately with regression equations such as that shown above for collections, and extensions may be dependent on sales, interest rates, and other economic conditions.

For financial institutions receivables (loans) would be the most important asset on the balance sheet, and the balance would be influenced by past balances, credit decisions, and economic events. Some bank models break the loan accounts into elaborate detail, showing many different types of loan categories according to their purpose and maturity.

There are numerous approaches to forecasting the level of loans for use in financial planning models. Two general approaches are: (1) to develop a forecast of total bank lending for the aggregate economy based on broad economic forecasts and variables, and then to forecast the particular bank's loans based on a forecast of the share of the loan market; or (2) to develop a forecasting model for the particular bank's loans based on vari-

EXHIBIT 6.12 Sales and Receivables Forecast by Equation (6.43)

Month(t)	1	2	3	4	5	6	7	8	9	10	11	12
Sales ($000)	100	150	200	250	300	350	400	350	300	250	200	150
Receivables ($000)	144	164	216	276	336	396	456	436	384	324	264	204

ables specific to the bank and its market. An example of the first approach is discussed by Roering and Smith (1978). The second approach is probably more useful for short-run planning because it develops a bank forecast that is keyed to the specific situation. The disadvantage is that it may require more input based on local forecasts as opposed to more readily available national forecasts. An example of such a forecasting model that can be based on specific bank data is presented by Thompson (1973) as

$$\begin{aligned} Loans_t = a &+ b_1 \cdot Loans_{t-1} + b_2 \cdot Lines\ of\ credit_t \\ &+ b_3 \cdot (Loans_{t-1} - Loans_{t-2}) \\ &+ b_4 \cdot (Prime\ rate_t - Commercial\ paper\ rate_t), \end{aligned}$$

where parameters a, b_1, b_2, b_3, b_4 are all estimated from past data. Thompson's model is separately estimated for loans of different maturities.

For short-term forecasting of loans the time series methodology that uses exponential smoothing, moving averages or autoregressive techniques, and seasonal adjustments may be very useful for planning applications. These techniques were introduced in the forecasting chapter.

Inventories. As with other current asset categories, there are numerous ways in which to model inventories, each one being suited to a particular purpose or situation. The simplest is to show inventories as a proportion of sales. In addition, more complex sales-driven models could be formulated, or alternatively, inventories can be related directly to a production sector of the model.

For the longer horizon model the simple proportional relation

$$Inventories_t = b \cdot Sales_t \tag{6.50}$$

may be sufficiently accurate because inventories at the end of each year may bear a stable relation to sales over a period of years, and the relation could be estimated easily from past data. For long-run strategic planning purposes where rough approximations prove sufficient, and where it is unnecessary to track the seasonal details of inventories, there is little reason to burden the model with greater complexity.

The relation between *Inventories* and *Sales,* such as (6.50), can be based on past relationships and estimated from past data using a linear regression approach, or it may be included in the model so as to reflect an inventory policy decision. As an example of the latter approach, the policy might be to maintain an inventory balance equivalent to 50 days' sales (evaluated at cost of goods sold). Assume cost of goods sold is 70 percent of sales, with sales per day of

$$\textit{Sales per day} = \textit{Annual sales}/365;$$

evaluated in terms of cost, the goods sold per day would be

$$0.70 \cdot \textit{Sales per day},$$

or

$$0.70 \cdot \textit{Annual sales}/365,$$

and to have inventory to meet 50 days' sales, the firm would have

$$\begin{aligned} \textit{Inventory} &= 50 \cdot 0.70 \cdot \textit{Annual sales}/365 \\ &= 0.096 \cdot \textit{Annual sales}, \end{aligned}$$

so this inventory policy would call for inventories being maintained at 9.6 percent of *Sales* to meet the 50-day requirement.

Greater detail and accuracy may be attainable by showing inventories in terms of the variables that most directly influence them—specifically, both production and sales. For example, as was shown in Exhibit 6.2B, the expression

$$\textit{Inventories}_t = \textit{Inventories}_{t-1} + (\textit{Units produced}_t - \textit{Units sold}_t) \cdot \textit{Cost per unit}_t \qquad \text{(B.4)}$$

is true by definition and could accurately track inventories if production, sales, and costs are accurately forecasted. This would be especially suited to a short horizon where seasonal variations in production and sales are important, and where there is a production sector that deals in physical units. For example, the Sun Oil Company model [Gershefski (1968)] has a production sector that determines the amount of crude oil production that is separate from the sales sector, so that inventories are the cumulative result of these separate sectors. Obviously, Expression (B.4) need not be expressed in terms of physical units. It can be expressed directly in terms of dollar value so as to bypass the difficulties of working with physical units and developing data from which to evaluate the cost per unit.

Because production is usually based on current and future expected sales, the inventory expression (B.4) may be rederived in a form so inventories are driven solely by sales. For example, a simple adaptive model of production could be of the form

$$\textit{Units produced}_t = \textit{Units sold}_t + a(\textit{Units sold}_t - \textit{Units sold}_{t-1}), \tag{6.51}$$

where current production is equal to current sales plus some proportion, *a,* of the current increase in sales so as to increase inventory to meet an anticipated sales increase next period. Substituting (6.51) for $\textit{Units produced}_t$ in (B.4) yields

$$\textit{Inventories}_t = \textit{Inventories}_{t-1} + a \cdot (\textit{Units sold}_t - \textit{Units sold}_{t-1}) \cdot \textit{Cost per unit}_t. \tag{6.52}$$

Macroeconomic models may prove helpful in specifying the inventory investment relation for the firm. For example, Evans (1969, p. 219) shows the increase (denoted by Δ) in manufacturer's inventories at the macro level as

$$\Delta\, \textit{Inventory}_t = a + b \cdot \textit{Sales}_{t-1} + c \cdot \textit{Inventory}_{t-2} + d \cdot \textit{Unfilled orders}_{t-1},$$

where the periods are quarters, and the coefficients were estimated as

$$a = -5.03,\ b = 0.0718,\ c = 0.0539, \text{ and } d = 0.422.$$

There are numerous decision models that are intended to specify an optimal inventory policy based on various factors of demand, interest rates, and ordering costs for goods held in inventory.[6] These optimization models can provide the basis for forecasting inventories in a simulation model when it is assumed the firm follows the optimal policy. For example, the simplest inventory model is the economic order quantity (EOQ) model that prescribes the optimal amount of inventory to order and implies that the average inventory will be

$$\textit{Inventory} = \textit{Sales}^{1/2} \cdot \tfrac{1}{2}\,[\textit{Ordering cost}/\textit{Cost per unit} \cdot \textit{Interest rate}]^{1/2},$$

where *Ordering cost* represents the fixed cost of placing one new order for the goods carried in inventory, and *Cost per unit* • *Interest rate* is the opportunity cost of carrying one unit in inventory for a year.

For the firm following the EOQ policy, the average inventory would increase with sales, but would increase at a decreasing rate as sales increase. Thus, inventories would not be strictly proportional to sales, and the inventory as a proportion of sales would decrease as forecasted sales increase. Note that this model relates the average inventory to the *Ordering cost* and the *Carrying cost,* so that to utilize it in the financial planning context would necessitate forecasting not just sales, but these costs (including interest rates) as well.

There are numerous other more sophisticated inventory models that potentially could be useful in modeling inventories in a simulation model. However, the sophistication may be self-defeating. The more sophisticated models may impose an impractical burden of forecasting on the planner if it requires that too many variables be forecast in excessive detail. Generally speaking, the simpler the model, the more useful it is.

Fixed Assets. With a long planning horizon and long periods comprising the horizon, a percent-of-sales approach to fixed assets is probably not too far wrong. In the long run the firm's ability to increase output of product is tied fairly closely to its productive capacity, so that any increases in output will require increases in the fixed assets that constitute its productive capac-

---

[6] Inventory policy models are explained in Wagner (1969, chaps. 9 and 19) and Hadley and Whiten (1963).

ity. Thus, the percent-of-sales relation is a good first approximation for fixed assets, where

$$\text{Net fixed assets}_t = a \cdot \text{Sales}_t, \tag{6.53}$$

and for investment one obtains

$$\text{Fixed asset investment}_t = a \cdot (\text{Sales}_t - \text{Sales}_{t-1}). \tag{6.54}$$

This simplified approach leads to immediate, concurrent responses of investment to changes in sales. This approach would be adequate for very aggregative models where the time periods are relatively long. On the other hand, it may be misleading in a more detailed model that focuses on shorter time periods and is more detailed in terms of the number of different asset categories. One difficulty is that if a sales decline is forecasted, this model would always show disinvestment in response to the sales decline, whereas, in the short run, a firm can cut production in response to a sales decline without selling off assets. Conversely, most firms have some limited capacity to increase sales without an immediate increase in assets.

There are numerous ways to modify the link between sales and investment so as to improve its accuracy. Francis and Rowell (1978) present a model where investment occurs only if the sales forecast exceeds the level of sales that can be produced with existing assets. For example, assume the minimum stock of assets that must be available to produce a given level of sales is

$$\text{Required fixed assets}_t = a \cdot \text{Sales}_t;$$

then asset investment can be specified as

$$\begin{aligned}\text{Fixed asset investment}_t &= \max\,[0, \text{Required fixed assets}_t - \text{Fixed assets}_{t-1}] \\ &= \max\,[0, a \cdot \text{Sales}_t - \text{Fixed assets}_{t-1}]\end{aligned} \tag{6.55}$$

If $\textit{Fixed assets}_{t-1}$ exceeds $a \cdot \textit{Sales}_t$, no new investment occurs in the model.

The technology of the production process may help one to model the link between sales and investment in fixed assets. The firm's production function, expressing its maximum output as a function of the factor inputs, can be utilized to derive the level of capital assets required to support a given level of sales. For example, in the planning model of AT&T [Davis, Caccappolo, & Chaudry (1973)], the firm's production function is estimated. Based on the production function, the required investment in capital assets can be expressed as a function of sales and the relative prices of the factors of production, including the cost of physical capital services.

One difficulty frequently encountered in defining the simulation model, and particularly in relating investment to sales, is whether to define output in physical units or in dollars. It can be useful to focus on the physical units of output because it is this that most directly affects the need for new investment, and is less likely to be confounded by the effects of inflation. In addition, the separation of units from product prices makes the model better suited to exploring pricing policies and the effects of competition and inflation.

For example, in the Sun Oil Company model, "The New Investments block first determines the amount of investment required in new service stations to achieve a specified market share for the coming year. The construction program is based on the expected performance of existing stations and those to be constructed." [Gershefski (1968), p. 23]. In the Francis and Rowell (1978) model the dollar amount of investment is linked to the forecast of *unit* industry sales with the following four simplified expressions:

$$\begin{aligned}
\textit{Unit company sales}_t &= \textit{Market share}_t \cdot \textit{Industry unit sales}_t && (6.56)\\
\textit{Capital units required}_t &= a \cdot \textit{Unit company sales}_t && (6.57)\\
\textit{Required fixed assets}_t &= P \cdot \textit{Capital units required}_t && (6.58)\\
\textit{Fixed asset investment}_t &= \max\,[0, \textit{Required fixed assets}_t - \\
&\qquad \textit{Fixed assets}_{t-1}], && (6.59)
\end{aligned}$$

where a is the ratio of physical capital to sales, and P is the price per unit of physical capital.

The problem with defining variables in physical units is that it can lead to a model that is excessively detailed, requiring too much data input and generating more output than is necessary to answer the questions that the model was intended to answer. This is especially true for a firm with many different product lines. The excessive detail demanded by unit definitions can be avoided either by sticking with a model defined in dollar amounts, or by using an index of unit output that summarizes the unit output of all the different product lines.

The modeling of fixed assets helps to emphasize a major difference between a planning model and an accounting model. An accounting model would usually be oriented toward keeping track of the costs of the assets and would track the accounts for specific classes of assets over their life. This would usually be too much detail to be useful in a planning context. For planning purposes, in most cases it is better to focus attention on the broad aggregate levels of the asset accounts, rather than develop excessive detail about the different account categories. An exception occurs when the purpose of the simulation is to analyze the acceptability and feasibility of specific investment proposals, as will be discussed in the next section.

Direct Investment Evaluation

When the purpose of the simulation is to evaluate specific investment projects, the modeling approach is different from the case where investment reacts passively to the sales forecast. In this case, the focus is on the specifics of the proposed investment, and the modeling problem is how to relate properly the details of the investment to the rest of the simulation model of the firm.

In the context of financial modeling and planning there are two aspects to the consideration of investment proposals. The first is the evaluation of the investment itself, and the second is relating the investment to the firm as a whole so that the user can evaluate how the investment affects the firm's financial statements. The evaluation will be considered first, and then we will discuss how to include the investment in the larger firm model.

Investment Evaluation. There are numerous techniques that have been advocated for evaluating capital investments by the firm. The two most generally acceptable techniques are net present value (NPV) and internal rate of return (IRR).[7] The net present value technique will be emphasized here.

[7]More detailed discussions of the techniques for investment evaluation can be found in Weston and Copeland (1986, chaps. 6, 7, and 21) and Franks, Broyles, and Carleton (1985, Chaps. 4, 5, and 6).

Net present value (NPV) is calculated according to the expression

$$NPV = \sum_{t=1}^{h} Cash\ flow_t\,[1/(1+k)^t] - Cost, \qquad (6.71)$$

where *Cost* denotes the present value of the net amounts invested in a project, $Cash\ flow_t$ is the increment in the cash flow that is generated by the investment project, h is the number of periods in the life of the project, and k denotes the rate of return that is required on the investment.

The decision criterion that is used for evaluating the acceptability of an investment project is that the NPV should not be less than zero, i.e., NPV $>$ 0. If the NPV is exactly equal to zero it means that the cash flows are just sufficient to return to the investor the original cost of the investment (return *of* investment) plus, yield a rate of return *on* the investment equal to the discount rate k. If k is the firm's required return on investment, NPV $=$ 0 means that the investment just meets the firm's standard by returning the original principal invested *and* yielding a rate of return equal to k. If NPV $>$ 0, the investment yields a rate of return greater than k and returns the original principal of the investment. Applying the NPV criterion is relatively simple so long as one is careful to use the correct definitions of cash flow, cost, and discount rate. In this regard, two alternative applications of NPV will be discussed: first, the weighted-average-cost-of-capital (WACC) approach and second, the equity approach.

The Weighted-Average-Cost-of-Capital Approach. The WACC approach to NPV investment evaluation tries to answer the question, Are the total (or overall) cash flows generated by the project sufficient to return the original total cost (return *of* investment principal) and provide the required returns *on* investment to *all* classes of security holders who helped finance the cost of the project? The total cost of the project is financed with equity capital and, perhaps, capital provided by lenders and other security holders. Thus, the total cost includes not just the investment by equity security holders, but also whatever funds were borrowed to finance the project. The cash flow that is relevant is not just the cash flow that is available to be distributed to the owners (stockholders), but also the flow that is available to be paid to the lenders. The discount rate, denoted by k_a (where subscript *a* denotes average), that is used to calculate NPV with the WACC approach is a weighted average of the return required by the equity investors (cost of equity, denoted by k_e) and the return required by the lenders (cost of debt, denoted by k_d).

For example, assume that an investment project will cost \$100,000 and that it will be financed by a loan of \$40,000 plus an equity investment of \$60,000. The debt has an interest rate of 10 percent ($k_d = 0.10$) and will be repaid in 15 years with equal annual payments of \$5,258.94 (principal and interest). The expected return (after corporate income tax) required by the equity investors is 15 percent ($k_e = 0.15$), and the tax rate on corporate income is 46 percent. The total cost of the investment is depreciated over 15 years on a straight-line basis. The investment will generate incremental earnings before depreciation, interest, and taxes (EBDIT) of \$20,301.67 over 15 years. No salvage value is anticipated.

To apply the WACC approach to this problem, the discount rate, cost, and cash flows must be calculated so they are all consistent with each other.

The discount rate to be used to calculate NPV is the weighted average cost of capital, and is normally calculated according to

$$k_a = \left(\frac{Debt}{Total\ capital}\right) \cdot k_d \cdot (1-T) + \left(\frac{Equity}{Total\ capital}\right) \cdot k_e, \qquad (6.72)$$

where

k_d is the interest rate (return required by lenders) at the date the investment is undertaken, which is 0.10 for this example;

k_e is the return required by the equity investors as of the date the investment is undertaken, which is 0.15 for this example;

Debt/Total capital is the proportion of interest-bearing debt in the firm's capital structure if the investment is undertaken;

Equity/Total capital is the proportion of equity used to finance the firm if the project is undertaken; and

T is the corporate income tax rate, which is assumed to be 0.46.

For this example, the WACC is

$$\begin{aligned} k_a &= \left(\frac{40{,}000}{100{,}000}\right)(0.10)\,(1-0.46) + \left(\frac{60{,}000}{100{,}000}\right)(0.15) \\ &= (0.40) \cdot (0.10) \cdot (0.54) + (0.60) \cdot (0.15) \\ &= 0.1116, \end{aligned}$$

or 11.16 percent.

The correct application of WACC requires that the proportions of debt and equity be the proportions of these capital sources for the *firm as a whole* as it would be financed if the project is adopted. It would be incorrect to use only the proportions that apply for the project financing rather than the whole firm. In this example it is assumed that the project *is* the whole firm so the 40 percent–60 percent mix is appropriate. On the other hand, if the project was part of a larger firm, it would be the firm's capital proportions that are relevant, not just the project's. Another important point about applying WACC is that the proportions of capital should be based on market values, not book values. That is, the amounts of debt and equity used in calculating the proportions should be market values at the time the project is undertaken.

The cash flow that should be matched to the WACC method for calculating the discount rate is the cash flow available to be distributed to those who contributed capital to finance the project. Since both lenders and equity investors contributed capital, this should be the after-tax cash flow available to be distributed to both lenders and equity investors, where, for purposes of cash flow calculation, the tax effects of interest are ignored because they will be taken into account in the calculation of k_a. For example, consider the modified income statement for the first period of the project:

Total revenue	$58,000.00
− Operating costs	37,698.33
EBDIT	20,301.67
− Depreciation	6,666.67
EBIT	13,635.00
− Interest	n/a
Taxable income	13,635.00
Income tax	6,272.10
Net income	$ 7,362.90

If it is assumed that total revenue represents an actual cash inflow to the firm and operating costs are all cash expenses, then EBDIT can be regarded as the amount of cash flow generated by the project that is available to be distributed to three different groups: the government (taxes), the lenders (principal and interest), and the owners. The part of this cash flow that is available after taxes to the lenders and owners is the portion that is relevant as cash flow to be discounted at the weighted average cost of capital. This cash flow is

$$\begin{aligned} \textit{Operating cash flow} &= \textit{EBDIT} - \textit{Tax} \\ &= \textit{EBDIT} - T \cdot [\textit{EBDIT} \\ &\quad - \textit{Depreciation}] \\ &= \textit{EBDIT} \cdot (1-T) + T \cdot \textit{Depreciation}, \\ &= \$20{,}301.67 \cdot (1-0.46) \\ &\quad + 0.46 \cdot (\$6{,}666.67) \\ &= \$14{,}029.57. \end{aligned} \tag{6.73}$$

Given the assumption that EBDIT will be the same amount every year over the 15-year life of the project, the operating cash flow available to both lenders and owners is also the same amount every period, $14,029.57.

The method shown above for calculating the cash flow does not show either interest or principal payments on the debt as deductions from the basic cash flow. Nor does it consider the tax deductibility of interest payments. The reason for this apparent omission is that by using the interest rate on the debt on an after-tax basis, $k_d \cdot (1\text{-}T)$, to calculate the WACC, the question being asked is whether the cash flows will be large enough to cover these costs.

For applying WACC, the cost of the project is the present value of the net cost of acquiring the relevant assets, regardless of how the purchase is financed. In this case, the cost is the total outlay of $100,000. It does not matter that part of the $100,000 is financed with debt and another part with equity; what matters is simply that the assets are purchased for $100,000.

For this very simple investment project we can easily evaluate its acceptability by calculating NPV. Using the weighted average cost of capital, $k_a = 0.1116$, to discount this overall cash flow of $14,029.57 that is received annually for 15 years, with a cost of $100,000, the net present value is

$$\text{NPV} = \$14{,}029.57\ (7.1278) - \$100{,}000 = 0,$$

where 7.1278 is the present value of an annuity of $1 per year for 15 years at a discount rate of 11.16 percent. Exhibit 6.13 also shows the calculation of NPV with each period's cash flow. With NPV of 0, the project has an overall return of 11.16 percent—high enough to give lenders their 10 percent return on investment (ROI), the equity investors their required 15 percent ROI, and return each group their original principal investment.

It is important to note that one must take care to be consistent in the method for calculating project cost, project cash flows, and the discount rate. In this example, the focus was placed on weighted average cost of capital so the cost, cash flows, and discount rate were all defined so they would be consistent for this approach. To understand the relevance of this comment, the WACC approach should be compared to what will be referred to as the equity approach.

The Equity Approach. The equity approach to investment evaluation asks whether the cash flows generated by the investment project are sufficient to return the original principal amount invested by the equity investor and provide the return on investment required by the equity investor.

In the context of NPV, the cost of the investment is the amount of capital contributed by the equity investor, the cash flow is that which is available to be distributed to the equity investor, and the discount rate is the minimum expected return required by the investor as compensation for the risk of the investment. Thus, NPV to equity is the present value of the cash flows available to stockholders (equity) less the cost incurred by them, discounted at the stockholders' required return.

Using the same example that was used for the WACC approach, but now focusing on equity, the income statement for period 1 would be as follows:

Total revenue	$58,000.00
− Operating costs	37,698.00
EBDIT	20,301.67
− Depreciation	6,666.67
EBIT	13,635.00
− Interest	4,000.00
Taxable income	9,635.00
− Income tax	4,432.10
Net income	$ 5,202.90

Now, the 10 percent interest on the $40,000 debt that is outstanding is shown in the income statement, and the interest and principal on the debt both are taken into account in calculating the cash flow. The cash flow available to equity can be calculated for period 1 as

Net income	$ 5,202.90
+ Depreciation	+ 6,666.67
− Debt principal payment	− 1,258.94
Equity cash flow	$10,610.63

Alternatively, this can be calculated as

EBDIT	$20,301.67
− Tax	− 4,432.10
− Interest	− 4,000.00
− Debt principal payment	− 1,258.94
Equity cash flow	$10,610.63

The cash flow and NPV calculations are shown in Exhibit 6.13. Note that the equity cash flow declines each year of the project even though EBDIT is assumed to be constant. This is because the portion of the debt service payment that is interest is declining each period as the outstanding principal is reduced, and consequently, the income tax bill increases, reducing the after-tax cash flow to equity.

With the cash flow calculated in this manner, the present value of the equity cash flow is approximately $60,000 when the discount rate is $k_e = 0.15$, and the net present value of the investment project is approximately zero. This means the cash flows are just high enough to yield the investor a 15 percent return on investment and to return the original invested principal of $60,000 to the equity investor.[8]

The major point is that one could use either the WACC approach or the equity approach to evaluating the investment. Each approach can be applied in a valid manner, but the cost, cash flows, and discount rate used must be defined consistently. The WACC approach to NPV is the method that is taught in

[8]In this example the NPV to equity differs slightly from zero first, because of rounding errors, and second because of a slight distortion due to a changing mix of debt and equity.

EXHIBIT 6.13 Net Present Value of Proposed Investment Using WACC and Equity Approaches

	Year						
	1	*2*	*3*	*4*	*5*	*6*	*7*
Weighted average cost of capital approach							
EBDIT × (1 − Tax rate)	$10,962.90	$10,962.90	$10,962.90	$10,962.90	$10,962.90	$10,962.90	$10,962.90
plus							
Depreciation × Tax rate	$ 3,066.67	$ 3,066.67	$ 3,066.67	$ 3,066.67	$ 3,066.67	$ 3,066.67	$ 3,066.67
equals							
Over all cash flow	$14,029.57	$14,029.57	$14,029.57	$14,029.57	$14,029.57	$14,029.57	$14,029.57
times							
WACC discount factor	0.8996	0.8093	0.7280	0.6549	0.5892	0.5300	0.4768
equals							
Present value	$12,621.06	$11,354.13	$10,213.53	$ 9,187.97	$ 8,266.22	$ 7,435.67	$ 6,689.30
Present value of cash flows	$100,000						
less							
Cost of project	− 100,000						
equals							
Net present value (over all)	0						
Equity approach							
EBDIT	$20,301.67	$20,301.67	$20,301.67	$20,301.67	$20,301.67	$20,301.67	$20,301.67
Depreciation	$ 6,666.67	$ 6,666.67	$ 6,666.67	$ 6,666.67	$ 6,666.67	$ 6,666.67	$ 6,666.67
EBIT	$13,635.00	$13,635.00	$13,635.00	$13,635.00	$13,635.00	$13,635.00	$13,635.00
Interest	$ 4,000.00	$ 3,874.11	$ 3,735.62	$ 3,583.29	$ 3,415.73	$ 3,231.41	$ 3,028.65
Taxable income	$ 9,635.00	$ 9,760.89	$ 9,899.38	$10,051.71	$10,219.27	$10,403.59	$10,606.35
Tax	$ 4,432.10	$ 4,490.01	$ 4,553.71	$ 4,623.79	$ 4,700.86	$ 4,785.65	$ 4,878.92
Net income	$ 5,202.90	$ 5,270.88	$ 5,345.67	$ 5,427.92	$ 5,518.41	$ 5,617.94	$ 5,727.43
plus							
Depreciation	$ 6,666.67	$ 6,666.67	$ 6,666.67	$ 6,666.67	$ 6,666.67	$ 6,666.67	$ 6,666.67
minus							
Debt principal	$ 1,258.94	$ 1,384.83	$ 1,523.32	$ 1,675.65	$ 1,843.21	$ 2,027.53	$ 2,230.29
equals							
Equity cash flow	$10,610.63	$10,552.72	$10,489.02	$10,418.94	$10,341.87	$10,257.08	$10,163.81
times							
Equity discount factor	0.86957	0.75614	0.65752	0.57175	0.49718	0.43233	0.37594
equals							
Present value	$ 9,226.69	$ 7,979.33	$ 6,896.74	$ 5,957.03	$ 5,141.77	$ 4,434.44	$ 3,820.98
Present value of cash flow	$59.811						
less							
Equity cost of project	− 60,000						
equals							
Net present value (equity)	− 189						

Year							
8	*9*	*10*	*11*	*12*	*13*	*14*	*15*
$10,962.90	$10,962.90	$10,962.90	$10,962.90	$10,962.90	$10,962.90	$10,962.90	$10,962.90
$ 3,066.67	$ 3,066.67	$ 3,066.67	$ 3,066.67	$ 3,066.67	$ 3,066.67	$ 3,066.67	$ 3,066.67
$14,029.57	$14,029.57	$14,029.57	$14,029.57	$14,029.57	$14,029.57	$14,029.57	$14,029.57
0.4290	0.3859	0.3471	0.3123	0.2809	0.2527	0.2274	0.2045
$ 6,018.69	$ 5,414.01	$ 4,869.66	$ 4,381.43	$ 3,940.91	$ 3,545.27	$ 3,190.32	$ 2,869.05
$20,301.67	$20,301.67	$20,301.67	$20,301.67	$20,301.67	$20,301.67	$20,301.67	$20,301.67
$ 6,666.67	$ 6,666.67	$ 6,666.67	$ 6,666.67	$ 6,666.67	$ 6,666.67	$ 6,666.67	$ 6,666.67
$13,635.00	$13,635.00	$13,635.00	$13,635.00	$13,635.00	$13,635.00	$13,635.00	$13,635.00
$ 2,805.62	$ 2,560.29	$ 2,290.43	$ 1,993.57	$ 1,667.04	$ 1,307.85	$ 912.74	$ 478.12
$10,829.38	$11,074.71	$11,344.57	$11,641.43	$11,967.96	$12,327.15	$12,722.26	$13,156.88
$ 4,981.51	$ 5,094.37	$ 5,218.50	$ 5,355.06	$ 5,505.26	$ 5,670.49	$ 5,852.24	$ 6,052.16
$ 5,847.87	$ 5,980.34	$ 6,126.07	$ 6,286.37	$ 6,462.70	$ 6,656.66	$ 6,870.02	$ 7,104.72
$ 6,666.67	$ 6,666.67	$ 6,666.67	$ 6,666.67	$ 6,666.67	$ 6,666.67	$ 6,666.67	$ 6,666.67
$ 2,453.32	$ 2,638.65	$ 2,968.51	$ 3,265.37	$ 3,591.90	$ 3,951.09	$ 4,346.20	$ 4,780.82
$10,061.22	$10,008.36	$ 9,824.23	$ 9,687.67	$ 9,537.47	$ 9,372.24	$ 9,190.49	$ 8,990.57
0.3269	0.28426	0.24718	0.21494	0.18691	0.16253	0.14133	0.12289
$ 3,289.01	$ 2,844.08	$ 2,428.35	$ 2,082.27	$ 1,782.65	$ 1,523.27	$ 1,298.89	$ 1,104.85

most standard finance texts, and it is recommended that the reader use it rather than the equity approach. Both are discussed here to help the reader understand the differences in approach. Generally speaking, the nonexpert would tend to make fewer mistakes in using the WACC approach for investment evaluation. Just be very careful how cash flows are calculated.

Working Capital in the Investment Evaluation. Regardless of which approach to investment evaluation is used, it is especially important to use the correct method for calculating the various factors that enter the NPV calculation. One aspect that is frequently handled improperly is the determination of the cost of the project for purposes of calculating NPV. A major source of confusion in this determination is the treatment of the investment in working capital.

The cost of adopting an investment project should include not just the direct costs of purchasing and installing the asset, but also any incremental investment in working capital necessary to make the investment operational. If the purchase and operation of a new plant requires that the plant be provided with an initial inventory of raw materials or an initial balance of cash or other current assets, the funds committed to these current assets must be considered part of the cost of the investment. In addition, the standard approach requires that the disinvestment in working capital when the project ends should be considered as a recovery of capital (a cash inflow to the firm analogous to salvage value of equipment).

To understand this, consider Exhibit 6.14, which shows the sequence of inventory purchases and subsequent sales of goods. Materials purchased for $100 at t_0 are sold for $150 at t_1, yielding EBIT of $50. Then in each period, goods are purchased at the beginning of the period for sale at the end of the period.

If the calculation of cash flow is based on EBDIT as in Expression (6.73), where cost of goods sold (CGS) is treated as a cash outflow, there is a mismatching of costs and cash payments. That is, in period 1 the goods sold at t_1 were actually purchased at t_0, and there is not actually a cash outflow at t_1 associated with this cost of goods sold. The cash outflow at t_1 covers the purchase of new inventory to be sold at t_2. Finally, at

EXHIBIT 6.14 Inventory Investment and Disinvestment in Capital Budgeting

1	Time	0	1	2	3
2	Materials purchased	100	100	100	0
3	Inventory sold		100	100	100
4	Sales		150	150	150
5	Cost of goods sold		−100	100	100
6	EBDIT		50	50	50
7	Sales		150	150	150
8	Cash paid for purchases	100	100	100	0
9	Net cash flow	(100)	50	50	150

t_3, when we show EBDIT of \$50 resulting from sales of \$150 and CGS of \$100, there is no cash outflow at all because no additional inventory is purchased. In this case, EBDIT = \$50 understates the net cash flow because it overstates the cash outflow by assuming that CGS involves a cash outflow. The actual cash outflow is shown as net cash inflow on line 9 of the exhibit.

The suggestion to treat an increase in inventory as part of the investment and a decrease in inventory as disinvestment (a cash inflow) is intended to correct these distortions to provide a proper estimate of cash flows from the investment project. For this example, the initial purchase of inventory is part of the initial cost of the investment project; the operating cash inflow will be based on EBDIT = \$50 for t_1, t_2, and t_3; and then at t_3 we assume we recover the investment in inventory of \$100. Thus, for t_3, we show \$100 inflow from inventory disinvestment, plus the \$50 EBDIT, for a total inflow of \$150, as confirmed in line 9.

This reasoning applies to any working capital account as it relates to evaluating an investment. Any increases in a working capital account (or any asset, for that matter) should be considered as an investment cost, and any decrease in the working capital account could be treated as a return of investment, and thus a cash inflow analogous to salvage value.

The foregoing discussion of methods for evaluating investments was intended to provide the general framework. Now, an extended example will be presented that will demonstrate some of the important aspects of modeling a capital budgeting problem.

A Case Study: Evaluating an Investment for Plastico Inc. ***The Problem:*** Plastico Inc. manufactures a wide variety of plastic parts and components on contract for other companies. Its products currently range from plastic toys to plastic components for automobiles and aircraft. The company is considering a project that would involve supplying the plastic body for a new sports car that will be marketed by Ford Motor Company. To supply the bodies in the quantity and quality required by Ford would require that Plastico construct a brand-new manufacturing plant. The land adjacent to their existing facilities would have to be purchased, a new building constructed, and new machinery, moulds, and equipment would have to be purchased and installed. These new facilities would be quite expensive for this small company, requiring an investment of almost $3 million spread over four years. There is little doubt that this contract with Ford would increase their share of market and their sales. The profitability of the project and its effect on the value of the company still need to be determined, however.

The Objective. The officers of Plastico agree that they would want to adopt the project only if it will make the value of the company greater; this value is reflected by the market price of the common stock, which is traded over-the-counter. George Simpson, the vice president for finance, says that even though the link between their decision to adopt the project and their main objective is vague and intangible, the firm can use as its decision criterion the net present value of the project, and that it should accept this project only if its net present value is positive. Positive net present value serves as an operational goal that, if attained, will help the firm reach its main objective of value maximization.

In calculating net present value, as a first approximation, the firm's current cost of equity capital will be used as the discount rate. Subsequently, the use of debt financing will be considered, and the weighted average cost of capital will be used as the discount rate. Current estimates indicate that Plastico's cost of equity capital is about 15.5 percent, based on its present capital structure, which is all equity.

The Constraints. The main constraints that are relevant for evaluating this project are the economic conditions and the technological relationships that limit the firm's ability to attain its objectives. The relevant economic conditions are those in its product market, the requirements in its contract to sell its product, and the costs of its factors of production.

The product market and the Ford contract determine the price of the product and the number of units that can be sold, and these factors can be considered as constraints that limit the firm. On the basis of the features of the contract for the first part of the planning horizon, and the forecast of the future of the market for moulded plastic auto bodies, the financial staff of Plastico estimates that the sales of the output will start out at \$2 million in 1988, rise to \$5 million in 1989, and then stabilize at \$6 million per year from 1989 through 1997.

The firm's production technology and conditions in the markets for labor and materials serve as constraints on production and costs. Estimates of the level of production, the costs of labor and materials, and the technical specification of the new plant lead to a forecast for incremental operating costs of \$1.65 million and \$4.26 million in 1988 and 1989, respectively, and \$5.13 million from 1990 through 1997.

The Planning Horizon. The officers of Plastico feel that the market for plastic auto bodies cannot be relied on to last for much more than 10 years, and that they cannot forecast beyond a 10-year horizon. Furthermore, plant and machinery of the required type tends to decline in productivity and value over about 10 years. Consequently, for purposes of evaluating the project, it is decided that it will be evaluated with a 10-year planning horizon, with sales assumed to begin in 1988 and to terminate at the end of 1997.

It is felt that annual data will provide sufficient detail for evaluation, so the planning horizon is broken up into 10 subperiods of one year each. The capital investment in the project is assumed to begin in early 1987 and continue throughout the

EXHIBIT 6.15 Expressions for Calculating Net Present Value

Project investment		
1.	*Gross investment$_t$*	= *Land purchase price$_t$ + Building purchase price$_t$ + Equipment purchase price$_t$*
2.	*Investment tax credit$_t$*	= 0.10 · *Equipment purchase price$_t$*
3.	*Fixed asset investment$_t$*	= *Gross Investment$_t$ − Investment tax credit$_t$*
4.	*Increase in cash balance$_t$*	= 0.05 · *Incremental revenue$_t$*
5.	*Increase in receivables$_t$*	= 0.14 · *Incremental revenue$_t$*
6.	*Increase in inventory$_t$*	= 0.23 · *Incremental revenue$_t$*
7.	*Investment in working capital$_t$*	= *Increase in cash balance$_t$ + Increase in receivables$_t$ + Increase in inventory$_t$*
8.	*Investment in net working capital$_t$*	= *Investment in working capital$_t$ − Increase in payables$_t$*
9.	*Net investment$_t$*	= *Fixed asset investment$_t$ + Investment in net working capital$_t$*
10.	*Present value of net investment*	$= \sum_{t=1}^{h=10} \text{Net investment}_t\,[1/(1+k)^t]$
Operating cash flows		
11.	*Incremental revenue$_t$*	= *Total revenue with project$_t$ − Total revenue without project$_t$*
12.	*Incremental operating costs$_t$*	= *Operating costs with project$_t$ − Operating costs without project$_t$*
13.	*Incremental EBDIT$_t$*	= *Incremental revenue$_t$ − Incremental operating costs$_t$*
14.	*Incremental depreciation expense$_t$*	= *Depreciation with project$_t$ − Depreciation without project$_t$*
15.	*Incremental operating cash flow$_t$*	= *Incremental EBDIT$_t$* · $(1-T)$ + *Incremental depreciation expense$_t$* · (T)
16.	*Present value of incremental operating cash flow*	$= \sum_{t=1}^{h=10} \text{Incremental operating cash flow}_t\,[1/(1+k)^t]$
Cash recovery at project end		
17.	*Land sale price$_h$*	= *Land purchase price* · (1 + *Land annual rate of appreciation*)^{10}
18.	*Building sale price$_h$*	= *Building purchase price* · (1 + *Building annual rate of appreciation*)^{10}

19. *$Equipment\ sale\ price_h$ = $Equipment\ purchase\ price \cdot (1 + Equipment\ annual\ rate\ of\ appreciation)^8$

20. $Land\ sale\ proceeds_h$ = $Land\ sale\ price - (0.28 \cdot Land\ sale\ price - Land\ purchase\ price)$

21. $Building\ tax_h$ = $0.28 \cdot (Building\ sale\ price - Building\ purchase\ price + Building\ accumulated\ depreciation)$

22. $Equipment\ tax_h$ = $0.28 \cdot (Equipment\ sale\ price - Equipment\ purchase\ price + Equipment\ accumulated\ depreciation)$

23. $Building\ sale\ proceeds_h$ = $Building\ sale\ price - Building\ tax$

24. $Equipment\ sale\ proceeds_h$ = $Equipment\ sale\ price - Equipment\ tax$

25. $Working\ capital\ recovery_h$ = $Project\ cash_h + Project\ receivables_h + Project\ inventory_h$

26. $Fixed\ asset\ proceeds_h$ = $Land\ sales\ proceeds_h + Building\ sale\ proceeds_h + Equipment\ sale\ proceeds_h$

27. $Project\ cash\ recovery_h$ = $Working\ capital\ recovery_h + Fixed\ asset\ proceeds_h$

Project evaluation

28. *Present value of project* = $Present\ value\ of\ incremental\ operating\ cash\ flow + Project\ cash\ recovery \cdot [1/(1+k)^h]$

29. *Net present value* = $Present\ value\ of\ project - Present\ value\ of\ net\ investment$

---

*Note: Not all the details of equipment transactions are shown because equipment is purchased at different dates over five years.

year. As an approximation for discounting, it is assumed that these expenditures are incurred in the middle of the first year. All subsequent expenditures and income are assumed to occur at the end of each year. It is assumed the plant and equipment are sold for salvage at the end of 1997.

The Model and the Input. The assumptions, forecasts, and structural input that were used to develop the model are shown by Exhibit 6.15, that shows the equations used to generate output that will be useful for evaluating the project. The details of the model and additional assumptions and forecasts are explained below.

Project investment. For the purpose of evaluating the acceptability of the project, the cost of the project should be the present value of all the incremental outlays necessary to complete the project and make it operational. The outlays that typically would be included would be expenditures for the purchase of plant and equipment and any investment necessary to increase the balances of working capital, net of any spontaneous increase in current liabilities. Exhibit 6.16 summarizes these investment outlays for the Plastico project. The *gross investment* in 1987 necessary to construct the new plant is $1,228,000, consisting of $500,000 for the land, $448,000 for the building, and $280,000 for new equipment. The equipment purchase qualifies for a 10 percent investment tax credit (ITC), which will reduce the taxes paid in 1987 by $28,000, so the outlay for fixed assets net of this tax reduction is $1,200,000.

The project will require that the stock of equipment be increased each year for the five-year period 1987–91. These equipment purchases each year qualify for a 10 percent ITC, which offsets the outlay for the equipment, so the net outlays for *fixed asset investment* are $1,200,000, $110,000, $115,000, $120,000, and $125,000 for years 1987–91, respectively.

The operations of the new plant and the expanding sales of the product will require that the balances in working capital (current assets) be increased. The *increase in working capital* is an investment just as is the increase in fixed assets, and it constitutes part of the investment required to make the project operational. The required investments in working capital are $840,000, $1,260,000, and $420,000 in 1988, 1989, and 1990, re-

EXHIBIT 6.16 Plastico Inc.: Investment Outlays for Proposed Project ($000)

	1987	*1988*	*1989*	*1990*	*1991*	*1992*
Project investment outlays						
Land	$ 500.00	—	—	—	—	—
Building	448.00	—	—	—	—	—
Equipment	280.00	$122.23	$127.78	$133.34	$138.89	—
Gross investment	1,228.00	122.23	127.78	133.34	138.89	$0.00
Investment tax credit	28.00	12.22	12.78	13.33	13.89	0.00
Fixed asset investment	1,200.00	110.01	115.00	120.01	125.00	0.00
Increase in cash balance	0.00	100.00	150.00	50.00	0.00	0.00
Increase in receivables	0.00	280.00	420.00	140.00	—	—
Increase in inventory	0.00	460.00	690.00	230.00	—	—
Investment in working capital	0.00	840.00	1,260.00	420.00	0.00	0.00
Less: Increase in payables	50.00	340.00	510.00	170.00	0.00	0.00
Investment in net working capital	−50.00	500.00	750.00	250.00	0.00	0.00
Net investment	1,150.00	610.00	865.00	370.01	125.00	0.00

spectively. The amounts are based on the forecast that the required increases in cash, receivables, and inventory will be in direct proportion to any increase in total revenue associated with the project, as shown by Expressions (4), (5), and (6) in Exhibit 6.15. Some of the increase in working capital will be financed spontaneously, however, as trade payables increase with the level of operations. This spontaneous increase in payables offsets some of the required increase in current assets, so that the required increases in net working capital that needs to be financed from other sources are $500,000, $750,000, and $250,000 for 1988, 1989, and 1990, respectively. This figure is negative for 1987 because there is a net increase in payables in 1987 and no increase in working capital, so there is a net generation of funds of $50,000.

When the required fixed asset investment is combined with the increase in net working capital, the net investment for the project that will require funding will total $1,150,000, $610,000, $865,000, $370,000, and $125,000 for the years 1987–91. These net investment outlays must be discounted to account for the fact that they are incurred at different times over several years.

Operating cash flows. One proper method for determining the operating cash flow for the project is to calculate the *incremental* cash flow according to

$$\textit{Operating cash flow} = \textit{EBDIT} \cdot (1-T) + \textit{Depreciation expense} \cdot T,$$

where the relevant figure is the *change* in this cash flow as a result of undertaking the investment. For example, for this project consider a partial income statement for 1988 for Plastico as it would appear with and without the project, as shown in Exhibit 6.17.

From Exhibit 6.17, assume that both *Total revenue* and *Operating costs* are cash income and cash expenses, so that *EBDIT* represents a cash inflow to the firm. After paying taxes, the cash flow that is available to be distributed to the stockholders is

EXHIBIT 6.17 Income and Cash Flow, 1988—Partial Income Statement ($000)

	Without Project	*With Project*	*Increment*
Total revenue	$3,000.0	$5,000.0	$2,000.0
Operating costs	2,700.0	4,350.0	1,650.0
EBDIT	300.0	650.0	350.0
Depreciation expense	64.0	126.3	62.3
EBIT	236.0	523.7	287.7
− Interest*	0	0	0
Taxable income	236.0	523.7	287.7
− Income tax	108.6	240.9	132.3
Net income	127.4	282.8	155.4

Incremental Cash Flow

	Without Project	*With Project*	*Increment*
EBDIT	$300.0	$650.0	$350.0
− Income tax	108.6	240.9	132.3
Cash flow	191.4	409.1	217.7

*Note: Interest expense is ignored in this context because interest and its tax effects will be considered in the calculation of the weighted average cost of capital.

\$191,400 without the project, and \$409,100 with the project, for an increase in cash flow of \$217,700 as a result of the project. This incremental cash flow is more directly calculated:

$$\begin{aligned} \textit{Incremental cash flow} &= \Delta\ \textit{EBDIT} \cdot (1-T) + \\ &\quad \Delta\ \textit{Depreciation expense} \cdot T \\ &= \$350 \cdot (1-0.46) \ + \ \$62.3 \cdot (0.46) \\ &= \$189 \qquad\qquad\quad + \ \$28.7 \\ &= \$217.7. \end{aligned}$$

Exhibit 6.18 shows the complete calculation of the incremental cash flows for years 1987–90, and the incremental cash flows for the remaining years are summarized in Exhibit 6.21 (where *depreciation expense* is based on ACRS as shown in Exhibit 6.19).

Other cash flows. In addition to the operating cash flows, there are other flows that need to be considered. The major ones are the proceeds from selling any assets at the end of the project (salvage value) and from the recovery of investment in working capital.

EXHIBIT 6.18 Plastico Inc.: Incremental Operating Cash Flow, 1987–1997 (\$000)

	1987		*1988*		*1989*		*1990*	
a. Total revenue with project	\$3,000		\$5,000		\$8,000		\$9,000	
b. Total revenue without project	3,000		3,000		3,000		3,000	
c. Incremental revenue		0		\$2,000		\$5,000		\$6,000
d. Operating expenses with project	2,700		4,350		6,960		7,830	
e. Operating expenses without project	2,700		2,700		2,700		2,700	
f. Incremental operating expenses		0		1,650		4,260		5,130
g. Incremental EBDIT		0		350		740		870
h. Incremental EBDIT • (1 − *T*)		0		189		399.6		469.8
i. Incremental Depreciation Expense	0		62.3		120.7		139.9	
j. Incremental depreciation expense • (1 − *T*)		0		28.7		55.5		64.4
k. Incremental operating cash flow		0		217.7		455.1		534.2

EXHIBIT 6.19 Plastico Inc.: Schedule of Depreciation on Building and Equipment ($000)*

Depreciable Basis	*Year of Acquisition*				
	1987	*1988*	*1989*	*1990*	*1991*
Building purchase	448.0	—	—	—	—
Depreciable basis—building	448.0	—	—	—	—
Equipment purchase	280.0	122.23	127.78	133.34	138.89
− (0.50) • ITC:	14.0	6.11	6.39	6.67	6.94
Depreciable basis—equipment	266.0	116.12	121.39	126.67	131.95

Depreciation Expense	*ACRS Depreciation on Equipment Acquired in:*					*Total Equipment Depreciation*	*Building Depreciation*	*Total Depreciation Expense*
	1987	*1988*	*1989*	*1990*	*1991*			
Year depreciation taken								
1988	$39.9	—	—	—	—	$ 39.9	$22.4	$ 62.3
1989	58.52	$17.42	—	—	—	75.94	44.8	120.74
1990	55.86	25.55	$18.21	—	—	99.64	40.32	139.94
1991	55.86	24.39	26.71	$19.0	—	125.96	35.89	161.80
1992	55.86	24.39	25.49	27.87	$19.79	153.40	31.36	184.76
1993	—	24.39	25.49	26.60	29.3	105.78	31.36	137.14
1994	—	—	25.49	26.60	27.71	79.8	26.88	106.68
1995	—	—	—	26.60	27.71	54.31	26.88	81.19
1996	—	—	—	—	27.71	27.71	26.88	54.59
1997	—	—	—	—	—	0	26.88	26.88

*Note: Using ACRS schedule 15 years for building, 5 years for equipment.

EXHIBIT 6.20 Plastico Inc.: Proceeds from Sale of Assets in 1997 ($000)

	Land		*Building*		*Equipment*		*Total*
Annual rate of price appreciation	+5%		−2%		−15%		—
Expected sale price, 1997		$815.		$366.		$160.	—
Purchase price	$500.		$448.		$802.2		—
Accumulated depreciation	0		313.6		762.4		—
Book value, 1997	500.		134.4		39.8		—
Gain	315.		231.6		120.2		—
Tax @ 28%		88.2		64.8		33.6	—
Net proceeds from sale		$726.8		$301.2		$126.4	$1,154.4

Exhibit 6.20 shows the net proceeds from the sale of the plant and equipment, totaling $1,154,400, at the end of 1997, the end of the 10-year life of the project. It is assumed the values of these assets change at the annual rates indicated, starting at the beginning of 1988, when the project begins operation. The land appreciates in value, but both the building and equipment decline in value from physical deterioration during their use.

The working capital balances that are released at the end of the project consist of $300,000 in cash balances that were built up over the life of the project, receivable balances of $840,000, and inventory amounting to $1,380,000, for a total of $2,520,000. Any inflation or appreciation is already built into these amounts because the incremental investment in inventory was assumed to be stated in nominal dollars. We assume that the firm follows a FIFO accounting policy, so the inventory balances are stated in terms of their market values; if the rate of price change is significant and the firm uses LIFO inventory accounting, however, the liquidation value of the stock of inventory remaining at the end of the project will be understated.

Evaluation of Project. The data representing net investment, operating cash flows, and salvage are summarized in Exhibit 6.21, which shows the calculation of the present value of the cash flows and the net present value. Based on the discount rate of 15.5 percent, the cash inflows generated by the project are worth $2,608,100, and the present value of net investment is $2,500,200, so the value of the cash inflows exceeds the cost by $107,900, which is the net present value of the project.

If the project had had an NPV equal to zero, it would have been just marginally acceptable in the sense that the rate of return earned on the investment would just equal the required return of 15.5 percent. With a positive NPV, however, the return earned exceeds the required return, and the NPV of $107,900 represents the increase in the value of stockholders' equity that will result from adoption of the project.

One question that would arise would be whether the firm will be better off with a financing arrangement that is different from the proposed all-equity financing alternative. This question will be considered in greater detail in the next section of the chapter, which deals with financing. However, one specific financing alternative will be examined here to demonstrate the use of weighted average cost of capital in capital budgeting, and to show how the financing decision may interact with the investment decision.

Assume that the project itself will be financed entirely with debt; that is, sufficient funds are borrowed to meet all the external financing needs. Without going into the specific details of the financing at this time, assume that this will cause 39 percent of Plastico's total capital to be debt, and 61 percent to be equity. The weighted average cost of capital will be

$$\begin{aligned} k_a &= \left(\frac{Debt}{Total\ capital}\right) k_d\,(1-T) + \left(\frac{Equity}{Total\ capital}\right) k_e \\ &= (0.39)\,(0.11)(1-0.46) + (0.61)(0.178) \\ &= 0.132. \end{aligned}$$

This is based on the forecast that the borrowing cost will be $k_d = 0.11$, and the cost of equity will be $k_e = 0.178$. The reason the cost of equity is higher than the 15.5 percent used in the all-equity case is that the use of debt financing increases the risk to the stockholders, and in response, they require a higher rate of return on their investment to compensate them for taking the extra risk.

The application of weighted average cost of capital, when k_a is calculated as done above, requires that the cash flows that are to be discounted are calculated according to the same method we previously used. That is, the operating cash flows are calculated according to

$$Operating\ cash\ flow = EBDIT \cdot (1 - T) + Depreciation \cdot T.$$

EXHIBIT 6.21 Plastico Inc.: Calculation of Net Present Value ($000)

Year	Periods Discounted	Net Investment	Operating Cash Flow	Salvage and Working Capital Recovery	Present Value Factor @15.5%	Present Value of Net Investment	Present Value of Project Cash Flows
1987	1/2	$1,150.0	—	—	0.9325	$1,072.4	—
1988	1	610.0	$217.7	—	0.8696	530.5	$189.3
1989	2	865.0	455.1	—	0.7561	654.0	344.1
1990	3	370.0	534.2	—	0.6575	243.3	351.2
1991	4	—	544.2	—	0.5718	—	311.2
1992	5	—	554.8	—	0.4972	—	275.8
1993	6	—	532.9	—	0.4323	—	230.4
1994	7	—	518.9	—	0.3759	—	195.0
1995	8	—	507.1	—	0.3269	—	165.8
1996	9	—	494.9	—	0.2843	—	140.7
1997	10	—	482.2	$1,154.4	0.2472	—	404.6
Present value of project:							$2,608.1
Present value of net investment:						$2,500.2	
Net present value of project:							+ 107.9

Thus, we use the same cash flows as shown in Exhibit 6.21, but discount them at $k_a = 0.132$. Applying this discount rate to the net investment, operating cash flows, and salvage, we get:

Present value of project	$2,840,360
Present value of net investment	2,549,900
Net present value	$ 290,460.

Based on this analysis, debt financing will result in the project's having a higher net present value than the equity financing alternative. The reason is that by using debt, a source of funds with lower cost has been substituted for a higher cost source, and the rate of return and the cash flow required to meet the expectations of the contributors of capital are lower than in the all-equity case. The cash flow in excess of the minimum necessary to satisfy both the lenders and equity investors accrues to the stockholders, and the present value of this excess cash flow represents the net present value. Thus, the positive net present value approximates the addition to the value of equity that will result from adoption of the project. Because the NPV is greater with the use of debt financing, a greater amount is added to stockholders' value by the project with debt financing, than when it is financed entirely with equity.

Accrual Accounting and Investment Evaluation. In addition to evaluating the investment with a standard criterion like net present value, management will want to assess the effect of the investment on the financial position of the firm as a whole. In some cases an investment project that is attractive when evaluated in isolation with the NPV criterion will have undesirable effects on other aspects of the firm. Management will want to know how the investment will affect the firm's sales, operating costs, earnings, ability to service debt, liquidity, and equity position, among others. Furthermore, it may be important to assess how the investment affects attainment of various other goals set by management and how it fits into the broader set of policies and strategies of the firm. Thus, the effect of the investment on the firm's financial position should be explored with a simulation model of the firm as a whole.

To integrate the investment evaluation into the model of the firm, the investment model should relate to the accounting module of the firm. Investment evaluation focuses on the cash flows relating to the investment, which may differ greatly from the accounting treatment of the investment process. Management will want to evaluate both the cash flow and the accounting impacts of the investment. Consequently, both cash flow effects and accounting effects must be presented in a consistent manner.

Most of the differences between investment evaluation and the accounting model are due to the differences between cash and accrual accounting. For the analysis of the short-run effects of investment, the modeling system should reconcile cash and accrual accounting using the data describing the investment project—sales, costs, and financing. If one is considering a long planning horizon that is broken up into periods such as years, the fine distinctions between cash flows and accrual accounting are unimportant. One could generally treat the broad categories of accrual accounting as though they represent cash-based accounts. That is, for example, in the context of a five-year planning model comprised of one-year intervals, sales can be considered as though they represent cash inflows, and operating expenses as though they are cash outflows from the firm.

On the other hand, when the planning horizon is comprised of shorter periods, say days, weeks, or months, the differences between accrual accounting and cash flows may be very important. The investment planning model should reconcile accrual and cash accounting so that the investment evaluation can be focused properly on cash flow, yet the model can show financial statements consistent with the firm's accrual-based accounting system.

In explaining the overall approach to investment evaluation it was noted that the operating cash flow to be used in calculating net present value can be expressed as

$$EBDIT\,(\mathrm{I} - T) + T \cdot Depreciation. \tag{6.73}$$

This method is intended to yield the cash flow from the investment project that is available to the security holders. This expression is a simplification, however, that may overlook some of the differences between accounting income and cash flow.

In Expression (6.73), EBDIT is intended to represent cash operating income before deductions for depreciation, interest, and taxes. But EBDIT taken from a standard income statement, measured over short periods, may not really represent cash flow, and several adjustments may have to be made to calculate operating cash flow. The major adjustments to convert accrual to cash would involve sales and operating costs because we define

$$\textit{EBDIT} = \textit{Total revenue} - \textit{Operating costs}.$$

Cash collections from sales may differ from sales shown according to accrual accounting. The major factor causing accrual sales to differ from cash sales is credit sales. A credit sale is shown as accrued revenue when it occurs, yet does not represent a cash inflow, so that accrued sales may overstate the cash inflow. Conversely, as accounts receivable are repaid by customers, there is a cash inflow that is not reflected by current sales.

The cash inflow from sales would be

$$\textit{Cash receipts} = \textit{Total revenue} - \textit{Increase in receivables}_t, \tag{6.74}$$

where *Total revenue* represents the accrual, and

$$\textit{Increase in receivables}_t = \textit{Accounts receivable}_t - \textit{Accounts receivable}_{t-1}. \tag{6.75}$$

For example, if all sales are on credit, then *Accounts receivable* will increase by an amount equal to *Total revenue,* and *cash receipts* would be zero. On the other hand, if there is a net repayment of receivables, the *Increase in receivables* will be negative, so *Cash receipts* will exceed total revenue because of these collections.

Of course, there are numerous ways to express these relationships. In the foregoing example, the focus was on changes in balance sheet accounts. The same relation may be shown with the focus on income and cash flow with the following expression:

$$\textit{Cash receipts} = \textit{Total revenue} - \textit{Credit sales} + \textit{Collections of receivables}. \tag{6.76}$$

Exhibit 6.22 shows an example of the relation between accrued revenue and cash receipts. Basic data are shown in the top half of the table, where subscripts denote the month. *Accounts receivable* at the end of last month ($t - 1$) were $76,000, and they increase by $45,000 during the current month (t) because $80,000 of sales are made on credit, and $35,000 of previously accrued receivables are paid off. The bottom half of the table shows the calculation of cash receipts during the current month according to three alternative expressions. These expressions are equivalent, and which one to be used depends on the type of data available and how one wants to structure the planning model.

The operating costs for an investment project may differ from actual cash outlays, and adjustments may be necessary to express accurately the cash operating costs of the project. Most of the discrepancies between accounting costs and cash operating costs will be related to accrued expenses not yet actually paid, prepaid expenses, and noncash expenses. In general, the adjustment necessary to convert expenses, as shown with accrual accounting, to cash operating expenses would be made according to the following expression:

$$\begin{aligned} \textit{Cash expenses} = {} & \textit{Operating expenses} - \textit{Unpaid accrued expenses} \\ & + \textit{Prepayments of future expenses} \\ & - \textit{Current expense prepaid in past periods} \end{aligned} \tag{6.77}$$

An example of *Unpaid accrued expenses* would be material expense that is recognized in the current period, although the materials were purchased on credit and the payable will not be paid until a future period. The purchase of materials on credit will increase *Accounts payable*, so that one way to adjust *Operating expenses* for unpaid accrued expenses is to deduct any increase in *accounts payable:*

$$\textit{Cash expenses} = \textit{Operating expenses} - \textit{Increase in accounts payable.} \tag{6.78}$$

This adjustment would take correct account of any credit purchases. If funds are used to repay the account, *Accounts payable* will decline, *Increase in accounts payable* will be negative, so that *Cash expenses* will exceed *Operating expenses.*

An example of *Prepayment of future expenses* is insurance. The insurance premium is prepaid for the coming period. The

EXHIBIT 6.22 Reconciliation of Accrued Revenue and Cash Receipts

Cash sales	\$20,000	
Credit sales	80,000	
Total revenue		\$100,000
Accounts receivable$_{t-1}$	\$76,000	
+ Credit sales$_t$	+80,000	
− Collections of receivables$_t$	−35,000	
Accounts receivable$_t$		\$121,000

$$\textit{Cash receipts}_t = \textit{Total revenue}_t - \textit{Increase in accounts receivable}_t$$
$$\$55{,}000 = \$100{,}000 - \$45{,}000$$

or

$$\textit{Cash receipts}_t = \textit{Total revenue}_t - \textit{Credit sales}_t + \textit{Collections of receivables}_t$$
$$\$55{,}000 = \$100{,}000 - \$80{,}000 + \$35{,}000$$

or

$$\textit{Cash receipts}_t = \textit{Cash sales}_t + \textit{Collections of receivables}_t$$
$$\$55{,}000 = \$20{,}000 + \$35{,}000$$

expense is recognized month by month after the premium is paid, and as the expense is recognized, the prepaid expense account declines. From the point of view of *Cash expense,* any *increase in prepaid expenses* is a cash outflow. A decrease in *prepaid expense* occurs because the expense is recognized in the current period, using up the prepayment, so there is no current cash outflow associated with the expense. To adjust *Operating expenses* for the effects of prepayments, the *increase in prepaid expenses* should be added to *operating expenses.*

Combining the effects of unpaid accrued expenses and prepaid expenses, cash expenses are related to operating expenses according to:

$$\textit{Cash expenses} = \textit{Operating expenses} - \textit{Increase in accounts payable} + \textit{Increase in prepaid expenses}. \tag{6.79}$$

There may be some other adjustments to cover a multitude of the sins of accrual accounting.

Returning to the discussion of the cash flow for an investment project, the *Operating cash flow* corresponding to EBDIT in Expression (6.73), can be calculated by combining Expressions (6.74) and (6.79):

$$\begin{aligned} \textit{Operating cash flow} &= \textit{Cash receipts} - \textit{Cash expenses} \\ &= \textit{Total revenue} \\ &\quad - \textit{Increase in receivables} \\ &\quad - \textit{Operating expenses} \\ &\quad + \textit{Increase in accounts payable} \\ &\quad - \textit{Increase in prepaid expenses} \end{aligned} \tag{6.80}$$

Remember that this operating cash flow is not yet presumed to have considered depreciation, interest, or tax expenses.

6.4 THE FINANCING MODULE

The financing module is the set of equations that represents the financing of the assets required in future periods to meet the sales forecast in the sales-driven model. Some aspects of financing would be endogenous to the model, such as spontaneous short-term financing, while other aspects of financing would be exogenous, and would have to be specified as decisions that would be entered as input to the simulation model. Whether exogenous or endogenous, the financing that is specified in the model is an important part of the equilibrating mechanism that balances assets and liabilities and assures that sources are equal to uses of funds.

The equations of the financing module are those that determine the flow of funds to and from creditors and owners and determine the amounts in the liability accounts. The liability accounts can be classified as spontaneous or discretionary, where spontaneous means that this particular source of financing grows more or less automatically with sales and the firm's assets, whereas discretionary means that a decision must be made to utilize a particular source of financing. Any given source could be either spontaneous or discretionary, depending on the type of business and the firm's policies. Liability accounts, such as those shown in Exhibit 6.2, are usually classified as follows:

Spontaneous sources of financing
- Cash flows from operations
- Accounts payable
- Accrued expenses

Discretionary sources of financing
Notes payable
Long-term debt
Common stock
Retained earnings

The equations of the financing module will normally be specified so as to reflect the spontaneous or discretionary character of the particular accounts.

Spontaneous Financing

The spontaneous sources of financing respond to growth or changes in the level of sales or, perhaps, the growth in assets, and are determined endogenously (internally) to the model. The equations in the model should reflect the spontaneous character of the source by relating the absolute amount of the cash flow or liability, or alternatively, the change in the amount of the liability, to another variable, such as sales, to which it responds.

Cash Flows from Operations. The cash flows generated by the firm's operations are usually considered to be the first source of funds to finance expansion, and this financing is spontaneous because it tends to grow with the firm's sales.

Consider the income statement shown as Exhibit 6.23, in which net income appears as $242,000. The question at hand is what amount of funds is available to help finance the firm's investment? For most kinds of firms *Sales* represents a cash inflow, *Operating expenses* are an outflow, and their difference, shown here as *Earnings before depreciation, interest, and taxes (EBDIT)* represents an inflow to the firm, which amounts to $585,000 in this example. Below the level of EBDIT on the income statement the expenses are depreciation, interest, and taxes, which leave the net income of $242,000. Depreciation is an expense that does not require any cash outlay, however; it is simply accounting for that portion of the cost of assets purchased in the past that is attributed to the costs of generating income this period.

Consequently, if the interest and tax expenses are actually cash outlays, the net income understates the amount of cash flowing into the firm by $58,000, the amount of the depreciation

EXHIBIT 6.23

Hypothetical Corporation
Income Statement
For Year Ended December 31, 1985
($000)

Sales	$4,500
Operating expenses	3,915
Earnings before depreciation, interest, and taxes	585
Depreciation expense	58
Earnings before interest and taxes	527
Interest expense	117
Earnings before tax	410
Income tax expense	168
Net Income	$ 242

expense shown, and the cash flow from operations in the current period are:[9]

Net income	$242,000
Depreciation expense	58,000
Cash flow from operations	$300,000

or, alternatively, the cash flow is calculated as

EBDIT	$585,000
− Interest expense	−117,000
− Income tax expense	−168,000
Cash flow from operations	$300,000.

This $300,000 from operations is available to help finance the purchase of assets needed to generate the forecasted increase in sales, and can be considered as the first source of funds that are spontaneously generated.[10]

[9]To the extent that sales are not actually a cash inflow or the expenses are not cash outflows, the cash flow from operations would have to be adjusted, as was explained in the earlier discussions of investment evaluation and accrual accounting.

[10]In many discussions of internally generated (spontaneous) financing, the internally generated funds are considered to be the cash flow from operations (as defined above) less dividends paid to the stockholders. That approach certainly is not incorrect. However, dividends involve an explicit decision (they are certainly not automatic nor spontaneous), so they will be discussed subsequently, under the heading of discretionary financing.

In a sales-driven planning model that utilizes financial ratios, especially with a percent-of-sales forecasting approach, the cash flows generated by operations can be calculated as

$$\begin{matrix}\textit{Cash flow}\\ \textit{from}\\ \textit{operations}_t\end{matrix} = \textit{Sales}_t \left[\begin{matrix}\textit{Net}\\ \textit{profit}\\ \textit{margin}\end{matrix} + \frac{\textit{Depreciation}}{\textit{Sales}} \right],$$

where the *Net profit margin* is the forecast of the margin (after interest and taxes) that is forecasted for the future period *t,* and *Depreciation/Sales* is the estimate of depreciation expense as a percentage of sales that will apply in the future period. Depreciation expense does not usually vary directly with the sales level. However, for long-range planning, where depreciable assets vary with sales and with depreciation expense proportional to the level of depreciable assets, it is not misleading to assume that depreciation expense will vary with sales.

The use of a net profit margin to calculate cash flows would be less useful in cases where the method of financing will affect net income. The use of debt financing implies interest expense, and the interest expense will vary with the amount and details of the debt, so that the net profit margin will vary with the method of financing. Consequently, care must be exercised when using the profit margin approach to determine the amount of internal financing available, since it will actually depend on the amount and costs of the external financing obtained.

Accounts Payable. *Accounts payable* is a good example of spontaneous financing from current liabilities. *Accounts payable* represents credit purchases of goods and materials used in producing the output that is sold. Thus, sales drives the purchases. In turn, purchases determines the balance in *Accounts payable.* In a very aggregative model with long periods comprising the planning horizon, these relationships would be summarized in a percent-of-sales model for payables of the form

$$\textit{Accounts payable}_t = a \cdot \textit{Sales}_t, \tag{6.81}$$

where a is the parameter that represents the payable as a percentage of sales. The parameter a would be determined from observations of past data, modified by judgments regarding the future relationship.

With respect to financing growth of sales and assets, it is the increase in current liabilities that is the relevant source of spontaneous financing. For accounts payable, the spontaneous increase, denoted by ΔAP_t, corresponding to (6.81), is expressed as

$$\Delta AP_t = a\,(Sales_t - Sales_{t-1}). \qquad (6.82)$$

As with other account balances, as the planning horizon and the periods comprising the horizon are shortened, it may be appropriate to model payables in greater detail. There are many different approaches, and a good starting point for any necessary elaboration is shown by Expression B.10 of Exhibit 6.2B as

$$\begin{aligned} Accounts\ payable_t = {} & Accounts\ payable_{t-1} \\ & - Payments\ on\ account_t \\ & + Credit\ purchases_t. \end{aligned} \qquad (B.10)$$

Each of the components, *Payments on account* and *Credit purchases,* would be modeled separately. For example, if the length of the periods is one week and accounts are always paid in four weeks we would have

$$Payments\ on\ account_t = Accounts\ payable_{t-4};$$

and if purchases are equal to 60 percent of sales forecasted for two weeks in the future, we have

$$Credit\ purchases_t = 0.60 \cdot Sales_{t+2}.$$

This example is based on a specific policy that is assumed to apply over the planning horizon. In other cases, it may be more appropriate to use observed past data to make econometric estimates of the relationships between payments or purchases and sales. An example of a linear regression relation that would be estimated using lagged variables is

$$\begin{aligned} Payments\ on\ account_t = {} & a + b_1 \cdot Accounts\ payable_{t+1} \\ & + b_2 \cdot Accounts\ payable_{t-2}. \end{aligned}$$

where the data are used to estimate parameters a, b_1, and b_2, and purchases are estimated from a relation such as

$$\begin{aligned} Credit\ purchases_t = {} & a + b_1 \cdot Sales_{t-1} + b_2 \cdot \text{Sales}_t \\ & + b_3 \cdot \text{Sales}_{t+1}. \end{aligned}$$

Other types of current liabilities, such as accrued expenses, are usually spontaneous and would be modeled in much the same manner as payables. There is seldom much benefit from modeling such accounts in great detail in a planning context.

For the very broad treatment of financing that focuses on the percent-of-sales ratios, we can combine the cash flow from operations with the spontaneous growth in current liabilities to yield an approximation of total spontaneous financing. This is expressed as

$$\begin{pmatrix} \textit{Total} \\ \textit{spontaneous} \\ \textit{financing}_t \end{pmatrix} = \left[\begin{pmatrix} \textit{Net} \\ \textit{profit} \\ \textit{margin} \end{pmatrix} + \left(\frac{\textit{Depreciation}}{\textit{Sales}} \right) \right] \cdot \textit{Sales}_t \qquad (6.83)$$

$$+ \left[\left(\frac{\begin{matrix} \textit{Spontaneous} \\ \textit{current} \\ \textit{liabilities} \end{matrix}}{\textit{Sales}} \right) \right] \cdot (\textit{Sales}_t - \textit{Sales}_{t-1}),$$

where *Spontaneous current liabilities/Sales* is the forecast of the ratio between the total of all current liabilities that increase with sales, and sales. This formulation does not yet reflect the effects of dividends paid.

Discretionary Sources of Financing

The discretionary sources of funds are those sources that require an explicit decision to access and positive action or application to obtain. Loans—either short- or long-term—are examples of discretionary sources, as are other sources such as equity financing.

Frequently, the primary purpose of a financial planning model is to determine the amount of financing that will be necessary to support the growth of the firm and to explore the consequences of alternative methods of obtaining those funds. Thus, it is often the case that the analysis of the discretionary sources is the primary reason for formulating the model.

Of course, the first task is to determine the amount of discretionary financing that will be required. In the sales-driven model this could be done in steps as follows:

1. $\textit{Required investment}_t = \textit{Total assets}_t - \textit{Total assets}_{t-1}$
2. $\textit{Spontaneous financing}_t = \textit{Cash flow from operations}_t$
   $+ \textit{Increase in accounts payable}_t$
   $+ \textit{Increase in other liabilities}_t$

$$3. \quad \textit{External financing}_t = \textit{Required investment}_t - \textit{Spontaneous financing}_t + \textit{Dividends paid}_t$$

Having determined the amount of funds that must be raised externally, the question is how to model and evaluate the different possible sources of external funds. Each alternative source will have a different effect on the firm and its objective, and the model should be structured so as to demonstrate these effects. The following sections will explain how to model the various sources of funds and discuss how each relates to the firm's financial position and objectives.

Debt Financing. Naturally, there are many different approaches to specifying the discretionary debt financing in the simulation model. The approach to be discussed first is quite aggregative and would be appropriate for long-term planning based on the overall simulation model presented as Exhibit 6.2. Exhibit 6.24 presents additional equations that could serve to expand the debt sector of the financing module.

This debt sector takes as input the amount of *External financing* that is required in each period in the horizon, and allows the user to specify with the *Target debt ratio,* the portion of the *External financing* that should be debt. Then, the amount of *Debt issued* is allocated between short-term and long-term debt according to decision parameters specified by the user. This model assumes the short-term debt matures in one period, as reflected in Expression (D.4). Long-term debt is repaid according to a schedule specified by the user with the parameter *Long-term repayment rate*, which is the proportion of the outstanding long-term debt that is repaid each period. The interest expense would be calculated using *Note rate* and *Long-term rate* parameters that reflect the average interest rate on short-term and long-term debts, respectively. These were discussed in greater detail in the section describing the income generation module.

This treatment of debt financing can be expanded or contracted according to the modeling needs of the user. For longer planning horizons, it may not be useful to distinguish between long- and short-term debt; for shorter term planning, this distinction may be much more important.

EXHIBIT 6.24 Debt Sector of Financing Module

Debt transactions		
D.1 *Debt issued$_t$*	=	(*Target debt ratio$_t$*) · (*External financing$_t$*)
D.2 *Short-term debt issued$_t$*	=	(*Short-term portion$_t$*) · *Debt issued$_t$*
D.3 *Long-term debt issued$_t$*	=	(*Long-term portion$_t$*) · *Debt issued$_t$*
D.4 *Short-term debt repaid$_t$*	=	*Notes payable$_{t-1}$*
D.5 *Long-term debt repaid$_t$*	=	(*Long-term repayment rate$_t$*) · *Long-term debt$_{t-1}$*
Interest and debt service		
D.6 *Short-term debt interest$_t$*	=	(*Note rate$_t$*) · *Notes payable$_{t-1}$*
D.7 *Long-term debt interest$_t$*	=	(*Long-term rate$_t$*) · *Long-term debt$_{t-1}$*
D.8 *Interest expense$_t$*	=	*Short-term debt interest$_t$* + *Long-term debt interest$_t$*
D.9 *Debt service$_t$*	=	*Interest expense$_t$* + *Short-term debt repaid$_t$* + *Long-term debt repaid$_t$*
Debt balance		
D.10 *Notes payable$_t$*	=	*Notes payable$_{t-1}$* + *Short-term debt issued$_t$* − *Short-term debt repaid$_t$*
D.11 *Long-term debt$_t$*	=	*Long-term debt$_{t-1}$* + *Long-term debt issued$_t$* − *Long-term debt repaid$_t$*

As the needs for greater detail increase, the detail can be expanded to show various types of debt financing having different features. An example of such an elaboration is given in Exhibit 6.25, which presents the expressions that would expand the detail of the debt financing sector of the model. This expansion would be appropriate for a model that focuses on short-term financing, where the distinctions between types of debt, debt prepayments, and maturity dates are important.

This debt model starts from the same base as Exhibit 6.24; the required *External financing* is generated elsewhere in the simulation model, and the user provides the *Target debt ratio* to determine the proportion of *External financing* that is to be financed with debt. This debt financing is divided into one part that is financed through a line of credit and another part that is

EXHIBIT 6.25 Detailed debt model for short-run planning

Debt transactions

Debt issued$_t$ = (*Target debt ratio*$_t$) · *External financing*$_t$

Credit line taken$_t$ = (*Line portion*$_t$) · *Debt issued*$_t$

Loan taken$_{jt}$ = (*Loan portion*$_{jt}$) · *Debt issued*$_t$

Credit line repaid$_t$ = (*Credit repayment portion*$_t$) · *Credit line balance*$_{t-1}$

Loan prepayment$_{jt}$ = (*Loan prepayment portion*$_{jt}$) · *Loan Balance*$_{jt-1}$

Loan maturity payment$_t$ = *Loan balance*$_{t,t-1}$

Total debt repaid$_t$ = *Credit line repaid*$_t$ + $\sum_{j=t+1}^{h}$ *Loan prepayment*$_{jt}$ + *Loan maturity payment*$_t$

Interest and debt service

Credit line interest$_t$ = *Credit line balance*$_{t-1}$ · (*Credit line rate*$_t$)

Loan interest$_{jt}$ = *Loan balance*$_{j,t-1}$ · (*Loan rate*$_j$)

Interest expense$_t$ = *Credit line interest*$_t$ + $\sum_{j=t}^{h}$ *Loan interest*$_{jt}$

Debt service$_t$ = *Total debt repaid*$_t$ + *Interest expense*$_t$

Debt balance

Credit line balance$_t$ = *Credit line balance*$_{t-1}$ + *Credit line taken*$_t$ − *Credit line repaid*$_t$

Loan Balance$_{jt}$ = *Loan balance*$_{jt-1}$ + *Loan Taken*$_{jt}$ − *Loan prepayment*$_{jt}$ − *Loan maturity payment*$_t$

Total loan balance$_t$ = $\sum_{j=t+1}^{h}$ *Loan balance*$_{jt}$

financed with loans with different maturities. The decision parameter *Line portion* determines the amount of the *Debt issued* that is financed with the line of credit, and the parameter *Loan portion*$_{jt}$ determines the part that is financed during period t with Loans that mature in period j. The double subscripts used here allow the user to identify loans that mature at different dates, with the first subscript j denoting the period when the loan matures. Thus, *Loan taken*$_{jt}$ represents the amount of loan obtained in period t that matures in period j. For a given period t, j will go from $t + 1$ to h (written as $j = t + 1, \ldots, h$), where h denotes a maturity date beyond the horizon. (Obviously, if the modeling software system being used will not handle subscripts, the same effect is obtained if each different maturity is given an appropriately descriptive name.) The decision parameters specified by the user would be *Target debt ratio*$_t$, *Line portion*$_t$, *Loan portion*$_{jt}$, *Credit repayment portion*$_t$, and *Loan prepayment portion*$_{jt}$, where the latter parameter provides for paying off the loans before the maturity date. The parameters *Loan rate*$_j$ and *Credit line rate*$_t$ are the forecasted interest rates that are input to the model.

The financing module will be doubly important for modeling and planning of financial institutions where the dichotomy of financing into spontaneous and discretionary sources carries over to banks, savings and loans, and similar institutions. For these depository institutions the spontaneous sources of financing are not spontaneous with respect to sales; rather, certain types of depository accounts will grow (or shrink) without management's making a decision to raise a specific amount of funds. For example, passbook accounts may grow based on seasonal factors, economic conditions, the general level of interest rates, and the rates and terms of specific account categories, yet this source of funds is not really discretionary because management does not decide in advance to borrow a given amount of funds by accepting passbook deposits. Management may be able to set certain terms, but then it must simply await the "spontaneous" growth of this source of funds.

There are many different ways to model these deposit sources. For longer range planning it may be satisfactory to show the spontaneous deposits as a percentage of total assets or to use a normalized loan-to-deposit ratio that is forecasted for future periods. For shorter planning horizons, alternative approaches may be more useful. Thompson (1973) notes that for short-run predictions "exponential smoothing provides a relatively effective technique" because deposit levels are relatively stable in the short run.[11] For intermediate-term forecasts of deposit levels, econometric models may provide a better fit: deposits would be shown as depending on interest rates, personal income, monetary policy, and variables measuring differences between regional and national economic growth rates.

While some deposit accounts may be spontaneous, other accounts and sources of funds can be considered discretionary. Large certificates of deposit, federal funds, notes and bonds, and, of course, new external equity funds are all sources that will require a conscious decision by management about the amount and terms to be issued.

In developing a model of the financial institution there are many different ways to handle the various sources. An example

---

[11]Exponential smoothing for deposit forecasting is discussed in Cramer and Miller (1973).

is presented in Exhibit 6.26, which shows part of the financing module of a commercial bank planning model that was developed by the author.[12] In this model the user provides a forecast of the rate of growth of each different category of deposit account, as shown by the growth parameters in Expressions (1)–(3). The inflow of deposits is the driving variable in this bank model. The *Operating cash inflow* in Expression (6) and *Other cash flow* are generated in the other sectors of the model, and the user specifies the components of *Long-term financing.* Expressions (7)–(16) model the short-term discretionary financing that is necessary to bring the system to equilibrium. The equilibrium is established by maintaining the cash balance at a level that is specified by the user. If *Trial cash* exceeds *Minimum cash,* the *Excess cash* is used to repay short-term borrowing from previous periods or to invest as federal funds. If *Trial cash* is less than *Minimum cash,* the *Cash deficit* is funded by borrowing *Fed funds,* issuing CDs, or *Other funds.* The user specifies which of these sources are used with the parameters FF, CD, and FB, which are the proportions of the deficit funded from the three sources, respectively.

It is worth emphasizing that a model of a financial institution, such as is partially shown in Exhibit 6.26, is driven by the financing module, rather than the income generating module, as would be the case for a sales-driven model of a nonfinancial firm. In this particular bank model, the primary inputs are growth rates in deposits, and the secondary input is data showing the loans funded by the bank. After all loans and investments are specified by the user, the financing module determines the amount of discretionary financing necessary to meet the forecasted growth in assets (loans, investments, and so forth).

Equity Financing. Equity financing comes from two sources, internal and external. Internal equity is the earnings that are retained in the firm instead of being paid out to the stockholders as dividends. External equity financing, the sale of new shares of stock to investors, will be considered first.

---

[12] Exhibit 6.26 is an abbreviated version of part of a much larger scale, adaptable bank model written in IFPS by the author to meet the general planning needs of a commercial bank.

EXHIBIT 6.26 Financing Module of Bank Planning Model

Spontaneous deposit inflow

1. *Demand deposit inflow*$_t$ = *Demand deposits*$_{t-1}$ • (*Demand deposit growth rate*$_t$)
2. *Savings deposit inflow*$_t$ = *Savings deposit*$_{t-1}$ • (*Savings deposit growth rate*$_t$)
3. *Time deposit inflow*$_t$ = *Time deposits*$_{t-1}$ • (*Time deposit growth rate*$_t$)
4. *Net deposit inflow*$_t$ = *Demand deposit inflow*$_t$ + *Savings deposit inflow*$_t$ + *Time deposit inflow*$_t$

Discretionary long-term financing

5. *Long-term financing*$_t$ = *Long-term debt issued*$_t$ + *Stock sold*$_t$
6. *Net cash inflow*$_t$ = *Net deposit inflow*$_t$ + *Operating cash inflow*$_t$ + *Other cash flow*$_t$ + *Long-term financing*$_t$

Funding of cash deficit with short-term discretionary sources

7. *Trial cash*$_t$ = *Cash*$_{t-1}$ + *Net cash inflow*$_t$
8. *Excess cash*$_t$ = Maximum (0, *Trial cash*$_t$ − *Minimum cash*)
9. *Cash deficit*$_t$ = Maximum (0, *Minimum cash* − *Trial cash*$_t$)
10. *Fed funds bought*$_t$ = FF • *Cash deficit*$_t$
11. *CD issued*$_t$ = CD • *Cash deficit*$_t$
12. *Other funds borrowed*$_t$ = FB • *Cash deficit*$_t$
13. *Fed funds repaid*$_t$ = Minimum (*Excess cash*$_t$, *Fed funds bought*$_{t-1}$)
14. *Other funds repaid*$_t$ = Minimum (*Excess cash*$_t$ − *Fed funds repaid*$_t$, *Other funds borrowed*$_{t-1}$)
15. *Fed funds sold*$_t$ = *Excess cash*$_t$ − *Fed funds repaid*$_t$ − *Other funds repaid*$_t$
16. *Cash*$_t$ = *Cash*$_{t-1}$ + *Net cash inflow*$_t$ + *Fed funds bought*$_t$ + *CD issued*$_t$ + *Other funds borrowed*$_t$ − *Fed funds repaid*$_t$ − *Other funds repaid*$_t$ − *Fed funds sold*$_t$

External Equity: Stock Issue. Most firms issue new shares of stock rather infrequently because of the expense involved in arranging and executing the issue, and because of a (frequently misplaced) concern for the dilution of ownership associated with issuing additional shares. Nevertheless, the financial plan and model should consider the possibility of raising capital from this source. Particularly in the long-run planning context, periodic issues of new stock may be necessary to provide a sufficient equity base to support the planned growth. The financial model will assist the planner to evaluate the consequences of the use of external equity financing.

Exhibit 6.27 shows the expressions necessary to elaborate on the equity financing shown as *Common Stock Issued* in Exhibit 6.2B. In this case, the user specifies the *Target debt ratio* (as was the case for the debt financing) so that whatever *External financing* is required is split between debt and external equity. In addition, the user specifies or the model calculates the *Issue price per share,* which is the forecast of the gross price at which the stock could be sold to the investing public, and the user forecasts the *Proportional issue costs* that represent the underwriting, accounting, and legal costs associated with selling new shares. For a finely tuned forecast, these costs may be important because, if the costs are substantial, they will affect the number of shares sold (*New common shares issued*) and, subsequently, the degree of dilution.

Obviously, one major problem with this detailed modeling approach is that it requires the user to forecast the *Issue price per share.* This may pose difficulties for at least a couple of reasons. First, as any investor knows it is especially difficult to forecast stock prices, even in the near term, and next to impossible in the long term. Second, there may be a problem of simultaneity imposed by the structure of the model.

The forecasting problem is present in any aspect of planning and modeling, and there are accepted ways to handle it. The objective is not necessarily to make a definitive forecast of the stock price at some future date. Rather, the objective in most planning models is only to approximate the future price, or, in the case of some simulations, to analyze the results for alternative scenarios that may involve varying the prices of the stock. Under these circumstances it may be satisfactory either to try out different stock price scenarios or to include a simple stock valuation model in the simulation to determine the value of the stock. Alternative approaches to modeling the stock valuations are explained in the following sections.

Price-Earnings Ratio Model of Stock Value. One of the simplest valuation models is based on the price-earnings ratio (PE) of the form:

$$\textit{Issue price per share}_t = PE_t \cdot \textit{Earnings per share}_t, \quad (6.90)$$

where the model generates the *Earnings per share*$_t$ and PE_t is

EXHIBIT 6.27 Equity Sector of Financing Module

Stock issue equations

1. *Equity issued*$_t$ = [1 − (*Target debt ratio*$_t$)] · *External financing*$_t$
2. *Stock issue costs*$_t$ = (*Issue price per share*$_t$) · *Proportional issue costs*$_t$
3. *Net issue price per share*$_t$ = *Issue price per share*$_t$ − *Stock issue costs*$_t$
4. *New common shares issued*$_t$ = *Equity issued*$_t$ / *Net issue price per share*$_t$

Balance sheet equations

5. *Common stock*$_t$ = *Common stock*$_{t-1}$ + (*New common shares issued*$_t$ · *Par value per share*)
6. *Paid-in capital*$_t$ = *Paid-in capital*$_{t-1}$ + (*Net issue price per share*$_t$ − *Par value per share*) · New common shares issued$_t$
7. *Retained earnings*$_t$ = *Retained earnings*$_{t-1}$ + (*Net income*$_t$ − *Dividends*$_t$)

Memoranda

8. *Shares outstanding*$_t$ = *Shares outstanding*$_{t-1}$ + *New common shares issued*$_t$
9. *Earnings per share*$_t$ = *Net income*$_t$ / *Shares outstanding*$_{t-1}$
10. *Dividends per share*$_t$ = *Dividends*$_t$ / *Shares outstanding*$_{t-1}$

the forecast of the price-earnings ratio that is expected to prevail at time t. The PE forecast could either be input by the model user, or it could be generated internally to the model. There have been many studies of the factors that influence the PE ratio of firms, and their results may provide a useful starting point for generating the PE in the model. A good example presented by Malkiel and Cragg (1970) relates the PE in a given period to growth, dividend payout, and the beta, which measures the systematic volatility of the stock. For 1965 the relation reported was

$$PE = 7.47 + 1.5\ Growth + 5.6\ Dividend\ payout - 0.95\ Beta. \tag{6.91}$$

This would be implemented in the simulation by generating estimates of the future values of the independent variables *Growth, Dividend payout,* and *Beta,* given the estimates of the parameters that are the coefficients of the independent variables. Obviously, the form of the relationship and the parameters would be expected to change over time, and it would have to be reestimated with recent data. Still, the Malkiel and Cragg expression is indicative of one way to generate the PE forecast.

The use of Expression (6.90) to generate the price in Exhibit 6.27 can present a problem of simultaneity that can give the modeler trouble if not recognized and handled properly. Simultaneity refers to the fact that variables are simultaneously determined so that to calculate variable number 1, you have to know the value of variable number 2, but, to calculate variable number 2 you have to know the value of variable number 1, so one appears to be caught in a trap of circular reasoning. In the present model, Exhibit 6.27, to use Expression (6.90) to determine the *Issue price per share,* one has to know the *Earnings per share,* but the calculation of this latter variable requires that we know the *Issue price per share.* This is because *Earnings per share* depends on the number of *Shares outstanding,* which will depend on the number of *New common share issued,* which, in turn, depends on the *Issue price per share.* Thus, one seems to be caught on a circular track that goes nowhere.

One simple method to handle the problem of simultaneity is to avoid it by having the user supply at least one of the simultaneous variables, such as the *Issue price per share.* Another way to avoid it is to structure the model to calculate the variables sequentially rather than simultaneously. For example, calculate one variable such as *Earnings per share*$_t$ for period t based on the number of shares outstanding at the beginning of the period (time $t - 1$, the end of the previous period); the second variable (or others), such as *Issue price per share*$_t$ in (6.90), depends on the earnings, but it is not simultaneous. Finally, one can meet simultaneity head on by recognizing that it is a characteristic of the real system and is more than just an artifact of the mathematical model. In this case, the simultaneous equations would not be circumvented. Rather, the solution process would have to incorporate a method for solving simultaneous equations.

Dividend Model of Stock Value. The dividend valuation model shows the value of the stock as the present value of the stream of dividends to be received by the stockholder.[13] Apply-

[13]For a more complete explanation of the dividend valuation model see Jacob and Pettit (1984, chapter 16).

ing this over the h-period planning horizon, the value of the stock would be

$$\begin{pmatrix} \textit{Price} \\ \textit{per} \\ \textit{share}_0 \end{pmatrix} = \sum_{t=1}^{h} \begin{pmatrix} \textit{Dividend} \\ \textit{per} \\ \textit{share}_t \end{pmatrix} \frac{1}{(1+k)^t} + \begin{pmatrix} \textit{Price} \\ \textit{per} \\ \textit{share}_h \end{pmatrix} \frac{1}{(1+k)^h}, \qquad (6.92)$$

where the model (or the user) calculates the *Dividend per share* for each period t in the planning horizon, *Price per share*$_t$ is the forecast of the price at which the shares will trade at the end of the planning horizon, and k is the discount rate representing the minimum expected return that is required by investors in order for them to be willing to invest in stock that has the risk that characterizes this firm. Expression (6.92) would apply, in modified form, to any period in the planning horizon. The *Price per share* at date t would be the present value of dividends expected from that date forward until, say, time h, the end of the planning horizon.

In the case of a finite horizon valuation model such as (6.92), one must forecast the value of the stock at the horizon date, shown as *Price per share*$_h$. One way to do this is to use the well-known constant-growth model of the form

$$\textit{Price per share}_h = \frac{\textit{Dividend per share}_{h+1}}{k - g}, \qquad (6.93)$$

where g is the forecast of the average, long-run rate at which dividends will grow, where $k > g$. For many situations this constant-growth model provides a good first approximation, especially where, after a period of rapid or unstable growth during the planning horizon, the firm matures and the growth rate slows down to a rate that can, on the average, be sustained over the long run. Furthermore, the constant-growth model could be used to generate the estimate of the stock value at any date during the planning horizon, if the assumptions on which the model is based apply to this firm. If the constant-growth assumption applied, then the value at any date t is

$$\textit{Price per share}_t = \frac{\textit{Dividend per share}_{t+1}}{k - g}. \qquad (6.93a)$$

The difficulty with using this model to apply to all periods during the planning horizon is that the decisions being analyzed in the simulation may cause the constant dividend growth rate assumption to be violated.

The next method of valuation to be explained is equivalent to the dividend valuation model. However, it focuses on the firm's income rather than dividends, and the particular version presented here calculates the aggregate value of the stock, which is independent of the number of shares outstanding. The value per share is determined simply by dividing by the number of shares outstanding. Miller and Modigliani (1961) developed this especially useful approach to equity valuation, which correctly takes account of the effects of both internal and external equity financing. The Miller and Modigliani model is of the form

$$\begin{aligned} \mathit{Equity\ value}_0 = \sum_{t=1}^{h} \left(\mathit{Net\ income}_t\right) - \left(\mathit{Equity\ financing}_t\right) \frac{1}{(1+k)^t} + \\ \left(\mathit{Equity\ value}_h\right) \frac{1}{(1+k)^h}, \end{aligned} \tag{6.94}$$

where *Net income* is as usually defined, and *Equity financing* is the total amount of financing provided from both internal equity (retained earnings) and external equity (new shares issued). This expression reflects the effects of dividend policy and the dilution due to the issue of new shares. If no external equity is issued and all the equity financing is through retained earnings, the difference between *Net income* and *Equity financing* is simply the aggregate amount of dividends paid to all the firm's stockholders. If new shares are issued to raise new equity capital, there is a dilution of ownership for the original stockholders. The dilution effect on the original stockholders' stock value is reflected by the *Equity financing* term. Thus, whether the equity financing comes from internal or external sources, Expression (6.94) will properly account for its effects on the value of shares held by stockholders at a given date.

Some clarification may be required for the term *Equity* $value_h$ in (6.94). Because *Equity* $value_0$ is intended to represent the value, evaluated at t_0, of all the shares held by stockholders at that date, care must be exercised to make the horizon value consistent. That is, *Equity* $value_h$ should be the aggregate value at the horizon date, *h,* of all shares held by the original stockholders, and it should exclude shares held by new stockholders who have been brought into the ownership circle between t_0 and h. One way to model this horizon value is to determine separately the value per share at h and let

$$Equity\ value_h = Price\ per\ share_h \cdot Number\ of\ shares_0, \qquad (6.95)$$

where the subscript 0 denotes the number of shares held at t_0. Obviously, one difficulty is determining *Price per share*$_h$. This could be modeled as recommended previously using either a PE ratio that is expected to apply at h, or alternatively, using a constant-growth-rate model that applies to periods after the planning horizon.

After *Equity value*$_0$ is calculated according to (6.94), the next step is to calculate *Price per share*$_0$ by dividing by the number of shares outstanding at t_0. At each subsequent date over the planning horizon, the value of the shares is calculated in a similar manner on the basis of the number of shares outstanding on that date.

Dividends. The discussion of dividends has been delayed until now because dividends are, in a sense, part and parcel of equity financing, and one should not consider one without the other because they are so closely interrelated. Dividends are payments of income to the owners of the firm, and in the long run, the reason stockholders are willing to purchase the firm's stock is to receive the dividend income. At first it may be difficult to see how dividends relate to the firm's discretionary, external financing requirements. However, it will become clear that dividends are analogous to "negative financing."

If investors purchase stock in a corporation, there is a flow of funds from these investors to the firm, and the firm can use the funds to acquire assets. On the other hand, if the dividends are paid by the corporation to the stockholders, there is a flow of funds from the firm to the stockholders, and those are the funds that could otherwise have been used by the firm to acquire assets. Each dollar of income that is paid out to stockholders as dividends could have been used as a source of funds to finance investment in new assets, and if the firm's investment plans are not to be scaled back in order to pay dividends, then these funds must be obtained elsewhere, either by some form of borrowing or by issuing new stock.

The trade-offs between dividends and financing are not always immediately apparent, and one of the contributions a simulation can make is to enable the decision maker to explore the implications of dividend policy in terms of its effects on the firm's investment plans, its financing requirements, and the value of its stock.

One facet of the dividend decision is to determine the best *Dividend payout ratio*; that is, the proportion of earnings that should be paid to the stockholders. In Exhibit 6.2 this variable determines dividends according to

$$\textit{Dividend}_t = \textit{Net income}_t \cdot \textit{Dividend payout ratio}, \quad \text{(A.10)}$$

where the payout ratio represents the firm's policy, and is usually supplied by the user.

The influence of dividend policy on financing needs is emphasized when Expression (6.85), which calculated *Total spontaneous financing,* is modified to reflect a constant dividend payout ratio:

$$\begin{aligned}\begin{array}{l}\textit{Total}\\\textit{spontaneous}\\\textit{financing}_t\end{array} = & \left[\begin{pmatrix}\textit{Net}\\\textit{profit}\\\textit{margin}\end{pmatrix} \cdot \left(1 - \begin{pmatrix}\textit{Dividend}\\\textit{payout}\\\textit{ratio}\end{pmatrix}\right)\right.\\ & \left. + \left(\frac{\textit{Depreciation}}{\textit{Sales}}\right)\right] \textit{Sales}_t\\ & + \left(\frac{\begin{array}{c}\textit{Spontaneous}\\\textit{current}\\\textit{liabilities}\end{array}}{\textit{Sales}}\right)(\textit{Sales}_t - \textit{Sales}_{t-1}). \quad \text{(6.83a)}\end{aligned}$$

The product (*Net profit margin*) • (1 − *Dividend payout ratio*) • (*Sales*) represents retained earnings, and obviously the larger the payout ratio, the smaller are retained earnings that are available to finance investment. For example, using the data from the *Combex Corporation* of Chapter 3, assume:

Net profit margin	= 0.055
Depreciation/Sales	= 0.013
Spontaneous current liabilities/Sales	= 0.12
$Sales_t$	= \$5,400,000
$Sales_t - Sales_{t-1}$	= \$900,000.

Applying (6.83a) for different payout ratios, we obtain the amounts of spontaneous (internal) financing after dividend payments shown in Exhibit 6.28.

In this case, if the firm required investment of, say, \$500,000, the required external financing would range from as low as \$24,800 to as high as \$321,800, depending on the proportion of earnings paid out as dividends.

For developing a long-run financial plan the assumption of a constant payout ratio may be an adequate approximation because many firms attempt to maintain dividends as a constant proportion of earnings in the long run. However, for modeling with a shorter planning horizon, the dividend decision may have to be modeled with greater detail that considers other complicating factors. For example, many firms attempt to maintain the absolute level of dividends without allowing dividends to decline with earnings. To provide for such a policy, dividends could be determined according to the rule

$$Dividends_t = \text{Maximum}\ [Dividends_{t-1},\ Dividend\ payout\ ratio \cdot Net\ income_t]. \qquad (6.97)$$

This prevents dividends from declining temporarily when earnings do, yet allows them to increase with earnings. More complex expressions may be necessary to limit dividends to no more than the balance in the retained earnings account in the balance sheet, or to limit dividends so as to be consistent with loan contract provisions.

The theory of finance would contend that the firm should pay dividends only if the investment opportunities available to the firm are less attractive than those available to the firm's stockholders (net of the effects of taxes). The stockholders' opportunity cost for these funds is presumably measured by the firm's cost of equity capital, so that if the firm cannot invest equity funds at a rate of return at least as great as the cost of equity capital, then any earnings should be paid out as divi-

EXHIBIT 6.28 Internal Financing Net of Dividends

Dividend Payout Ratio	*Retained Earnings*	*Other Spontaneous Financing*	*Total Internal Financing Net of Dividends*
0	$297,000	$178,200	$475,200
0.20	237,600	178,200	415,800
0.40	178,200	178,200	356,400
0.60	118,800	178,200	297,000
0.80	59,400	178,200	237,600
1.00	0	178,200	178,200

dends to the stockholders. This idea is referred to as the "residual theory of dividends,"[14] in which dividends are regarded as the residue that is left over after making the necessary investments in new assets. If the firm follows this policy, the dividends could be calculated with the following expressions:

$$\textit{Required equity financing}_t = [\textit{Required investment}_t - \textit{Spontaneous financing}_t] \cdot [1 - \textit{Target debt ratio}] \quad (6.98)$$

$$\textit{Dividend}_t = \text{Maximum}\ [0, \textit{Net income}_t - \textit{Required equity financing}_t] \quad (6.99)$$

$$\textit{Addition to retained earnings}_t = \textit{Net income}_t - \textit{Dividend}_t. \quad (6.100)$$

$$\textit{Equity issued}_t = \textit{Required equity financing}_t - \textit{Addition to retained earnings}_t \quad (6.101)$$

In this case, it is assumed that external financing is split between debt and equity sources, and dividends are paid only if there is no need for the equity funds for financing new investment.

A Case Study Analyzing the Financing Decision

The decisions about investment and financing for the firm are not made in a vacuum. There are always some interactions be-

[14]The effects of dividend policy and the residual theory have been discussed extensively in the finance literature; for example, see Weston and Copeland (1986, chap. 22 and accompanying references).

tween management's decisions and events in the security markets. These interactions are what the field of managerial finance is all about, and they must be considered in the financial planning process. That is, the sensible use of a model for financial planning requires more than just the mechanical application of the equations comprising the model. Rather, the lessons of the theory of finance must be brought to bear in the modeling and planning process. The lessons that are of present concern are those that deal with the effects of alternative financial structures on the value of the firm. These issues will be explored by way of an example that utilizes the model represented by Exhibits 6.2A, B, and C.

Let us return to the example of the Plastico Company, whose investment decision was analyzed earlier. Recall that Plastico manufactures plastic parts and components and is considering an expansion of its capacity. While Plastico has not been especially profitable in recent years, it has managed to meet almost all of its financing needs through internal equity financing, and, with the exception of trade payables, at the moment it has no debt in its capital structure.

Plastico presently has 150,000 shares of stock outstanding. The officers own about 35 percent of the stock, and the remainder is held by the public. It is traded over the counter, and recently its price has been in the range of $3.50 to $5.25 per share, or at a price-earnings ratio of 4 to 6 times earnings.

The Problem. Plastico has just been granted a contract to supply the plastic body for a new model of sports car that will be manufactured by Ford Motor Company. To supply these bodies in the quantity and quality required will require a major capital investment program, and management is considering alternative ways to finance this expansion. To evaluate the alternative ways to finance the expansion, the proper objective of the decision must be defined, the decision alternatives must be enumerated, the linkages between the decisions and the goals need to be specified, and the various constraints that impinge on reaching the goal must be described.

The Decision Alternatives. As a first pass at the problem the planning staff will consider three alternative financing schemes: (*a*) all-equity financing, (*b*) a 50-50 mix of debt and equity financing, and (*c*) using debt as the only source of new funds for the project. There are many other possible alternatives that could be considered, but considering these three first should help to clarify some of the issues that are important, and may help to generate ideas about which other alternatives should be explored.

The Objective. Discussions among officers and managers about how the financing alternatives should be evaluated have produced confusion and disagreement at Plastico. Each officer appears to have a different goal in mind when he considers how he would compare the alternatives. Joe, the president and founder of the company, states that he wants the firm to continue to have a "strong balance sheet," with very little debt. Sam, the vice president for operations, states that he thinks the firm could increase earnings by using greater financial leverage; and George, the vice president for finance, contends that the value of the firm's common stock could be increased with the judicious use of debt financing. These officers have requested their staff to explore the consequences of the financing alternatives in terms of each of these objectives. After seeing the results they will discuss further which objective should take precedence.

Without a clear statement of the goal of the decision, it is much harder to formulate the planning model, because it is not clear what kind of information is necessary for the evaluation, nor is it clear how to define the links between the decision and the goal. Nevertheless, with the three main bases for evaluation specified—financial strength, earnings, and stock value—the model can be developed to explore each of these factors.

Data Input: The Current State of the System. The starting point for analyzing the financing decision is to describe the current state of the firm. The firm's current condition is best described by its financial statements, which show its resources and obligations and the nature of its income and expenses. The balance sheet and income statement for the most recent period, ending December 31, 1986, are shown as Exhibit 6.29.

Plastico presently appears to be a relatively safe but not spectacularly profitable company. It has no debt, and it has

EXHIBIT 6.29 Plastico Inc.: Current State of the System (financial statements)

PLASTICO INC.
Income Statement
Year Ended December 31, 1986
($000)

Total revenue	$3,000.00
Operating costs	2,700.00
Operating income	300.00
Depreciation	58.00
EBIT	242.00
Interest expense	0.00
Taxable income	242.00
Income tax	111.32
Net income	$ 130.68
Dividends	$ 52.27
Earnings retained	78.41

PLASTICO INC.
Balance Sheet
December 31, 1986
($000)

Cash	$ 70.00
Marketable securities	25.00
Receivables	420.00
Inventories	471.00
Current assets	986.00
Gross fixed assets	2,212.00
Accumulated depreciation	380.00
Fixed assets	1,832.00
Total assets	$2,818.00
Accounts payable	$ 460.00
Notes payable	0.00
Current liabilities	460.00
Long-term debt	0.00
Common stock	1,500.00
Retained earnings	858.00
Total liabilities	$2,818.00

earned steady profits in recent years, but the annual return on stockholders' equity (based on book value) has been about 5.5 percent, which is particularly low compared to other firms in the industry, which earn about 16 percent on equity. Part of the reason for Plastico's low return is that it has been generating a low level of sales relative to its investment in assets. While other firms in its industry have a total asset turnover of about 2.0, Plastico had a turnover rate of 1.06 in 1986.

Investors in the stock market have not favored Plastico stock, and it recently has been trading at a price of about $4.50 per share, which is a price-earnings ratio of about 5.2 × earnings, as compared to a PE ratio of about 10× for the average stock. Based on the dividend yields and annual rate of price appreciation in recent periods, the stock has returned investors an annual average rate of return of about 15.5 percent, which is about right for a stock with the level of risk inherent in Plastico.

Additional input that describes the state of the system includes data describing current conditions in the economy and industry. These are discussed as they relate to developing the forecasts of future conditions.

Data Input: Forecasts. The evaluation of the alternative financing decisions will depend on the forecast of the relevant economic variables that affect the firm and the firm's investment and revenues over the planning horizon. These forecasts are shown in Exhibit 6.30. The level of interest rates at which the firm can meet its borrowing needs is shown, along with the *Total revenue* that is the forecasted variable that drives the model. In addition, the forecast of relations between this driving variable and other variables are defined in the exhibit. The expense variables and current asset balances are all tied to the revenue forecast with parameter estimates based on past data (it is assumed that *Operating costs* will decrease to 87 percent of *Total revenue* from the recent historical level of 90 percent).

The problem to be addressed in this modeling effort is to assess the consequences of alternative financing schemes. To accomplish this, the amounts of required financing must be determined in each period over the planning horizon, and the effects of meeting the needs with alternative plans must be determined. The major outputs that will help in this assessment are the financial statements that are presented as models in Exhibits 6.2A, B, and C. The thing that is missing in Exhibits 6.2 is the mechanism for balancing the system, or reaching equilibrium. This equilibrating mechanism is provided by the set of equations presented as Exhibit 6.31, which is similar to the cash balance adjustment model presented as Exhibit 6.8.

The simulation model is a cash balance adjustment model that determines the required financing by adjusting the cash balance at the end of each period in the planning horizon to a specified value. Any *Excess cash* is invested in *Marketable securities,* and a *Cash deficit* is financed by issuing *common stock* or incurring long-term debt. The amounts of these sources are specified by the user with the decision variable *Target debt ratio,* which for this case will be either 0, 0.50, or 1.0. In this example, the *Target debt ratio* specifies just the proportion of external financing that is funded with debt; it does not refer to the firm's overall debt ratio.

EXHIBIT 6.30 Plastico Inc.: Forecasts and Assumptions (1987–1991)

Forecasts

	1987	*1988*	*1989*	*1990*	*1991*
The economic environment					
Borrowing rate—short-term	0.09	0.09	0.09	0.09	0.09
Borrowing rate—long-term	0.11	0.11	0.11	0.11	0.11
Required return on average stock	0.16	0.16	0.16	0.16	0.16
The firm					
Fixed asset investment ($ millions)	$1.2	$0.11	$0.115	$0.12	$0.125
Revenue (without investment) ($ millions)	3.0	3.0	3.0	3.0	3.0
Incremental revenue (with investment) ($ millions)	0	2.0	5.0	6.0	6.0
Total revenue (with investment) ($ millions)	3.0	5.0	8.0	9.0	9.0

Relations between variables

$\textit{Operating costs}_t = 0.87 \cdot \textit{Total revenue}_t$
$\textit{Depreciation}_t = 0.035 \cdot \textit{Fixed assets}_t$
$\textit{Income tax}_t = 0.46 \cdot \textit{Taxable income}_t$
$\textit{Dividends}_t = 0.40 \cdot \textit{Net income}_t$
$\textit{Credit purchases}_t = 0.17 \cdot \textit{Total revenue}_t$
$\textit{Desired cash}_t = 0.05 \cdot \textit{Total revenue}_t$
$\textit{Receivables}_t = 0.14 \cdot \textit{Total revenue}_t$
$\textit{Inventories}_t = 0.23 \cdot \textit{Total revenue}_t$

Other assumptions

Excess cash is invested in *marketable securities.*
Marketable securities mature in one period.
Cash deficit is financed by issuing stock or debt.
Accounts payable are paid off in one period.

Modeling Output. Based on the data input, the assumptions about the relations between variables, and the forecasts of the future, the planning staff constructed the financial model represented by Exhibits 6.2 and 6.31. These were used to generate pro forma statements over a five-year planning horizon, 1987–91, broken into one-year subperiods. Exhibits 6.32, 6.33, and 6.34 (A, B, and C) show these statements.

Using the Output to Analyze the Problem. The pro forma financial statements were presented to the officers for

EXHIBIT 6.31 Cash Balance Adjustment Sector

Cash flow from operations$_t$	= *Net income* + *Depreciation$_t$* − *Dividend$_t$*
Increase in payables$_t$	= *Credit purchases$_t$* − *Payments on account$_t$*
Security proceeds$_t$	= *Securities matured$_t$* + *Securities sold$_t$*
Sources of cash$_t$	= *Cash flow from operations$_t$* + *Increase in payables$_t$* + *Security proceeds$_t$*
Increase in working capital$_t$	= *Receivables increase$_t$* + *Inventory increase$_t$*
Fixed asset investment$_t$	= (forecast input by user)
Uses of cash$_t$	= *Increase in working capital$_t$* + *Fixed asset investment$_t$*
Trial cash flow$_t$	= *Sources of cash$_t$* − *Uses of cash$_t$*
Trial cash balance$_t$	= *Cash$_{t-1}$* + *Trial cash flow$_t$*
Desired cash$_t$	= 0.05 · *Total revenue$_t$*
Trial excess cash$_t$	= *Trial cash balance$_t$* − *Desired cash$_t$*
Excess cash$_t$	= *Trial excess cash$_t$* if *Trial excess cash$_t$* > 0 = 0 if *Trial excess cash$_t$* ≤ 0
Cash deficit$_t$	= 0 − *Trial excess cash* if *Trial excess cash$_t$* < 0 = 0 if *Trial excess cash$_t$* ≥ 0
Securities purchased$_t$	= *Excess cash$_t$*
Long-term debt issued$_t$	= *Target debt ratio* · *Cash deficit$_t$*
Common stock issued$_t$	= [1 − *Target debt ratio*] · *Cash deficit$_t$*
Net cash inflow$_t$	= *Trial cash flow$_t$* − *Securities purchased$_t$* + *Long-term debt issued$_t$* + *Common stock issued$_t$*
Cash$_t$	= *Cash$_{t-1}$* + *Net cash inflow$_t$*

their evaluation and decision. Joe's response was that the equity financing plan left the firm with a cleaner balance sheet, and the total net income is greater in each year because the firm is not obligated to pay interest on the debt. Also, Joe remarked that he had difficulty assimilating this large amount of data.

Sam, who initially advocated debt financing, responded that while the total net income is greater with the use of equity financing, this does not properly take account of the dilution of ownership that will result from the issue of new shares. He thinks that the earnings per share should be the measure for evaluating the alternatives. The stock of Plastico has recently been trading at a price between $3.50 and $5.25 per share, or in terms of price-earnings ratios, between 4× and 6× earnings.

EXHIBIT 6.32A Plastico Inc.: Income Statements All-Equity Financing ($000)

	Actual	*Forecast*				
	1986	*1987*	*1988*	*1989*	*1990*	*1991*
Total revenue	$3,000.00	$3,000.00	$5,000.00	$8,000.00	$9,000.00	$9,000.00
Operating costs	2,700.00	2,700.00	4,350.00	6,960.00	7,830.00	7,830.00
EBDIT	300.00	300.00	650.00	1,040.00	1,170.00	1,170.00
Depreciation	58.00	64.12	103.88	104.09	104.47	105.02
EBIT	242.00	235.88	546.12	935.91	1,065.53	1,064.98
Interest expense	0.00	0.00	0.00	0.00	0.00	0.00
Taxable income	242.00	235.88	546.12	935.91	1,065.53	1,064.98
Income tax	111.32	108.50	251.22	430.52	490.14	489.89
Net income	$ 130.68	$ 127.38	$ 294.91	$ 505.39	$ 575.39	$ 575.09
Dividends	$ 52.27	$ 50.95	$ 117.96	$ 202.16	$ 230.15	$ 230.04
Earnings retained	78.41	76.43	176.94	303.23	345.23	345.05

EXHIBIT 6.32B Plastico Inc.: Cash Balance Adjustments All-Equity Financing ($000)

	Forecast				
	1987	*1988*	*1989*	*1990*	*1991*
Cash flow from operations	$ 140.55	$280.82	$ 407.32	$449.70	$450.07
Increase in payables	50.00	340.00	510.00	170.00	0.00
Security proceeds	25.00	0.00	0.00	0.00	79.70
Sources of cash	215.55	620.82	917.32	619.70	529.77
Increase in working capital	219.00	740.00	1,110.00	370.00	0.00
Fixed asset investment	1,200.00	110.00	115.00	120.00	125.00
Uses of cash	1,419.00	850.00	1,225.00	490.00	125.00
Trial cash flow	−1,203.45	−229.18	−307.68	129.70	404.77
Plus: Cash ($t-1$)	70.00	150.00	250.00	400.00	450.00
Trial cash balance	−1,133.45	−79.18	−57.68	529.70	854.77
Less: Desired cash	150.00	250.00	400.00	450.00	450.00
Trial excess cash	−1,283.45	−329.18	−457.68	79.70	404.77
Excess cash	0.00	0.00	0.00	79.70	404.77
Cash deficit	1,283.45	329.18	457.68	0.00	0.00
Securities purchased	0.00	0.00	0.00	79.70	404.77
Long-term debt issued	0.00	0.00	0.00	0.00	0.00
Common stock issued	1,283.45	329.18	457.68	0.00	0.00
Net cash inflow	80.00	100.00	150.00	50.00	0.00
Plus: Cash ($t-1$)	70.00	150.00	250.00	400.00	450.00
Cash balance (ending)	150.00	250.00	400.00	450.00	450.00

EXHIBIT 6.32C Plastico Inc.: Balance Sheets
All-Equity Financing ($000)

	Actual	*Forecast*				
	1986	*1987*	*1988*	*1989*	*1990*	*1991*
Assets						
Cash	$ 70.00	$ 150.00	$ 250.00	$ 400.00	$ 450.00	$ 450.00
Marketable securities	25.00	0.00	0.00	0.00	79.70	404.77
Receivables	420.00	420.00	700.00	1,120.00	1,260.00	1,260.00
Inventories	471.00	690.00	1,150.00	1,840.00	2,070.00	2,070.00
Current assets	986.00	1,260.00	2,100.00	3,360.00	3,859.70	4,184.77
Gross fixed assets	2,212.00	3,412.00	3,522.00	3,637.00	3,757.00	3,882.00
Accumulated depreciation	380.00	444.12	548.00	652.09	756.56	861.57
Fixed assets	1,832.00	2,967.88	2,974.00	2,984.91	3,000.44	3,020.43
Total assets	$2,818.00	$4,227.88	$5,074.00	$6,344.91	$6,860.15	$7,205.20
Liabilities						
Accounts payable	$ 460.00	$ 510.00	$ 850.00	$1,360.00	$1,530.00	$1,530.00
Notes payable	0.00	0.00	0.00	0.00	0.00	0.00
Current liabilities	460.00	510.00	850.00	1,360.00	1,530.00	1,530.00
Long-term debt	0.00	0.00	0.00	0.00	0.00	0.00
Common stock	1,500.00	2,783.45	3,112.63	3,570.31	3,570.31	3,570.31
Retained earnings	858.00	934.43	1,111.37	1,414.60	1,759.84	2,104.89
Total Liabilities	$2,818.00	$4,227.88	$5,074.00	$6,344.91	$6,860.15	$7,205.20

EXHIBIT 6.33A Plastico Inc.: Income Statements
Combination Debt and Equity Financing ($000)

	Actual	*Forecast*				
	1986	*1987*	*1988*	*1989*	*1990*	*1991*
Total revenue	$3,000.00	$3,000.00	$5,000.00	$8,000.00	$9,000.00	$9,000.00
Operating costs	2,700.00	2,700.00	4,350.00	6,960.00	7,830.00	7,830.00
EBDIT	300.00	300.00	650.00	1,040.00	1,170.00	1,170.00
Depreciation	58.00	64.12	103.88	104.09	104.47	105.02
EBIT	242.00	235.88	546.12	935.91	1,065.53	1,064.98
Interest expense	0.00	0.00	70.59	89.95	116.73	116.73
Taxable income	242.00	235.88	475.53	845.96	948.80	948.26
Income tax	111.32	108.50	218.75	389.14	436.45	436.20
Net income	$ 130.68	$ 127.38	$ 256.79	$ 456.82	$ 512.35	$ 512.06
Dividends	$ 52.27	$ 50.95	$ 102.72	$ 182.73	$ 204.94	$ 204.82
Earnings retained	78.41	76.43	154.07	274.09	307.41	307.24

Sam estimates that under the all-equity financing alternative, new shares could be sold to the public at a price-earnings ratio of about 5× earnings, based on the most recent earnings of $0.87 per share, or about $4.35 per share, net to the company; and that the shares could be sold at a net price of about $4.00

EXHIBIT 6.33B Plastico Inc.: Cash Balance Adjustments Combination Debt and Equity Financing ($000)

	Forecast				
	1987	*1988*	*1989*	*1990*	*1991*
Cash flow from operations	$140.55	$257.95	$378.18	$411.88	$412.25
Increase in payables	50.00	340.00	510.00	170.00	0.00
Security proceeds	25.00	0.00	0.00	0.00	41.88
Sources of cash	215.55	597.95	888.18	581.88	454.13
Increase in working capital	219.00	740.00	1,110.00	370.00	0.00
Fixed asset investment	1,200.00	110.00	115.00	120.00	125.00
Uses of cash	1,419.00	850.00	1,225.00	490.00	125.00
Trial cash flow	−1,203.45	−252.05	−336.82	91.88	329.13
Plus: Cash (*t*−1)	70.00	150.00	250.00	400.00	450.00
Trial cash balance	−1,133.45	−102.05	−86.82	491.88	779.13
Less: Desired cash	150.00	250.00	400.00	450.00	450.00
Trial excess cash	−1,283.45	−352.05	−486.82	41.88	329.13
Excess cash	0.00	0.00	0.00	41.88	329.13
Cash deficit	1,283.45	352.05	486.82	0.00	0.00
Securities purchased	0.00	0.00	0.00	41.88	329.13
Long-term debt issued	641.73	176.03	243.41	0.00	0.00
Common stock issued	641.73	176.03	243.41	0.00	0.00
Net cash inflow	80.00	100.00	150.00	50.00	0.00
Plus: Cash (*t*−1)	70.00	150.00	250.00	400.00	450.00
Cash balance (ending)	150.00	250.00	400.00	450.00	450.00

per share for the mixed financing alternative. According to Sam, this price is lower because the increased debt will impose greater risk on the stockholders, and they will not be willing to pay as high a price (PE ratio of about 4.6×) for shares that have greater risk. For the all-debt alternative, obviously, the issue price per share is not applicable to determining the number of shares. Based on these assumed prices, Sam produced estimates of earnings per share (EPS) as shown in Exhibit 6.35. The effects on earnings of the new project do not show up until 1988; for that period the EPS are $0.566, $0.724, and $1.458 for the all-equity, the mixed, and the all-debt financing alternatives, respectively. Sam draws attention to the level of EPS under the all-debt alternative, which is about twice as large as with the mixed financing, and is about 2.6 times as large as EPS under the all-equity alternative. On the basis of these estimates of earnings per share, Sam supports the all-debt financing plan; at the same time, he cautions that these EPS calculations are to-

EXHIBIT 6.33C Plastico Inc.: Balance Sheets
Combination Debt and Equity Financing ($000)

	Actual	Forecast				
	1986	*1987*	*1988*	*1989*	*1990*	*1991*
Assets						
Cash	$ 70.00	$150.00	$ 250.00	$ 400.00	$ 450.00	$ 450.00
Marketable securities	25.00	0.00	0.00	0.00	41.88	329.13
Receivables	420.00	420.00	700.00	1,120.00	1,260.00	1,260.00
Inventories	471.00	690.00	1,150.00	1,840.00	2,070.00	2,070.00
Current assets	986.00	1,260.00	2,100.00	3,360.00	3,821.88	4,109.13
Gross fixed assets	2,212.00	3,412.00	3,522.00	3,637.00	3,757.00	3,882.00
Accumulated depreciation	380.00	444.12	548.00	652.09	756.56	861.57
Fixed assets	1,832.00	2,967.88	2,974.00	2,984.91	3,000.44	3,020.43
Total assets	$2,818.00	$4,227.88	$5,074.00	$6,344.91	$6,822.33	$7,129.56
Liabilities						
Accounts payable	$ 460.00	$ 510.00	$ 850.00	$1,360.00	$1,530.00	$1,530.00
Notes payable	0.00	0.00	0.00	0.00	0.00	0.00
Current liabilities	460.00	510.00	850.00	1,360.00	1,530.00	1,530.00
Long-term debt	0.00	641.73	817.75	1,061.16	1,061.16	1,061.16
Common stock	1,500.00	2,141.73	2,317.75	2,561.16	2,561.16	2,561.16
Retained earnings	858.00	934.43	1,088.50	1,362.59	1,670.00	1,977.23
Total liabilities	$2,818.00	$4,227.88	$5,074.00	$6,344.91	$6,822.33	$7,129.56

EXHIBIT 6.34A Plastico Inc.: Income Statements
All Debt Financing ($000)

	Actual	Forecast				
	1986	*1987*	*1988*	*1989*	*1990*	*1991*
Total revenue	$3,000.00	$3,000.00	$5,000.00	$8,000.00	$9,000.00	$9,000.00
Operating costs	2,700.00	2,700.00	4,350.00	6,960.00	7,830.00	7,830.00
EBDIT	300.00	300.00	650.00	1,040.00	1,170.00	1,170.00
Depreciation	58.00	64.12	103.88	104.09	104.47	105.02
EBIT	242.00	235.88	546.12	935.91	1,065.53	1,064.98
Interest expense	0.00	0.00	141.18	182.42	239.27	239.27
Taxable income	242.00	235.88	404.94	753.49	826.26	825.72
Income tax	111.32	108.50	186.27	346.60	380.08	379.83
Net income	$ 130.68	$ 127.38	$ 218.67	$ 406.88	$ 446.18	$ 445.89
Dividends	$ 52.27	$ 50.95	$ 87.47	$ 162.75	$ 178.47	$ 178.35
Earnings retained	78.41	76.43	131.20	244.13	267.71	267.53

tally dependent on his assumptions regarding the price at which new shares can be issued, and he has made no explicit calculation of the price per share under each alternative.

George, the vice president for finance, pointed out that the use of financial leverage could, indeed, help generate higher

EXHIBIT 6.34B Plastico Inc.: Cash Balance Adjustments
All Debt Financing ($000)

	Forecast				
	1987	*1988*	*1989*	*1990*	*1991*
Cash flow from operations	$ 140.55	$235.08	$348.22	$372.18	$372.55
Increase in payables	50.00	340.00	510.00	170.00	0.00
Security proceeds	25.00	0.00	0.00	0.00	2.18
Sources of cash	215.55	575.08	858.22	542.18	374.73
Increase in working capital	219.00	740.00	1,110.00	370.00	0.00
Fixed asset investment	1,200.00	110.00	115.00	120.00	125.00
Uses of cash	1,419.00	850.00	1,225.00	490.00	125.00
Trial cash flow	−1,203.45	−274.92	−366.78	52.18	249.73
Plus: Cash (*t*−1)	70.00	150.00	250.00	400.00	450.00
Trial cash balance	−1,133.45	−124.92	−116.78	452.18	699.73
Less: Desired cash	150.00	250.00	400.00	450.00	450.00
Trial excess cash	−1,283.45	−374.92	−516.78	2.18	249.73
Excess cash	0.00	0.00	0.00	2.18	249.73
Cash deficit	1,283.45	374.92	516.78	0.00	0.00
Securities purchased	0.00	0.00	0.00	2.18	249.73
Long-term debt issued	1,283.45	374.92	516.78	0.00	0.00
Common stock issued	0.00	0.00	0.00	0.00	0.00
Net cash inflow	80.00	100.00	150.00	50.00	0.00
Plus: Cash (*t*−1)	70.00	150.00	250.00	400.00	450.00
Cash balance (ending)	150.00	250.00	400.00	450.00	450.00

EXHIBIT 6.34C Plastico Inc.: Balance Sheets
All Debt Financing ($000)

	Actual	Forecast				
	1986	*1987*	*1988*	*1989*	*1990*	*1991*
Assets						
Cash	$ 70.00	$ 150.00	$ 250.00	$ 400.00	$ 450.00	$ 450.00
Marketable securities	25.00	0.00	0.00	0.00	2.18	249.73
Receivables	420.00	420.00	700.00	1,120.00	1,260.00	1,260.00
Inventories	471.00	690.00	1,150.00	1,840.00	2,070.00	2,070.00
Current assets	986.00	1,260.00	2,100.00	3,360.00	3,782.18	4,029.73
Gross fixed assets	2,212.00	3,412.00	3,522.00	3,637.00	3,757.00	3,882.00
Accumulated depreciation	380.00	444.12	548.00	652.09	756.56	861.57
Fixed assets	1,832.00	2,967.88	2,974.00	2,984.91	3,000.44	3,020.43
Total assets	$2,818.00	$4,227.88	$5,074.00	$6,344.91	$6,782.62	$7,050.15
Liabilities						
Accounts payable	$ 460.00	$ 510.00	$ 850.00	$1,360.00	$1,530.00	$1,530.00
Notes payable	0.00	0.00	0.00	0.00	0.00	0.00
Current liabilities	460.00	510.00	850.00	1,360.00	1,530.00	1,530.00
Long-term debt	0.00	1,283.45	1,658.38	2,175.16	2,175.16	2,175.16
Common stock	1,500.00	1,500.00	1,500.00	1,500.00	1,500.00	1,500.00
Retained earnings	858.00	934.43	1,065.63	1,309.76	1,577.47	1,845.00
Total liabilities	$2,818.00	$4,227.88	$5,074.00	$6,344.91	$6,782.62	$7,050.15

EXHIBIT 6.35 Plastico Inc.: Earnings per Share with Each Financing Alternative

	1986	1987	1988	1989	1990	1991
Equity financing						
Common stock issued	—	$1,283,450	$329,180	$457,680	—	—
Net issue price per share		$4.35	$4.35	$4.35	—	—
New common shares issued	—	295,046	95,674	105,214	—	—
Shares outstanding (beginning)	150,000	150,000	445,046	520,720	—	—
Shares outstanding (ending)	150,000	445,046	520,720	625,934	625,934	625,934
Net income	$130,680	$127,380	$294,910	$505,390	$575,390	$575,090
Earnings per share	$ 0.8712	$ 0.2862	$ 0.5664	$ 0.8074	$ 0.9193	$ 0.9188
Combination debt and equity						
Common stock issued	—	$641,730	$176,030	$243,410	—	—
Net issue price per share	—	$4.00	$4.00	$4.00	—	—
New common shares issued	—	160,433	44,008	60,853	— —	
Shares outstanding (beginning)	150,000	150,000	310,433	354,441	—	—
Shares outstanding (ending)	150,000	310,433	354,441	415,294	415,294	415,294
Net income	$130,680	$127,380	$256,790	$456,820	$512,350	$512,060
Earnings per share	$ 0.8712	$ 0.4103	$ 0.7245	$1.10	$1.2337	$1.233
All-debt financing						
Common stock issued	—	—	—	—	—	—
Shares outstanding	150,000	150,000	150,000	150,000	150,000	150,000
Net income	$130,680	$127,380	$218,670	$406,880	$446,180	$445,890
Earnings per share	$ 0.8712	$ 0.8492	$ 1.4578	$ 2.7125	$2.9745	$ 2.9726

earnings per share and higher return on equity when the firm did well. He further noted that leverage also magnified any decline in earnings when the firm performed poorly. In fact, not only would financial leverage magnify the gains and losses to equity, the use of leverage would make the return on equity and the earnings per share more uncertain, and would make their year-to-year variations greater.

To demonstrate the effect of debt financing on the sensitivity of net income to changes in revenues, George produced Exhibit 6.36, which show net income, earnings per share, and return on equity for 1988 based on total revenues of $1 million, $3 million, $5 million, $7 million, and $9 million. Exhibits 6.37A and B show graphically the same relationships. For a given total revenue, the firm's EBIT for 1988 is the same regardless of which financing alternative is used. For example, if total rev-

EXHIBIT 6.36 Earnings per Share and Return on Equity for 1988 Based on Various Total Revenue Scenarios for Three Financing Alternatives ($000)

	Revenue Scenario				
Total revenue	$1,000.00	$3,000.00	$5,000.00	$7,000.00	$9,000.00
Operating costs	870.00	2,610.00	4,350.00	6,090.00	7,830.00
Depreciation	103.88	103.88	103.88	103.88	103.88
EBIT	26.12	286.12	546.12	806.12	1,066.12
All-equity financing					
EBIT	$26.12	$286.12	$546.12	$806.12	$1,066.12
Interest expense	—	—	—	—	—
Income tax	12.02	131.62	251.22	370.82	490.42
Net income	14.11	154.51	294.91	435.31	575.71
Earnings per share ($)	0.27	0.297	0.566	0.836	1.106
Return on equity (%)	0.3%	3.6%	7.0%	10.3%	13.6%
Combination debt and equity					
EBIT	$26.12	$286.12	$546.12	$806.12	$1,066.12
Interest expense	70.59	70.59	70.59	70.59	70.59
Income tax	(20.45)	99.15	218.75	338.35	457.95
Net income	(24.01)	116.39	256.79	397.19	537.59
Earnings per share ($)	(0.068)	0.328	0.724	1.12	1.517
Return on equity (%)	(0.7%	3.4%	7.5%	11.7%	15.8%
All-debt financing					
EBIT	$ 26.12	$286.12	$546.12	$806.12	$1,066.12
Interest expense	141.18	141.18	141.18	141.18	141.18
Income tax	(52.93)	66.67	186.27	305.87	425.47
Net income	(62.13)	78.27	218.67	359.07	499.47
Earnings per share ($)	$(0.414)	$0.522	$1.458	$2.394	$3.33
Return on equity	(2.4%	3.1%	8.5%	14.0%	19.5%

enue is $1 million, EBIT is $26,210 for all three financing alternatives. This is because revenue and all expenses above the level of EBIT on the income statement are independent of the way in which the firm is financed. Thus, EBIT is $26,120, $286,120, $546,120, $806,120, and $1,066,120 for each of the assumed revenues, regardless of the financing used. Because the interest costs are fixed for a given financing alternative regardless of the level of EBIT, however, the net income varies more in response to variations in revenue and EBIT when more debt is used. Examining the period-to-period variations in sales that might occur, from Exhibits 6.37 it is evident that both EPS and return on equity will be more stable and predictable with equity financing than with the debt financing alternatives.

This point is also made by looking at the degree of financial

EXHIBIT 6.37A Earnings per Share at Different Levels of Total Revenue with Alternative Financing Plans

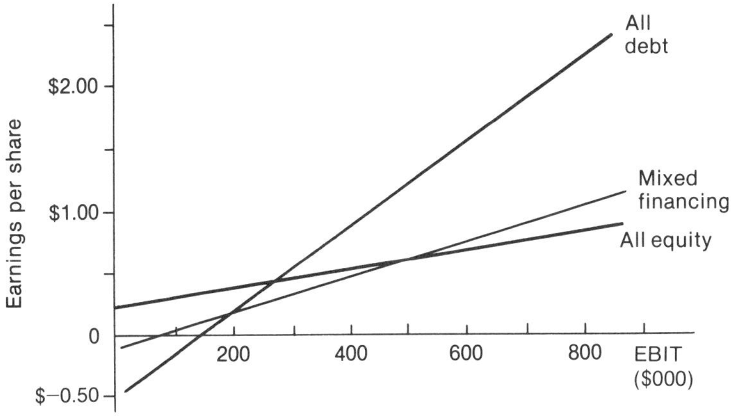

leverage (DFL), which measures the elasticity of net income with respect to variations in EBIT, and can be calculated according to the formula

$$EBIT/(EBIT - Interest).$$

At a total revenue of $5 million for 1988 for the all-debt alternative, this is 546,120/(546,120 − 141,180) = 1.348, which means that if EBIT changes by 1 percent, net income will change by 1.348 percent. For the mixed financing, DFL is 1.148, and for the all-equity case it is 1.0. The conclusion to be drawn from this is that the use of debt financing can increase the *quantity* of expected EPS and return on equity, but it also decreases their *quality* by making them more variable and unpredictable.

George says that lower quality of the leveraged income associated with the greater use of financial leverage means that a dollar of future expected income that is of lower quality is worth less today than if the income was of higher quality. That is, for investors who are risk averse, a stream of *expected* future income of $1 per year will be discounted at a higher rate if it is more uncertain. Consequently, this stream of income will be of lower *value* than a stream of expected income of $1 per year that is of higher quality, that is, if there is greater certainty that the income will, in fact, be $1 each year.

EXHIBIT 6.37B Return on Equity at Different Levels of Total Revenue with Alternative Financing Plans

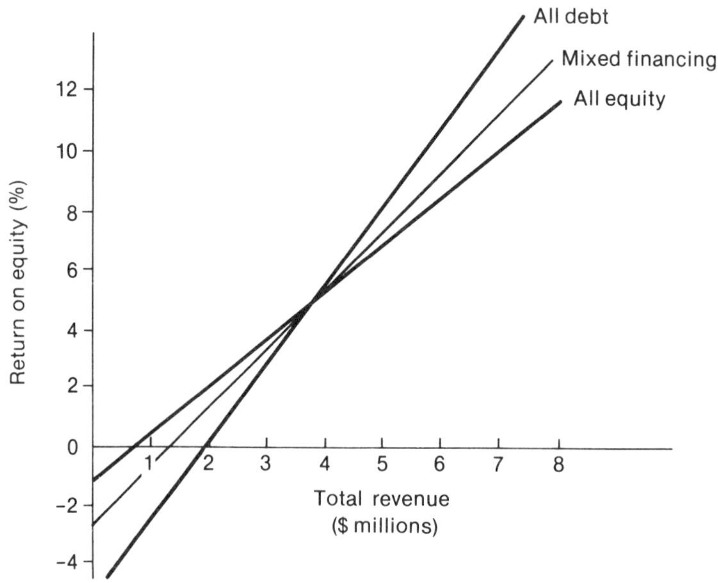

The implication of this relation between quality and the discount rate is that to evaluate the financing alternatives one must determine the present discounted value of the stream of income for each alternative and pick the alternative with the *highest present value,* rather than just considering the level of expected income for a given year.

To evaluate each financing alternative, George calculated the value of the shares to the current stockholders (those who own the stocks before new shares are sold to finance the new project). To determine the value, the appropriate discount rate must be determined, and a valuation model must be developed that will properly take account of the dilution effects of issuing new stock.

The capital asset pricing model (CAPM) was chosen by George as the basis for calculating the discount rate. According to the CAPM, the return that is required on an investment should be the risk-free interest rate, r_f, plus a risk premium that is proportional to the "systematic," or "market" risk of the investment. The systematic risk is measured by the volatility of the returns on the investment relative to the returns earned from a well diversified portfolio of stocks such as the Standard & Poor's composite 500-stock index. More precisely, the required return for the equity stock of a company, denoted by k_e (subscript e denotes equity), would be calculated according to

$$k_e = r_f + (k_m - r_f)\,\beta, \tag{6.102}$$

where $k_m - r_f$ is the risk premium (return in excess of the risk-free rate, r_f) expected (or required) on an investment in the market portfolio such as the S&P 500, and β (beta), measures the stock's systematic risk.[15]

Using Expression (6.102) with current data, George calculates the required return on Plastico's stock as

$$k_e = 0.09 + (0.08)(0.81) = 0.155,$$

where the current risk-free rate is 9 percent, the firm's beta is about 0.81 (based on past observations of the relation between returns on Plastico's stock and the S&P 500), and the historical average market risk premium of about 8 percent is used as a current estimate of $(k_m - r_f)$.[16]

The estimate of 15.5 percent for Plastico's cost of equity capital applies to the firm as it exists in its presently unleveraged condition. That is, Plastico has not used debt financing in recent years, and the estimate of its beta is based on observations from recent periods, so that beta estimate is implicitly the beta for Plastico financed as an all-equity firm.

If Plastico's capital structure is changed by using debt financing, this additional leverage will increase the risk borne by the stockholders, and the stockholders will require a higher return to compensate them for bearing this additional risk. The additional risk premium associated with financial leverage can be calculated by revising the beta according to the formula[17]

---

[15]For more complete explanations of the CAPM see Jacob and Pettit (1984, chap. 9–11, 13, and 16).

[16]The historical annual average risk premium on the S&P 500 Index has been estimated to be about 8.3 percent by Ibbotson and Sinquefield (1982).

[17]The adjustment of beta for financial leverage is derived in Hamada (1969) and Rubinstein (1973).

$$\beta_L = \beta_U \left[1 + \frac{Debt}{Equity}(1 - T)\right], \qquad (6.103)$$

where β_U denotes the beta for the firm when it is unleveraged (subscript U denotes unleveraged), β_L denotes the beta for the leveraged firm (subscript L denotes leveraged), T is the firm's corporate income tax rate, and *Debt/Equity* measures the amount of financial leverage.

With the mixed financing alternative, the firm's debt-to-equity ratio will stabilize at about 0.24 and with the all-debt alternative it will be 0.65. Applying (6.103) the revised betas will be

$$\begin{aligned}\beta_L &= 0.81\,[1 + 0.24(1 - 0.46)] \\ &= 0.915\end{aligned}$$

for the mixed financing, and

$$\begin{aligned}\beta_L &= 0.81\,[1 + 0.65\,(1 - 0.46)] \\ &= 1.094\end{aligned}$$

for the all-debt plan. Using these revised betas in the CAPM Expression (6.102), the estimates of the cost of equity capital for the leveraged firm are

$$\begin{aligned}k_e &= 0.09 + (0.08)(0.915) \\ &= 0.163\end{aligned}$$

for the mixed financing, and

$$\begin{aligned}k_e &= 0.09 + (0.08)(1.094) \\ &= 0.178\end{aligned}$$

for the all-debt financing. These estimated costs of equity capital are then used as discount rates for evaluating the financing alternatives.

The next step is to formulate a valuation model that can be used to assess the alternatives. One approach is to calculate the present value of expected dividends per share over the life of the firm, using the discount rates already calculated. A major difficulty is that this presents the problem of simultaneity. Finding the dividend per share requires that the number of shares outstanding be known, but this, in turn, depends on the price at which any new shares will be issued—and this is related to value, which is the thing to be determined. A superior approach that bypasses the simultaneity problem is the one developed by Miller and Modigliani (1961) that was already discussed.

In the present application George formulated the Miller and Modigliani model of stock value as

$$\begin{aligned} \mathit{Equity\ value}_0 = \sum_{t=1}^{5} \left(\mathit{Net\ income}_t - \mathit{Earnings\ retained}_t - \mathit{Common\ stock\ issued}_t \right) \frac{1}{(1+k_e)^t} \\ + \left[\frac{1}{(1+k)^5} \left(\frac{\mathit{Dividend}_6}{k_e} \right) \right]. \end{aligned} \quad (6.104)$$

Over the first five years (1987–91) the net income, earnings retained, and common stock issued are the aggregate amounts based on the pro forma statements in Exhibits 6.32, 6.33, and 6.34. Exhibit 6.38 shows the computation of the aggregate value of equity and the value per share based on this model.

For present purposes, George made the simplifying assumption that after 1991 the firm's net income would stabilize with no subsequent growth, and all net income would be paid out as dividends every year from 1992 forward. Thus, $\mathit{Dividend}_6$ is assumed to be equal to *Net income* for 1992 (and 1991), and the dividend stream is valued as a perpetuity as of 1991—($\mathit{Dividend}_6/k_e$)—and then discounted from 1991 back to the beginning of 1987 using the terms $[1/(1+k_e)^5(\mathit{Dividend}_6/k_e]$.

In the exhibit the "Net" line represents *Net income − Earnings retained − Common stock issued,* which multiplied by the present value factor, $1/(1+k)^t$, gives the present value of the net amount. The sum of these present values gives the *Equity value* of each alternative as of the beginning of 1987. The *Equity value* divided by the number of shares outstanding at the beginning of 1987 generates the value per share to the stockholders at that date.

Based on this calculation of *Equity value* and *Value per share,* George concludes that the all-debt financing strategy will generate greater value for the current stockholders. He argues that this approach to evaluating the alternatives properly takes account of dilution of ownership due to the issue of new shares, and the increased risk resulting from the use of debt financing. The fact that the *Common stock issued* is subtracted from *Net income* takes account of any dilution in ownership for the original stockholders due to the issue of new shares, and the discount

EXHIBIT 6.38 Value of Plastico Stock for Each Financing Alternative ($000)

		1987	*1988*	*1989*	*1990*	*1991*	*1992*
Equity financing							
Net income		$ 127.38	$ 294.91	$ 505.39	$575.39	$575.09	$575.0
− Earnings retained		76.43	176.94	303.23	345.23	345.00	0
− Common stock issued		1,283.45	329.18	457.68	0	0	0
"Net"		−$1,232.50	−$211.21	−$255.52	$230.16	$230.04	$575.0
× Present value factor @k_e = 0.155		0.8658	0.7496	0.6490	0.5619	0.4865	(0.4865/0.155)
Present value of "net"		−1,067.1	−158.32	−165.83	129.33	111.91	1,804.75
Equity value*: $654.75							
Value per share: $4.36	(= $654,750/150,000 shares)						
Combination debt and equity							
Net income		$127.38	$256.79	$456.82	$512.35	$512.06	$512.0
− Earnings retained		76.43	154.07	274.00	307.41	307.24	0.
− Common stock issued		641.73	176.03	243.41	0	0	0
"Net"		−$590.78	$−73.31	−$60.68	$204.94	$204.82	512.0
× Present value factor @k_e = 0.163		0.8598	0.7393	0.6357	0.5466	0.4700	(0.47/0.163)
Present value of "net"		−507.95	−54.20	−38.57	112.02	96.26	1,476.32
Equity value*: $1,083.88							
Value per share: $7.23	(= $1,083,880/150,000 shares)						

All-debt financing						
Net income	$127.38	$218.67	$406.88	$446.18	$445.89	$445.0
− Earnings retained	76.43	131.20	244.13	267.71	267.53	0.
− Common stock issued	0	0	0	0	0	0
"Net"	50.95	87.47	162.75	178.47	178.35	445.0
× Present value factor @k_e = 0.178	0.8489	0.7206	0.6117	0.5193	0.4408	(0.4408/0.178)
Present value of "net"	43.25	63.03	99.55	92.68	78.62	1,102.00

Equity value*: $1,479.13

Value per share: $9.86 (= $1,479,130/150,000 shares)

*Calculated from Equation 6.104.

rate, which ranges from 15.5 percent for the all-equity case to 17.8 percent for the all-debt case, takes account of the increased risk for stockholders due to the use of debt financing.

As an additional point in support of his position, George says that another way to evaluate these financing alternatives is to calculate the firm's weighted average cost of capital. This cost is a weighted average of the after-tax interest cost of the debt and the required return on equity, and it usually is calculated according to

$$k_a = \left[\frac{Debt}{Debt + Equity}\right] k_d (1 - T) + \left[\frac{Equity}{Debt + Equity}\right] k_e,$$

where k_d is the currently prevailing interest rate on the debt, k_e is the required return to equity after adjustment for the risks of financial leverage, and the weights are the long-run proportions of total capital financed by debt and equity, respectively. (These weights should be based on market values, but George used book values as an adequate first approximation.)

George says that the financing alternative that results in the lowest weighted average cost of capital is the one that will make the value of the firm its largest and that will also maximize the value of the stockholders' shares of equity. For these three financing alternatives George calculated the weighted average costs of capital shown in Exhibit 6.39. From these figures, he concludes that the all-debt alternative is best for the stockholders.

Joe listened to George and Sam and acknowledged that their arguments made sense, but he was still uncomfortable with the idea of increasing the firm's financial leverage. He fears that the use of debt financing will result in a deterioration of the firm's credit rating, will tend to depress the value of the firm's stock, and may threaten the firm's future financial flexibility.

With respect to the problem of credit rating, Sam acknowledged that increasing debt would increase the stockholders' risk, and any potential lenders would also bear increasing risk as the amount of debt is increased. He notes that their credit rating currently is excellent, and they should be able to borrow funds at close to the prime rate, even for the all-debt alternative because even in that case, the amount of debt will still be moder-

EXHIBIT 6.39 Weighted Average Cost of Capital for Each Financing Alternative

Financing Alternative	*Proportion of Debt*	*Cost of Debt, k_d*	*Proportion of Equity*	*Cost of Equity, k_e*	*Weighted Average, k_a*
Equity financing	0	0.11	1.00	0.155	0.155
Combination debt and equity	0.19	0.11	0.81	0.163	0.143
All-debt financing	0.39	0.11	0.61	0.178	0.132

ate. He says that it is pointless to worry about their credit rating if they aren't going to take advantage of it.

In response to Joe's fear that the stock value will suffer, George says that most of the adverse effects of debt financing are already considered in the adjustment of the required return to equity for different amounts of debt. If the cash flow available to equity did not increase sufficiently to generate the higher return required with debt financing, then the value of the stock would decline. However, by using the higher required return associated with debt financing as a rate for discounting the cash flow available to equity, one is testing whether the returns with debt financing are high enough to compensate for the extra risk.

Finally, both Sam and George admit that the use of debt financing does potentially decrease their future financial flexibility because it may decrease their ability to borrow in the future. However, they do not think the proposed amount of borrowing is so extreme that it limits their opportunities to borrow in the future, and besides, they note, they have no idea how much future flexibility they need, and by undertaking profitable investment now, they may actually open up new investment opportunities in the future.

6.5 SUMMARY

This chapter is the centerpiece of this book about financial modeling. It has discussed methods for structuring financial simulation models. Obviously, not all models could be presented and explained, so the purpose of this chapter has been to present and discuss the basic form of a "generic" financial simulation model. The types of equations that constitute such a model were explained. This generic model consists of modules that serve different functions in the model. The modules are the accounting module, the income generation module, the investment module, and the financing module. Each module consists of equations that express the relationships within the firm, and between the firm and its environment.

It was noted that a very important component of any such model is the system or mechanism for balancing the model—that is, helping the model to reach an equilibrium. Two major approaches to equilibrating the model were explained: a cash flow balancing system, and an asset-liability balancing system. Each approach represents a way to balance investment and financing and to maintain consistency in the model.

Many different approaches to structuring the different modules and to generating input to the modules were discussed, so the reader should now have some idea how to handle a variety of financial modeling tasks. In many cases the model will require that parameters be estimated with past data, and suggestions were made for ways to estimate the necessary parameters using statistical-econometric techniques.

Finally, an extended example was presented to demonstrate modeling the investment and financing decisions for a hypothetical company, Plastico Inc. The Plastico example shows how we can use a simulation model for evaluating investments. In addition, it also shows how difficult it still may be to evaluate the data and make a decision. One disadvantage of many simulation models is that they can generate a mountain of output and data that is confusing and difficult to evaluate. What is needed in many cases is a systematic way to compare the decision alternatives. Chapter Eight will explain how optimization models can be of help in this regard.

REFERENCES

BELL, F. W., and N. B. MURPHY. *Costs in Commercial Banking: A Quantitative Analysis of Bank Behavior and Its Relationships.* Research Report No. 41, Boston: Federal Reserve Bank of Boston, April 1968.

BLUMENTHAL, P. *Financial Model Preparation.* New York: American Institute of Certified Public Accountants, 1983.

BROWN, J., and D. LOW. "Interactive Simulation for Banking." *IBM Systems Journal* 12, no.2 (1973).

BRYANT, J. W., ed. *Financial Modeling in Corporate Management.* New York: John Wiley & Sons, 1982.

BREALEY, R., and S. MYERS. *Principles of Corporate Finance.* 2nd ed. New York: McGraw-Hill, 1984.

CARLETON, W. T.; C. L. DICK; and D. DOWNES. "Financial Policy Models: Theory and Practice." *Journal of Financial and Quantitative Analysis,* December 1973, pp. 691–709.

COHEN, K., and S. GIBSON. *Management Science in Banking.* Boston: Warren, Gorham and Lamont, 1978.

CRAMER, R. H., and R. MILLER. "Development of a Deposit Forecasting Procedure for Use in Bank Financial Management." *Journal of Bank Research,* Summer 1973, pp. 122–38.

DAMON, W. and R. SCHRAMM. "Simultaneous Decision Model for Production, Marketing and Finance." *Management Science,* October 1972.

DAVIS, B. E.; G. J. CACCAPPOLO; and M. A. CHAUDRY. "An Econometric Planning Model for American Telephone and Telegraph Company." *Bell Journal of Economics and Management Science,* Spring 1973, pp. 29–56.

DUESENBERRY, J.; G. FROMM; L. KLEIN; and E. KUH, eds. *The Brookings Quarterly Econometric Model of the United States.* Chicago: Rand McNally, 1965.

DZIELINSKI, B. "A Guide to Financial Planning Tools and Techniques." *IBM Systems Journal,* 12, no. 2 (1973).

EVANS, M. *Macroeconomic Activity: Theory, Forecasting, and Control.* New York: Harper & Row, 1969.

FRANCIS, J. C. *Investments: Analysis and Management.* 4th ed. New York: McGraw-Hill, 1986.

———. "Financial Planning and Forecasting Models: An Overview." *Journal of Economics and Business,* 1983, pp. 185–300.

FRANCIS, J. C., and D. ROWELL. "A Simultaneous Equation Model of the Firm for Financial Analysis and Planning." *Financial Management,* Spring 1978, pp. 29–44.

FRANKS, J. R.; J. E. BROYLES; and W. CARLETON. *Corporate Finance: Concepts and Applications.* Boston: Kent Publishing Co., 1985.

GERSHEFSKI, G. "Building a Corporate Financial Model." *Harvard Business Review,* July-August 1969, pp. 61–72.

———. "Corporate Models: The State of the Art." *Management Planning,* November-December 1969, pp. 1–6.

———. *The Development and Application of a Corporate Financial Model.* Oxford, Ohio: The Planning Executives Institute, 1968.

GORDON, R. J. "Financial Modeling on Small Systems." *IBM Systems Journal,* 12, no. 2 (1973).

HADLEY, G., and T. WHITEN. *Analysis of Inventory Systems.* Englewood Cliffs, N.J.: Prentice-Hall, 1963.

HAMADA, R. S. "Portfolio Analysis, Market Equilibrium, and Corporation Finance." *Journal of Finance,* March 1969, pp. 13–32.

HIGGINS, R. C. *Analysis for Financial Management.* Homewood, Ill.: Richard D. Irwin, 1984.

IBBOTSON, R., and R. SINQUEFIELD. *Stocks, Bonds Bills and Inflation: The Past and the Future.* Charlottesville, Va.: Financial Analysts Research Foundation, 1982.

JACOB, N., and R. PETTIT. *Investments.* Homewood, Ill.: Richard D. Irwin, 1984.

JOHNSON, R. W., and R. W. MELICHER. *Financial Management.* 5th ed. Boston: Allyn & Bacon, 1982.

LIFSON, K. A., and B. BLACKMARR. "Simulation and Optimization Models for Asset Deployment and Funds Sources Balancing Profit, Liquidity and Growth." *Journal of Bank Research,* Autumn 1973, pp. 239–44.

LACASCIO, V. "Financial Planning Models." *Financial Executive,* March 1972.

LONGBRAKE, W. "Statistical Cost Analysis." *Financial Management,* Spring 1973.

MALKIEL, B., and J. CRAGG. "Expectations and the Structure of Share Prices." *American Economic Review,* September 1970, pp. 601–17.

MEYER, H. I. *Corporate Financial Planning Models.* New York: John Wiley & Sons, 1977.

MILLER, M., and F. MODIGLIANI. "Dividend Policy, Growth, and the Valuation of Shares." *The Journal of Business,* October 1961, pp. 411–33.

MILLER, M. and D. ORR. "A Model of Demand for Money by Firms." *Quarterly Journal of Economics,* August 1966, pp. 413–35.

MURPHY, N. "The Implications of Econometric Analysis of Bank Cost Functions for Bank Planning." *Journal of Bank Research,* Autumn 1973, pp. 203–6.

NAYLOR, T. "Corporate Simulation Models." *Simulation,* August 1973.

_______. *Corporate Planning Models.* Reading, Mass: Addison-Wesley Publishing, 1979.

_______. *Computer Simulation Experiments with Models of Economic Systems.* New York: John Wiley & Sons, 1971.

NAYLOR, T., and H. SCHAULAND. "A Survey of Users of Corporate Planning Models." *Management Science,* May 1976, pp. 927–57.

NORTON, J. "Simulation for Planning and Control." *Management Review,* February 1972.

ORGLER, Y. "An Unequal Period Model for Cash Management Decisions." *Management Science,* October 1969, pp. B77–92.

_______. *Cash Management: Methods and Models.* Belmont, Calif.: Wadsworth, 1970.

ROBINSON, R. S. "Bank Mod: An Interactive Simulation Aid for Bank Financial Planning." *Journal of Bank Research,* Autumn 1973, pp. 212–24.

ROERING, K. J., AND P. E. SMITH. "A Distributed Lag Forecasting Model for Bank Loans and the Money Supply." *Journal of Bank Research,* Summer 1978, pp. 104–11.

RUBINSTEIN, M., "A Mean Variance Synthesis of Corporate Financial Theory." *Journal of Finance,* March 1973.

SCHRIEBER, A. *Corporate Simulation Models.* Seattle: University of Washington Press, 1970.

SMITH, KEITH. *Guide to Working Capital Management.* New York: McGraw-Hill, 1979.

SNIDER, W. "Building an On-Line Financial Planning Model." *Journal of Bank Research,* Autumn 1973, pp. 232–38.

THOMSON, M. "Forecasting for Financial Planning." *Journal of Bank Research,* Autumn 1973, pp. 225–31.

TRAENKLE, J.; E. COX; and J. BULLARD. *The Use of Financial Models in Business.* New York: Financial Executives Research Foundation, 1975.

TYRAN, M. W. *Computerized Financial Forecasting and Performance Reporting.* Englewood Cliffs, N.J.: Prentice-Hall, 1980.

VANDERWEIDE, J., and S. MAIER. *Managing Corporate Liquidity: An*

Introduction to Working Capital Management. New York: John Wiley & Sons, 1985.

WAGNER, H. *Principles of Operations Research—With Applications to Management Decisions.* Englewood Cliffs, N.J.: Prentice-Hall, 1969.

WARREN, J., and J. SHELTON. "A Simultaneous Equation Approach to Financial Planning." *Journal of Finance,* December 1971, 1123–42.

WESTON, J. F., and T. COPELAND. *Managerial Finance.* 8th ed. Hinsdale, Ill.: Dryden Press, 1986.

CHAPTER SEVEN

Dealing with Uncertainty

7.1 INTRODUCTION

Presumably, one of the reasons we are inclined to go to the trouble of building financial models and developing plans for the future is to deal with uncertainty. That is, we don't know what will happen in the future, and we want to be prepared for most eventualities. Building models and developing plans is our way to minimize the pain and costs of encountering our uncertain future in business. However, to this point we have discussed how we might build simulation models, but we have not really considered how we will use them to deal with the uncertain world of business. That is what this chapter is about: We will consider different methods for analyzing and dealing with uncertainty by the use of financial planning models.

The kinds of uncertainty that we could consider are uncertainties about future economic events: prices, sales levels, market shares, costs, lives of assets and projects, interest rates, and even availability of financing. All these factors, and more, are important to the success of most business ventures, and most of them vary over time—we do not know what they will be in the future. Without knowing what will happen, it is difficult to be sure we are making the right decision. Yet, we want to make the best decision possible under the circumstances of our limited knowledge and considerable ignorance. In this regard, models can help us. All the modeling and planning in the world can not assure us that we will have made the best decision when we look back at it after the fact, with the benefit of hindsight. All we can hope to do is to arrive at the best decision possible given the information we have available before the fact, without the benefit of hindsight.

The key word is *information.* With the best information, properly evaluated, we can improve the likelihood that we are making the best decision. What modeling and planning do is provide a way to process and analyze the available information so we can get a maximum amount of insight about our uncertain future. The model simply helps us organize what we know about our firm, its relation to its environment, and the possible events that will influence our firm. Planning involves the evaluation of that information so we are prepared with some decisions as the future rolls toward us.

No matter how thorough our models, nor how careful our plan, our decisions will turn out to be completely correct only with monumentally good luck. Generally, when we look back on our decisions, they will turn out to have been wrong. What modeling and planning can do for us is help us minimize the costs of being wrong. If we prepared for our uncertain future, if we have anticipated that the best laid plans are bound to go awry, then we can be ready to respond to events that turn out to be different from those we expected. That is, we need not only to plan, but we need to plan for being wrong about our plan.

One way we can plan for being wrong is to consider the various events that can possibly occur and develop contingency plans. We can play out different scenarios ahead of time and consider how we should react with these different scenarios. We can explore the various possible events and assess our situation with these different events. This is where modeling pays off. A model provides a mechanism to explore the future ahead of time. The simulation model exists so we have an inexpensive way to play out the different events and assess their effects.

One way we can use the simulation model is what we will call *scenario simulation,* or sensitivity analysis, which tries out different scenarios, asking What if this happens? and What if that happens? Scenario simulation allows us to trace through the intricate relations that make up our firm. Another way to simulate is to use what is called *Monte Carlo* simulation. Monte Carlo simulation requires that we estimate the probabilities of different outcomes and then have the model make random draws of the relevant random variables according to the relative frequencies prescribed by the probabilities. This way we not only trace through the effects of different scenarios, but we utilize information about the relative likelihood of these scenarios so we can determine the relative likelihoods of different outcomes for our firm.

There are other ways to deal with risk and uncertainty besides scenario simulation and Monte Carlo simulation. The methods we will discuss we will call *risk adjustment* methods. These are techniques for estimating values, particularly for firms or investment projects, that take account of the uncertainty by adjusting or penalizing the value of an investment for the amount of risk. More risky or uncertain investments are typically regarded as less valuable than less risky investments, and the risk adjustment methods assess a penalty that shows how much less valuable the more risky investment should be. The price we would be willing to pay for the investment would then be low enough so we aren't hurt as badly when the adverse outcomes occur.

We will discuss each of these methods for dealing with uncertainty, but the main focus of our discussion will be on simulation. Examples will be presented that point out the main features of simulation, and we will discuss how to interpret the results of our simulations.

7.2 SCENARIO SIMULATION

Obviously, we do not know what will happen in the future—we don't know if we will have a recession, we don't know what will happen to stock prices or whether oil prices will drop. The essence of business is taking risks, but we want to be able to earn rewards that outweigh the risks. One way we can earn such rewards is to be lucky, but luck is notoriously unreliable. Another way is to study the risks so we have superior knowledge of the possibilities—the risks and rewards—and be able to reject those ventures where the tradeoff is unattractive. Scenario simulation allows us to analyze, in as much depth and detail as we like, the various possible outcomes of our decisions so that we can be sure of all the risks and take them into account in our decision making.

Scenario simulation is quite straightforward. We assume a probable set of circumstances about the business environment, about our firm, and about our decisions, and work out the implications with the aid of our model. Thus, we assume a scenario and determine how things would work out with that scenario. Then, because we don't know what will actually come to pass, we change the assumptions and work out the implications of a different scenario. We simply try out different combinations of environments and decisions to evaluate the results.

An easy example of scenario simulation, or sensitivity analysis, is an extension of the discussion of the Mogul Corporation presented in Chapter Three. If you will recall, the Mogul Corporation manufactured skis that were sold on a seasonal basis, leading to a seasonal pattern of needs for funds. The determination of the expected required financing was based on a set of assumptions that included an expected pattern of collections of receivables. The assumptions about collections were that 10 percent of sales were on a cash basis, and 90 percent were on credit, with 40 percent of sales being collected the first month after the sale, 30 percent collected the second month after the sale, 15 percent collected the third month, and 5 percent never collected. Based on these assumptions, we developed a statement of cash receipts and disbursements that was presented in complete form as Exhibit 3.1, and which is presented here in abbreviated form as Exhibit 7.1. Under the initial assumptions the *required financing* builds up to a peak of $79,274 in October. However, this statement is based on a set of forecasts and assumptions, about none of which we can be sure. Almost all the variables that go into the statement are forecasts that are sure to be incorrect.

One forecast that will prove crucial is the assumed collection experience. We cannot be sure that we will collect receivables in the pattern anticipated. A very large firm with many relatively small credit accounts such as Sears Roebuck, Exxon, or even GMAC cannot be sure about the collections on any single account, but for their total receivables they can quite accurately determine the proportion that will be collected each month. A

EXHIBIT 7.1 Mogul Corporation: Cash Receipts and Disbursements, July 1986–June 1987 (Base case)

	July	*Aug*	*Sept*	*Oct*	*Nov*	*Dec*	*Jan*	*Feb*	*Mar*	*April*	*May*	*June*
Sales	$3,000	$ 8,000	$18,000	$40,000	$60,000	$35,000	$20,000	$15,000	$ 5,000	$ 3,000	$ 2,000	$ 1,000
Receipts												
Cash sales	300	800	1,800	4,000	6,000	3,500	2,000	1,500	500	300	200	100
Collections, Month 1	400	1,200	3,200	7,200	16,000	24,000	14,000	8,000	6,000	2,000	1,200	800
Collections, Month 2	600	300	900	2,400	5,400	12,000	18,000	10,500	6,000	4,500	1,500	900
Collections, Month 3	450	300	150	450	1,200	2,700	6,000	9,000	5,250	3,000	2,250	750
Total receipts	1,750	2,600	6,050	14,050	28,600	42,200	40,000	29,000	17,750	9,800	5,150	2,550
Total disbursements	8,700	15,758	33,768	45,499	28,261	20,258	14,075	6,859	6,774	5,500	3,800	7,700
Net cash flow	−6,950	−13,158	−27,718	−31,449	339	21,942	25,925	22,141	10,976	4,300	1,350	−5,150
Plus: Beginning cash	5,000	−1,950	−15,108	−42,825	−74,274	−73,935	−51,992	−26,067	−3,926	7,049	11,349	12,699
Equals: Cumulative cash	−1,950	−15,108	−42,825	−74,274	−73,935	−51,992	−26,067	−3,926	7,049	11,349	12,699	7,549
Less: Desired cash	5,000	5,000	5,000	5,000	5,000	5,000	5,000	5,000	5,000	5,000	5,000	5,000
Equals: Required financing	6,950	20,108	47,825	79,274	78,935	56,992	31,067	8,926	0	0	0	0
Excess cash	0	0	0	0	0	0	0	0	2,049	6,349	7,699	2,549

small firm such as Mogul that has relatively few accounts receivable, each of which may be large relative to the total, cannot so accurately estimate the proportion that will be collected each month. One customer missing a payment will make a larger difference in the proportion collected than it would for Sears Roebuck.

Clearly we don't know exactly how much will be collected each month, but we can make some plausible guesses how much we can collect. Suppose, based on judgment and past experience, we are quite confident that the worst we would do would be to collect 20 percent of sales in the first month (instead of 40 percent), and 50 percent in the second month (instead of 30 percent), with the rest of the collection parameters unlikely to change. On the optimistic side we feel the best we could do would be to have *cash sales* equal to 15 percent of sales (instead of 10 percent), and we could collect 50 percent in the first month and 15 percent the second month, with the third-month collections and bad debts remaining unchanged. With these varied assumptions we can work out the implications of our uncertainty to determine the likely range of *required financing*. We won't know what will happen, but by exploring the upper and lower ends of what is possible, we can be better prepared for these different scenarios.

Exhibits 7.2 and 7.3 show the results of working out the implications of these pessimistic and optimistic assumptions. Whereas the original set of assumptions that we considered most likely (the base case), showed a peak financing need of $79,274 occurring in October, the pessimistic scenario for collections shows a peak need of $86,983 in November, and the optimistic scenario shows a peak required financing of $74,548. Thus, we know that if the collections are the only critical uncertainty and our estimates of high and low values are correct, we should be prepared to meet a minimum financing need of $74,548, but we could need as much as $86,983. If we can deal with our banker with these estimates available, we will be in a much better position to obtain the required financing.

Clearly, there are bound to be many other uncertain variables that will affect our required financing. Sales, prices, collections, operating costs, and interest rates are some of the

EXHIBIT 7.2 Mogul Corporation: Cash Receipts and Disbursements, July 1986–June 1987 (Pessimistic scenario)

	July	*Aug*	*Sept*	*Oct*	*Nov*	*Dec*	*Jan*	*Feb*	*Mar*	*April*	*May*	*June*
Sales	$3,000	$ 8,000	$18,000	$40,000	$60,000	$35,000	$20,000	$15,000	$ 5,000	$ 3,000	$ 2,000	$ 1,000
Receipts												
Cash sales	300	800	1,800	4,000	6,000	3,500	2,000	1,500	500	300	200	100
Collections, Month 1	400	600	1,600	3,600	8,000	12,000	7,000	4,000	3,000	1,000	600	400
Collections, Month 2	600	300	1,500	4,000	9,000	20,000	30,000	17,500	10,000	7,500	2,500	1,500
Collections, Month 3	450	300	150	450	1,200	2,700	6,000	9,000	5,250	3,000	2,250	750
Total receipts	1,750	2,000	5,050	12,050	24,200	38,200	45,000	32,000	18,750	11,800	5,550	2,750
Total disbursements	8,700	15,758	33,773	45,512	28,291	20,325	14,176	6,919	6,810	5,511	3,800	7,700
Net cash flow	−6,950	−13,758	−28,723	−33,462	−4,091	17,875	30,824	25,081	11,940	6,289	1,750	−4,950
Plus: Beginning cash	5,000	−1,950	−15,708	−44,430	−77,892	−81,983	−64,108	−33,284	−8,203	3,737	10,026	11,776
Equals: Cumulative cash	−1,950	−15,708	−44,430	−77,892	−81,983	−64,108	−33,284	−8,203	3,737	10,026	11,776	6,826
Less: Desired cash	5,000	5,000	5,000	5,000	5,000	5,000	5,000	5,000	5,000	5,000	5,000	5,000
Equals: Required financing	6,950	20,708	49,430	82,892	86,983	69,108	38,284	13,203	1,263	0	0	0
Excess cash	0	0	0	0	0	0	0	0	0	5,026	6,776	1,826

EXHIBIT 7.3 Mogul Corporation: Cash Receipts and Disbursements, July 1986–June 1987 (Optimistic scenario)

	July	*Aug*	*Sept*	*Oct*	*Nov*	*Dec*	*Jan*	*Feb*	*Mar*	*April*	*May*	*June*
Sales	$3,000	$ 8,000	$18,000	$40,000	$60,000	$35,000	$20,000	$15,000	$ 5,000	$ 3,000	$ 2,000	$ 1,000
Receipts												
Cash sales	450	1,200	2,700	6,000	9,000	5,250	3,000	2,250	750	450	300	150
Collections, Month 1	400	1,500	4,000	9,000	20,000	30,000	17,500	10,000	7,500	2,500	1,500	1,000
Collections, Month 2	600	300	450	1,200	2,700	6,000	9,000	5,250	3,000	2,250	750	450
Collections, Month 3	450	300	150	450	1,200	2,700	6,000	9,000	5,250	3,000	2,250	750
Total receipts	1,900	3,300	7,300	16,650	32,900	43,950	35,500	26,500	16,500	8,200	4,800	2,350
Total disbursements	8,700	15,757	33,760	45,481	28,221	20,182	13,984	6,805	6,741	5,500	3,800	7,700
Net cash flow	−6,800	−12,457	−26,460	−28,831	4,679	23,768	21,516	19,695	9,759	2,700	1,000	−5,350
Plus: Beginning cash	5,000	−1,800	−14,257	−40,717	−69,548	−64,869	−41,102	−19,586	109	9,869	12,569	13,569
Equals: Cumulative cash	−1,800	−14,257	−40,717	−69,548	−64,869	−41,102	−19,586	109	9,869	12,569	13,569	8,219
Less: Desired cash	5,000	5,000	5,000	5,000	5,000	5,000	5,000	5,000	5,000	5,000	5,000	5,000
Equals: Required financing	6,800	19,257	45,717	74,548	69,869	46,102	24,586	4,891	0	0	0	0
Excess cash	0	0	0	0	0	0	0	0	4,869	7,569	8,569	3,219

uncertain factors. To get a better idea about Mogul's needs for the next few months, we should work through numerous scenarios that show the joint effects of all these uncertain variables. We can combine the variables in various scenarios, and with the aid of a spreadsheet program[1] easily develop plans to meet almost any eventuality.

While this type of scenario simulation can be useful, one of its weaknesses is that it doesn't take into account the fact that some scenarios are more likely than others. It is important to work out the implications of the worst case scenario, but it should not necessarily drive the firm's decision when that worst case is extremely unlikely to occur. We should base our decisions on what is most likely, tempered by a prudent consideration of both the pessimistic and optimistic possibilities. One of the ways we can include this balance in our modeling and planning is to take into account the relative likelihoods of the different scenarios. This is what we do with Monte Carlo simulation.

7.3 MONTE CARLO SIMULATION

Monte Carlo simulation is just an extension of what we have called scenario simulation, except that we take explicit account of the probabilities of different scenarios, and determine the likelihood of different outcomes. If we assume that a variable, such as prices, sales, or collections, could take any one of many possible different values, then a scenario approach would assume that one of these many values prevailed and trace out the consequences. With Monte Carlo simulation we may assume this same variable is a random variable with a known probabil-

---

[1]The spreadsheet software used to develop this example was IFPS/Personal, available from Execucom Systems Corporation, 3410 Far West Blvd., Austin, TX 78731. IFPS is a very powerful and flexible system that offers many features superior to the better known, smaller spreadsheets. However, IFPS/Personal is more difficult to learn, requires greater memory on the personal computer, and is much more expensive. IFPS on mainframe computers is a superlative financial planning software product that is easy to learn and use, and has only the disadvantage that it is expensive and requires a mainframe computer. Both IFPS/Personal and the mainframe IFPS offer the useful capability to try "What If" scenario simulation. Simply by choosing the "What If" option, one can quickly work through innumerable scenarios.

ity distribution, so that we know the relative likelihood of each possible value of the random variable. Then we randomly generate or draw many values of this variable to trace out the consequences of each draw, where the proportional number of times we draw a particular value of the variable approximates its probability. In this way we can generate a frequency distribution of consequences that approximates the true relative likelihoods of the different consequences.

Let us return to the Mogul Corporation example to demonstrate Monte Carlo simulation. Assume that all the variables have the same values as in the base case discussed earlier, except that the proportions of cash and credit sales are random variables, with *Cash proportion* being a normally distributed random variable with expected value

$$E\ (\textit{Cash proportion}) = 0.10$$

and standard deviation,

$$\sigma\ (\textit{Cash proportion}) = 0.02.$$

Thus, the proportion of sales made on a cash basis each month is assumed to be drawn randomly from a probability distribution as shown in Exhibit 7.4, and consequently the *Cash sales* and *Credit sales* will be random each month.

EXHIBIT 7.4

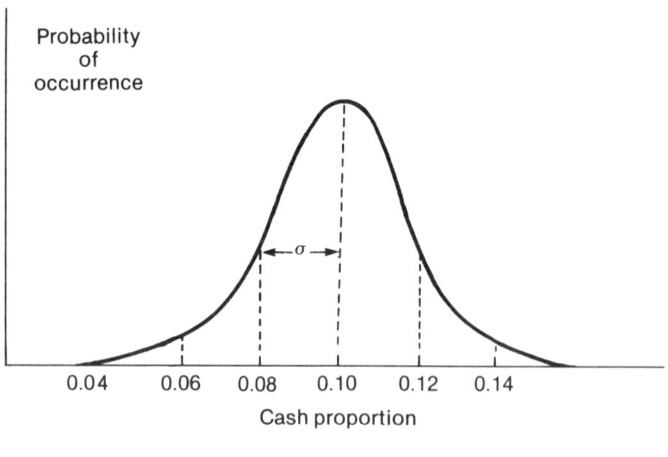

EXHIBIT 7.5

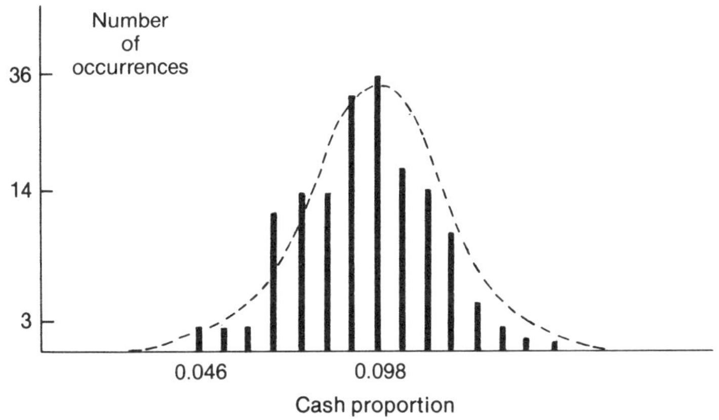

With Monte Carlo simulation we draw randomly many different values of the variable *Cash proportion,* and on each draw trace out the consequences of that particular value with our model. Each value is drawn from the described probability distribution, so that values close to the mean, *E* (*Cash proportion*), have a much higher likelihood of being picked, and values far from the mean are less likely to be drawn. For this example, the *Cash proportion* was drawn randomly 200 times to see what the range of possible outcomes might turn out to be and what the relative frequencies of different outcomes are.[2] Exhibit 7.5 shows a histogram of the number of observations of *Cash proportion* drawn out of 200 trials, with the *Cash proportion* shown on the horizontal axis and the number of observations on the vertical axis. This graph corresponds to the probability distribution shown as Exhibit 7.4, except Exhibit 7.4 represents the theoretical frequencies that we should observe from the different outcomes, and the histogram represents the actual observed frequencies. For example, out of 200 draws, 36 observations of *cash proportion* were in the interval 9.7 percent to 10.5 percent

[2]The IFPS software on a mainframe computer was used for this simulation. It offers the user a "Monte Carlo" option where the user specifies the nature of the probability distributions, and the system generates random drawings from the distributions to be fed into the spreadsheet financial model.

and only one observation was in the interval between 15.4 percent and 16.3 percent and none was higher than that. From this we can see that, by the chance of the draw we can get outcomes more or less frequently than the strict probabilities would

EXHIBIT 7.6 Monte Carlo Simulation of Collections of Receivables

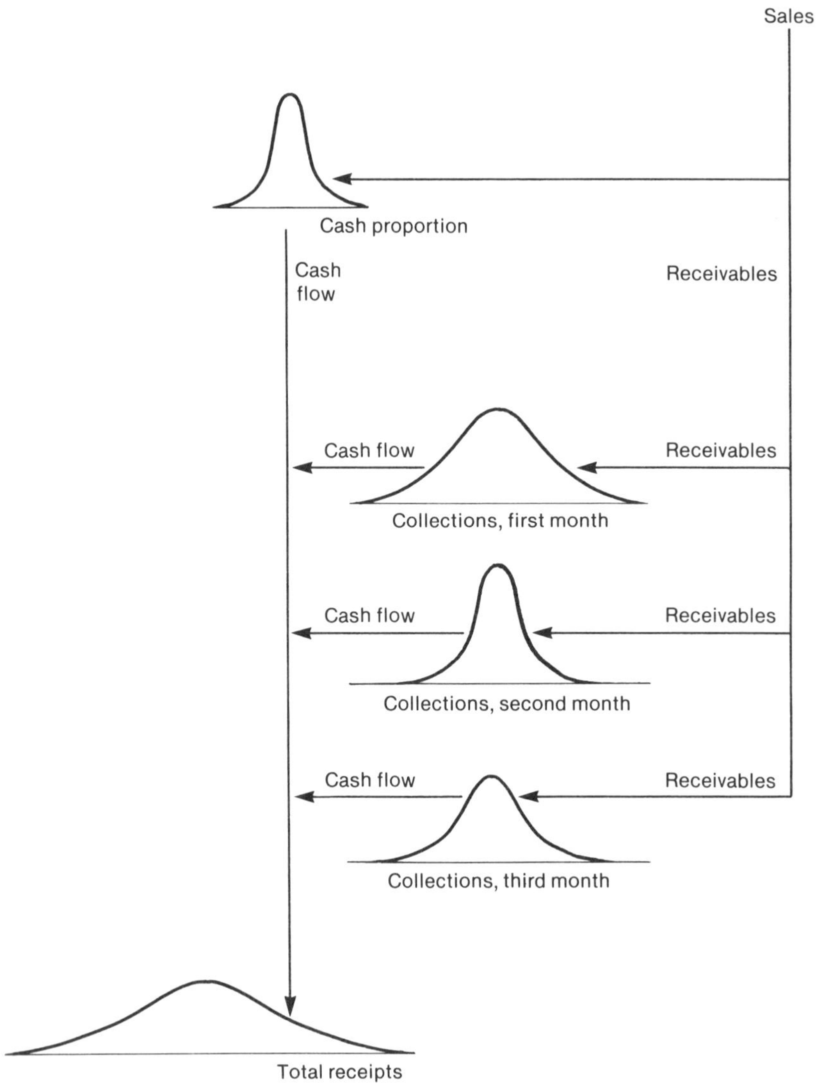

suggest, but over all, the frequency outcomes in many trials should approximate the probability distribution as shown in Exhibit 7.4.

The real value of making the random draws from probability distributions and then working the results through the model is that we can combine and explore the consequences of a number of different random variables in the system. If there are many different random variables that affect the outcomes of our decisions, it is extremely difficult to discern directly how these variables will interact. But, by simulating their random behavior we can begin to understand the combined effects of randomness. Exhibit 7.6 demonstrates the idea. With a given level of *sales,* the *Cash proportion* is a random variable (as is the *Credit proportion*), determining the immediate *Cash flow* from *Sales.* Then, from the *Credit sales* the amount of *collections* in the first month is a random variable, providing a cash flow the first month after the sale. Whatever is left in receivables may be collected in the second or third months, but these amounts collected are also random variables. Thus, the *Total receipts* derived from *Sales* will be the combined random result of the split between *Cash sales* and *Credit sales,* and the timing of the customers' payments. In this way, the amount collected and the timing of the collections are random variables. However, it is extremely difficult to have a very good idea of the amounts that will be received without working through the problem with a simulation.

To see how this might work, assume that these variables have probability distributions with the following parameters.

Variable	*Expected Value*	*Standard Deviation*
Cash proportion	0.10	0.02
Collections, first month	0.444	0.05
Collections, second month	0.60	0.10
Collections, third month	0.75	0.07

In this case the collection variables are the proportions of the declining balance of receivables that are collected each month. Of the credit sales, 44.4 percent are expected to be collected in the first month after the sale, but this amount is uncertain, so we represent the uncertainty by assigning the standard deviation of 5 percent. Of the receivables still uncollected, we assume that the probability distribution of collections has an expected value of 60 percent and standard deviation of 10 percent, and similarly, the parameters for *Collections, third month* are an expected value of 75 percent of remaining receivables with standard deviation of 7 percent. Since each level of collection is unknown beforehand, and is drawn by chance from the distribution, we must simulate the collection process to determine the pattern of cash flow from our customers.

Based on the assumed parameters of the probability distributions of *Cash sales, Collections, first month, Collections, second month,* and *Collections, third month,* 200 random drawings were made from each distribution to simulate the *Total receipts* collected by the Mogul Corporation each month over their planning horizon. Exhibit 7.7 displays the histograms of the *Collections* and *Total receipts* just for the month of December.

For comparison and evaluation, the total receipts from this simulation and the base case figures from Exhibit 7.1 are shown below for July through December.

	July	*Aug*	*Sept*	*Oct*	*Nov*	*Dec*
Base case						
Total receipts	1,750	2,600	6,050	14,050	28,600	42,200
Simulation						
Total receipts (mean)	1,747	2,601	6,062	14,006	28,668	42,218
Standard deviation	61	181	468	1,046	1,729	2,100

The means (expected values) of *Total receipts* were quitė close to the values of the base case (because the random variables in the simulation was specified with means equal to values in the base case). What is of interest is the spread, or range, of possible outcomes as measured by the standard deviation of *Total receipts.*

For a normally distributed random variable, there is almost no chance that the value of a variable will actually occur more

EXHIBIT 7.7 Frequency Histograms of Cash Sales, Collections, and Receipts (December)

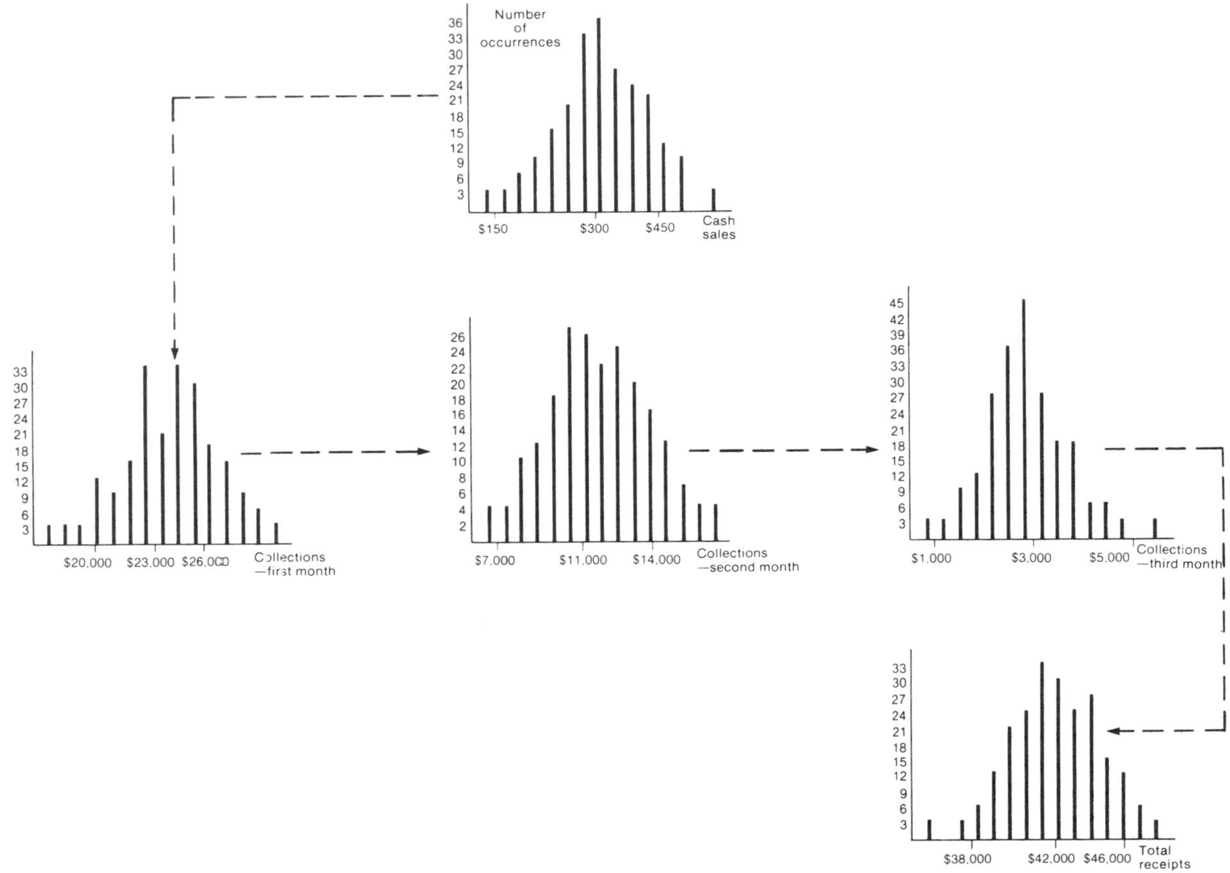

than three standard deviations above or below the mean. So for example, for December, with mean *Total receipts* of \$42,218 and standard deviation of \$2,100, the lowest that can reasonably be expected to occur is

$$\begin{aligned} & E\,(\textit{Total receipts}) - 3 \cdot \sigma\,(\textit{Total receipts}) \\ = {} & 42{,}218 - 3 \cdot (2{,}100) \\ = {} & 42{,}218 - 6{,}300 \\ = {} & \$35{,}918 \end{aligned}$$

and the highest is

$$\begin{aligned} & E\,(\textit{Total receipts}) + 3 \cdot \sigma\,(\textit{Total receipts}) \\ & 42{,}218 + 6{,}300 \\ & \$48{,}518. \end{aligned}$$

Thus, we can say that there is almost no chance that *Total receipts* for December will be less than \$35,918 or more than \$48,518.

Another feature of the normal distribution is that we know, with about two chances out of three, the value actually observed will be within the range of the expected value plus or minus (±) one standard deviation. For December *Total receipts* this range would be

$$E\,(\textit{Total receipts}) \pm \sigma\,(\textit{Total receipts}),$$

which for the low side is

$$\$42{,}218 - 2{,}100 = \$40{,}118,$$

and for the high side is

$$\$42{,}218 + 2{,}100 = \$44{,}318.$$

From this we can say that there is a good chance (two chances out of three) that the actual *total receipts* will most likely occur in the range between \$40,118 and \$44,318.

In making our plans, if we believe our estimates of the parameters of the probability distributions, *Total receipts* will not drop below \$35,918, nor exceed \$48,518, and we can regard its most likely value to lie between \$40,118 and \$44,318, with an expected value of about \$42,218.

The statement "If we believe our estimates of the parameters of the probability distributions" is central to the usefulness of

Monte Carlo simulation. We have at least two levels of uncertainty. First, if we know the parameters of the probability distributions, we still don't know what outcome will occur. Second, we typically don't really know the parameters or even the form of the probability distributions. We can only estimate or guess at these parameters. To deal with this uncertainty, it is suggested that we use sensitivity analysis on the parameters to explore the effects of different parameters. For example, we aren't really sure that the *Cash proportion* has expected value of 10 percent and standard deviation of 2 percent. We can vary these parameters and work through a new Monte Carlo simulation to get some idea of the effects of different parameters on our *Total receipts,* and ultimately, on our financing requirements.

This method of analysis cannot eliminate the uncertainty. After all, it is not magical. Its value is that it helps us get a better idea of range of possibilities, and allows us to make our contingency plans that take into account the range of possibilities.

Simulation of NPV

Another application of Monte Carlo simulation that deserves some explanation is its use in investment analysis in determining the parameters of the probability distribution of the net present value of an investment. This method views an investment as potentially having many different possible net present values, depending on which particular cash flows actually occur. We don't know which sequence of cash flows will occur, but assuming we know their probabilities, we can associate a probability with each possible cash flow scenario and describe a probability distribution of net present values of these different cash flows.

As an example, first consider a very simple investment that will generate cash flow at the end of one period that could take any one of the following three values with the probabilities as indicated:

Cash flow at t_1	\$400	\$450	\$500
Probability of occurrence	0.20	0.60	0.20

If the *cash flow* turns out to be \$500 at t_1, then its present value today is \$500(1/1.07) = \$467.29, using a risk-free rate of r_f = 0.07 as the discount rate. Similarly, if the *cash flow* turns out to be \$400, its present value is \$373.83, and if the *cash flow* is \$450 at t_1, its value is \$420.56. Based on these values that used r_f as the discount rate, the distribution of values is:

Value at t_1	\$373.83	\$420.56	\$467.29
Probability of occurrence	0.20	0.60	0.20

From these results, the cash flow has expected value of \$420.56 with standard deviation of \$29.56. In this context, however, we don't directly determine a value from these figures. Rather, we say we do not directly know its value because we don't know what cash flow it may generate. We say its value is either \$373.83, or \$420.56, or \$467.29, depending on which *cash flow* eventually occurs at t_1.

While this approach doesn't lead to a value assessment, it does provide one additional bit of perspective for deciding how much the investment is worth. We know that if we pay more than \$420.56 there is an 80 percent chance that the value of the cash flow we will earn will be less than we paid. If we pay \$373.83, then the worst that can happen is that we will earn the riskless rate of 7 percent, and we may do much better, so presumably we should be willing to pay something more than \$373.83, and less than \$420.56.

Now let us extend this approach to a multiperiod example, using Monte Carlo simulation.

Assume that we are considering an investment that costs \$1,000 today, and will generate cash flows at times t_1, t_2, and t_3. The cash flows are unknown as of today, but we have figured out the parameters of the probability distributions from which they will be drawn. The cash flows are assumed to be drawn from normal distributions with parameters as follow:

	Period 1	*Period 2*	*Period 3*
E (*Cash flow*)	\$450	\$500	\$400
σ (*Cash flow*)	50	100	150

The Monte Carlo simulation will make many different draws from these distributions, calculating the NPV for each draw, using the risk-free rate as the discount rate, which is assumed to be $r_f = 0.07$. Suppose, for example, that on one of these draws, just by luck of the draw, the cash flows turned out to be \$400, \$563, and \$250 at t_1, t_2, and t_3, respectively. The net present value would be

$$\begin{aligned} \text{NPV} &= -1{,}000 + 400\,(1/1.07) + 563\,(1/1.07)^2 + 250\,(1/1.07^3 \\ &= -1{,}000 + 1{,}069.65 \\ &= +\ \$69.65. \end{aligned}$$

The Monte Carlo simulation will make many such draws from the distributions, so we will get an idea of the frequency distribution of the possible NPV outcomes.

In this example, it was assumed that the draws were independent between periods (i.e., period 1's draw does not affect the draw in period 2).[3] The frequency distribution of draws for each period that were observed with 200 draws is shown as Exhibit 7.8, with the resulting frequency distribution of net present value shown as the histogram at the bottom. The NPV values ranged from −\$240 to \$600, with a mean of $E(\text{NPV}) =$ \$166 and standard deviation of $\sigma(\text{NPV}) =$ \$157.

One of the ways this simulation can help us with our decision is to evaluate the probability that NPV will be less than zero. With the parameters for NPV of 166, and $E(NPV) =$ $\sigma\,(NPV) =$ \$157, zero NPV is 1.057 standard deviations below the mean, calculated as

$$\frac{0 - E\,(NPV)}{\sigma\,(NPV)} = \frac{0 - 166}{157} = -1.057.$$

Inspecting a table of the standard normal distribution we find that the relevant probability is 14.5 percent, meaning that there is a probability of 14.5 percent that NPV will be less than zero, and an 86.5 percent chance that NPV will be positive, at a 7 percent discount rate. Thus, we not only know the expected NPV and the range of possible outcomes, but we get a good idea of the likelihood that the project will not even earn a return as high as 7 percent.

---

[3]For an analysis of the cases where the cash flows are not independent between periods, see Hillier (1963) and Van Horne (1986, chap. 6 and 7).

EXHIBIT 7.8 Monte Carlo Simulation of Cash Flows and Net Present Value

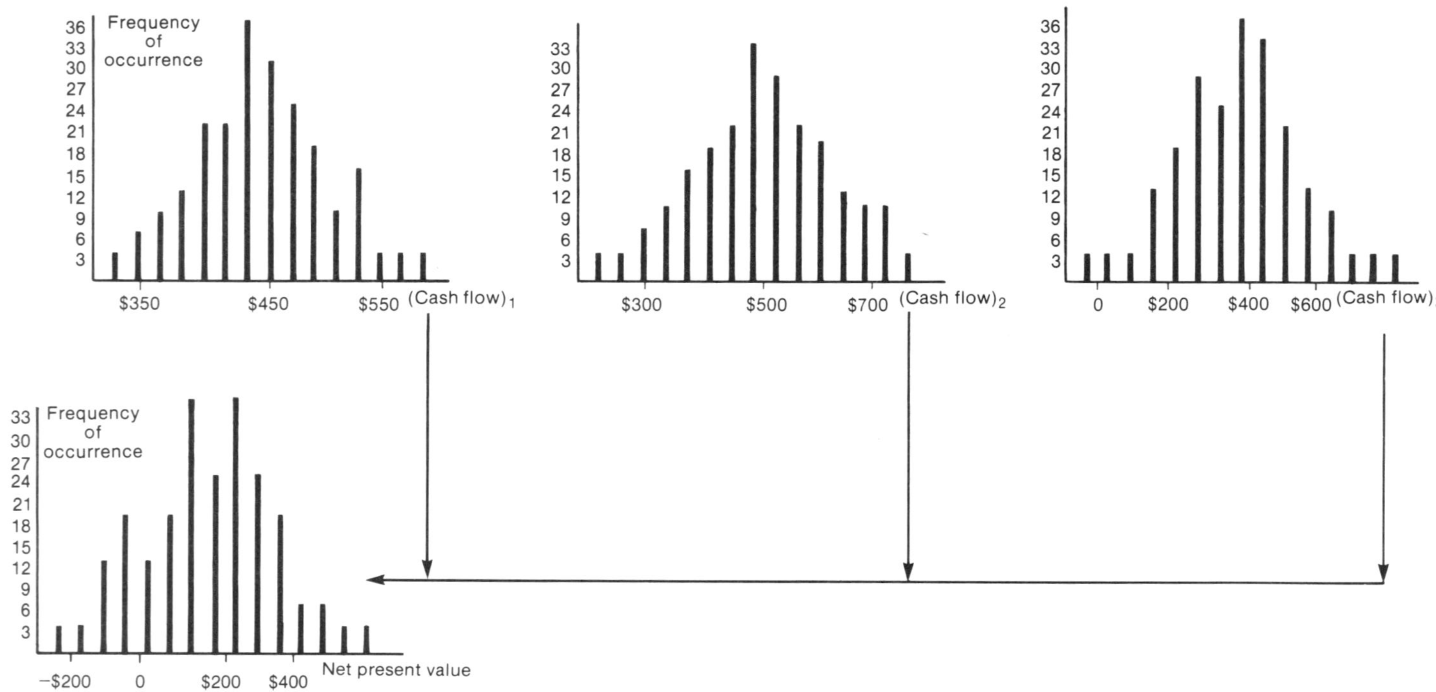

This example is quite simple, but it shows the idea. In more complex situations Monte Carlo simulation is very useful because it is about the only way to take into account all the different elements of uncertainty and organize the results so we can evaluate them. When sales, collection rates, costs, and so on are all uncertain, it is particularly difficult to see how these random variables combine. Monte Carlo simulation can help us clarify the situation.

7.4 RISK ADJUSTMENT

While both scenario simulation and Monte Carlo simulation are useful for exploring the range of possible events, neither one necessarily tells us which decision to make—they only show us what might happen if we make a particular decision. What is needed is a method for summarizing the information about the possible outcomes so that we can compare one decision with another. One way to do this is to determine the *value* of a particular course of action that takes uncertainty into account. That is what the "risk adjustment" methods do: they provide an estimate of value, adjusted for the uncertainty. That way, we can compare the risk-adjusted value of alternative decisions and choose the one with the highest risk-adjusted value.

Risk adjustment refers to adjusting or penalizing our estimates to take account of the uncertainty of some prospect. For example, if we conclude that an investment with no risk is worth $100, then a similar investment may be evaluated as worth $80 when its risk is taken into account. We have penalized its value by $20 to adjust for its risk.

The two most frequently discussed methods for making such a risk adjustment are the risk-adjusted discount rate, and the certainty-equivalent approach. While the certainty-equivalent approach is valid in principle, it is quite difficult to apply in practice. Consequently, our discussion will focus on the risk-adjusted discount rate.

We have alluded to the risk-adjusted discount rate already in discussing methods for evaluating investments in Chapter Six. What the risk-adjusted discount rate does is increase the discount rate used for discounting expected future cash flows as the riskiness or uncertainty of these cash flows is increased. For example, suppose an investment is expected to generate \$450, to be received in one year. If this \$450 is certain to be received, then we would discount this expected cash flow at the risk-free interest rate of, say, $r_f = 0.07$, which is the current rate on riskless investments like U.S. Treasury securities. The present value of this expected cash flow would be

$$\begin{aligned} 450\,(1/(1 + r_f)) &= 450\,(1/1.07) \\ &= \$420.56. \end{aligned}$$

On the other hand, suppose we have an investment that will generate a cash flow at the end of one year, but we don't know how much cash will be received. We can think of this cash flow as though it is a random variable that is drawn like a lottery ticket at the end of the year. We don't know its value, but we can make some plausible guesses about the probability distribution of the outcomes. That is, we assume we can estimate the probabilities of the different possible outcomes of the draw. Based on this, we estimate the expected value or most likely value of the cash flow. We can discount that expected cash flow at a rate that is higher than the risk-free rate to determine its value today.

Assume we have used Monte Carlo simulation to determine the probability distribution of outcomes for this investment. Exhibit 7.9 shows the simulated proportional number of outcomes

EXHIBIT 7.9 Simulated Probability Distribution of Cash Flow

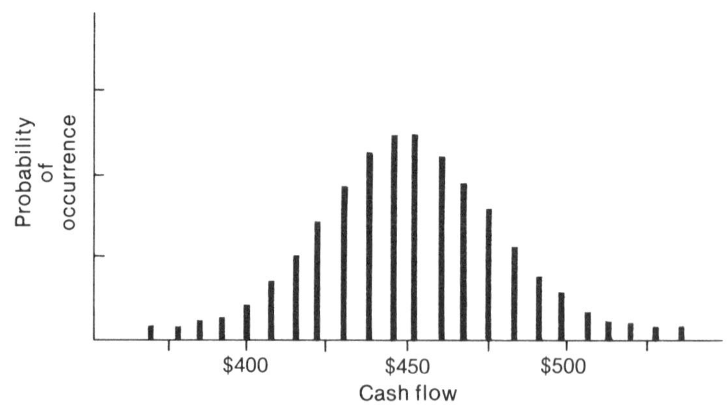

of the random cash flow for t_1. The simulated outcomes range from \$320 to \$613, with an average value of \$450 and standard deviation of \$50. Based on our best estimates, then, the actual cash flow at t_1 will be drawn from a probability distribution that is approximated by this simulated distribution that has expected value E (*Cash flow*) = \$450 and standard deviation σ(*Cash flow*) = \$50.

The question is, how much is it worth today to be able to receive at t_1 an amount of money that is unknown today but which we can view as having the probabilities indicated by the simulated probability distribution?

The risk-adjusted discount rate approach to determining value for this investment uses a discount rate that is adjusted upward for more risky investments. For this investment, with a risk-free rate of $r_f = 0.07$, assume that we have determined that the appropriate risk adjustment is to add a risk premium of 0.09 (9 percent) to the risk-free rate, for a risk-adjusted discount rate of

$$\begin{aligned} k &= r_f + \textit{Risk premium} \\ &= 0.07 + 0.09 \qquad = 0.16, \end{aligned}$$

so the risk-adjusted present value of the cash flow is

$$\begin{aligned} \textit{Present value} &= E\ (\textit{Cash flow}) \cdot (1/(1+k)) \\ &= 450 \cdot (1/1.16) \\ &= 450 \cdot (0.8621) \\ &= \$387.95 \end{aligned}$$

This value means that we should be willing to pay, today, any amount up to, but not greater than, \$387.95 to buy the right to receive whatever random amount is generated by the investment at t_1.

It would be quite difficult to say that one uncertain, risky investment is better than another unless we can reduce all the possible outcomes of each investment to one value. That is what risk-adjusted discount rate does. Even though the first period's cash flow could turn out to be any one of many different amounts, we use a risk-adjusted rate to discount the *expected* amount of the cash flow. In this way, if we have two investments that each have expected cash flow of \$450 but different levels of risk, we use a higher discount rate on the more risky one to penalize its value for its greater risk. In this example we saw that if the investment was completely riskless its value would be $420.56, but if the cash flow was uncertain, warranting a discount rate of 16 percent, its value would be $387.95.

When the cash flows occur over many periods, we generally apply the risk-adjusted discount rate to each period's cash flow, and then sum the present values.[4] For example, suppose an investment will generate unknown random cash flows at the end of each of the next three years, and the expected values of these random cash flows are $450, $500, and $400 at times t_1, t_2, and t_3. If we use the risk-adjusted discount rate of

$$k = r_f + \textit{Risk premium} = 0.07 + 0.09 = 0.16,$$

the risk-adjusted present value would be

$$\begin{aligned} \textit{Present value} &= 450\,(1/1.16)^1 + 500\,(1/1.16)^2 + 400\,(1/1.16)^3 \\ &= 450\,(0.8621) + 500\,(0.7432) + 400\,(0.6407) \\ &= 387.95 \quad + 371.60 \quad 256.28 \\ &= \$1{,}015.83, \end{aligned}$$

which is just the sum of the three risk-adjusted present values. We say this investment with three periods of cash flows has a risk-adjusted present value of $1,015.83.

The obvious question is, How do we determine the proper discount rate? There are many different approaches to calculating the appropriate discount rate, ranging from the purely subjective to more technical approaches. On the subjective or judgmental end, you can simply add on a risk premium that you regard as sufficiently high to make the investment attractive. In this regard, it may be helpful to know that common stocks have generated average annual returns that typically have been about 6 percent to 8 percent above the rate on U.S. Treasury securities (see Ibbotson and Sinquefield [1977 and 1982]). This suggests that if you regard an investment as being of about the same level of risk as an average share of stock, a risk premium of 6 percent to 8 percent would be appropriate.

---

[4]It has been argued that using a risk-adjusted present value in this manner over several periods has the effect of compounding the risk adjustment, so that the cash flow received further in the future are penalized excessively for their risk. For further detail, see Robichek and Myers (1966).

At the technical end of the spectrum is the capital asset pricing model (CAPM) that is discussed to some extent in Chapter Six.[5] The CAPM gives us a framework for calculating risk premiums for investments based on an index of the investment's volatility relative to the volatility of the average stock portfolio. The index is the beta coefficient of the investment; if the investment is of average volatility, the beta is $\beta = 1$, and if the investment is half as volatile as the average stock, then $\beta = 0.5$. Based on this, the risk premium should be

$$\textit{Risk premium} = (k_m - r_f)\,\beta,$$

where $(k_m - r_f)$ is the risk premium required to be earned on a market portfolio that is a cross section of the investments available in the market as a whole. With this model, the required return or discount rate would be

$$\begin{aligned} k &= r_f + \textit{Risk premium} \\ &= r_f + (k_m - r_f)\,\beta. \end{aligned}$$

To apply the CAPM to our problem, assume that we have analyzed data on other investments similar to the one we are presently evaluating, and assessed their returns to be about 1.5 times as volatile as the average portfolio of securities. We will use this as our estimate of β for our investment. In addition, estimating the average risk premium to be $(k_m - r_f) = 0.06$, our estimate of the required return on our investment is

$$\begin{aligned} k &= r_f + (k_m - r_f)\,\beta \\ &= 0.07 + (0.06) \cdot (1.5) \\ &= 0.07 + 0.09 = 0.16, \end{aligned}$$

which we would use as the discount rate for evaluating the investment.

7.5 CONCLUSION

The two methods we have discussed for dealing with uncertainty in the modeling context are what we have called scenario

[5]For a more detailed explanation of this CAPM framework see Jacob and Pettit (1984, chap. 10 and 11).

simulation and Monte Carlo simulation. Each approach is an attempt to assess the consequences of our decisions when we are unsure of the future, which is almost all of the time. Scenario simulation is simply the process of working through the model with different uncertain events as the input, but it typically does not deal with the probabilities of the different events. Monte Carlo simulation takes the probabilities into account by making random draws of the relevant events, where the chance of drawing a particular outcome is proportional to its probability.

Obviously there are many other methods of dealing with uncertainty. The methods discussed here are just the beginning, but they are the methods that are easiest to use in the modeling context.

REFERENCES

CHEN, H. Y. "Valuation under Uncertainty." *Journal of Financial and Quantitative Analysis,* September 1967, pp. 313–25.

HERTZ, D. B. "Risk Analysis in Capital Investment." *Harvard Business Review,* January–February 1964, pp. 95–106.

HILLIER, F. "The Derivation of Probabilistic Information for the Evaluation of Risky Investments." *Management Science,* April 1963, pp. 443–57.

IBBOTSON, R., and R. SINQUEFIELD. *Stocks, Bonds, Bills, and Inflation: The Past 1926–1976 and the Future.* Charlottesville, Va.: Financial Analysts' Research Foundation, 1977.

———. *Stocks, Bonds, Bills, and Inflation: The Past and the Future.* Charlottesville, Va.: Financial Analysts' Research Foundation, 1982.

JACOB, N., and R. R. PETTIT. *Investments.* Homewood, Ill: Richard D. Irwin, 1984.

ROBICHECK, A., and S. C. MYERS. "Conceptual Problems in the Use of Risk-Adjusted Discount Rates." *Journal of Finance,* December 1966, pp. 727–30.

VAN HORNE, J. C. *Financial Management and Policy.* 7th ed. Englewood Cliffs, N.J.: Prentice-Hall, 1986.

WESTON, J. F., and T. COPELAND. *Managerial Finance.* 8th ed. Hinsdale, Ill.: Dryden Press, 1986.

CHAPTER EIGHT

Optimization Models for Financial Planning

One of the main concerns of the modern theory of finance is to explain how we can determine optimal investment and financing decisions for a firm, where optimal is taken to mean maximizing the wealth of the firm's stockholders. The more immediate objective is to make investment and financing decisions that will maximize the market value of the firm's stock. The body of financial theory that has been developed is intended to explain the link between decisions and the value of the firm. If the effect of decisions on value can be explained, then we should be able to determine which particular policy or set of decisions will maximize the firm's value. The theory of finance, however, is still not so perfected that we have a completely accepted and verified theory of valuation. Consequently, we are not yet in a position to make perfect financial decisions that are the simple result of some calculation. Nevertheless, we do have much of the necessary valuation framework that can help us describe the links between decisions and the objective of value maximization. Armed with that framework we should be able to improve financial decision making by constructing decision models that calculate optimal decisions. This is the topic of this chapter—the construction and use of optimization models that can aid us in financial planning and decision making by providing the mechanism for calculating the optimal decisions in the context of our financial model. This chapter will build on the modeling concepts presented in Chapter six to develop optimization models.

8.1 THE PROCESS OF OPTIMIZATION

Chapter Six explained the construction and use of simulation models for financial planning. Simulation models are being used more widely all the time, and they are quite useful for exploring the consequences of decisions. As was evident from the examples in that chapter, however, simulation models can generate a lot of output, yet it is frequently very hard to evaluate the output and determine which decision is really the best. The user of the model tends to be overwhelmed and is unable to see which decision is best. You will recall the very large amount of financial data generated to evaluate the investment and financing decisions for Plastico Inc. Financial statements were produced for each year from 1987 through 1991 for each financing alternative. It is difficult enough to evaluate a single financial statement, but it is overwhelming to be faced with the task of evaluating all these statements. Most decision makers simply cannot digest and evaluate this much data. A major attraction of the optimization approach is that it tends to force the model user to define the objective of the decision more carefully so the results of the decision are summarized and can be evaluated.

Moreover, when a problem presents many different decision alternatives, the number of different decisions that can be considered may be too large for a person to analyze and evaluate each one. For example, suppose there are just 11 investment projects available, and your task is to choose the best combination of projects to be included in the firm's capital budget. The portfolio of projects could have one project or it could have any number up to all 11 projects. The number of different combinations that could be considered would be 2,047. Most decision makers would rather not be faced with the task of sifting through all 2,047 alternatives to find the best combination. Optimization models are specifically designed to analyze in a systematic manner all these combinations and to determine which one will be best for reaching the goal of the decision. Some optimization techniques are intended simply to search systematically and efficiently through all the alternatives, and others use our knowledge about the conditions characterizing an optimum to determine directly which solution is the optimum.

The dictionary defines an optimum as "the best or most favorable point," or "the best result obtainable under specific conditions." Optimization, then, is the process of finding the optimum. That is, optimization is the process of searching or solving for a decision variable that will yield the best result obtainable under the conditions faced by the decision maker. For example, Expressions (4.1) and (4.2) from Chapter Four constitute a simple model of the firm's total revenue that can be combined as one equation of the form

$$\begin{aligned} \textit{Total revenue} &= 500 \cdot \textit{Price per unit} \\ &\quad - 30 \cdot \textit{Price per unit}^2, \end{aligned} \tag{8.1}$$

where the decision variable is the *Price per unit.* If the objective of the decision is to make *Total revenue* as large as possible, then one can determine the *Price per unit* that will generate the largest value of the objective. Optimization is the process or technique of finding this optimal value of the decision variable.

A search technique would enumerate the various possible values of the decision variable and the value of the objective function that results from that decision, and then search through the list to determine which was best. For example, suppose the prices to be considered range from \$5 to \$10 in increments of \$1. From Expression (8.1) the *Total revenue* associated with each *Price per unit* would be:

Price per unit	\$5	\$6	\$7	\$8	\$9	\$10
Total revenue	\$1,750	\$1,920	\$2,030	\$2,080	\$2,070	\$2,000

A search for the highest *Total revenue* shows a value of \$2,080 and the *Price per unit* that yields this value is \$8. There is no assurance, however, that there is not another *Price per unit* between \$7 and \$9 that yields an even higher *Total revenue.* The search could be continued to consider prices in this interval that would yield even better results.

One drawback of searching for the best alternative is that there may be too many alternatives, and the search process becomes too time-consuming and expensive. Then we may turn to another method for finding the optimum. One such method that is familiar to most people is the use of derivatives from calculus to determine an extreme point in a mathematical function such as Expression (8.1). By taking the derivative of (8.1) with respect to the variable *Price per unit,* equating to zero and solving, one obtains the solution that the optimal *Price per unit* must be set equal to $8.33. At this price, *Total revenue* is $2083.33, which is the largest revenue possible, and any other price would yield a smaller revenue.

Exhibit 8.1 is a graph that shows *Total revenue* on the vertical axis as a function of the *Price per unit,* which is shown on the horizontal axis. The process of searching for a best price simply calculates values at different points along the curve that represents the *Total revenue* earned at each different *Price per unit.* On the other hand, calculus finds the best point by using our knowledge that the maximum is reached when the slope of the curve is zero, and solving directly for that point.

The techniques of calculus are useful for many problems, but in many other situations the problem is not amenable to this approach. The problems of financial modeling are usually too complex to be formulated in a way that they can be solved with calculus. However, there are other techniques that are well suited to determining an optimal solution to a financial planning problem. These techniques come under the heading of mathematical programming—linear programming (LP), nonlinear programming, and dynamic programming. This chapter is focused on the use of linear programming to find optimal solutions to financial planning problems.

Constrained Optimization

Mathematical programming is a technique for solving "constrained optimization" problems. Constrained optimization is the process of finding an optimal solution to a problem where there are constraints that limit the choices of the decision variables. An example of an optimization problem is to determine the quickest way to get from New York to San Francisco, and the quickest way is clearly to travel in a straight line at the speed of light—perhaps being beamed there by the Starship Enterprise—but there are technological limitations on our ability

EXHIBIT 8.1 Total Revenue as a Function of Price per Unit

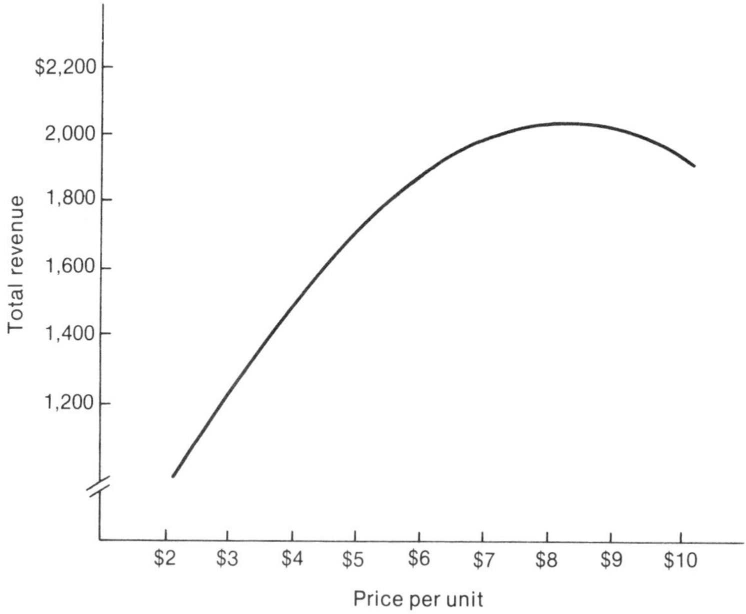

to do that. That is, there are some constraints that limit our choices and limit our ability to reach our goal. The problem should be restated, saying that we want to find the quickest way to get from New York to San Francisco subject to several constraints. The first constraint is that we are limited by the technology so that our choices consist of airplane, train, and automobile. Second, we may want to impose a constraint on our expenditures, limiting our travel expenses to $500. Third, we want to make a stop in Bishop, California, to visit relatives. Given the choices, the airplane is clearly the fastest mode of transportation, but the commercial airlines don't stop in Bishop, so we must consider chartering a plane. That would cause our expenditure constraint of $500 to be exceeded, however, so we can reject the airplane as a choice. The train does not go through Bishop either, so obviously we have to consider driving. The car would be a feasible choice if we can make the trip for no more than $500; if not, then the trip is not feasible within our limitations. Given these constraints on our choices, the problem is one of finding the quickest route by car that still is within our budget.

The pricing problem discussed earlier can also be formulated as a constrained optimization. Assume the objective is to maximize *Total revenue* but the *Price per unit* must be at least $9 in order to cover our costs. This problem would be stated mathematically as

Maximize

$$\textit{Total revenue} = 500 \cdot \textit{Price per unit} - 30 \cdot \textit{Price per unit}^2 \qquad (8.2)$$

subject to

$$\textit{Price per unit} \geq 9.00 \qquad (8.3)$$

The expression to the right of the equal sign is the "objective function," which expresses the relationship between the decision variable—that is, *Price per unit*—and the objective. The second expression is the constraint, that limits our choice of the decision variable to values that are $9 or greater. In Exhibit 8.1 it is obvious that a price of $9 will yield the largest revenue, because *Total revenue* declines as the *Price per unit* is increased for all prices greater than $8.33, and $9 is the lowest price that can be charged without violating the constraint. In more complex problems, however, the solution is not so obvious, and the solution can be very difficult. The techniques used to solve such problems come under the heading of *nonlinear programming.* The problem is nonlinear because it involves relationships between variables that are nonlinear. In this case, the graph of the relation between *Price per unit* and *Total revenue* is a curve, instead of a straight line, so we say that the problem is nonlinear, hence the term *nonlinear programming.* On the other hand, if we could have drawn this relationship as a straight line, we would say the problem is linear, and we could use the techniques of *linear programming* to find the solution.

Linear Programming

Linear programming is a method for formulating and solving certain kinds of constrained optimization problems. It is similar to the constrained maximization pricing example given above but the problem has a linear objective function that is to be either maximized or minimized, it has one or more decision variables, and it has one or more constraints that limit our choice among decision variables. There are a number of different algorithms (procedures) for solving linear programming problems that are quick and efficient, and quite large and involved problems can be solved easily, particularly on a computer. Consequently, if a problem can be formulated as a linear programming problem, it can usually be solved quite easily. Even many problems that are nonlinear can be approximated as linear programming problems and can be solved for a solution that is satisfactorily close to the true optimal solution.

A short example will help demonstrate how a linear programming problem is formulated. Assume that you have \$500 of your own money to invest, and you can borrow an additional \$175. There are three different investment projects that can be undertaken (projects 1, 2, and 3). You can invest any amount in a project up to a limit: The most any one person can invest in project 1 is \$300, the limit for 2 is \$600, and there is no limit on 3. Project 1 will generate future cash flows with a present value of \$1.50 for each \$1 invested, project 2 will generate a present value of \$1.20 for each \$1 invested, and project 3, \$1.10 for each \$1 invested. Assume that your goal is to choose the investment plan that will make the present value of your investment portfolio as large as possible.

All three projects are attractive, so you obviously would like to put as much money as possible into the investment. There are a number of limitations, or constraints, however, that impinge on your choice of investments. There are limitations on borrowing and on the investment expenditures. These constraints must be taken into account in deciding the best mix of investments and financing. This decision problem can be set up and solved as a linear program. The linear program will consist of four decision variables contained in five mathematical expressions: an objective function and four constraints. Let's see how to develop these expressions.

First, define the decision variables: let *Invest 1, Invest 2,* and *Invest 3* be the amounts to be invested in projects 1, 2, and 3, respectively, and let *Borrow* represent the amount that is to be borrowed. The problem is to choose the values of *Invest 1, Invest 2, Invest 3,* and *Borrow* that will optimize our objective. Assume the objective is to maximize the present value of the cash flows from our investment portfolio. The objective function is the mathematical expression that shows how each decision variable affects the objective. In this case the objective function is written as

$$1.5(\textit{Invest } 1) + 1.2(\textit{Invest } 2) + 1.1(\textit{Invest } 3) - 1.02(\textit{Borrow}), \tag{8.4}$$

where the coefficient of each decision variable represents the present value per dollar invested, or in the case of borrowing, the present value per dollar borrowed.[1] That is, each dollar invested in project 1 yields $1.50 in present value, and the decision variable *Invest* 1 is the number of dollars invested, so that the product, 1.5(*Invest* 1), represents the present value of cash flows generated from the total expenditure in project 1. For example, if $300 is spent on project 1, the present value derived from the investment is

$$1.5(\textit{Invest } 1) = 1.5\ (300) = \$450.$$

Next, we need to write the constraint equations. The four constraint expressions are:

$$\begin{aligned}
&\textit{Invest 1} + \textit{Invest 2} + \textit{Invest 3} - \textit{Borrow} \le 500 && (8.5)\\
&\textit{Invest 1} \le 300 && (8.6)\\
&\textit{Invest 2} \le 600 && (8.7)\\
&(\textit{Borrow}) \le 175 && (8.8)
\end{aligned}$$

Expression (8.5) constrains net expenditures (net of borrowing) to be no greater than $500. (When the variable *Borrow* is transposed to the right side the gross expenditures are $500 plus the amount borrowed.) Expressions (8.6) and (8.7) limit the expenditures for projects 1 and 2, respectively, and (8.8) limits the amount borrowed.

[1]The borrowing coefficient is the present value of principal and interest repaid on the debt. It is assumed that the interest rate on the debt is 12 percent and the discount rate is 10 percent, which for one period yields the present value per dollar borrowed of $-\$1(1.12)/1.10 = -1.02$, with the sign negative to indicate a cash outflow.

When the objective function and constraints are combined the problem is shown as:

Max

$$1.5(\textit{Invest 1}) + 1.2(\textit{Invest 2}) + 1.1(\textit{Invest 3}) - 1.02(\textit{Borrow})$$

s.t.

$$\begin{aligned}
\textit{Invest 1} + \textit{Invest 2} + \textit{Invest 3} - \textit{Borrow} &\leq 500 \\
\textit{Invest 1} &\leq 300 \\
\textit{Invest 2} &\leq 600 \\
\textit{Borrow} &\leq 175,
\end{aligned}$$

where "Max" means to pick the decision variables so as to maximize, and "s.t." means "subject to" the constraints.

This problem can be solved using the *simplex algorithm,* which is the standard mathematical procedure for solving a linear program. Just a couple of seconds on the computer yield the optimal solution that

$$\textit{Invest 1} = \$300, \textit{Invest 2} = \$375, \textit{Invest 3} = 0, \text{ and } \textit{Borrow} = \$175.$$

This problem is so simple that one does not need a linear program to figure out that project 1 should be undertaken to its limit, that 2 should be expanded as far as borrowing allows, and that borrowing should be undertaken to its limit. However, the problem does help to demonstrate linear programming and to highlight some of the features of the technique.

When a problem is stated in the standard form of linear programming, it would appear in the following form:

Max

$$Z = c_1x_1 + c_2x_2 + c_3x_3 + c_4x_4 \tag{8.9}$$

s.t.

$$a_{11}x_1 + a_{12}x_2 + a_{13}x_3 + a_{14}x_4 \leq b_1 \tag{8.10}$$
$$a_{21}x_1 + a_{21}x_2 + a_{23}x_3 + a_{24}x_4 \leq b_2 \tag{8.11}$$
$$a_{31}x_1 + a_{32}x_2 + a_{33}x_3 + a_{34}x_4 \leq b_3 \tag{8.12}$$

where Expression (8.9) is the objective function, and (8.10), (8.11), and (8.12) are the constraints; the x's are the decision variables whose optimal values are to be found by solving the problem; the c_i's and a_{ij}'s represent the numbers that are the coefficients (the subscripts just distinguish among the coefficients so that, for example, a_{32} denotes the coefficient in the third row and second column); and the b_i's are the constant numbers that are the constraint limitations. This problem is shown with just four decision variables and three constraints. There could be many variables and constraints; however, the only limitation is the size of the computer and software available to solve the problem.

If the problem can be stated in the general form shown, then it can be solved as a linear programming problem. For example, the investment problem fit this format: the decision variables corresponding to the x_i's were x_1 = *Invest 1*, x_2 = *Invest 2*, x_3 = *Invest 3*, and x_4 = *Borrow;* the coefficients in the objective function were $c_1 = 1.5$, $c_2 = 1.2$, $c_3 = 1.1$, and $c_4 = -1.02$; the coefficients in the first constraint expression were $a_{11} = 1$, $a_{21} = 1$, $a_{13} = 1$, and $a_{14} = 1$; and the constants on the right hand side of the inequalities that represented the constraint limits were $b_1 = 500$, $b_2 = 300$, $b_3 = 600$, and $b_4 = 175$.

Once the problem is correctly formulated, it can be solved quite easily on a computer. Solution algorithms such as the simplex method are used to solve the problem, and these algorithms are readily available as computer software. For example, the linear programming software package used by the author on a personal computer will handle problems with as many as 2,255 variables and 255 constraints, and at the time that this was written this software cost only $99. While knowledge seldom hurts, one does not necessarily have to be knowledgeable in the technical details of the solution process. The reader who is interested in the mathematics of solving the linear program is referred to the operations research books cited at the end of the chapter, such as Hadley (1962), Hillier and Lieberman (1967), and Wagner (1969).

To solve the problem, it is important that it be properly formulated. The most basic requirement is that the problem be linear, as opposed to being nonlinear. Nonlinear problems can be solved, but they are much more difficult, and the algorithms and software are not so readily available.

What makes the problem linear is that in each expression in the problem every decision variable is multiplied by a coefficient, but no decision variable is multiplied by any other decision variable, nor is it multiplied by itself. That is, a decision variable such as x_1 can be multiplied by a scalar coefficient, such as 1.5, so it appears in the objective function or a constraint in a form such as $1.5x_1$, but it cannot be multiplied by itself (i.e., it cannot be shown in a form such as $1.5x_1^2$ nor can it be multiplied by another decision variable so that it appears in a form such as x_1x_2. If the variables are multiplied by themselves or each other, the problem becomes nonlinear, and then it cannot be solved by the solution algorithms used for linear programming. That was the case in the pricing problem presented earlier: the decision variable *Price per unit* appeared in the objective function in a squared term, *Price per unit*^{2}, with the result that the objective function would appear on a graph as a curve, as it did in Exhibit 8.1. In that case, the problem is nonlinear, and it could not be solved with the techniques of linear programming.

Naturally, not all problems of financial planning require linear programming—or any kind of optimization technique, for that matter—for their solution. But there are many planning problems that are handled best with an optimization technique, and they often can easily be fitted into the linear programming format. There are many examples of financial planning problems that have been solved with linear programming, and some of these are referenced at the end of this chapter. These include problems of working capital management, capital budgeting under conditions of capital rationing, and more general long-range financial planning.

Examples of LP models of working capital management are those developed by Robichcck, Teichroew, and Jones (1965) and Orgler (1970). The Robicheck, Teichroew, and Jones model addresses the problem of planning the strategy for meeting the short-term needs for funds that are imposed by the seasonal fluctuations in the firm's sales. Over the yearly cycle the firm must finance its production costs, inventory accumulation, and the buildup in receivables, until cash is collected on the receivables. The decision problem is to choose the combination of financing sources that will minimize the net costs of financing over the annual cycle. The constraints are that there is a limit on each source of financing, and, of course, debt repayments cannot exceed the amount of debt outstanding.

Orgler's model is similar, but it is somewhat more detailed and comprehensive. It addresses the problem of deciding on the sources of short-term financing and investment so as to maximize the earnings from the management of working capital over a planning horizon that can be as long as a year. The decision variables include the amount of trade credit to be repaid, the amount of funds to be borrowed and repaid for each of the various sources of short-term credit, the amounts to be invested in short-term securities, the amounts of these securities to be sold before they mature, and the amount of funds that should be carried in the cash account at each date in the planning horizon. Each source of financing has an interest cost, and each short-term security has an interest yield, and these costs and yields are included in the objective function. The constraints that limit the decisions are that each short-term credit source is limited, that compensating balances must be maintained, that debt repayment cannot exceed the balance of the loan, purchases of securities cannot exceed the amount of excess cash that is available, security sales cannot exceed the balance of securities held, that a minimum cash balance must be maintained, and most importantly, that sources of cash must equal uses of cash.

Another application of linear programming to a problem of financial planning involves the choice of investment projects when there are limitations on the amount of funds available for investment. Weingartner (1967) presented the pioneering model of capital budgeting under conditions of capital rationing. Capital rationing refers to the situation in which there is a limitation on the amount of funds available, and the decision problem is to choose the portfolio of capital investment projects that will provide the maximum net present value for the portfolio as a whole without exceeding the budget limitation. This LP model of the capital budgeting problem can be useful. In its simplest form it is limited, however, because it does not take into account the possibility of obtaining additional financing. It takes very little elaboration of the model to add various forms of financing so that it can become a more general model for long-term financial planning.

8.2 INVESTMENT DECISIONS ON A LIMITED BUDGET

One of the best-known and easiest to understand applications of linear programming to financial decision problems is the capital investment decision model first presented by Weingartner. This model assists us in making optimal investment decisions under conditions of capital rationing.

The capital budget may be limited for several reasons: the officers of the firm may have set a maximum limit on capital expenditures in each period; the capital expenditures may be limited to the amount of funds generated internally by the operations of the firm; the officers may assume that there is a limit on the amount of funds that can be raised externally in a given period; it may be felt that there is a limit on the rate of expansion of the firm so that if the firm tries to expand too rapidly it will overload the firm's managerial resources; or the firm may set a limit on the amount of funds that each division may spend for capital projects. Whatever the reason for the limitation on the capital budget, once the limitation is specified, the task is to choose the best mix of investment projects while, at the same time, assuring that the budget allocation is not exceeded.

An Example of Capital Rationing

An example will help to demonstrate the problems of capital rationing and the linear programming approach to solving these problems.

The top management of the Xatos Corporation has asked the managers of its different divisions to submit proposals for major capital expenditures. The managers of the various divisions have submitted their proposals, and now the decision must be made as to which of the various projects should be adopted.

The divisional managers have already screened most of the projects so they generally meet the firm's standards for acceptance. These standards are that they should have a positive NPV when evaluated at a discount rate that is appropriate for their level of risk. For projects that don't differ in terms of risk from the rest of the firm, this discount rate is currently 15 percent, which is the firm's cost of capital. If projects are regarded as having risks substantially different from the rest of the firm, then the discount rate would be adjusted to reflect that risk.

The major project proposals are all quite detailed and involved, but the staff at headquarters has summarized some of the relevant data relating to the costs and expected cash flows of the projects. Exhibit 8.2 shows this summary data. There are 11 major proposals, designated as project 1 through project 11. The body of the table in Exhibit 8.2 shows the estimates of the cash flows for each project (expressed in thousands of dollars). Negative numbers denote cash outlays, and positive numbers indicate cash inflows generated by the project at each of the dates indicated in the left hand column. Time t_0 indicates the present, time t_1 is one year from now, and so on. The longest projects are assumed to end in 10 years. The data at the bottom of the exhibit present summary figures for each project: present values of costs, present value of cash inflows, NPV, internal rate of return (IRR), and the present value index (PVI). All projects were evaluated at the 15 percent cost of capital. For example, project 1 requires investment outlays of \$200,000 and \$150,000 at times t_0 and t_1, respectively. These outlays (costs) have a present value of \$330,500. Project 1 is expected to generate cash inflows starting with \$20,000 at time t_2, building up to a peak of \$180,000 at t_6, and then declining to \$50,000 by t_9. The cash inflows have a present value of \$364,500. Some projects, such as 6 and 11, involve cash outlays at their end; these are included as negative cash flows, not as part of the initial cost of the project.

All 11 projects meet the firm's acceptance criteria: They have positive NPV, their rates of return equal or exceed 15 percent, and for each the present value index, defined as (*Present value of cash flows*)/(*Present value of costs*), exceeds 1. If there were no limitations on the firm's ability to accept projects, all 11 projects would be adopted, but, the board of directors has set a limit on capital expenditures. For the present (t_0) the maximum that can be spent is set at \$800,000, for the next year (t_1) the limit is \$300,000, and for t_2 the limit is \$200,000. These limits for the next couple of years are set with reference to obligations undertaken now because the directors do not want to commit now to large expenditures in the next two years that might limit the firm's ability to consider new projects later that are currently still unknown.

EXHIBIT 8.2 Xatos Corporation: Cash Flow Estimates for Major Investment Proposals ($000)

	Project										
Time	*1*	*2*	*3*	*4*	*5*	*6*	*7*	*8*	*9*	*10*	*11*
0	−$200	−$600	−$100	−$150	−$420	−$200	−$10	0	−$500	−$80	−$50
1	−150	+150	−400	+30	+80	−800	−4	−100	−200	0	+400
2	+20	200	−200	35	90	+280	+5	−400	−200	+150	+50
3	80	350	+290	40	180	280	8	−200	+300	0	−510
4	120	350	290	40	180	280	8	+290	360		0
5	150	250	290	40	130	280	8	290	400		
6	180	0	290	40	0	280	0	290	400		
7	90		290	40		280		290	400		
8	70		0	40		280		290	0		
9	50			35		280		0			
10	0			10		−200					
Present value of:											
Cash flows	$364.5	$836.5	$733.7	$181.3	$423.6	$1,043.6	$17.7	$638.3	$922.3	$133.4	$50.2
Initial costs	−330.5	−600.0	−599.2	−150.0	−420.0	−896.0	−13.5	−521.3	−825.2	−80.0	−50.0
NPV	$34.0	$236.5	$134.5	$31.3	$3.6	$147.6	$4.2	$116.9	$97.1	$33.4	$0.2
IRR	17.1%	28.7%	21.7%	20%	15.3%	19.9%	25%	21.7%	18.1%	36.9%	15%
PVI	1.1	1.39	1.22	1.21	1.009	1.16	1.3	1.22	1.12	1.42	1.0

Given the limits on capital expenditures set by the directors, management must now decide which of these 11 projects should be undertaken. They want to choose the package, or portfolio, of projects that will make the portfolio as valuable as possible while not exceeding the capital budgets. The planning staff sets to work to formulate and solve this capital budgeting problem.

The choice of the best portfolio of capital investment projects can be formulated as a linear programming problem. The objective is to choose the mix of projects that will generate the highest net present value for the portfolio as a whole. The main constraints are that the limits on capital expenditures should not be exceeded. The decision variables are which projects should be adopted and which should be rejected.

To set this model up in linear programming format, the variables must be defined. Number the projects 1 through 11, and let subscript i designate a project, so that $i=3$ refers to project number 3. A decision variable is designated as x_i. The value of x_i in the solution of the problem will tell whether project i would be adopted or not. For example, if $x_3=1$ in the solution it means project 3 should be adopted and if $x_3=0$, project 3 would be rejected. With 11 projects ($i=1,2, \ldots, 11$) there will be 11 decision variables, $x_1, x_2, \ldots, x_{11}$, each one of which will be either 0 or 1 in the solution.

Let NPV_i denote the net present value of project i. For example, for project 3, from Exhibit 8.2 we have $\text{NPV}_3=\$134.5$, and for project 5, $\text{NPV}_5=\$3.6$. With this notation, the net present value of the package, or portfolio, of projects can be expressed in general form as

$$\sum_{i=1}^{11} \text{NPV}_i \cdot x_i, \tag{8.13}$$

or in specific form as

$$\begin{aligned}\sum_{i=1}^{11} \text{NPV}_i \cdot x_i &= 34\,x_1 + 236.5\,x_2 + 134.5\,x_3 + 31.3\,x_4 \\ &+ 3.6\,x_5 + 147.6\,x_6 + 4.2\,x_7 + 116.9\,x_8 \\ &+ 97.1\,x_9 + 33.4\,x_{10} + 0.2x_{11}.\end{aligned}$$

The numbers shown as coefficients of the x_i's are the net present values of the projects, NPV_i, and the product $\text{NPV}_i\,x_i$ represents the contribution of project i to the NPV of the portfolio of projects. For example, if in the solution $x_3=1$ we have

$$\text{NPV}_3 \cdot x_3 = 134.5 \cdot 1 = \$134.5,$$

and if $x_4 = 0$, we have

$$\text{NPV}_4 \cdot x_4 = 31.3 \cdot 0 = 0.$$

The sum of $\text{NPV}_i \cdot x_i$, that is, $\sum_{t=1}^{11} \text{NPV}_i \cdot x_i$, is the NPV for the whole portfolio.

Suppose, for example, the solution values of the decision variables are $x_1 = 1$, $x_3 = 1$, $x_5 = 1$, and all other decision variables are zero; then the NPV for the whole package is

$$\begin{aligned} &34\,x_1 + 236.5\,x_2 + 134.5\,x_3 + 31.3\,x_4 + 3.6\,x_5 + 147.6\,x_6 + \\ &\quad 4.2\,x_7 + 116.9\,x_8 + 97.1\,x_9 + 33.4\,x_{10} + 0.2\,x_{11} \\ &= 34(1) + 236.5(0) + 134.5(1) + 31.3(0) + 3.6(1) + 147.6(0) \\ &\quad + 4.2(0) + 116.9(0) + 97.1(0) + 33.4(0) + 0.2(0) = \$172.1. \end{aligned}$$

Note that the portfolio NPV could be made larger by adopting all projects ($x_i = 1$ for $i = 1.2, \ldots, 11$)—the portfolio NPV would be \$839.3. Because all 11 projects have positive net present value, they are all acceptable, and the value of the firm would be maximized by adopting all 11 projects if that were feasible. The essence of the problem at hand, however, is that because of budget limitations, not all projects can be adopted. The decision problem is to choose the mix of projects that will be as valuable as possible without exceeding the budget.

In the mathematical programming context, the limitations imposed by the budget would be expressed as constraint equations or inequalities. The budget constraint would be a mathematical statement that the amount spent for capital investment could not exceed the budget. That is, the budget constraint is an expression in mathematical terms that, for period t,

$$\textit{Total capital expenditures}_t \leq \textit{Budget ceiling}_t. \tag{8.14}$$

Some type of budget constraint is present in virtually all financial LP models. It is essential that a constraint be included that requires sources of funds to equal uses of funds, and that is the purpose served by Expression (8.14).

To express the budget constraint, define $\textit{Expend}_{tj}$ as the net cash outflow in period t for project j. If there is a net cash outflow for the project, $\textit{Expend}_{tj}$ is positive, and if there is an inflow of funds, $\textit{Expend}_{tj}$ is negative. For example, from Exhibit

8.2 we have $Expend_{01}=200$, meaning that at time t_0 project 1 involves a cash outlay of $200; $Expend_{11}=150$ means there is an additional outlay of $150 during period 1 for project 1, and $Expend_{21}=-20$ means that, during period 2, project 1 will generate a net cash inflow of $20 (a negative expenditure of funds). For the purpose of expressing the budget constraint, $Expend_{tj}$ shows the net incremental cash outflow for whatever purpose, regardless of whether or not it is a capital expenditure. For example, project 1's outlay of $150 at t_1 may consist of $120 for plant and equipment, and $30 that is incremental investment in working capital. Similarly, the net cash inflow in period 2 for project 1, shown as $Expend_{21}=-20$, could represent a capital expenditure of $90 offset by a cash inflow of $110 from operating the project.

Using this notation, the cash outflow in period t from project j will be

$$Expend_{tj} \cdot x_j,$$

where x_j is the 0, 1 decision variable. If $x_j=0$, the product, $Expend_{tj} \cdot 0$ equals zero, and if the project is accepted, so that $x_j=1$, the product $Expend_{tj} \cdot 1 = Expend_{tj}$.

In period t the total expenditures for all 11 projects will be

$$\sum_{j=1}^{11} Expend_{tj} \cdot x_j.$$

The constraint that total project expenditures not exceed the budget ceiling would be written for period t as

$$\sum_{j=1}^{11} Expend_{tj} \cdot x_j \leq Budget\ ceiling_t, \qquad (8.15)$$

and there would be such a constraint for each period that had a budget ceiling. For example, the immediate (t_0) constraint for Xatos Corporation is that expenditures not exceed $800, so the t_0 constraint would be written as

$$200\,x_1 + 600\,x_2 + 100\,x_3 + 150\,x_4 + 420\,x_5 + 200\,x_6 + 10\,x_7 + 0x_8 + 500\,x_9 + 80\,x_{10} + 50\,x_{11} \leq 800,$$

where the numerical coefficients are the values of $Expend_{0j}$ for $j=1, \ldots, 11$. Because the firm has set budget limits for times 0,

1, and 2, the linear program would be set up with three budget constraints, one for each period.

A second type of constraint would be one that limits the values of the decision variables, x_j. In a standard linear programming approach to such a problem, the solution value of the decision variable, x_j, represents the amount of project j that should be adopted. If $x_j=0.5$ one half of project j should be undertaken, and $x_j=3.2$ means that project j should be adopted at a level that is 3.2 times as large as one unit of the project. However, it makes sense to assume that the firm can adopt only whole projects and it cannot adopt partial projects.

To reflect the fact that only whole projects will be considered, the decision variables that are considered can be confined to integer values (0, 1, 2, 3, etc.) by using an *integer programming* method of solving the problem. Integer programming is a variation of linear programming that searches for the positive integer values of the decision variables that yield the optimal solution. If integer programming is used, the only additional constraints that are necessary take the form

$$x_j \leq 1.$$

Because integer programming considers only positive integer values, this constraint assures that the only values of the decision variables that are considered are $x_j=0$ or $x_j=1$, where $x_j=0$ indicates we reject the project and $x_j=1$ that we accept the project.

Having considered the essential components of the programming approach to capital budgeting, these components are combined to represent the complete formulation. The general form of the integer program to solve the 11-project, 3-constraint capital budgeting problem is

$$Z = \sum_{j=1}^{11} NPV_j \cdot x_j \tag{8.16}$$

subject to

$$\sum_{j=1}^{11} Expend_{tj} \cdot x_j \leq Budget\ ceiling_t \qquad t = 1,2,3 \tag{8.17}$$

$$x_j \leq 1 \qquad j = 1,\ldots,11. \tag{8.18}$$

The specific form requires that the numerical values of the coefficients NPV_j, $Expend_{tj}$ and the constraint, *Budget ceiling*$_t$ be supplied. For the present example, these values are obtained from Exhibit 8.2, and the complete integer programming problem is shown in Exhibit 8.3. The objective function is shown as line *Z*, and the constraints are shown as lines 0 through 13. Line 0 is the constraint for the time 0 budget ceiling, and lines 1 and 2 apply to times 1 and 2. Constraints 3 through 13 limit the values of the integer decision variables x_j to be 0 or 1.

When this integer programming problem is solved, the solurion values of the decision variables are as shown in Exhibit 8.4.[2] This solution shows that projects 2, 3, 7, and 10 should be adopted, and the others should be rejected. With this solution the net present value of the optimal portfolio of projects is

$$\begin{aligned} Z &= NPV_2 \cdot 1 + NPV_3 \cdot 1 + NPV_7 \cdot 1 + NPV_{10} \cdot 1 \\ &= 236.5 \quad + 134.5 \quad + 4.2 \quad + 33.4 \\ &= \$408.6, \end{aligned}$$

where the 1s in the first line denote the optimal values of decision variables x_2, x_3, x_7, and x_{10}. Any other *feasible* solution would generate a smaller net present value for the portfolio.

With this optimal solution, with the t_0 *Budget ceiling* of \$800, the net expenditures amount to \$790:

$$600x_2 + 100x_3 + 10x_7 + 80x_{10} = 790.$$

Then, at time t_1 when the budget is limited to \$300, the accepted projects utilize a *net* amount of \$254; even though projects 3 and 7 require \$404, project 2 generates a cash inflow of \$150 that helps cover part of the costs of projects 3 and 7, leaving \$46 unused from the t_1 budget. The next budget limitation is \$200 at t_2, and the optimal capital plan actually generates a net cash inflow so that none of the allowed budget must be used. That is, project 3 utilizes \$200, but projects 2, 7, and 10 generate an inflow of \$355 that can be used to meet the needs of project 3.

The linear programming approach is powerful because it si-

---

[2]The routine used to solve this problem was MILP88, a mixed integer programming package for IBM PC and IBM compatibles that will handle 255 constraints, 64 integer variables, and 1,255 noninteger variables. The package is available from Eastern Software Products, P.O. Box 15328, Alexandria, VA 22309.

EXHIBIT 8.3 Xatos Corporation: Linear (Integer) Programming Tableau for Capital Budgeting Problem

	x_1	x_2	x_3	x_4	x_5	x_6	x_7	x_8	x_9	x_{10}	x_{11}		
Z	$34\ x_1$ +	$236.5x_2$ +	$134.5x_3$ +	$31.3x_4$ +	$3.6x_5$ +	$147.6x_6$ +	$4.2x_7$ +	$116.9x_8$ +	$97.1x_9$ +	$33.4x_{10}$ +	$0.2x_{11}$		
0	$200x_1$ +	$600\ x_2$ +	$100\ x_3$ +	$150x_4$ +	$420x_5$ +	$200\ x_6$ +	$10x_7$ +	$0\ x_8$ +	$500x_9$ +	$80x_{10}$ +	$50x_{11}$	$\leq$	800
1	$150x_1$ −	$150\ x_2$ +	$400\ x_3$ +	$30x_4$ −	$80x_5$ +	$800\ x_6$ +	$4x_7$ +	$100\ x_8$ +	$200x_9$ +	$0\ x_{10}$ −	$400x_{11}$	$\leq$	300
2	$-20x_1$ −	$200\ x_2$ +	$200\ x_3$ −	$35x_4$ +	$90x_5$ −	$280\ x_6$ −	$5x_7$ +	$400\ x_8$ +	$200x_9$ −	$150x_{10}$ −	$50x_{11}$	$\leq$	200
3	x_1											$\leq$	1
4		x_2										$\leq$	1
5			x_3									$\leq$	1
6				x_4								$\leq$	1
7					x_5							$\leq$	1
8						x_6						$\leq$	1
9							x_7					$\leq$	1
10								x_8				$\leq$	1
11									x_9			$\leq$	1
12										x_{10}		$\leq$	1
13											x_{11}	$\leq$	1

EXHIBIT 8.4 Optimal Solution to Xatos Corporation Capital Budgeting

Project	1	2	3	4	5	6	7	8	9	10	11
Decision Variable	x_1	x_2	x_3	x_4	x_5	x_6	x_7	x_8	x_9	x_{10}	x_{11}
Optimal Value	0	1	1	0	0	0	1	0	0	1	0

multaneously takes account of the benefits and costs of each project relative to all other projects. For example, project 10 which has NPV of only 33.4, is preferred to project 6, which has NPV of 147.6, because 10 uses very little cash ($80) at $t=0$ when funds are scarce, whereas 6 would require an investment of $200, and an expenditure of $200 would require that other projects that are much more productive, such as 2, would have to be forgone.

Elaborations on the Basic Model

This example demonstrates the basic features of the Weingartner type of linear programming model of capital budgeting under conditions of capital rationing. It serves as a very instructive basis for expanding the LP to consider other useful elaborations and extensions that provide a more general planning model. Some of these elaborations that can be added include:

- Mutually exclusive projects and contingent projects.
- Lending and borrowing.
- A more general schedule of investment opportunities.
- Policy constraints on minimum rates of growth of earnings and dividends.
- The issuance of new common stock.

Mutually Exclusive Projects. Mutually exclusive projects occur when you can adopt one out of two (or more) projects, but not both (or all). That is, you must choose between the projects. In the Xatos Corporation example, projects 3 and 8 are intended to be mutually exclusive because 8 is just 3 delayed by one year. (Note that the cash flows for 8 in Exhibit 8.2 are the same as 3, except 8's cash flows occur one year later.) By including both in the set of possible projects, we are allowing the LP to compare the desirability of delaying 3 one year. As it turns out in this particular example, 3 is chosen without considering the mutual exclusiveness of these two projects. However, if the LP solution had recommended both 3 and 8 be adopted, at the very least it would have been confusing advice.

With the 0,1 decision variables it is easy to handle mutual exclusion of projects in the LP. Constraints are added to insure that one but not both projects are adopted. The constraint would be of the form

$$x_3 + x_8 \leq 1, \tag{8.20}$$

for mutually exclusive projects 3 and 8. Because the decision variables must be either 0 or 1, constraint Expression (8.20) insures that we won't have both $x_3 = 1$ and $x_8 = 1$, because if that were the case $x_3 + x_8 = 2$, which is prohibited by (8.20). With (8.20) both projects can be rejected, or just one of the projects can be accepted but not both. Similarly, if there is a set of projects among which we can choose only one, a constraint of the form

$$x_2 + x_3 + x_7 + x_8 \leq 1 \tag{8.21}$$

would suffice for mutually exclusive projects 2, 3, 7, and 8. If (8.21) is added to the Xatos problem, obviously the LP must reject projects that it previously accepted. In this case it will choose projects 1 and 2, for a smaller portfolio NPV of $270.5.

Contingent Projects. Investments are contingent when they are related so that one project can't be accepted unless another project is also accepted. For example, suppose project 11 is the purchase of a new computer, and 10 is the purchase of a software system to be used on the computer. The computer could be purchased without that particular software, but it would make no sense at all to purchase the software without also purchasing the computer. In this case, project 10 (software) is contingent on the acceptance of 11 (computer). This type of contingency can be included in the LP with the addition of the constraint

$$x_{10} \leq x_{11}, \tag{8.22}$$

which would actually be included in the LP as

$$x_{10} - x_{11} \leq 0. \tag{8.23}$$

If the solution has $x_{11} = 0$, then (8.22) also requires that $x_{10} = 0$. But if $x_{11} = 1$ in the solution, x_{10} can be 0 or 1, depending on its merits. Suppose another project, 12, is an alternative software system competing with 10 so they are mutually exclusive, but both are contingent on the acceptance of 11. This would be reflected in the constraint

$$x_{10} + x_{12} \leq x_{11},$$

so if $x_{11} = 1$, 10 or 12 could be accepted, but not both.

Lending and Borrowing. The LP formulation of the capital budgeting problem that we have considered up until now was deficient in that it doesn't provide for funds to be transferred between periods. That is, if the excess funds that are available at t_1 could be transferred to t_0 or t_2, perhaps more projects could be undertaken. Borrowing and lending are mechanisms for transferring funds between periods, and when borrowing and lending opportunities are added to the problem, we get the beginnings of a complete financial planning model. To see how borrowing and lending opportunities can be added to the model, return to the Xatos example.

Lending. Lending (investment in marketable securities such as U.S. Treasury securities) allows the transfer of funds forward from one period to the next so that, for example, surplus funds at t_1 can be carried to t_2. Assume that there is no limit on the amount that can be lent except for limitations imposed by funds available for lending. Let $Lend_0$ and $Lend_1$ represent the decision variables that are the amounts invested in marketable securities at t_0 and t_1, respectively; and assume that the rate of return earned on funds invested for one period is denoted by

$$Lend\ rate = 0.10,$$

and with a tax rate of $T = 0.46$, the after-tax return is

$$Lend\ rate \cdot (1-T) = 0.10(1-0.46) = 0.054.$$

In the objective function the coefficients of the lending decision variables must be defined in the same terms as they were for the capital investment projects. The coefficients of x_i for the investment projects were the net present values (NPV_i) of the after-tax cash flows generated by these projects. Consequently, the coefficients of the $Lend_t$ decision variables must also be in terms of the net present values of the after-tax cash flows. Lending \$1 at t_0 is a cash outflow of \$1 at t_0 and will generate a cash inflow after taxes of

$$\$1\ [1 + (Lend\ rate)\ (1-T)]$$

at t_1. The net present value of the cash flows from lending \$1 is

$$\left[-1 + \frac{1 + Lend\ rate\ (1-T)}{1 + Discount\ rate}\right]. \tag{8.24}$$

For our example, assume the *Discount rate* is the rate at which funds can be borrowed,[3] which will be 12 percent, so the NPV per dollar lent is

$$\left[-1 + \frac{1 + 0.10(1-0.46)}{1.12}\right] = -\ 0.059$$

and, discounting these cash flows for one more period yields the NPV for lending at t_1 as -0.053. Thus, investing in short-term securities does not add net value to the investment portfolio, but it allows the transfer of funds from a period when they are idle to a period in which they may be used in more productive capital investments.

Adding lending to the Xatos LP requires the following additions to the objective function and constraints:

Line in Exhibit 8.3	*Terms added*
Z	$-0.059 \cdot Lend_0 - 0.053\ \ Lend_1$
0	$+\ \ Lend_0$
1	$-1.054 \cdot Lend_0 + \ \ Lend_1$
2	$-\ 1.054 \cdot Lend_1$

Because the constraints are expressed in terms of cash outflows, $Lend_0$ has a positive coefficient of $+1$ in expression 0 because it is a cash outflow at the time of the investment, but at t_1 there will be a net after-tax inflow of \$1.054 for each dollar lent, hence

[3]The borrowing rate would be appropriate as the discount rate because it represents the highest return that can be earned on an extra \$1 at this level of risk. That is, an extra \$1 can be used to repay debt and save (i.e., earn) the borrowing rate.

the negative coefficient in expression 1. A similar interpretation applies to the coefficients of $Lend_1$.

The lending variables are assumed not to be integer variables, so they can be any positive value permitted by the constraints. The solution process requires a *mixed integer linear programming* solution technique when these variables are added to the problem.

Borrowing. Assume that even though a budget limit has been imposed on capital expenditures, management will allow a limited amount of borrowing to take place, provided that total borrowing does not exceed $200 in any period and all borrowing must be repaid from project cash flows by time t_2. Assume that the current interest rate on borrowed funds is 12 percent, denoted by

$$Borrow\ rate = 0.12.$$

Borrowing is for one period only (from t_0 to t_1 or from t_1 to t_2), so a loan taken out at t_0 is repaid at t_1, and a new loan can be arranged at t_1 to be repaid at t_2.

Let $Borrow_0$ and $Borrow_1$ represent the decision variables that are amounts to be borrowed at t_0 and t_1; respectively. $Borrow_0$ is a cash inflow to the firm at t_0 that is available to help finance other investment projects. The cash outflow at t_1 is the principal and interest net of taxes; that is,

$$\begin{aligned}[1 + (Borrow\ rate)\ (1-T)]\ Borrow_0 &= [1+0.12(1-0.46)] \\ &\quad \cdot Borrow_0 \\ &= [1.065] \cdot Borrow_0\end{aligned}$$

Similarly, the cash inflow from borrowing at t_1 is $Borrow_1$ and the cash outflow at t_2 is

$$[1 + (Borrow\ rate)\ (1-T)] \cdot Borrow_1.$$

The coefficients of the borrowing decision variables in the objective function should be the net present value per dollar borrowed. Borrowing $1 at t_0 generates a cash inflow of $1 at t_0 and a cash outflow after taxes of

$$\$1\ [1 + (Borrow\ rate)\ (1-T)].$$

The net present value of the cash flows from borrowing $1 at t_0 is

$$+1 - \frac{1 + \textit{Borrow rate}\,(1-T)}{1 + \textit{Discount rate}},$$

where *Discount rate* denotes the "opportunity rate" at which these cash flows are discounted, and, when the amount borrowed is $Borrow_0$, the NPV of the total amount borrowed at t_0 is

$$\left[1 - \frac{1 + \textit{Borrow rate}\,(1-T)}{1 + \textit{Discount rate}}\right] Borrow_0 \qquad (8.25)$$

For example, assume that *Borrow rate* = 0.12, and *Discount rate* = 0.12 (because the borrowing rate is the opportunity cost of funds). The coefficient (the NPV per dollar borrowed) of $Borrow_0$ in the objective function will be

$$\left[1 - \frac{1 + 12(1-0.46)}{1.12}\right] = 0.0493;$$

the coefficient of $Borrow_1$ (the NPV evaluated at t_0 of $1 borrowed at t_1 will be

$$\left[1 - \frac{1 + 0.12(1-0.46)}{1.12}\right]\left(\frac{1}{1.12}\right) = 0.044;$$

and the borrowing variables would be shown in the objective function as

$$0.0493\ Borrow_0 + 0.044\ Borrow_t.$$

When the lending and borrowing opportunities are added to the Xatos LP, the objective function and constraints are expanded with the new terms shown in Exhibit 8.5. In the exhibit the negative coefficients of the borrowed amounts, $-1 \cdot Borrow_0$ in constraint (0) and $-1 \cdot Borrow_1$ in constraint (1), indicate that cash flows *in* from borrowing at t_0 and t_1, respectively (to understand this, transpose $-1 \cdot Borrow_0$ to the right side of (0) to note that $Borrow_0$ adds to the funds available for investment). The positive coefficients $1.065 \cdot Borrow_0$ in constraint (1) and $1.065 \cdot Borrow_1$ in constraint (2) represent the after-tax cash outflow resulting from repayment of the debt. Constraints 3 and 4 represent the limitation that the total amount that can

EXHIBIT 8.5 Xatos Corporation: Terms Added to LP for Lending and Borrowing

Line in Exhibit 8.3	*Lending Terms Added*	*Borrowing Terms Added*
Z	-0.059 Lend$_0$ $-$ 0.053 Lend$_1$	+ 0.0493 Borrow$_0$ + 0.044 Borrow$_1$
0	+ Lend$_0$	$-$Borrow$_0$
1	-1.054 Lend$_0$ + Lend$_1$	+ 1.065 Borrow$_0$ $-$ Borrow$_1$
2	$-$ 1.054 Lend$_1$	+1.065 Borrow$_1$
14		Borrow$_0$
15		Borrow$_1$

be borrowed must not exceed $200 in any period. The fact that all borrowing is repaid at t_1 and t_2, coupled with the fact that there is no further borrowing at t_2, assures that all borrowing is repaid from the cash flows generated by the investment projects.

With the expansion of the problem to reflect the opportunities to borrow and lend, the solution changes, as shown in Exhibit 8.6. When borrowing is available, projects 4, 8, and 11 are added to the portfolio of accepted investments. This is possible because, as shown for *Borrow*$_0$, borrowing at t_0 is $190, expanding the capital budget by $190 beyond the $800 limit to $990. Even with the expansion of the number of projects accepted, there are still excess funds at t_1, so the solution calls for lending $163.20. With this solution, the NPV for the portfolio of projects is $553.56, as compared with $408.60 without the opportunity to borrow or lend.

One of the more perplexing problems in developing an LP model for financial planning is the treatment of debt financing. What is necessary is a way to reflect the advantages of debt financing and at the same time properly take account of the risks imposed by debt financing. The theory of finance says that, starting from the base of a firm financed entirely with equity, moderate and prudent increases in debt financing can increase the value of the firm, due primarily to the tax advantages of debt financing. There is a point, however, where the risks and potential costs of financial distress begin to outweigh the advantages, and debt financing should not be expanded beyond that point. The ideal planning model would be able to assess these

EXHIBIT 8.6 Xatos Corporation: Optimal Solution with Borrowing and Lending

Investment Project	*Decision Variable*	*Optimal Value*
1	x_1	0
2	x_2	1
3	x_3	1
4	x_4	1
5	x_5	0
6	x_6	0
7	x_7	1
8	x_8	1
9	x_9	0
10	x_{10}	1
11	x_{11}	1
	$Borrow_0$	\$190
	$Borrow_1$	0
	$Lend_0$	0
	$Lend_1$	\$163.20

trade-offs and arrive at an optimal mix of equity and debt financing. It is especially difficult to construct this ideal model.

The first hurdle for including debt in the ideal financial planning model is to reflect the advantages of debt financing and maintain the model's linear form so it can be solved as a linear program.[4] One approach that was suggested by Myers and Pogue is to discount, at the cost of equity, cash flows generated by investments as if the project is financed entirely with equity, and to show separately the effect of debt financing by calculating the present value of the tax savings from the interest on the debt.

For example, for an investment financed entirely with equity

[4]The standard method for evaluating investments and financing alternatives is to discount expected future cash flows at the firm's weighted average cost of capital, denoted by k_a. To the extend that k_a depends on the proportional mix of debt and equity financing, the present value of a cash flow, discounted at k_a, is a nonlinear function of the financing mix. That is, if the proportion of debt is changed, the present value of a future cash flow changes in a nonlinear way, violating the requirement that the model be linear with respect to the decision variables, one of which is the proportion of debt financing.

capital, assume that the investment has a level of risk that would require that its cash flows be discounted at a rate k_u (subscript u denotes that it is "unleveraged," i.e., has no debt financing). The unleveraged value of the cash flows would be

$$\sum_{t=1}^{n} \textit{Cash flow}_t \cdot 1/(1 + k_u)^t. \tag{8.26}$$

To the extent that the project does use debt financing, rather than adjusting the discount rate to show the effects of financial leverage, these effects are taken into account by adding a term that is the present value of the tax savings resulting from the tax deductibility of interest. The value of the leveraged cash flows would be

$$\sum_{t=1}^{n} \textit{Cash flow} \cdot 1/(1+k_u)^t + T \cdot \sum_{t=1}^{n} \textit{Interest}_t\,(1/1+k_d)^t, \tag{8.27}$$

where the term on the right is the present value of these tax savings, because the tax shield from interest in a given year is $T \cdot \textit{Interest}$, where T is the tax rate and k_d is the interest rate on the debt. This approach allows us to avoid the complications of nonlinearity caused when we use the weighted average cost of capital as the discount rate, but will assess the same value for cash flows as if we did use the weighted average cost of capital.[5] However, this value will be linearly related to the amount of debt financing because $T \cdot \textit{Interest}$ is a linear function of the amount of debt financing.

To see how these ideas would be applied in an LP model, return to the 11-project investment decision problem represented by Exhibit 8.3, where $x_1, x_2, \ldots, x_{11}$ are the investment decision variables. Assume that the firm can borrow to help finance these projects, and $Borrow_0$ and $Borrow_1$ are the decision

---

[5]This approach has the same effect as if the cash flows were discounted at the firm's weighted average cost of capital, where the cost of equity changes with the debt-to-equity ratio according to the expression

$$k_e = k_u + (k_u - r_f)(1-T)(\textit{Debt}/\textit{Equity}),$$

where k_u is the discount rate for a pure equity (unleveraged) cash flow, and r_f is the risk-free rate of interest. This expression, developed by Modigliani and Miller (1958), leads to the result that the weighted average cost of capital declines as the proportional amount of debt financing increases.

variables representing the number of dollars to be borrowed at t_0 and t_1, respectively.

If the NPV$_i$'s calculated from Exhibit 8.2 were based on the cost of equity capital *as if* the firm were financed entirely with equity, then even with the addition of borrowing to the problem we still use the same NPV$_i$'s in the objective function of the LP.

The effect of borrowing on the weighted average cost of capital and on the value of the firm will be taken into account by the coefficient of the decision variable *Borrow* in the objective function. This coefficient should be the net present value per dollar borrowed, which over the *m*-period life of the debt would be, in general terms

$$T \cdot \sum_{t=1}^{m} \textit{Borrow rate} \cdot 1/(1+ \textit{Borrow rate})^t, \qquad (8.28)$$

where *Borrow rate* is the interest rate on the debt. In our example, with one-period borrowing at a rate of 12 percent and a 46 percent tax rate, the coefficients would be

$$\begin{aligned} & T \cdot \textit{Borrow rate} \cdot 1/\ (1 + \textit{Borrow rate}) \\ = \ & (0.46)(0.12) \cdot (1/1.12) \\ = \ & 0.0493 \end{aligned}$$

per dollar borrowed at t_0 and, for t, the coefficient would be 0.044 after discounting for one more period. Thus, the borrowing decision variables appear in the objective function as

$$0.0493\ (\textit{Borrow})_0 + 0.044\ (\textit{Borrow})_1.$$

The shortcoming of this approach is that it encourages the use of debt beyond the point most practitioners would consider prudent. Without some restraints, an LP planning model will tend to generate solutions that recommend excessive expansion of debt financing. Debt will appear to be especially attractive as a source of funds in the planning model for two reasons. First, even without the tax advantage of debt, borrowing relaxes the budget constraint, providing funds for expansion of investments. Second, the positive effects of the tax savings from tax deductible interest will further encourage the use of debt financing. But, as everyone but linear program knows, excessive borrowing can be hazardous to a firm's financial health. So, like cigarettes, debt should carry warnings of impending doom so the LP should limit its use.

There are numerous ways to limit the use of debt financing in the LP model, none of them is entirely satisfactory. The first, to which you've already been introduced, is a limitation on the amount to be borrowed, written as

$$Borrow_t \leq Borrowing\ limit_t. \tag{8.29}$$

This approach is appropriate when the lender sets a limit, as in the case of a revolving credit agreement with a maximum amount that can be taken down. But, because of the apparent advantage of borrowing, the LP will usually push right to this limit without telling the user when it is best to borrow less than the maximum.

Financial ratios also can serve to set borrowing limits. For example, it is common to set a target for the ratio of total debt to total assets. This is easily done in the LP constraints. Suppose you regard the prudent limit for debt to be 25 percent of total assets. The over-all constraint would be

$$Total\ debt_t \leq 0.25\ (Total\ assets)_t.$$

To include this constraint in the LP you must consider that $Total\ debt_t$ consists of debt that is already outstanding, denoted by $Debt_0$, plus any new funds raised as specified by the decision variable $Borrow_t$. In addition, $Total\ assets_t$ will consist of initial assets, $Assets_0$, plus additions specified by the investment decisions recommended by the model. For example, at time t_0 we have

$$Total\ debt_0 = Debt_0 + Borrow_0$$

and

$$Total\ assets_0 = Assets_0 + \sum_{i=1}^{11} Asset_i\ x_i,$$

where $Asset_i$ is the amount of assets purchased at t_0 for investment project i. With these definitions of assets and debt, the constraint for t_0 would be written as

$$Debt_0 + Borrow_0 \leq 0.25\ [Asset_0 + \sum_{i=1}^{11} Asset_i\ x_i].$$

Putting all decision variables on the left side of the inequality and constants (nondecision variables) on the right, the constraint for t_0 is

$$Borrow_0 - 0.25 \sum_{i=1}^{11} Asset_i \cdot x_i \leq 0.25\ Asset_0 - Debt_0. \quad (8.30)$$

Similar constraints would be used for other periods in the planning horizon.

Another type of constraint that can impose a realistic restraint on debt financing is a risk constraint. With this approach, management subjectively determines the maximum acceptable probability that the firm will be unable to service the debt. A constraint is imposed that prohibits debt from expanding to the point at which the probability of insolvency is unacceptable.

Define the risk of insolvency as the probability that the cash flow will be insufficient to service the debt. Suppose we are willing to live with the risk that there is a 10 percent probability that our firm will be unable to service its debt from its operating cash flow. With information about the probability distribution of the cash flows, we can impose a constraint on the amount of debt so we don't exceed the acceptable risk of insolvency.

For example, as a first approximation, assume that the probability distribution of our firm's cash flow that is available to service debt is normal with expected value

$$E\ (Cash\ flow) = \$100{,}000,$$

and standard deviation

$$\sigma\ (Cash\ flow) = \$60{,}000.$$

From a standard normal probability table we can determine that the point that is 1.28 standard deviations below the expected value is the point where there is a 10 percent probability that the cash flow will be less, and a 90 percent probability that the cash flow will be more. In this case this point is

$$\begin{aligned} E\ (Cash\ flow) &- 1.28\ \sigma\ (Cash\ flow) &&= \\ 1000{,}000 &- (1.28) \cdot 60{,}000 &&= \\ 100{,}000 &- 76{,}800 &&= \$23{,}200. \end{aligned}$$

That is, there is 10 percent probability that the cash flow will be less than \$23,200 and 90 percent chance that the cash flow will be greater than \$23,200. By picking the debt level so debt service is no more than \$23,200 we are limiting the chance that we will be unable to service the debt to 10 percent. Assume for example, that the annual debt service is equal to 37 percent of the outstanding debt; then at t_0 the constraint on debt would be

$$0.37\ (Debt_0 + Borrow_0) \leq 23{,}200. \tag{8.31}$$

or, putting the constant terms on the right,

$$0.37 \cdot Borrow_0 \leq 23{,}200\ - 0.37\ Debt_0. \tag{8.32}$$

The difficulty with this approach is that the probability distribution of cash flows may be dependent on the investment projects accepted, and it may be necessary to incorporate this in our constraints. Myers and Pogue (1974, p. 593) explain how to treat this type of complication.

A Generalized Investment Schedule. One difficulty of the Weingartner model is that it requires a complete specification of the different investments that are available. In a more general planning context, the planner does not really know which particular investment opportunities will be available in the future, and certainly, the specifics of the cash flows are not known or even forecasted yet. Consequently, the Weingartner approach is not as useful for a longer range planning model. Alternative approaches that deal with a more general schedule of investment opportunities have been discussed by Myers and Pogue (1974) and Carleton (1970).

Myers and Pogue suggest defining a continuous (as opposed to integer) decision variable that we will denote as *Invest* that represents the amount it is planned to invest in a given future period in "yet-to-emerge investment projects." With *Invest* a decision variable, a task of the LP is to determine how much the firm should plan on investing in this unknown opportunity.

To solve the problem some sort of description must be made of the returns from this investment. Here, one must take care how the opportunities are specified. If it is assumed that any arbitrary amount can be invested in a profitable future opportunity without affecting its return, the model is unrealistic and the LP can generate unrealistic answers that recommend investing arbitrarily large amounts. A more realistic assumption is that as the amount invested is increased, the return earned on the investment declines. However when the returns earned on the investment depend on the amount invested, the problem is nonlinear, and it cannot be solved with LP techniques. The model must be formulated in a way to detour this nonlinearity.

One (of many possible) ways to show the return as a decreasing function of the amount invested is to specify the future investment opportunity schedule as a step function, such as shown by Exhibit 8.7. As the total amount invested is increased, the marginal return earned on the investment declines in discrete steps. For example, define continuous (noninteger) decision variables $Invest_1$, $Invest_2$, $Invest_3$, and $Invest_4$. $Invest_1$ represents the amount to be invested over the interval from 0 to l_1 as shown in Exhibit 8.7, and similarly, $Invest_2$, $Invest_3$, and $Invest_4$ correspond to the second, third, and fourth intervals in the exhibit. In the LP, $Invest_1$ can be found to be any value up to l_1; the next amount invested will be $Invest_2$, that can have a value up to an amount $l_2 - l_1$, and so on.

The rate of return earned on an investment declines in discrete steps. Define R_1, R_2, R_3, and R_4 as the rates of return earned on amounts invested in intervals 1, 2, 3, and 4, where $R_1 > R_2 > R_3 > R_4$. Any amount between zero and l_1 earns rate R_1, investments between l_1 and l_2, that is, $Invest_2$, earn rate R_2, and so forth.

This stairstep investment opportunity schedule can be included in the LP by adding the expressions shown in Exhibit 8.8 to the other LP expressions such as those shown in Exhibit 8.3. In Exhibit 8.8 line Z represents the part of the objective function relating to this investment problem. The coefficients of the decision variables in the objective function, as denoted by NPV_1, NPV_2, and so on, as the abbreviation suggests, are the net present values *per dollar* invested,[6] and the product, $NPV_j \cdot Invest_j$ is the net present value derived from investing an amount equal to $Invest_j$.

[6]One way to define the NPV for these general investment opportunities is to treat them as perpetuities that earn an annual cash flow of R per dollar invested, each year over an infinite horizon. In that case, the net present value of investing \$1 is $-1 + R/k$, where R is the rate of return and k the discount rate. Otherwise, a specific investment life must be assumed to determine the investment's NPV.

EXHIBIT 8.7 Investment Opportunity Schedule as a Step Function

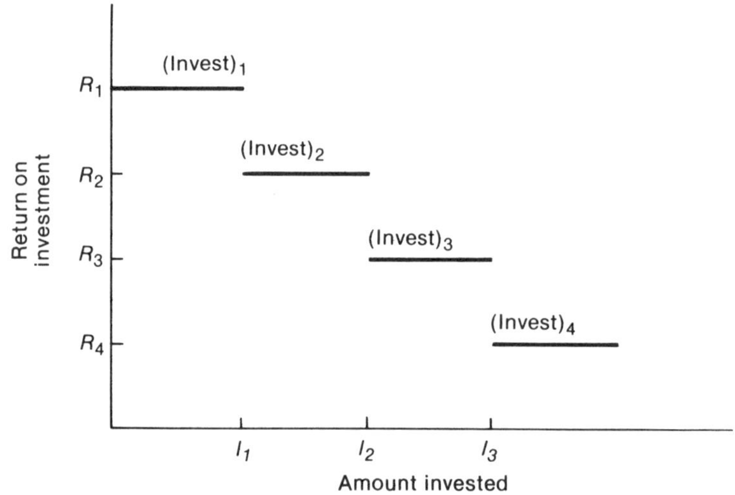

The total amount invested is the sum of the $Invest_j$ variables shown in line 1. Line 2 limits the amount invested in interval 1 (between 0 and l_1), and line 3 limits $Invest_2$ to interval 2, an amount equal to $l_2 - l_1$, similar interpretations apply to the other expressions. Additional expressions would be necessary to show the effects in subsequent periods of the cash flows generated by these investments.

With the investment intervals ranked in decreasing order of rates of return, the LP will automatically expand a higher return investment—such as $Invest_1$—to its limit before undertaking any of a lower return opportunity—such as $Invest_2$. The LP will recommend expanding the total amount of investment so long as there are no other uses for funds that generate a higher return.

The Transition to a Long-Range Planning Model

It is just a small step from the basic capital budgeting model to a comprehensive planning model. A comprehensive LP model for long-range planning should reflect the firm's long-range decisions about investment, financing with both debt and equity,

EXHIBIT 8.8 Expressions Added to the Planning LP to Show Investments with Decreasing Rates of Return

Z	$NPV_1 \cdot Invest_1$ +	$NPV_2 \cdot Invest_2$ +	$NPV_3 \cdot Invest_3$ +	$NPV_4 \cdot Invest_4$	
1	$Invest_1$ +	$Invest_2$ +	$Invest_3$ +	$Invest_4$	$\leq$ Budget ceiling
2	$Invest_1$				$\leq I_1$
3		$Invest_2$			$\leq I_2 - I_1$
4			$Invest_3$		$\leq I_3 - I_2$
5				$Invest_4$	$\leq I_4 - I_3$

and payment of dividends. Debt financing and the generalized investment schedule are two elaborations that help make the transition. Other features that should be added include equity financing and dividend payments. A relatively short example will now be presented to demonstrate the development of a planning model that has some of the features we have already discussed; it will also incorporate equity financing and dividends.

A Two-Year Planning Model. ***Initial Conditions.*** Our small firm has total assets of \$50,000, which generate an annual return of \$7,500 after taxes, but before considering the interest paid on debt. This is a 15 percent return on investment, and it is expected that we would continue to earn 15 percent on these assets. The firm has debt of \$12,000 that pays interest at 12 percent, but no principal payments are due for several years. Thus, the annual interest payments on this existing debt are \$1,440 before tax, but with the tax deductibility of interest expenses, the after tax cost of this debt is \$777.60 based on a 46 percent tax rate, that is, \$1,440 × (1−0.46). The net worth of the firm currently is \$38,000, which includes earnings from the period just ended that were retained in the business.

The Decision Problem and Planning Horizon. We want to develop a broad plan for investment and financing for a two-year planning horizon. By "broad plan" it is meant that we only want to specify, without too much detail, the total amounts that should be invested in the purchase of new assets (both current and long-term), how this should be financed, and what total amounts of dividends should be paid to stockholders. Our decisions will be assumed to specify our actions over periods that are one year in length. Decisions for the first year are assumed to be implemented immediately (time t_0), and decisions for the second year will be implemented at the end of the first year (time t_1).

The Decision Variables. The decision variables included in this model will be defined in aggregate terms, with a minimum of detail, to represent decisions to be made right now (time t_0) and at the end of one year (time t_1). The investment decisions are how much should be invested at t_0 and t_1 to increase the firm's total assets. (For purposes of simplicity, in this very aggregative model, the assets are not even separated into categories such as current assets and fixed assets.) The funds necessary to finance this asset expansion can come from retained earnings, borrowing, or from issuing new common stock. The planning model includes as decision variables, the total amounts of funds that should be raised from borrowing and new equity at each date, t_0 and t_1. In addition, the firm's earnings can be retained or paid to stockholders as dividends, and dividends are included as choice variables. In this particular case, it will be assumed that dividends have already been paid at t_0; the amount of dividends to be paid at t_1 must be decided. These decision variables, which are $Invest_{10}$, $Invest_{20}$, $Invest_{11}$, $Invest_{21}$, $Borrow_0$, $Borrow_1$, $Equity_0$, $Equity_1$, and $Dividend_1$, will be explained in more detail shortly.

The Objective. The goal or objective of our planning model is assumed to be to devise a schedule of investment and financing that will make the value or the stockholders' claims on the firm as large as possible—that is, we want to maximize the value of the common stock. This objective is made operational by maximizing the present value of the firm's cash flows that are potentially available to be distributed to the stockholders. The objective function of our LP model must be defined in a way that will link the decision variables to this objective. Thus, the coefficient of any decision variable in the objective function should be the contribution, per unit of the decision variable, to the present value of the cash flow potentially available to the stockholders. In this example the objective function will be written in general form as

$$NPV_{10} \cdot Invest_{10} + NPV_{20} \cdot Invest_{20} + NPV_{11} \cdot Invest_{11} + NPV_{21} \cdot Invest_{21} + b_0 \cdot Borrow_0 + b_1 \cdot Borrow_1 + e_0 \cdot Equity_0 + e_1 \cdot Equity_1 + d_1 \cdot Dividend_1, \quad (8.41)$$

where the decision variables are the dollar amounts that are to be invested or financed, and the coefficients are defined as the net present values *per dollar* of the decision variables. The values of these coefficients are explained and derived subsequently, and the actual objective function is shown in Exhibit 8.9 that shows the completed LP model with all the constraints.

Investment. The investment opportunities are assumed to take the form of a step function as was explained earlier. Assume that at the beginning of each period, funds up to a maximum amount of $8,000 can be invested in long-term opportunities that generate an internal rate of return of 17 percent. After the maximum of $8,000 is reached for step-1 investments, up to $10,000 additional funds can be invested at a return of 16 percent (these are step-2 investments). For step 1, each dollar invested at the beginning of period t will have net present value[8] (evaluated at t_0)

$$NPV_{1t} = [-1 + 0.17/0.15]\, 1.15^{-t},$$

which, for investments undertaken at t_0 and t_1, coefficients are $NPV_{10} = 0.133$ and $NPV_{11} = 0.116$, where the first subscript denotes step 1 (up to $8,000) and the second subscript denotes the time at which the investment is undertaken and where 15 percent is the discount rate appropriate for discounting the cash flows generated by the investments. For investments at step 2, which earns 16 percent, we have

[8] In this simple example, it is assumed that the investment generates a perpetual annual cash flow equal to $R \cdot Invest$, where R is the rate of return, so the present value of the cash flows is $(R/k)\,(Invest)$, where k is the discount rate. Thus, the net present value is $(-1 + R/k) \cdot Invest$.

EXHIBIT 8.9 Linear Programming Model for Two-Period Planning Horizon

Z	$0.133 \cdot Invest_{10} + 0.06 \cdot Invest_{20} + 0.116 \cdot Invest_{11} + 0.052 \cdot Invest_{21} + 0.1284 \cdot Borrow_0 + 0.1147 \cdot Borrow_1 - 0.10 \cdot Equity_0 - 0.87 \cdot Equity_1 + 0 \cdot Dividend_1$	
1	$Invest_{10}$	$\leq 8{,}000$
2	$Invest_{20}$	$\leq 10{,}000$
3	$Invest_{11}$	$\leq 8{,}000$
4	$Invest_{21}$	$\leq 10{,}000$
5	$Invest_{10} + Invest_{20}$	$\leq 12{,}000$
6	$Invest_{11} + Invest_{21}$	$= 12{,}000$
7	$Invest_{10} + Invest_{20} - Borrow_0 - 0.90 \cdot Equity_0$	$= 0$
8	$0.83 \cdot Invest_{10} + 0.84 \cdot Invest_{20} + Invest_{11} + Invest_{21} - 0.7352 \cdot Borrow_0 - Borrow_1 - 0.90 \cdot Equity_0 - 0.90 \cdot Equity_1 + Dividend_1$	$\leq 6{,}722$
9	$Borrow_0$	$\leq 7{,}000$
10	$0.80 \cdot Borrow_0 + Borrow_1$	$\leq 7{,}000$
11	$-0.25 \cdot Invest_{10} - 0.25 \cdot Invest_{20} + Borrow_0$	≤ 500
12	$-0.25 \cdot Invest_{10} - 0.25 \cdot Invest_{20} - 0.25 \cdot Invest_{11} - 0.25 \cdot Invest_{21} + 0.80 \cdot Borrow_0 + Borrow_1$	≤ 500
13	$-0.068 \cdot Invest_{10} - 0.064 \cdot Invest_{20} + 0.026 \cdot Borrow_0 + Dividend_1$	$\leq 2{,}689$

$$NPV_{2t} = [-1 + (0.16/0.15)]\ 1.15^{-t},$$

which yields $NPV_{20} = 0.06$ and $NPV_{21} = 0.052$.

In the objective function of our linear programming model, the investment decision variables will be shown as

$$NPV_{10} \cdot Invest_{10} + NPV_{20} \cdot Invest_{20} + NPV_{11} \cdot Invest_{11} + NPV_{21} \cdot Invest_{21},$$

where $Invest_{it}$ is the decision variable representing the amount to be invested during period t at step i. Using the coefficients developed, this part of the objective function would be written as

$$0.133 \cdot Invest_{10} + 0.06 \cdot Invest_{20} + 0.166 \cdot Invest_{11} + 0.052 \cdot Invest_{21}.$$

The investment decision variables will appear in constraints representing the step function of investment opportunities, in budget constraints that limit capital expenditures, in constraints that balance the system by requiring assets to equal liabilities, and, in constraints related to target financial ratios. These constraints are shown in Exhibit 8.9, which shows the completed LP planning model.

Lines of 1–4 of Exhibit 8.9 are the step function constraints that say funds can be invested each period in 17 percent opportunities up to \$8,000 (step 1), and then funds up to an additional \$10,000 can be invested to earn 16 percent.

Because of the difficulty of managing expansion, a limit has been imposed on the total amount of investment that the firm can undertake each year. It has been decided to limit total investment to \$12,000 in each of the two years of the planning horizon. Lines 5 and 6 of Exhibit 8.9 express this limitation.

Borrowing. Funds can be borrowed at an interest rate of 12 percent, with interest paid annually, and the principal is repaid in equal principal payments over five years. Because the objective function is defined in terms of net present value, the coefficients, b_0 and b_1, of the borrowing variables in the objective function should represent the net present value (evaluated at t_0) per dollar borrowed, which would be calculated as

$$b_t = (1 + Rate)^{-t} - \sum_{i=t+1}^{h} \left\{ (Rate)(1 - T) \left[1 - \sum_{j=t+1}^{i-1} \left(\frac{Proportion}{Repaid_t} \right) \right] + \frac{Proportion}{repaid_i} \right\} [1 + (Rate)]^{-i-t}, \qquad (8.42)$$

where $Rate = 0.12$ is the interest rate and $Proportion\ repaid_I = 0.20$ is the principal payment at t_i as a proportion of the initial amount borrowed. With the 12 percent interest rate and 20 percent repaid each year, the coefficients would be

$$b_0 = (1.12)^0 - \sum_{i=1}^{5} \{0.12(1 - 0.46)\ [1 - \sum_{j=1}^{i-1} 0.20] + 0.20\}\ (1.12)^{-i}$$

$$= 0.1284$$

and

$$b_1 = 0.1147,$$

which says that \$1 borrowed at t_0 makes cash flows (after taxes) available for investment and dividends that, over five years, have a net present value of 0.1284. Thus, the borrowing decision variables would appear in the objective function as

$$+ 0.1284 \cdot Borrow_0 + 0.1147 \cdot Borrow_1.$$

These positive coefficients in the objective function will lead the LP to recommend borrowing, so a limit must be placed on the amount borrowed. For this example, assume the lenders limit the amount they will lend to \$7,000. The constraints reflecting this limitation would be written as

$$\begin{aligned} Borrow_0 \qquad\qquad & \leq 7{,}000 \\ P_{01} \cdot Borrow_0 + Borrow_1 & \leq 7{,}000, \end{aligned}$$

where coefficient P_{01} represents the proportion of the principal amount borrowed at t_0 that is still outstanding at t_1, and would be calculated as

$$P_{01} = 1 - Proportion\ repaid.$$

These constraints are shown in Exhibit 8.9, on page 332, as lines 9 and 10.

The other constraints that involve borrowing are those that balance the system by making *assets* equal *liabilities* and, for this example, a constraint imposed by a target debt-to-equity ratio. First, though, the *Equity* and *Dividend* variables must be introduced.

Raising New Equity Capital. Assume the firm can raise new equity capital by selling shares of stock to the public. Let $Equity_t$ be the decision variable representing the gross amount of new capital raised by issuing stock in period t. When shares are sold, there is a transaction cost of underwriting and stock flotation that is assumed to be proportional to the size of the stock issue. The proportional flotation cost is denoted by f, and the net amount of funds available to the firm is $(1-f)\ Equity_t$.

In the objective function, the coefficient of the $Equity_t$ decision variable would be

$$e_t = -f(1+k)^{-t}$$

which, for, say, $f = 0.10$ and $k = 0.15$, would be

$$e_0 = -0.10(1.15)^{-0} = -0.10$$

and

$$e_1 = -0.10(1.15)^{-1} = -0.087,$$

and the $Equity_t$ variables would appear in the objective function as

$$-0.10 \cdot Equity_0 - 0.087 \cdot Equity_1.$$

The explanation of this treatment of *Equity* is that issuing new equity provides funds at the date of issue, but it dilutes ownership for the present owners, and as Miller and Modigliani (1961) show, the dilution of ownership exactly offsets the addition of funds at t when there are no transaction costs of issuing new shares. When transaction costs are considered, the addition to value from issuing \$1 of equity at t is $-f(1+k)^{-t}$, where k is the cost of equity capital (for proof and discussion see Morris [1975]).

In the various constraints, issuing equity provides funds equal to

$$(1-f)\ Equity_t$$

and adds to the net worth of the firm in the same amount.

Dividend Payments. One of the objectives of the long-range planning model is to determine the dividend policy that takes rational account of the various alternative uses and sources of funds. Let $Dividend_t$ be the decision variable representing the total dividends paid to stockholders in period t. In the objective function, the coefficient of $Dividend_t$ is $d_t = 0$. This does not mean that dividends have zero value; rather, the reason for this is that the other terms in the objective function represent the funds available to pay dividends, and once all other variables—*Invest, Borrow,* and *Equity*—are determined, dividends are automatically determined as a residual. To include these other variables *and* dividends in the objective function with nonzero coefficients would be double counting.[9]

Payment of dividends will appear in the constraints as a cash outflow from the firm, and will affect the net worth of the firm because it reduces the earnings that are retained.

Constraints. Now that all the decision variables of this simple model have been introduced, we can complete the descrip-

---

[9]We can write the value of the stock as

$$\sum_{t=1}^{\infty} (Dividend_t - Equity_t)\ (1+k)^{-t},$$

(see Miller and Modigliani [1961]). The sources of funds available to pay dividends are

$$\begin{aligned} EBIT(1-T) + Depreciation - Investment - (Interest)(1-T) \\ - Principal\ repayment + Borrowing \\ + (Equity)(1-f). \end{aligned}$$

When these sources are substituted for $Dividend_t$ in the valuation expression we obtain

$$\begin{aligned} \sum_{t=1}^{\infty} [EBIT_t\ (1-T) + Depreciation_t - Investment_t \\ - (Interest_t)\ (1-t) - Principal\ repayment_t \\ + Borrowing_t - f \cdot Equity_t]\ (1+k)^{-t}. \end{aligned}$$

The capital budgeting variables determine the terms $EBIT\ (1-T) + Depreciation - Investment$; the debt financing variables determine the terms $-\ Interest \cdot (1-T) - Principal\ repayment + Borrowing$; and the equity financing is represented by $Equity\ (1-f)$. When these variables are all determined in the model, *Dividends* are determined as a residual.

tion of the remaining constraints. As with any financial model, the crucial constraint is the one that balances the system, requiring uses of funds to equal sources of funds or assets to equal liabilities. There must be such a constraint for each period in the planning horizon, and there must be a link between the periods. This linkage is usually accomplished by having the ending balances from one period equal the beginning balances the next period. In this model, the balancing constraints will be expressed as

$$Assets_t - Liabilities_t = 0,$$

which can be shown as

$$\begin{aligned} Assets_{t-1} + Investment_t - Debt_{t-1} - Borrow_t - Net\ Worth_{t-1} \\ - Earnings\ retained_t - (1 - f)\ (Equity_t) = 0, \end{aligned} \tag{8.43}$$

which not only balances the system, but also links the balances from one period to the next. Of course, these broad categories must be expressed more specifically as detailed functions of the decision variables.

In this model, this balancing constraint for t_0 is expressed as

$$\begin{aligned} Assets_0 + Invest_{10} + Invest_{20} - Debt_0 - Borrow_0 \\ - Net\ worth_0 - (1+f)\ (Equity_0) = 0 \end{aligned} \tag{8.44}$$

where $Assets_0$, $Debt_0$, and $Net\ worth_0$ are the initial balances at t_0 prior to any investment or financing that takes place at t_0; $Invest_{j0}$ represents the assets purchased (step j) at t_0, and of course, $Borrow_0$ and $Equity_0$ are the financing variables for t_0. Putting the constant terms on the right-hand side of the equality, this t_0 constraint is written as

$$\begin{aligned} Invest_{10} + Invest_{20} - Borrow_{20} - (1 - f)\ (Equity_0) = \\ - Assets_0 + Debt_0 + Net\ worth_0, \end{aligned} \tag{8.45}$$

where the right-hand side is zero because initial assets must equal initial liabilities. This constraint is shown as line 7 in Exhibit 8.9.

For t_1 (and subsequent periods in a larger model) the balancing constraint is more complicated, primarily because the assets and net worth at t_1 must reflect investment at t_0, and earnings retained in the first period add to net worth at t_1. After new investment is undertaken at t_1, the total assets will be[10]

$$Assets_0 + Invest_{10} + Invest_{20} + Invest_{11} + Invest_{21}.$$

The firm's net earnings during period 1 will be

$$R_0 \cdot Assets_0 + R_{10} \cdot Invest_{10} + R_{20} \cdot Invest_{20} - I_0 \cdot Debt_0 - i_0 Borrow_0 \tag{8.46}$$

where the coefficients R represent the net return earned on investment (prior to considering interest expense, but after income taxes), so that $R \cdot Invest$ is net income earned from the investment; and I and i are the average interest rates, after taxes, paid on the initial debt ($Debt_0$) and new funds borrowed at t_0 ($Borrow_0$), respectively. The addition to net worth of the firm at t_1 would be net earnings from Expression (8.46), less $Dividend_1$, plus new equity issued at t_1, and of course, total net worth at t_1 is $Net\ worth_0$ plus $(1-f)$ $(Equity_0)$ plus this addition to net worth at t_1.

The total debt outstanding at t_1 will be

$$Debt_0 + Borrow_0 + Borrow_1 - Principal\ repaid_1,$$

which for our example will be assumed to be

$$Debt_0 + Borrow_0 + Borrow_1 - 0.20\ Borrow_0,$$

where we assume no principal is repaid on the initial $Debt_0$.

When all terms are combined and constant terms transposed to the right-hand side, our t_1 balancing constraint is written as

$$\begin{aligned}&(1 - R_{10})\ (Invest_{10}) + (1 - R_{20})\ (Invest_{20}) + Invest_{11}\\&+ Invest_{21} - (0.80 - i_0)\ Borrow_0 - Borrow_1 - (1 - f)\ Equity_0\\&- (1 - f)\ Equity_1 + Dividend_1\\&= (1 - I_0)\ (Debt_0) + Net\ Worth_0 - (1 - R_0)\ (Assets_0),\end{aligned} \tag{8.47}$$

which, with $R_{10} = R_{11} = 0.17$, $R_{21} = R_{20} = 0.16$, $R_0 = 0.15$, $i_0 = I_0 = 0.12(1-0.46) = 0.0648$, $f = 0.10$, and initial balances of $Assets_0 = 50{,}000$, $Debt_0 = 12{,}000$, and $Net\ worth_0 = 38{,}000$, we obtain the constraint shown as line 8 in the Exhibit.

---

[10]In this simple example, it is assumed that assets are replaced at the same rate at which they depreciate, with the replacement financed by the funds generated by depreciation deductions. Consequently, we do not show balances declining over time, and cash flows do not explicitly reflect depreciation because the funds are being reinvested.

Another way (that won't be used in this model) to balance the system would be to have a budget equation expressed in terms of cash flows. This cash flow constraint would require that uses of cash equal sources of cash, and could be written in general form as

$$Cash_t - Cash_{t-1} - Operatings\ cash\ flow_t + Investment_t \\ - New\ financing_t = 0, \quad (8.48)$$

where, as before, each component of (8.48) must be expanded to be expressed in terms of the decision variables in the problem.[11]

Another type of constraint that can be included to limit the firm's borrowing is one that requires the firm to maintain a target financial ratio. In this case, it is assumed that the firm's debt-to-total-asset ratio must not be allowed to exceed 25 percent. This requires

$$Debt_t / Assets_t \leq 0.25$$

or

$$-0.25\ (Assets_t) + Debt_t \leq 0.$$

When this constraint is expressed in terms of the decision variables and initial balances, the first constraint is

$$-0.25\ (Invest_{10}) - 0.25\ (Invest_{11}) + Borrow_0 \\ \leq .25\ (Assets_0 - Debt_{0},) \quad (8.49)$$

and the second constraint is similar, as is shown on lines 11 and 12 in Exhibit 8.9.

The last constraints included in this model are those that regulate dividends. First, assume that dividends paid each period must not exceed a target proportion, denoted by *W*, of earnings from that period, or

$$Dividend_t \leq W \cdot Earnings_t, \quad (8.50)$$

where for t_1

---

[11]Expression (8.48) is derived from $Cash_t = Cash_{t-1} + Operating\ cash\ flow_t - Investment_t + New\ financing_t$, which, when these components are expanded, is written as $Cash_t - Cash_{t-1} - EBIT_t(1-\mathrm{T}) - Depreciation_t + Interest(1-T) + Principal\ repayment_t - Borrowing_t - Equity_t + Dividend_t = 0$.

$$Earnings_1 = R_0 \cdot Assets_0 + R_{10} \cdot Invest_{10} + R_{20} \cdot Invest_{20} - I_0 \cdot Debt_0 - i_0 \cdot Borrow,$$

which yields the constraint

$$-W \cdot R_{10} \cdot Invest_{10} - W \cdot R_{20} \cdot Invest_{20} + W \cdot i_0\ Borrow_0 + Dividend_1 \leq W \cdot R_0\ Assets_0 - W \cdot I_0 \cdot Debt_0, \qquad (8.51)$$

where, for this example, the target dividend payout ratio is $W = 0.40$, and with $R_0 = 0.15$, $R_{10} = 0.17$, and $R_{20} = 0.16$ and $i_0 = I_0 = 0.12(1-0.46) = 0.0648$, we end up with the constraint shown as line 13 of the Exhibit.

Other dividend constraints that could be included (but in this case, are not) could be based on a minimum growth rate of dividends, or constraints that limit the potential variability of dividends. For example, it may be regarded as essential to keep dividends increasing at 5 percent per year, and this is shown with a constraint of the form

$$Dividend_t \geq 1.05\ Dividend_{t-1}$$

or

$$-1.05 \cdot Dividend_{t-1} + Dividend_t \geq 0.$$

The variability of dividends could be mitigated by limiting dividend growth to be less than some upper limit, of, say, 8 percent per year.

It may not always be possible to meet any given goal such as 5 percent dividend growth, especially when there are many other constraints on decisions. In that case, the linear program is infeasible and cannot be solved. The infeasibility is itself valuable information—it is helpful to know when the various constraint or targets cannot be met without violating the logic of the plan. If a program is not feasible, the constraints can be varied until a feasible program is found, and the user can evaluate the revised feasible plan. Most LP solution software does not directly tell the user which particular constraint causes the infeasibility; one must usually find it by trial and error—a method that will confound the user unless the model is kept as simple as possible.

The Solution to the Planning Model. Now that the LP model has been formulated, we need only to solve it. The input to the LP solution software is the array of coefficients of the variables. We refer to this array as the tableau, and it is displayed for this small problem as Exhibit 8.10. The variable names appear at the heads of the columns, and the numbers in the first row are the coefficients in the objective function. The coefficients of the nine decision variables are shown in the body of the table; each line corresponds to a constraint, and the constraint limitations are shown on the right-hand side. The names on the left refer to the constraints.

When this problem is solved, it generates the recommended investment and financing plan as is shown by the following list of optimal values of the decision variables:

Decision Variable	*Solution Value*
Investment	
Invest_{10}	\$8,000
Invest_{20}	4,000
Invest_{11}	8,000
Invest_{22}	4,000
Financing	
Borrow_0	3,500
Borrow_1	3,700
Equity_0	9,444.44
Equity_1	560.89
Dividend_1	0

Investment is expanded up to the maximum of \$12,000 in each period. This investment is financed at t_0 by borrowing \$3,500 and issuing stock for a net amount of \$8,500 (\$9,444.44 gross amount less \$944.44 flotation costs). At t_1, \$3,700 is borrowed, and net equity of \$504.80 (\$560.89 − \$56.09) is issued. The remainder at t_1 is financed by internal financing (retained earnings), as is shown by the sources and uses of funds statement:

EXHIBIT 8.10 Tableau of Coefficients for Linear Programming Model

	Variable									
	(Invest)$_{10}$	*(Invest)*$_{20}$	*(Invest)*$_{11}$	*(Invest)*$_{21}$	*(Borrow)*$_0$	*(Borrow)*$_1$	*(Equity)*$_0$	*(Equity)*$_1$	*(Dividend)*$_1$	
Objective Function	0.133	0.06	0.116	0.052	0.1284	0.1147	−0.10	−0.087	0	
Constraints										
1 17% Investment limit, $t = 0$	1	—	—	—	—	—	—	—	—	≤ $ 8,000
2 16% Investment limit, $t = 0$	—	1	—	—	—	—	—	—	—	≤ 10,000
3 17% Investment limit, $t = 1$	—	—	1	—	—	—	—	—	—	≤ 8,000
4 16% Investment limit, $t = 1$	—	—	—	1	—	—	—	—	—	≤ 10,000
5 Total Investment limit, $t = 0$	1	1	—	—	—	—	—	—	—	≤ 12,000
6 Total Investment limit, $t = 1$	—	—	1	1	—	—	—	—	—	≤ 12,000
7 Assets = Liabilities, $t = 0$	1	1	—	—	−1	—	−0.9	—	—	= 0
8 Assets = Liabilities, $t = 1$	0.83	0.84	1	1	−0.7352	−1	−0.9	−0.9	0.1	≤ 6,722
9 Borrowing limit, $t = 0$	—	—	—	—	1	—	—	—	—	≤ 7,000
10 Borrowing limit, $t = 1$	—	—	—	—	0.8	1	—	—	—	≤ 7,000
11 Debt equity ratio requirement, $t = 0$	−0.25	−0.25	—	—	1	—	—	—	—	≤ 500
12 Debit equity ratio requirement, $t = 1$	−0.25	−0.25	−0.25	−0.25	0.8	1	—	—	—	≤ 500
13 Dividend payout target	−0.068	−0.064	—	—	0.026	—	—	—	1	≤ 2,689

Sources and Uses of Funds, Time t_1

Sources of Funds		*Uses of Funds*	
Earnings from assets		Investment	$12,000.
0.15 • $Assets_0$	$ 7,500.	Net interest on debt	
0.17 • $Invest_{10}$	1,360.	0.0648 • $Debt_0$	777.
0.16 • $Invest_{20}$	640.	0.0648 • $Borrow_0$	227.
New equity issued (net)	504.	Principal repaid:	
$Borrow_1$	3,700.	0.20 • $Borrow_0$	700.
Total sources	$13,704	Total uses	$13,704.

When the decision variables are at their optimal values as shown above, the value of the objective function is as large as is possible, and the constraints are not violated. In this case, the value of the optimal objective function will be calculated as

$$\begin{aligned} &0.133 \cdot Invest_{10} + 0.06 \cdot Invest_{20} + 0.116 \cdot Invest_{11} \\ &+ 0.052 \cdot Invest_{22} + 0.1284 \cdot Borrow_0 + 0.1147 \cdot Borrow_1 \\ &- 0.10 \cdot Equity_0 - 0.087 \cdot Equity_1 + 0 \cdot Dividend_1, \end{aligned}$$

which with the optimal values of the decision variables is

$$\begin{aligned} 0.133(8{,}000) &+ 0.06(4{,}000) + 0.116(8{,}000) + 0.052(4{,}000) \\ &+ 0.1284(3{,}500) + 0.1147(3{,}700) \\ &- 0.10(9{,}444.44) - 0.087(560.89) + 0(0) \\ &= \$3{,}220.55, \end{aligned}$$

which is the largest value feasible within the constraints.

The objective function was defined in terms of the contribution each decision variable made to the present value of cash flows available to be paid as dividends to the stockholders, or more directly, the contribution to the value of the stockholders' equity. Consequently, the choice of this optimal plan of investment and financing should contribute $3,220.55 to the value of the stockholders' equity. Any other plan that is feasible would contribute less.

The dual variables. One very useful product of the linear programming solution is what is called the *dual variable* or *shadow price.*[12] There is a dual variable corresponding to each constraint in the LP, and it measures the change in the optimal value of the objective function that would occur if the constraint was relaxed by one unit.

For example, the first constraint is the limitation on step 1 investments that earn a return of 17 percent, and this limit is set at \$8,000, meaning that no more than \$8,000 can be invested in opportunities yielding 17 percent at t_0. The next dollar must be invested at 16 percent. What if we could invest up to \$8,001 instead of \$8,000? Would the opportunity to invest one additional dollar at 17 percent make any difference to the value of the equity, and if so, how much difference?

The answer is provided by the dual variable that corresponds to this first constraint. The value of this dual variable turns out to be 0.0739, meaning that the optimal value of the objective function would increase by \$0.0739 if just one additional dollar could be invested in this step 1 opportunity that yields 17 percent. Most of this additional value is attributable to the difference between the net present value of step 1 versus step 2 opportunities. Step 1 has $NPV_{10} = 0.133$, while for step 2, $NPV_{20} = 0.06$, a difference of 0.073, that is, an additional dollar invested at 17 percent and generating an $NPV = 0.133$ is a dollar that doesn't have to be invested at 16 percent, so we gain \$0.073 in value. But there is additional value that is determined in the LP. Part of the source of funds for investment at t_1 is the earnings retained in the business at t_1—earnings that are generated by investment at t_0. If we can invest more at t_0 at a higher rate of return, there are more funds available at t_1 to help finance investment at that date, and a smaller amount of funds need to be raised externally at t_1. In this case, a smaller amount of new equity capital would have to be raised at t_1, saving the firm from paying the transactions (underwriting or flotation) costs that would be necessary if shares had to be sold at t_1.

Tracing through all these potential interactions and relationships would be very difficult by hand. The LP does it auto-

---

[12] A detailed discussion of dual variables is beyond the scope of this book. The interested reader who wants additional information should consult any of the operations research books referenced at the end of the chapter, or, for more specific discussion of financial applications, see articles by Morris (1975) and Carleton, Kendall, and Tandon (1974).

matically as it solves the problem. Thus, we get information from the output that helps us to evaluate our plan and the constraints that limit it. For this problem the dual variables corresponding to each constraint are shown in Exhibit 8.11.

A constraint is said to be nonbinding when the solution does not reach the limit imposed by the constraint. For example, in this case, because total investment at t_0 is $12,000, the step 2 constraint that limits 16 percent investments to be less than $10,000, is not binding because the step 2 investment is only $4,000. In this case, the $10,000 limit on step 2 investments is no limit at all—it does not affect the solution because it is nonbinding. That is, stretching the constraint to $10,001 would not change anything. This is what is shown by the dual variable shown for line 2: the dual variable is zero.

On the other hand, a binding constraint will usually lead to a positive value for its dual variable. For example, constraint number 12 is the one that requires the debt-to-asset ratio to be no greater than 25 percent, and as is shown in Exhibit 8.11, its dual variable is 0.2114. This means that relaxing this constraint by one unit would add $0.2114 to the value of the stockholders' equity. Since the constraint is formulated as

$$\textit{Debt} \leq 0.25\ (\textit{Assets}),$$

one unit refers to an increase in assets of $4, resulting in a $1 increase in debt capacity (i.e., 0.25 × $4.00). In this example, this is the most costly constraint. It is costly because it causes us to give up $0.2114 in value. If it were relaxed, we could add to value for the stockholders.

This discussion helps to highlight the practical usefulness of the dual variables. We can use them to evaluate the opportunity cost imposed by various constraints. We can see what we have given up by having to live within the constraint. In this way, we can see what it would be worth to us to be able to relax the constraint.

This example, while very simple, helps to demonstrate how an LP model could be used to develop a longer term financial plan. Periods and variables can be added to handle larger and more realistic problems. However, care should be exercised in expanding the model. It is very easy to build a model that is so large that it is unmanageable. It is easy to make mistakes at

EXHIBIT 8.11 Dual Variables for Planning Model

Line Number in Exhibit 8.9	*Type of Constraint*	*Value of Dual Variable*
1	Investment limit, Step 1, t_0	0.0739
2	Investment limit, Step 2, t_0	0
3	Investment limit, Step 1, t_1	0.064
4	Investment limit, Step 2, t_1	0
5	Total investment budget, t_0	0.0284
6	Total investment budget, t_1	0.0082
7	Assets = Liabilities, t_0	0
8	Assets = Liabilities, t_1	0
9	$\text{Borrow}_0 \leq 7000$, t_0	0
10	$\text{Borrow}_1 \leq 7000$, t_1	0
11	Debt $\leq$ 0.25 Assets, t_0	0.0448
12	Debt $\leq$ 0.25 Assets, t_1	0.2114
13	$\text{Dividend}_1 \leq 0.40$ Earnings, t_1	0

each stage: in formulating the model, in determining the coefficients, and in putting the data into the computer. And, it is often extremely difficult to detect errors and to determine what the correction should be. You should always check your model and its output for errors. The starting point is just a matter of asking whether the solution makes sense. Then, a more detailed check can be made by developing financial statements based on the plan: Sources should equal uses, assets should equal liabilities, and there should not be any really extreme recommendations that violate your commonsense.

8.3 A LINEAR PROGRAMMING MODEL FOR THE PLANNING AND MANAGEMENT OF CURRENT ASSETS AND LIABILITIES

One of the tasks of a financial manager is to develop and execute plans for managing current assets and current liabilities. This involves deciding what minimum amount of cash should be maintained, how to invest excess cash, which marketable securities should be purchased, which should be sold, how receivables and payables should be managed, how much funds should be borrowed and in what maturity, and when outstanding debt should be repaid. The planning and management of the current accounts involves a plethora of problems with a myriad of potential solutions. Various approaches have been offered for the handling of individual problems such as cash management. The current accounts are interrelated, however, and the separate management of each account as an independent problem may be incorrect. What is necessary is a method for considering the numerous interrelationships and making decisions that would be consistent with a valid objective.

Linear programming is ideally suited to handling some of the problems and interdependencies of current assets and liabilities. Numerous linear programming models of the current accounts have been presented; two of the best known are those by Robicheck, Teichroew, and Jones (1965) and Orgler (1970). A simplified example based on Orgler will be discussed here.

WORKING CAPITAL DECISIONS FOR THE COUGAR CORPORATION

The manager of the working capital accounts of the Cougar Corporation faces the task of planning the firm's short-term security investments and the short-term financing, and managing the cash account.

Over the next six months the firm's operating cash flows will alternate between inflows and outflows, with some very large outflows occurring during the months when production is high as inventories are built up for future seasonal sales. A substantial inflow of funds, amounting to \$265,000, is expected over the next two days, but then there will be a period of about 12 weeks during which the operating outflows will total \$2.5 million. After that, receivables will begin to be collected, reversing the cash outflow. The details of this forecast are shown in Exhibit 8.12. In any case, the ebb and flow of funds must be planned for and managed.

The resources that are available to help meet the needs for funds include a current cash balance of \$900,000, marketable securities with face value of \$1,040,000, and a line of credit with the bank that allows it to borrow up to \$500,000.

The manager would like to develop a method that would allow him to analyze systematically and rationally the complex

EXHIBIT 8.12 Cougar Corporation: Forecast of Resources and Obligations over Planning Horizon

Period	*Number of Days until End of Period*	*Exogenous Net Cash Flow*	*Face Value of Maturing Securities*	*Principal Amount of Debt Maturing*
1	1	$ 200,000	$ 10,000	
2	2	65,000	10,000	
3	10	−800,000	120,000	
4	30	−1,300,000	50,000	
5	90	−400,000	100,000	$80,000
6	180	1,900,000	250,000	
7	Beyond Horizon		500,000	

interactions and trade-offs between the numerous investment and financing alternatives. He has decided that a linear programming model of his working capital management decisions would help to provide the best assistance for his decision making. Such a model would take into account the current balances of cash and securities and the amount of debt outstanding, and it could recommend strategies for the future purchase and sale of securities and plans for borrowing against the firm's line of credit to meet the short-term financing needs. The various structural and data inputs to this model are described below, along with the recommended actions over the firm's planning horizon.

Planning Horizon

The planning horizon spans six months, and it is broken into six unequal subperiods as follows:

Period	*Length of Period*
1	1 day
2	1 day
3	8 days
4	20 days
5	60 days
6	90 days

The decision problem is solved to generate decision recommendations for the next two days, and tentative decisions for the longer periods after that. Then the problem is solved again as time passes and market conditions change. In this way it is generating recommendations every couple of days for current decisions. The recommendations for periods further in the future are tentative and are revised as those periods approach the present.

The advantage of the unequal-period planning horizon is that it is unnecessary to make decisions regarding daily actions, say, four months hence, but it is necessary to worry about tomorrow and the next day. This unequal-period approach decreases the unnecessary detail of the plan for periods further in the future, while allowing more detailed consideration of the near term.

Based on the definition of the periods in the planning horizon, the cash flows, security balances, and currently outstanding debt are shown in Exhibit 8.12.

Decision Alternatives

The decision alternatives relate to the balance carried in the cash account, the purchase and sales of marketable securities, and the amount of short-term financing to use. Each decision involves some return or cost that affects the payoff at the end of the planning horizon, and each decision is affected by some constraints.

The decision variables used in the LP will be defined as follows:

- C_t is the decision variable representing the balance of *cash* held at the end of period *t,* for $t = 0,1,2,3,4,5,6$; C_0 denotes the balance held at the beginning of the planning horizon.
- SP_{jt} is the amount of *securities purchased* at the *end* of period *t* that mature at the *end* of period *j,* for $t = 0,1,2,$-. . .,6, and $j = 1,2,. . .,6,7$ (there are 28 SP_{jt} variables). SP_{j0} denotes the balance held at t_0 and t_7 refers to time 30 days beyond the end of the planning horizon. This decision variable is defined in terms of the face (maturity) value of securities that are purchased at a discount from face value. For

example, SP_{41} is the face value of securities purchased at t_1 that mature at t_4, which is an investment period of 29 days.

In this case, the amount actually invested at t_1 is less than SP_{41} because the securities are purchased at a discount. It is assumed the annual yield earned on short term investments is 10 percent, which would be 0.0278 percent per day, before taxes (taxes are ignored in this example). For the 29-day investment, SP_{41}, the amount spent at t_1 is $0.9919 \times SP_{41}$.

- SS_{jt} is the amount of *securities sold* during period t that would mature in period j, for $t = 1,2,\ldots,6$ and $j = 2,3,\ldots,7$ (there are 21 SS_{jt} variables). It is assumed that securities are sold at the end of period t, so the sale results in loss of yield that would otherwise be earned from t until j. For example, for variable SS_{41}, sale at t_1 of securities that would mature at t_4 would result in loss of yield from the end of period 1 until the end of period 4, a period of 29 days, which at 0.0278 percent per day is a loss of yield of $29 \times 0.000278 =$ \$0.00806 per dollar (face value) sold. The variable SS_{jt} is defined in terms of face (maturity) value of the discount security, so for each dollar of securities sold, the cash realized at the sale date is the discounted value (net of transaction cost).
- B_{jt} is the amount *borrowed* during period t that will be repaid during period j, for $t = 1,2,3,\ldots,6$ and $j = 1,2,\ldots,6,7$ (28 variables B_{jt}) where $t = 0$ refers to amounts borrowed before the start of the planning period. It is assumed that funds are borrowed at an annual rate of 12 percent (before taxes), for a cost 1 per day of 0.033 percent. Repayment prior to maturity is not considered. The decision variable B_{jt} is defined in terms of the amount borrowed at t, and the amount repaid at j will be principal plus interest from t until j. It is assumed that debt outstanding at t_0 has had interest paid to date, so additional interest will accrue from t_0; and debt maturing at t_7 is assumed to mature 30 days past the horizon.

The decision variables are summarized in Exhibit 8.13. There are 84 decision variables in this model: 7 symbolized as C (cash balances); 28 *SP (securities purchased)*; 21 *SS (securities sold)*; and 28 *B (borrowing)*. The decision variables are defined

EXHIBIT 8.13 Cougar Corporation: Decision Variables for Linear Program

	Period in which Action Is Taken							
Action	*0*	*1*	*2*	*3*	*4*	*5*	*6*	
Cash balance	C_0	C_1	C_2	C_3	C_4	C_5	C_6	
Securities purchased	SP_{10}							1
	SP_{20}	SP_{21}						2 Period *j*
	SP_{30}	SP_{31}	SP_{32}					3 in Which
	SP_{40}	SP_{41}	SP_{42}	SP_{43}				4 Securities
	SP_{50}	SP_{51}	SP_{52}	SP_{53}	SP_{54}			5 Mature
	SP_{60}	SP_{61}	SP_{62}	SP_{63}	SP_{64}	SP_{65}		6
	SP_{70}	SP_{71}	SP_{72}	SP_{73}	SP_{74}	SP_{75}	SP_{76}	7
Securities sold		SS_{21}						2 Period *j*
		SS_{31}	SS_{32}					3 in Which
		SS_{41}	SS_{42}	SS_{43}				4 Securities
		SS_{51}	SS_{52}	SS_{53}	SS_{54}			5 Mature
		SS_{61}	SS_{62}	SS_{63}	SS_{64}	SS_{65}		6
		SS_{71}	SS_{72}	SS_{73}	SS_{74}	SS_{75}	SS_{76}	7
Borrowing	B_{10}							1 Period *j*
	B_{20}	B_{21}						2 in Which
	B_{30}	B_{31}	B_{32}					3 Loan Will
	B_{40}	B_{41}	B_{42}	B_{43}				4 Be Repaid
	B_{50}	B_{51}	B_{52}	B_{53}	B_{54}			5
	B_{60}	B_{61}	B_{62}	B_{63}	B_{64}	B_{65}		6
	B_{70}	B_{71}	B_{72}	B_{73}	B_{74}	B_{75}	B_{76}	7

only for feasible combinations of periods. For example, the period in which securities are purchased must precede the period in which they mature.

Objective

The objective function of the linear program should be consistent with the objective of making the value of the firm as large as possible. In this case, the objective function is chosen to be the net value of the relevant working capital accounts at the end of the planning horizon. The working capital accounts being considered are *Cash, Securities,* and *Borrowing,* and the net value at the end of the planning horizon is the value of *Cash* + *Securities* − *Borrowing.* The terminal values in these accounts consist of the initial balances plus any earnings and less any costs or debt repayments over the planning horizon. Because the earnings from security investments and costs of transactions and borrowing over the planning horizon are taken into account, maximizing the terminal value is consistent with maximizing present value, and is, therefore, consistent with maximizing firm value.

In terms of the notation that has been introduced, the objective function that is to be maximized is written as

$$C_6 + \sum_{t=0}^{6} a_{7t}\, SP_{7t} - \sum_{t=1}^{6} a_{7t}\, SS_{7t} - \sum_{t=0}^{6} b_{7t}\, B_{7t}, \tag{8.60}$$

where

$\sum_{t=0}^{6} a_{7t}\, SP_{7t}$ is the market value at t_6 of *Securities purchased* in periods 0 through 6 that will mature beyond the planning horizon (t_7). The coefficients a_{7t} represent the discount factors that convert face values to market values at t_6;

$\sum_{t=1}^{6} a_{7t}\, SS_{7t}$ is the market value at t_6 of securities sold in previous periods that would mature at t_7, where a_{7t} is the discount factor converting face value SS_{7t} to market value; and

$\sum_{t=0}^{6} b_{7t}\, B_{7t}$ is the total amount owed (principal and interest) at t_6 from amounts borrowed in periods 0 through 6 that mature beyond the horizon (t_7); the coefficients b_{7t} are the compounding factors that convert the principal amount borrowed at time t to principal and interest owed at t_6.

The Link between Decisions and Goals

To weigh the relative attractiveness of taking different actions we need to define the contribution the action will make to helping us attain the goal. With the goal of maximizing the net value of working capital at the horizon date, the objective function will include only the account balances at the horizon date, and the other decision variables will not be shown in the objective function. That is, all decision variables and account balances that apply to dates prior to the horizon date will have zero coefficients in the objective function. This does not mean that these variables are not linked to the objective, however. The balances in the various accounts at the horizon date will be related to all previous decisions and balances by way of the constraints, particularly the cash flow constraints that require that sources of cash equal uses of cash. For example, sales of securities at t_5 will not be shown directly in the objective function, but the sale will generate cash that will either be included in the cash balance at t_6 or will be used to purchase securities held at t_6 or to reduce the debt outstanding at t_6. In a similar manner, every decision variable will be linked with working capital balances at the horizon date.

Constraints

The choices of actions available for managing working capital are limited by four types of constraints. First is a constraint imposed by the firm's policies, which is that the cash balance is not allowed to drop below a minimum level. Second, there are constraints imposed by the firm's resources. The main resource constraints in this model relate to security purchases and sales. Securities can be purchased only if the firm has the funds available to make the purchase, and securities can be sold only if the firm already has securities to sell. Third, there are limitations on the firm's actions imposed from outside the firm. In this case external constraint is imposed by lenders who set an upper limit on the amount they will lend to the firm. Fourth, and most important, there is the budget constraint that uses of cash must equal sources of cash, which we will refer to as the cash flow constraint. We will discuss how each set of decision variables is included in the constraints.

Cash Balances. The policy constraint that is shown in this model is the requirement that the cash balance not be allowed to drop below a minimum level. In this case the constraint is that for each date t,

$$C_t \geq \$100{,}000. \tag{8.61}$$

This constraint allows cash to exceed the minimum of \$100,000, but it can't drop below that level. Because there are alternative uses for cash that can generate income, it would be quite unusual for the model to recommend that cash balances be allowed to exceed the minimum.

Securities. At the beginning of the planning horizon, t_0, the firm has a portfolio of marketable securities that mature during and beyond the planning horizon. The face values of the securities held in the initial portfolio are indicated by the values of variables SP_{10}, SP_{20}, . . ., SP_{70}, where the second subscript, 0, indicates securities held at t_0, with the following expressions showing the amounts held at t_0:

Security Purchase Variable		*Value of Securities Maturing during Period*	*Period in Which Securities Mature*	
SP_{10}	=	\$ 10,000	1	(8.62A)
SP_{20}	=	10,000	2	(8.62B)
SP_{30}	=	120,000	3	(8.62C)
SP_{40}	=	50,000	4	(8.62D)
SP_{50}	=	100,000	5	(8.62E)
SP_{60}	=	250,000	6	(8.62F)
SP_{70}	=	500,000	7	(8.62G)

We can view the variables SP_{j0} as decision variables that are constrained to be equal the amounts of securities held, so Expressions (8.62A) through (8.62G) are equality constraints in the linear program.

At any date the securities held in the portfolio consist of the initial securities, plus securities purchased up to that date, less any securities sold. For example, at t_2 (just prior to t_2 security purchases or sales) the securities held that mature at t_4 are

$$SP_{40} + SP_{41} - SS_{41}. \tag{8.63}$$

The constraint on security sales is that securities can be sold prior to maturity only from the portfolio already held on the sale date (short sales are not considered). For example, security sales at t_2 of securities maturing at t_4 are constrained not to exceed the securities held:

$$SS_{42} \leq SP_{40} + SP_{41} - SS_{41},$$

or, putting all decision variables on the left side of the inequality, we have

$$-SP_{40} - SP_{41} + SS_{41} + SS_{42} > 0, \qquad (8.64)$$

where it is assumed that securities purchased at t_2 are not also sold at t_2. For each of the security sale variables, SS_{jt}, there must be a constraint such as (8.64), so there will be 21 constraints like (8.64).

The *security purchase* and *security sale* decision variables must appear in the constraints that require uses of cash to equal sources of cash. These constraints will ensure that securities can be purchased only if funds are available. With respect to security transactions, the cash flows in period t consist of cash outflows due to security purchases and cash inflows from maturing securities and the sales of securities prior to maturity.

The uses of cash associated with security transactions will be the cash outflows from purchases of securities. For example, in period 2 the total cash outflow from security purchases is

$$c_{32}SP_{32} + c_{42}SP_{42} + c_{52}SP_{52} + c_{62}SP_{62} + c_{72}SP_{72},$$

where the coefficients c_{j2} are the prices paid per dollar of face value purchased, which is simply the discounted price of the security per dollar of face value. Assume the nominal annual yield on securities is 10 percent. The coefficients c_{jt} are calculated here as 1 − (0.10/360) • (Days to maturity). For example, a \$1 security purchased at t_2 to mature at t_5 has 88 days to maturity, and would be purchased at a discounted price of 1 − (0.10/360) • (88) = 1 − 0.0222 = 0.9756, so $c_{52} = 0.9756$. With the face value of the security purchase being SP_{52}, the total cash outflow at t_2 from this purchase would be $c_{52}SP_{52} = 0.9756 \cdot SP_{52}$. These coefficients c_{jt} of decision variables SP_{jt} are shown in Exhibit 8.14.

The sources of cash from security transactions are the proceeds from maturing securities and the sales of securities. For example, at t_2 the cash flow from maturing securities is

$$SP_{20} + SP_{21} - SS_{21},$$

which are the securities maturing at t_2 that were purchased at t_0 (initial portfolio) and t_1, less the securities sold at t_1 that would have matured at t_2. The proceeds at t_2 from selling securities that would otherwise mature at t_3, t_4,. . .,t_7 are

$$a_{32}SS_{32} + a_{42}SS_{42} + a_{52}SS_{52} + a_{62}SS_{62} + a_{72}SS_{72},$$

EXHIBIT 8.14 Cougar Corporation: Price Paid per $1 Face Value for Security Purchases (coefficients c_{jt} of variables SP_{jt} in cash flow constraint)

Period in Which Security Matures	*Period in Which Purchase Occurs*					
	1	*2*	*3*	*4*	*5*	*6*
2	0.9997					
3	0.9975	0.9978				
4	0.9919	0.9922	0.9944			
5	0.9753	0.9756	0.9778	0.9833		
6	0.9503	0.9506	0.9528	0.9583	0.975	
7	0.9419	0.9422	0.9444	0.950	0.9667	0.9917

where the coefficients a_{j2} represent the discounted price per dollar of the securities that is realized on the sale because they are sold prior to maturity. In the absence of transaction costs, the prices of securities sold that would mature on a given date should be equal to the purchase price, so coefficients a_{jt} would be identical to the purchase coefficients c_{jt}. In this example, however, it is assumed that there is a transaction cost associated with selling (bid-ask spread) so the prices received from selling are lower than the price paid for the purchase. Specifically, it is assumed the transaction cost lowers the sale price by 0.001 per dollar of face value relative to the purchase price of the same security. Thus, $a_{jt} = c_{jt} - 0.001$, so the coefficients a_{jt} are obtained from Exhibit 8.14 by substracting 0.001. For example, the price received from the sale at t_2 of a security maturing for $1 at t_5 is assumed to be $a_{52} = 0.9756 - 0.001 = 0.9746$.

The main reason the transaction costs are included is that without a penalty for sales, the LP may tend to recommend the purchase of securities with longer maturities, followed by subsequent sales of these securities prior to maturity, as opposed to simply purchasing securities that mature as funds are needed. Imposing a transaction cost on the sale will cause the LP to prefer to purchase securities of an appropriate maturity rather than unnecessary sales of securities with longer maturity.

There must be a cash flow equation for each period in the planning horizon, and for period t, the cash inflows from maturing securities and sales of securities are combined with cash outflows from purchases of securities. In the cash flow constraint for period t, these terms would be combined as:

Maturing securities + Security sales − Security purchases

$$\sum_{i=0}^{t-1} (SP_{ti} - SS_{ti}) + \sum_{j=t+1}^{7} a_{jt} SS_{jt} - \sum_{j=t+1}^{7} c_{jt} SP_{jt}. \quad (8.65)$$

Borrowing. The borrowing variables will appear in two types of constraints, the constraints that limit the amount of borrowing and the cash flow constraints.

Assume that the firm can obtain funds through a line of credit with any maturity up to 30 days beyond the planning horizon. However, the lenders limit the total amount to be borrowed to \$500,000. This limit includes funds already borrowed at t_0.

At the beginning of the planning horizon the firm already has debt outstanding (denoted by decision variables $B_{j0}, j=1,\ldots, 7$). Assume that the only debt outstanding in this case consists of funds borrowed in previous periods that is due at the end of period 5. As of t_0 the total (principal and interest) due the lender is

$$B_{50} = \$80{,}000. \quad (8.66)$$

The variable B_{50} will be treated as a decision variable in this formulation, and equation (8.66) will be included as a constraint. The other variables B_{j0} could be included, but it is unnecessary.

The limitation on the total amount of debt requires that at the end of each period the total debt principal not exceed \$500,000, where total debt consists of debt outstanding at the end of the last period, plus any new funds borrowed, less any amount repaid. Assume funds are borrowed at the end of the period, and repayment occurs at the end of the maturity period. For example, at t_1 (end of period 1), the outstanding debt consists of:

- Debt outstanding at t_0:

$$B_{10} + B_{20} + B_{30} + B_{40} + B_{50} + B_{70}$$

- plus borrowing during period 1:

$$B_{21} + B_{31} + B_{41} + B_{51} + B_{61} + B_{71}$$

- less debt repaid at t_1:

$$- B_{10},$$

- all of which can be rewritten as

$$\sum_{i=2}^{7} B_{i0} + \sum_{i=2}^{7} B_{i1}. \tag{8.67}$$

With B_{50} the only debt outstanding at t_0, the constraint on total borrowing at t_1 is

$$B_{50} + \sum_{i=2}^{7} B_{i1} \leq 500{,}000. \tag{8.68}$$

For any date t this constraint in general form would be

$$\sum_{i=0}^{t} \sum_{j=t+1}^{7} B_{ji} \leq \$500{,}000. \tag{8.69}$$

With these constraints, the cumulative amount borrowed is maintained at a level at or below the limit. In this particular formulation early repayment is not considered, but a repayment variable could easily be added.

The cash flows related to borrowing must be shown in the cash flow constraint that requires sources to equal uses. Borrowing provides a cash inflow at the date of the borrowing, and a cash outflow occurs when the debt is repaid. For example, borrowing amount B_{53} generates an inflow of B_{53} dollars at the end of period 3 and an amount equal to $b_{53} \cdot B_{53}$ is repaid at t_5, where the coefficient b_{53} is the principal and interest paid to the lender at t_5 per dollar borrowed at the beginning of period 3. With a 12 percent borrowing rate, the coefficients b_{it} are shown in Exhibit 8.15, where it is assumed nothing is paid to the lender until the debt matures. From the exhibit we have $b_{53} = 1.027$, which means that for each \$1 borrowed at the end of period 3, \$1.027 is repaid at t_5, including principal and interest. If, in the LP solution, $B_{53} = 1{,}000$, there is an inflow of \$1,000 at the beginning of period 3, and an outflow of $b_{53} \cdot B_{53} = 1.027 \cdot 1{,}000 = \$1{,}027.00$ at t_5.

For debt that matures beyond the planning horizon (t_7) the LP is formulated to consider only the amount owed (principal and interest) at the end of the planning horizon (t_6). Consequently, the coefficients shown in Exhibit 8.15 for debt maturing

EXHIBIT 8.15 Amount Repaid at Maturity per Dollar Borrowed

Period in Which Borrowing Is Repaid	*Period in Which Borrowing Occurs*						
	0	*1*	*2*	*3*	*4*	*5*	*6*
1	1.0003						
2	1.0007	1.0003					
3	1.0033	1.0030	1.0027				
4	1.0101	1.0097	1.0094	1.0067			
5	1.0304	1.0301	1.0298	1.0270	1.0202		
6	1.0618	1.0614	1.0611	1.0583	1.0513	1.0304	
7	1.0618	1.0614	1.0611	1.0583	1.0513	1.0304	1.00

beyond the horizon are identical to debt maturing at t_6. The difference between debt maturing at t_6 and t_7 is that the t_6 cash flows include repayment of t_6 debt, whereas the t_7 debt (principal plus accrued interest) is assumed still to be outstanding at t_6.

The borrowing variables would appear in each period's cash flow equation with both cash inflows from borrowing and cash outflows from repayment. For example, for period 2 we have the net cash flow from borrowing as

$$-b_{20}B_{20} - b_{21}B_{21} + B_{32} + B_{42} + B_{52} + B_{62} + B_{72},$$

which, with the coefficients from Exhibit 8.15, is

$$-1.0007B_{20} - 1.0003B_{21} + B_{32} + B_{42} + B_{52} + B_{62} + B_{72},$$

where the first two terms represent repayment of principal and interest at t_2 of debt incurred in past periods.

There will be a cash flow constraint for each period in the planning horizon. Each constraint will contain the relevant borrowing variables to reflect both debt repayment and new borrowing.

Combining Terms in the Cash Flow Constraint. As has been the case with the other models explained in this book, it is essential to have a mechanism that balances the model. In this case, this task is performed by the cash flow constraints that require that sources of cash equal uses of cash. All the decision variables will be shown in the cash flow constraints. The cash flow constraint is based on the following definitional expression:

$$\begin{aligned} Cash_t = {} & Cash_{t-1} + Sources\ of\ cash_t \\ & - Uses\ of\ cash_t, \end{aligned} \tag{8.70}$$

which, in words, says that the *Cash* balance at the end of period t is composed of the beginning balance plus the net cash inflows generated during the period. The sources of cash will consist of sources that depend on the decision variables, which will be called *endogenous sources,* and sources that are independent of the decision variables, and are called *exogenous sources;* similar definitions apply to *endogenous uses* and *exogenous uses.* Using these definitions Expression (8.70) can be rewritten as

$$\begin{aligned} Cash_t - Cash_{t-1} - Endogenous\ sources_t + Endogenous\ uses_t \\ = Exogenous\ net\ cash\ flow_t, \end{aligned} \tag{8.71}$$

where

$$\begin{aligned} Exogenous\ net\ cash\ flow = {} & Exogenous\ sources \\ & - Exogenous\ uses. \end{aligned}$$

In our model, the *endogenous sources* are maturing securities, security sales, and borrowing, while the *endogenous uses* are security purchases and debt repayment. From our previous discussion we can write these endogenous sources and uses for period t in terms of the decision variables as follows:

Endogenous Sources

Maturing securities: $\sum_{j=0}^{t-1} SP_{tj} - \sum_{j=1}^{t-1} SS_{tj}$

Security sales: $\sum_{j=t+1}^{7} a_{jt} SS_{jt}$

Borrowing: $\sum_{j=t+1}^{7} B_{jt}$

Endogenous Uses

Security purchases: $\sum_{j=t+1}^{7} c_{jt}\, SP_{jt}$

Debt repayment: $\sum_{j=0}^{t-1} b_{tj}\, B_{tj}.$

When these terms are combined to fit (8.71), the cash flow constraint for period t is

$$C_t - C_{t-1} - \left(\sum_{j=0}^{t-1} SP_{tj} - \sum_{j=1}^{t-1} SS_{tj}\right) - \sum_{j=t+1}^{7} a_{jt}\, SS_{jt}$$
$$- \sum_{j=t+1}^{7} B_{jt} + \sum_{j=t+1}^{7} c_{jt}\, SP_{jt} + \sum_{j=0}^{t-1} b_{tj}\, B_{tj}$$
$$= \textit{Exogenous net cash flow}_t, \tag{8.72}$$

or, simplifying, we get

$$C_t - C_{t-1} - \sum_{j=0}^{t-1} SP_{tj} + \sum_{j=t+1}^{7} c_{jt}\, SP_{jt} + \sum_{j=1}^{t-1} SS_{tj}$$
$$- \sum_{j=t+1}^{7} a_{jt}\, SS_{jt} + \sum_{j=0}^{t-1} b_{tj}\, B_{tj} - \sum_{j=t+1}^{7} B_{jt}$$
$$= \textit{Exogenous net cash flow}_t. \tag{8.73}$$

The *exogenous net cash flows* are those flows that were forecasted over the six-month planning horizon and were shown in Exhibit 8.12 at the beginning of this section.

The Completed Model

Exhibit 8.16 shows the general form of the completed linear programming model. There are 78 decision variables and 48 constraints. The objective function at the top of the table represents the value of the net working capital balances held at the end of the planning horizon, t_6. The coefficients, c_{7t}, of variables SP_{7t} and SS_{7t} represent the value of securities held at t_6 that mature beyond the horizon (t_7). The coefficients, b_{7t}, of the borrowing variable, B_{7t}, are the principal plus accrued interest owed at t_6 on debt that matures beyond the end of the planning horizon. The constraints correspond to the expressions we have already developed and shown in their general form. Each type of constraint appears after the heading that identifies it, and the notation in parentheses under the heading (e.g., lines 1–7) relates to the line numbers of these constraints in the LP tableau to be discussed below. The first set of constraints set the initial balances of the marketable securities, the second set limit the security sales not to exceed the securities held at each date, which was explained as expression (8.64). The third and fourth

EXHIBIT 8.16 Cougar Corporation: Objective Function and Constraints in General Form of Linear Programming Model of Working Capital Management Problem

	Variables						
	Cash	*Security Purchases*	*Security Sales*	*Borrowing*	*Constraint limit*	*Range of Indexes*	*Number of Constraints*
Objective Function	C_6	$+\sum_{t=0}^{6} c_{7t} SP_{7t}$	$-\sum_{t=1}^{6} c_{7t} SS_{7t}$	$-\sum_{t=0}^{6} b_{7t} B_{7t}$			
Constraints							
Initial security balance (lines 1–7)		SP_{j0}			$=$ Initial security balance	$j=1, \ldots, 7$	7
Security sales (lines 8–28)		$-\sum_{t=0}^{t-1} SP_{jt}$	$+\sum_{t=1}^{t} SS_{jt}$		≤ 0	$j=t+1, \ldots, 7$ $t=1, \ldots, 6$	20
Initial debt balance (line 29)				B_{50}	$=$ Initial debt balance		1
Borrowing limit (lines 30–35)				$\sum_{i=0}^{t} \sum_{j=i+1}^{7} B_{ji}$	$\leq$ Borrowing limit	$t=1, \ldots, 7$	7
Cash flow (lines 36–41)	$C_t - C_{t-1}$	$-\sum_{j=0}^{t=1} SP_{tj} + \sum_{j=t+1}^{7} a_{jt} SP_{jt}$	$+\sum_{j=1}^{t-1} SS_{tj} - \sum_{j=t+1}^{7} a_{jt} SS_{jt}$	$+\sum_{j=0}^{t-1} b_{tj} B_{tj} - \sum_{j=t+1}^{7} B_{jt}$	$=$ Exogenous net cash flow	$t=1, \ldots, 6$	6
Cash balance (lines 42–48)	C_t				$\geq$ Minimum cash balance	$t=0, \ldots, 6$	7

sets of constraints relate to borrowing—first is the initial debt balance, and second are the limits set on the total borrowing that are imposed by the lenders. The fifth set of constraints are the cash flow constraints corresponding to Expression (8.73) that require the uses of cash to equal the sources of cash. Finally, the cash balance constraints require that the cash balance not be allowed to drop below the minimum level set by management policy.

Exhibit 8.17 is the tableau of coefficients for the LP representing the Cougar Corporation problem. The tableau is shown in four sections for ease of display, with successive sections being a continuation of each line shown in the previous section. The variables are shown across the top in each previous section, and the first line below the variables shows the coefficients in the objective function. The lines labeled 1 through 48 are the constraints. Lines 1–7 are the initial security balances, lines 8–28 are the security sale constraints, line 29 is the initial debt balance, lines 30–35 are the debt limitations, lines 36–41 are the cash flow constraints, and lines 42–48 are the minimum cash balance constraints. Of course, the coefficient 1 refers to a variable multiplied by 1, such as $1 \cdot SP_{71}$. The right-hand-side constants that limit the decisions are shown as the last column of the fourth section.

The Solution

When the LP is solved, the actions recommended to meet the firm's needs over the next six months are a sequence of *security purchases, security sales,* and *borrowing,* as shown in Exhibit 8.18. Exhibit 8.19 shows the cash flows that result from the recommended actions. At each date in the planning horizon, the actions are balanced so the cash remains at the minimum level of $100,000. These actions result in a terminal net value of working capital of $1,472,250, which is larger than would be obtainable from any other feasible strategy. This terminal value consists of account balances as follows:

Cash	$ 100,000
Securities	1,661,340
− Debt	289,090
	$1,472,250.

EXHIBIT 8.17 Cougar Corporation: Tableau of Coefficients for Linear Program

Variable:	C.0	C.1	C.2	C.3	C.4	C.5	C.6	SP.10	SP.20	SP.30	SP.40	SP.50	SP.60	SP.70	SP.21	SP.31	SP.41	SP.51	SP.61	SP.71
Objective Function Coefficients:							1							.9917						.9917
.1								1												
.2									1											
.3										1										
.4											1									
.5												1								
.6													1							
.7														1						
.8									−1											
.9										−1										
.10											−1									
.11												−1								
.12													−1							
.13														−1						
.14										−1						−1				
.15											−1						−1			
.16												−1						−1		
.17													−1						−1	
.18														−1						−1
.19											−1						−1			
.20												−1						−1		
.21													−1						−1	
.22														−1						−1
.23												1						−1		
.24													−1						−1	
.25														−1						−1
.26													−1						−1	
.27														−1						−1
.28														−1						−1
.29																				
.30																				
.31																				
.32																				
.33																				
.34																				
.35																				
.36	−1	1						−1							.9997	.9975	.9919	.9753	.9503	.9419
.37		−1	1						−1						−1					
.38			−1	1						−1						−1				
.39				−1	1						−1						−1			
.40					−1	1						−1						−1		
.41						−1	1						−1						−1	
.42	1																			
.43		1																		
.44			1																	
.45				1																
.46					1															
.47						1														
.48																				

	SP.32	SP.42	SP.52	SP.62	SP.72	SP.43	SP.53	SP.63	SP.73	SP.54	SP.64	SP.74	SP.65	SP.75	SP.76	SS.21	SS.31	SS.41	SS.51	SS.61
					.9917				.9917			.9917		.9917	.9917					
.1																				
.2																				
.3																				
.4																				
.5																				
.6																				
.7																				
.8																1				
.9																	1			
.10																		1		
.11																			1	
.12																				1
.13																				
.14																	1			
.15																		1		
.16																			1	
.17																				1
.18																				
.19		−1																1		
.20			−1																1	
.21				−1																1
.22					−1															
.23			−1				−1												1	
.24				−1				−1												1
.25					−1				−1											
.26				−1				−1			−1									1
.27					−1				−1			−1								
.28					−1				−1			−1		−1						
.29																				
.30																				
.31																				
.32																				
.33																				
.34																				
.35																				
.36																−.9987	−.9965	−.9909	−.9743	−.9493
.37	.9978	.9922	.9756	.9506	.9422											1				
.38	−1					.9944	.9778	.9528	.9444								1			
.39		−1				−1				.9833	.9583	.95						1		
.40			−1				−1			−1			.975	.9667					1	
.41				−1				−1			−1		−1		.9917					1
.42																				
.43																				
.44																				
.45																				
.46																				
.47																				
.48																				

EXHIBIT 8.17 *(concluded)*

	SS.71	SS.32	SS.42	SS.52	SS.62	SS.72	SS.43	SS.53	SS.63	SS.73	SS.54	SS.64	SS.74	SS.65	SS.75	SS.76	B.50	B.21	B.31	B.41
	−.9917					−.9917				−.9917			−.9917		−.9917	−.9917				
.1																				
.2																				
.3																				
.4																				
.5																				
.6																				
.7																				
.8																				
.9																				
.10																				
.11																				
.12																				
.13	1																			
.14		1																		
.15			1																	
.16				1																
.17					1															
.18	1					1														
.19			1				1													
.20				1				1												
.21					1				1											
.22	1					1				1										
.23				1				1			1									
.24					1				1			1								
.25	1					1				1			1							
.26					1				1			1		1						
.27	1					1				1			1		1					
.28	1					1				1			1		1	1				
.29																	1			
.30																	1	1	1	1
.31																	1		1	1
.32																	1			1
.33																	1			
.34																				
.35																				
.36	−.9409																	−1	−1	−1
.37		−.9968	−.9912	−.9746	−.9496	−.9412												1.001		
.38		1					−.9934	−.9768	−.9518	−.9434									1.003	
.39			1				1				−.9823	−.9573	−.949							1.01
.40				1				1			1			−.974	−.9657		1.03			
.41					1				1			1		1		−.9907				
.42																				
.43																				
.44																				
.45																				
.46																				
.47																				
.48																				

	B.51	B.61	B.71	B.32	B.42	B.52	B.62	B.72	B.43	B.53	B.63	B.73	B.54	B.64	B.74	B.65	B.75	B.76		
			−1.061					−1.06				−1.058			−1.051		−1.03	−1		
.1																			=	10
.2																			=	10
.3																			=	120
.4																			=	50
.5																			=	100
.6																			=	250
.7																			=	500
.8																			<=	0
.9																			<=	0
.10																			<=	0
.11																			<=	0
.12																			<=	0
.13																			<=	0
.14																			<=	0
.15																			<=	0
.16																			<=	0
.17																			<=	0
.18																			<=	0
.19																			<=	0
.20																			<=	0
.21																			<=	0
.22																			<=	0
.23																			<=	0
.24																			<=	0
.25																			<=	0
.26																			<=	0
.27																			<=	0
.28																			<=	0
.29																			=	80
.30	1	1	1																<=	500
.31	1	1	1	1	1	1	1	1											<=	500
.32	1	1	1		1	1	1	1	1	1	1	1							<=	500
.33	1	1	1			1	1	1		1	1	1	1	1	1				<=	500
.34		1	1				1	1			1	1		1	1	1	1		<=	500
.35			1					1				1			1		1	1	<=	500
.36	−1	−1	−1																=	200
.37				−1	−1	−1	−1	−1											=	65
.38				1.003					−1	−1	−1	−1							=	−800
.39					1.009				1.007				−1	−1	−1				=	−1300
.40	1.03					1.029				1.027			1.02			−1	−1		=	−400
.41		1.061					1.061				1.058			1.051		1.03		−1	=	1900
.42																			=	900
.43																			>=	100
.44																			>=	100
.45																			>=	100
.46																			>=	100
.47																			>=	100
.48																			>=	100

EXHIBIT 8.18 Cougar Corporation: Optimal Actions Recommended by LP

Period	Decision Variables ($000)		Action
1	SP_{31}	= $ 331.50	Purchase securities to mature at t_3.
	SP_{41}	= 833.35	Purchase securities to mature at t_4.
	B_{61}	= 147.27	Borrow to be repaid at t_6.
2	SP_{32}	= 348.50	Purchase securities to mature at t_3.
	B_{72}	= 272.73	Borrow to be repaid at t_7.
3			
4	SS_{64}	= 250.00	Sell securities that mature at t_6.
	SS_{74}	= 186.86	Sell securities that mature at t_7.
5	SS_{75}	= 313.14	Sell securities that mature at t_7.
	B_{65}	= 80.00	Borrow to be repaid at t_6.
6	SP_{76}	= 1,675.25	Purchase securities to mature at t_7.

Analysis of Results

After constructing and solving the model, we shouldn't stop as soon as we get the solution results. The results should be analyzed and checked. The first step is to organize the results into a format that will help us to assess whether or not they make sense. It is helpful to construct pro forma financial statements based on the model's results so we can check for logical consistency and balance. Do assets equal liabilities? Do sources of funds equal uses of funds? Do the balances of various accounts make sense—for example, are the relative amounts of debt and equity consistent with the firm's desired mix? Are the levels of operating expenses consistent with what you'd expect? The cash flow statement of the Cougar Corporation shown as Exhibit 8.19 helps to determine that the model makes sense: sources in fact do equal uses. If we had found an imbalance, it would indicate that there might be an error in the way the model was constructed or in the data that was fed into the computer software.

A second step in analyzing our results is sensitivity analysis. Sensitivity analysis consists of varying the coefficients and constraints of our model to see how these changes affect the solution. This is important for several reasons, a major one is that both our forecasting ability and our knowledge of the relation-

EXHIBIT 8.19 Cougar Corporation: Cash Flow Resulting from Optimal Solution ($000)

	Period					
Sources of Cash	*1*	*2*	*3*	*4*	*5*	*6*
Exogenous net cash flow	$200.00	$65.00	$800.00	−$1,300.00	−$400.00	$1,900.00
Securities sold				416.65	302.40	
Borrowing	147.27	272.73			80	
Maturing securities	10.00	10.00	800.00	883.35	100.00	
Total	$ 357.27	$347.73	$ 0	$ 0	$ 82.40	$1,900.00
Uses of cash						
Security purchases	$1,157.27	$347.73				$1,661.35
Debt repaid					$ 82.40	$ 238.65
Total	$1,157.27	$347.73	$ 0	$ 0	$ 82.40	$1,900.00
Net cash flow	−$800.00	$ 0	$ 0	$ 0	$ 0	$ 0
Beginning cash	$900.00	$100.00	$100.00	$100.00	$100.00	$100.00
Ending cash	$100.00	$100.00	$100.00	$100.00	$100.00	$100.00

ships portrayed in the model are limited so that there is invariably a lot of error in our estimates of the coefficients and constraints in the model. By varying the coefficients and resolving the model we can see just how sensitive the solution is to variations or errors in these coefficients.

For example, assume we are unsure what the interest rate on borrowing will be in future periods. By varying this borrowing rate and computing a new solution, we can determine how sensitive the optimal decision would be to our error in forecasting the borrowing rate. We initially assumed that funds were borrowed at 12 percent annually. What is the effect on our solution if the rate is as high as 18 percent? Increasing the rate on borrowing requires that the coefficients b_{jt} be changed throughout the model. The old values of the coefficients were shown in Exhibit 8.15, and by recalculating these coefficients and revising the model, we can see whether a higher interest rate will have much influence on our decisions and on the value of the optimal payoff represented by the objective function.

In this particular case, the higher interest rate makes quite a substantial difference. Now, the problem does not have a feasible solution. What this means is that there is no way to solve the problem without violating the constraints. If the interest rate on the borrowing is substantially increased, the firm cannot repay its debts from the funds available from other sources, and without borrowing, it cannot meet the demands for funds in those periods where there are large cash outflows.

This is valuable information. It is important to know what kinds of risk to which the firm is exposed. It is evident here that a substantial increase in interest rates could put the firm in an untenable position, and we need to evaluate the likelihood of rates rising this much, and make contingency plans to handle that threat.

The next step in this sensitivity analysis would be to find out how high interest rates could go and still allow the firm to operate within its constraints. By trying out different rates and solving the LP, we can determine what the firm's actions would be under different scenarios, and how high interest rates could go and still be tolerated.

The dual variables are another source of valuable information for evaluating the results of the LP model. As was explained earlier, there is a dual variable corresponding to each constraint in the LP, and it measures the increment in the optimal value of the objective function resulting from a unit change in the constant amount shown on the right-hand side of the constraint. The dual variable can be interpreted as an opportunity cost. For example, if the amount shown on the right-hand side of the constraint equation happens to represent the amount of a resource that is available to the firm, its dual variable is the opportunity cost or value of that resource, because it measures the amount of our objective (value or profit or whatever) that we give up because we are limited in the amount of that resource that is available. In this sense, then, the dual variable (also called a shadow price) is the marginal value or opportunity cost of that resource in our operation. Suppose the objective function were defined in terms of profit: the dual variable can be interpreted as the maximum amount of profit we could give up to get an additional unit of that resource. If the actual price of the resource were any amount less than this opportunity cost, then we can say we could buy an additional unit and it would increase our profit.

When the constraint is a financial limitation, the dual variables can have a particularly interesting and useful interpretation that relates to the interest rate we can afford to pay. For example, suppose our objective function is defined in terms of the annual rate of profit, and we are evaluating the constraint that limits the amount we can borrow. The dual variable will represent the increment in profit that would result if we were permitted to borrow an additional dollar. If we were to borrow an additional dollar and pay interest expense equal to the value of the dual variable, we would just break even in terms of profit. If our interest expense is anything less than that, our profit will increase. Thus, the dual variable would represent the largest interest expense we could afford to pay, and we can easily translate that into an interest rate.

In a case where the objective is stated in terms of value, as it was in the two-period planning model, similar results apply, but the interpretation is not quite as straightforward. For example, in the Cougar Corporation example of working capital management the objective function was defined in terms of the net value of the working capital accounts at the end of the six-month planning horizon, and there were constraints on the amount that could be borrowed at each date. The dual variable associated with the borrowing constraint for the fourth period was 0.03605. This means that if the firm could have borrowed an additional \$1 at t_4, it would have added \$0.3605 to the value of net working capital at t_6. The length of the period from t_4 to t_6 is 150 days, so the Cougar Corporation could have afforded to pay an interest rate that was 8.6 percentage points ([360/150] × 0.030605) greater than the rate they actually had to pay. This particular dual value would only apply over a range of values for the constraint limitations, so one should not assume it represents a general value that is appropriate for all periods or all situations the firm faces.

SUMMARY

This chapter has introduced you to the ideas and techniques of using linear programming for solving financial planning problems. The advantages of using a constrained optimization technique like linear programming are that it forces the planner to be specific about the objective, to determine the constraints, and to specify the linkages between the decision variables and the objective; and most important, it provides a systematic way to identify the best set of decisions.

The essential features of an LP model for financial planning include the decision variables that represent the amounts or levels of the different decisions that the planner must make, the objective function that expresses mathematically the links between the decisions and the objective, and the constraints that express the various limitations on our decisions.

The constraints in a financial planning model usually include constraints that balance the system and link one period to the next, that express limitations on our access to financing, that represent limitations set by the firm's policies, and others that express accounting definitions or technical relations between variables. The crucial constraints are those that balance the system by requiring assets to equal liabilities, or sources of funds to equal uses of funds. The limitation of access to financing usually refers to limitations on our borrowing when that is one of the decision variables. Without such a limitation, the model will frequently push borrowing beyond what would be considered a prudent limit. Policy constraints take many forms; examples would be dividend payout ratios, target growth rates in earnings and dividends, and cash balance requirements.

If too many constraints are imposed on the model, the problem may not be feasible. That is, there may be no solution that could simultaneously satisfy all the constraints. Consequently, the user should not proliferate constraints unless they are absolutely necessary to model the problem. In fact, the modeler should make every effort to keep the model as simple as possible, with a minimum number of constraints and decision variables. The more complex the model, the more likely that it will confuse the user and have errors in its construction that go undetected.

Any model is simply a guide to decision making, and should not have its results enshrined. The user should constantly be alert for errors and illogical results, and the results should be recalculated as frequently as new information would lead to a revision of the model.

REFERENCES

Bernhard, Richard H. "Mathematical Programming Models for Capital Budgeting—A Survey, Generalization, and Critique." *Journal of Financial and Quantitative Analysis,* June 1969, pp. 111–58.

Carleton, W. "An Analytical Model for Long Range Financial Planning." *Journal of Finance,* May 1970, pp. 291–315.

Carleton, W.; C. L. Dick; and D. H. Downes. "Financial Policy Models: Theory and Practice." *Journal of Financial and Quantitative Analysis,* December 1973, pp. 691–710.

Carleton, W.; G. Kendall, and S. Tandon. "An Application of the Decomposition Principle to the Capital Budgeting Problem in a Decentralized Firm." *Journal of Finance,* June 1974, pp. 815–27.

Charnes, A. and W. Cooper. "Chance Constrained Programming." *Management Science,* October 1959, pp. 73–79.

Charnes, A. A.; W. W. Cooper; and M. H. Miller. "Application of Linear Programming to Financial Budgeting and the Costing of Funds." *Journal of Business,* January 1959, pp. 20–46.

Cohen, K, and F. Hammer. *Analytical Methods in Banking.* Homewood, Ill: Richard D. Irwin, 1966.

Dantzig, G. Linear Programming and Extensions. Princeton, N.J.: Princeton University Press, 1963.

Dorfman, R., P. Samuelson, and R. Solow. *Linear Programming and Economic Analysis.* New York: McGraw-Hill, 1985.

Hadley, George. *Linear Programming.* Reading, Mass: Addison-Wesley Publishing, 1962.

Hillier, F., and G. Lieberman. *Introduction to Operations Research.* San Francisco: Holden-Day, 1967.

Iriji, Y.; F. K. Levy; and R. C. Lyon. "A Linear Programming Model for Budgeting and Financial Planning." *Journal of Accounting Research,* Autumn 1963, pp. 198–212.

Merville, L., and L. Tavis. "Long Range Financial Planning." *Financial Management,* Summer 1974, pp. 56–63.

________. "A Total Real Asset Planning System." *Journal of Financial and Quantitative Analysis,* January 1974, pp. 107–15.

Miller, M., and F. Modigliani. "Dividend Policy, Growth, and the Valuation of Shares." *Journal of Business,* October 1961, pp. 411–33.

MORRIS, J. R. "An Application of the Decomposition Principle to Financial Decision Models." *Journal of Financial and Quantitative Analysis,* March 1975, pp. 37–65.

MYERS, S. "Interactions of Corporate Financing and Investment Decisions—Implications of Capital Budgeting." *Journal of Finance,* March 1974, pp. 1–25.

MYERS, S., and G. POGUE. "A Programming Approach to Corporate Financial Management." *Journal of Finance,* May 1974, pp. 579–99.

NASLUND, B. "A Model of Capital Budgeting under Risk." *Journal of Business,* April 1966, pp. 257–71.

ORGLER, YAIR. *Cash Management: Methods and Models.* Belmont, Calif: Wadsworth Publishing Co., 1970).

———. "An Unequal Period Model for Cash Management Decisions." *Management Science,* October 1969, pp. B77–92.

POGUE, G., and R. BUSSARD. "A Linear Programming Model for Short Term Financial Planning under Uncertainty." *Sloan Management Review,* Spring 1972, pp. 69–98.

ROBICHECK, A. A.; D. TEICHROEW; and J. M. JONES. "Optimal Short Term Financing Decision." *Management Science* 12 (September 1965), pp. 1–36.

SARTORIS, W., and M. SPRUILL. "Goal Programming and Working Capital Management." *Financial Management,* Spring 1974.

WAGNER, HARVEY M. *Principles of Operations Research: With Applications to Managerial Decisions.* Englewood Cliffs, N.J.: Prentice-Hall, 1969.

WEINGARTNER, H. M. *Mathematical Programming and the Analysis of Capital Budgeting Problems.* Chicago: Markham Publishing Co., 1967.

———. "Capital Budgeting of Interrelated Projects: Survey and Synthesis." *Management Science,* March 1966, pp. 485–516.

———. "Criteria for Programming Investment Project Selection." *Journal of Industrial Economics,* November 1966, pp. 65–76.

CHAPTER NINE

Monitoring the Financial Plan

The main focus of this book has been on how we can develop models for financial planning, and the main purpose of any modeling effort is to aid in making decisions to reach our goals. The modeling process itself and the result generated by the model can help us make better decisions to get where we want to go. However, none of this will be of much use unless we periodically check our results to see whether we are on the right track.

Planning a trip is only part of the process of getting where we want to go. After planning the trip and starting out, it is obvious that we need to check our progress as we go. We need to watch the road signs to see if we are still on the right route, how far we are from our destination, and what corrections need to be made to maintain our progress.

Similarly, in implementing our financial plan we need constantly to monitor our progress to see if we are still on our way to our goal, and we need to revise our plan and make the right corrections if we have wandered off course.

That is what this concluding chapter is about—monitoring our progress so that we can stay on the course toward the goal that was prescribed by our planning.

Throughout the book the overall financial objective that has been assumed was maximization of the value of the stockholders' equity. That is, it is assumed that as managers, our job is to make decisions so as to make the owners of the firm as wealthy as possible, subject to the constraints and limitations imposed by resources, regulations, good judgment, and ethics. However, this overall objective is rather vague in terms of day-to-day decisions. We cannot easily observe whether our decision has led to value maximization, and we cannot easily determine our progress toward such a nebulous, intangible, and abstract goal.

In making our plans we usually need to formulate a set of goals that are subordinate to our overall objective and that, when attained, will help us get to the overall objective of value maximization. For example, in capital investment decisions, we say that we want to accept investments with positive net present values, and that this is consistent with value maximization. In this way, the analyst who prepares the project analysis need not know anything about value maximization, he need only know about net present value. Similarly, with respect to financing decisions, we can concern ourselves most directly with minimizing the cost of capital, rather than maximizing value, because this subgoal usually is consistent with maximizing the value of the owners' claims.

Furthermore, in terms of measuring progress toward our goals, these subgoals are too broad. We still need more mundane road signs to watch for to determine if we are still on the right road. Thus, subservient to goals such as net present value and cost of capital should be measures of performance and progress that are easily observed and monitored. Measures such as rates of return, earnings, and variances from budget are examples of observables that can be used as guide for monitoring our progress.

The standards that are set as targets for performance should be set in a way that relates to the broader objectives, and should be set in conjunction with the financial plan itself.

At the time the financial plan is developed, a set of goals and performance measures should also be specified that are consistent with the broader objective and will help measure progress toward the broader objective. After the plan is implemented the firm's performance needs to be compared periodically with the subgoals and performance measures set in the plan. If performance is not on course, corrective actions must be taken, and the plan itself may need to be revised to meet the changing conditions.

For example, in evaluating and planning for a capital investment proposal, we presumably calculated the project's net present value based on a forecast of investment costs, cash flows, and discount rates. These forecasts were, in turn, dependent on our estimates of prices, sales volume, production costs, interest rates, and even stock prices. All of these elements that went into determining whether the project was acceptable in the first place are the same elements that should be monitored throughout the life of the project to see if the project continues to be acceptable, or if we would be better off abandoning it.

Exhibit 9.1 shows the general format for calculating net present value for evaluating an investment project; it also shows the broad categories of forecasted revenues, costs, and so on, that are input to the capital budget and to the calculation of NPV. These are the same items that need to be monitored after the project is implemented to see if it should be continued or abandoned. At each stage the actual costs and revenues must be compared to the budgeted amounts to see if the project is on target. If it is not on target, remedial actions should be taken to put it back on track, and if they don't work, abandonment must be considered.

The targets and standards for evaluation should be set at the time the project is first accepted. The forecasts and data on which its acceptance is based should be used to set standards for subsequent performance evaluation. For example, recall the first investment example introduced in the direct investment evaluation section of Chapter Six. That investment was expected to cost $100,000, was to be financed with $40,000 of borrowed funds and $60,000 of equity, and was forecasted to generate annual sales of $58,000 and annual EBDIT of $20,301 over its 15 year life, as was shown in Exhibit 6.13. Exhibit 9.2 summarizes some of the data that were used to evaluate this investment. Based on the equity investment of $60,000, the cash flow available to equity generates an internal rate of return to equity of about 15 percent, which meets the acceptance criterion that the return must be at least 15 percent. If the cash flows turn out to be less than these forecasted amounts, the project will not earn the required return of 15 percent and it will not turn out to have been worthwhile. Consequently, it is important to monitor the project during its life to ascertain that it is meeting the minimum standard.

EXHIBIT 9.1 Input to the Capital Investment Decision

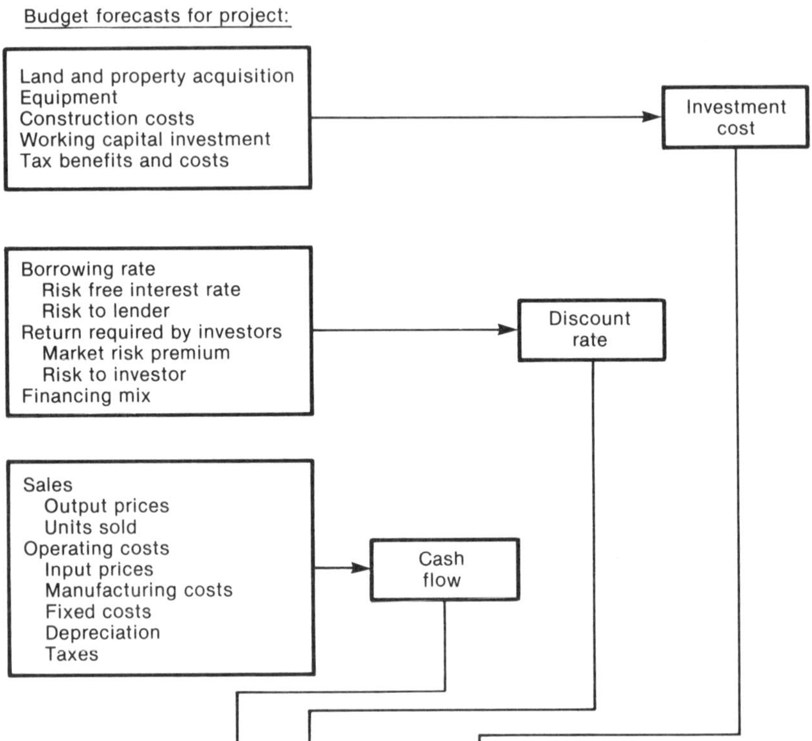

$$NPV = \sum_{t=1}^{n} \left(\begin{matrix}\text{Cash}\\ \text{Flow}\end{matrix}\right)_t (1+k)^{-t} \quad \sum_{t=0}^{n} \left(\begin{matrix}\text{Investment}\\ \text{cost}\end{matrix}\right)_t (1+k)^{-t}$$

One measure commonly used for monitoring performance is the return on investment. However, care must be taken in measuring return on investment and comparing it to the required return, such as 15 percent in this example. The differences between required internal rate of return and return on investment based on accounting data are often misunderstood and consequently these measures may be misused in the monitoring process. For example, what we will call the accounting return on equity is calculated as *Net Income/Equity,* where *Net Income* is the income after taxes reported according to generally accepted accounting principals, and *Equity* is the stockholders' net worth. The accounting return on equity is shown at the bottom of Ex-

EXHIBIT 9.2 Income, Invested Capital, and Rate of Return for Proposed Investment Project

	Period							
	1	*2*	*3*	*4*	*5*	*6*	*7*	*8*
EBDIT	$ 20,301.67	$ 20,301.67	$ 20,301.67	$ 20,301.67	$ 20,301.67	$ 20,301.67	$ 20,301.67	$ 20,301.67
Net Income	5,202.90	5,270.88	5,345.67	5,427.92	5,518.41	5,617.95	5,727.43	5,847.87
Equity Cash Flow	10,610.62	10,552.71	10,489.00	10,418.93	10,341.85	10,257.06	10,163.79	10,061.20
Debt	40,000.00	38,741.05	37,356.20	35,832.87	34,157.21	32,313.98	30,286.42	28,056.12
Equity	60,000.00	54,592.28	49,310.46	44,167.12	39,176.11	34,352.67	29,713.56	25,277.19
Total Capital	100,000.00	93,333.33	86,666.66	79,999.99	73,333.32	66,666.65	59,999.98	53,333.31
Return On Equity	8.67%	9.65%	10.84%	12.29%	14.09%	16.35%	19.28%	23.13%

	Period						
	9	*10*	*11*	*12*	*13*	*14*	*15*
EBDIT	$ 20,301.67	$ 20,301.67	$ 20,301.67	$ 20,301.67	$ 20,301.67	$ 20,301.67	$ 20,301.67
Net Income	5,980.35	6,126.08	6,286.38	6,462.71	6,656.68	6,870.04	7,104.73
Equity Cash Flow	9,948.35	9,824.21	9,687.65	9,537.45	9,372.22	9,190.47	8,990.54
Debt	25,602.78	22,904.10	19,935.56	16,670.17	13,078.23	9,127.11	4,780.86
Equity	21,063.86	17,095.87	13,397.74	9,996.46	6,921.73	4,206.18	1,885.76
Total Capital	46,666.64	39,999.97	33,333.30	26,666.63	19,999.96	13,333.29	6,666.62
Return On Equity	28.39%	35.83%	46.92%	64.65%	96.17%	163.33%	376.76%

hibit 9.2 for each year over the project's life, based on the data forecast for the project. Note that if the project goes according to plan, the accounting return on equity varies from year to year, starting out at 8.7 percent and increasing to over 300 percent by the last year. It increases because the cash flow available to equity is assumed to be paid to the stockholders so that the amount of equity decreases over the life of the project, while the net income is slowly increasing.

The main point is that if the project is evaluated using the accounting return on equity each year, even if the project is on target, in the early years the accounting return on equity could be interpreted as showing that the project is underperforming the target return of 15 percent, and in later years, as far outperforming the target. Obviously, we are measuring two different aspects of performance with internal rate of return and accounting return on investment.

There are many problems with using accounting rates of return to evaluate performance.[1] Nevertheless, these measures are widely used, so if we must use them, we should at least include them in our plan so they will not be used incorrectly. In this case, the plan for the investment project should include a period-by-period specification of the accounting rates of return on investment, such as shown in Exhibit 9.2, that are to be the targets for performance. This will help prevent misinterpretation and incorrect decisions when it is found that the accounting rates of return differ from the required internal rate of return.

At every stage there should be an evaluation of whether the project should be continued. For this purpose, the relevant analysis must concentrate on the *incremental* costs and opportunity costs of continuing the project and the benefits remaining in the project. An important point is that *sunk costs never count*! It does not matter if $5 billion have already been sunk into a project—that is water under the bridge. What matters is that if an additional $1 yet to be invested in the project would not generate benefits equal to $1, so it doesn't pay to invest that

---

[1]An informative discussion of accounting rates of return and their relation to the internal rate of return is presented in Franks, Broyles and Carleton (1985, chap. 11).

$1, and the project should be abandoned. On the other hand, if another billion dollars could be invested to remedy the situation and the benefits of spending this one billion outweigh the costs, then the incremental investment is worthwhile.

We can return to the example of the $100,000 project to see how we might analyze the potential abandonment of a project. Suppose we have undertaken this project and are at the end of the third year in the life of the project. Based on new information about our markets, we find that we must revise downward our forecasts of the *EBDIT* for the remaining 13 years of the project from $20,301 to $15,000 annually, so the overall operating cash flows are revised to be $11,167 per year instead of $14,029 as was shown originally in Exhibit 6.13. Based on this revision of our forecast, we reestimate the present value of the remaining over all cash flows to be $71,951, using the weighted average cost of capital as the discount rate. In addition, using the method of calculation as was shown for the equity approach in Exhibit 6.13, we revise our estimate of the present value of the cash flows to equity to be $38,763.

On the other hand, suppose we can sell the project's assets on the open market for $78,000, from which we would net $42,167 for the stockholders after paying back the remaining balance on the debt. With the revision of the cash flow forecasts, the project is worth more dead than alive because it will generate cash flows that have a present value that is less than what we could realize from the sale of the assets. We could sell the assets and earn a greater cash flow from investing the proceeds elsewhere than we could earn from continuing the project. In essence, we can evaluate the continuation of the project as if it is like any other investment—it has a cost and a benefit and we want to weigh one against the other. The cost of continuing this project is the opportunity cost of forgoing the proceeds from the sale of the assets and the benefit of continuation is the present value of the expected future cash flows. Using the weighted average cost of capital approach with these revised cash flow estimates, the *NPV* of continuing the project is

$$NPV = \$71{,}951 - \$78{,}000 = -\$6{,}049,$$

where the first term is the present value of the cash flows and the second term is the opportunity cost—the amount that could be realized from the sale of the assets. Using the equity approach, the *NPV* is

$$NPV = \$38{,}763 - \$42{,}167 = -\$3{,}404$$

Thus, even though $100,000 has already been invested in the project and continuation of the project does not involve any additional outlay, the project should be discontinued and the asset sold.

For longer-run planning, a useful way of looking at the problem of monitoring and controlling the firm is provided by the field of control theory.[2] One of the concerns of control theory is the guidance of a system along a planned path. For example, consider a space ship traveling through space, subject to random forces and shocks causing it to deviate from its planned path. Assume there are costs associated with controlling the space ship to restore it to the planned path. Given these costs, it is too expensive to control the ship continuously. It makes sense to monitor its progress, and periodically incur the costs of taking remedial actions that will restore it to its path. In this control process the deviation from the path is checked periodically. If the deviation is small, it isn't economical to incur the costs of controlling the ship back to the path, for if many small corrections are made, the costs of control become excessive. It is better to wait until the deviation from the path is large enough to warrant a correction. In this way the costs are incurred less frequently, and the ship is maintained on its path with a series of less frequent but larger corrections. The control-theoretic approach to the problem analyzes the nature of the random disturbances, the costs of control, and derives a set of control policies that maintain the path and also manage the costs of monitoring and taking remedial action.

The firm's long-run financial plan can be viewed as analogous to the space ship's problem. The planning and modeling problem is to determine the best path. The path for the firm is described by the time sequence of investments, financing with

[2]For a more detailed look at control theory applications, see Bensoussan, Hurst, and Naslund (1974), Kamien and Schwartz (1981), Krouse (1972), and Inselbag (1973).

debt and equity, and the payment of dividends, with the objective of making the value of the firm's stock as large as possible. Periodic shocks and disturbances such as changes in interest rates, prices, and competition cause the firm to deviate from its planned path. It is the task of the planner to set up a system of measures that will monitor progress along the path and to provide for taking the necessary corrective actions as they are required. To reach the proper balance of control and costs, it is also necessary to consider the costs of monitoring progress and making the corrections.

The measures that are used for monitoring progress should be readily observable and should relate to the plan. When the plan is first developed, these measures should be described and their target values should be specified. The types of measures that can be used are many of the normal metrics of business performance: rates of return on investment, profit margins, asset turnover, financial leverage, growth rates, price-earnings ratios, and stock prices.

For example, in Chapter Three we discussed the five-year financial plan of the Combex Corporation. The projection of the firm's future financial position was based on a set of assumptions, shown in Exhibit 3.16, including a 20 percent annual growth rate of sales, operating costs that were 87 percent of sales, and many of the balance sheet accounts that were forecasted as a percentage of sales. The validity and success of any plans based on this percent-of-sales approach depends on the continuation of these relationships in future periods, and these relationships should be monitored as time passes to see whether, and how far, the firm is departing from the plan.

One of the decision alternatives considered for Combex was the use of equity financing to meet future needs for external funds. Based on this decision, the return on equity was projected for each year in the five-year planning horizon. As time passes, the realized return on equity should be compared with the value originally projected. Any significant variance from the projected value should be investigated to determine the source of the deviation. Is the profit margin different from that projected? Is the asset turnover too low? Is the sales level much different from the forecast? By examining the results and searching for the source of any important variances, we should

EXHIBIT 9.3 Du Pont Framework for Financial Analysis

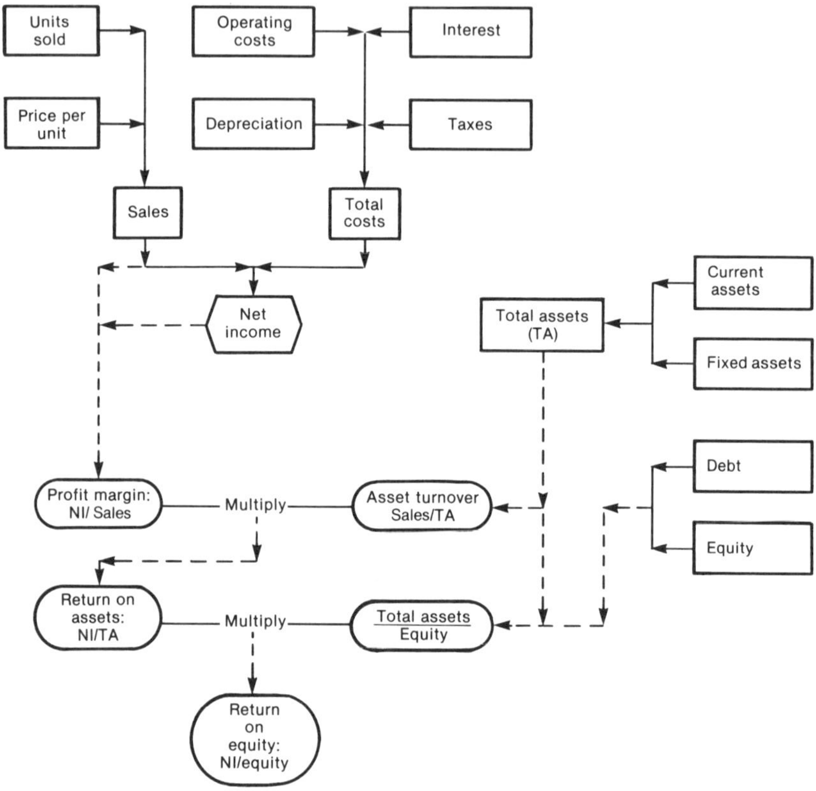

be able to devise some corrective actions that will put the firm back on its planned course—if that is still desired.

As this discussion suggests, in searching for the source of problems and deviations from the plan, it is helpful to decompose the different measures of progress into their components, as is done in a conventional financial analysis. Exhibit 9.3 diagrams the well known Du Pont framework for financial analysis.[3] The point of the Du Pont approach is that return on assets is the product of asset turnover and profit margin, and return on equity is the product of return on assets and the ratio of total

[3]A more thorough explanation of the Du Pont framework is presented in Weston and Copeland (1986, chap. 9) and Johnson and Melicher (1982, chap. 4).

assets to equity. If we are monitoring our firm's progress, and it turns out that the return on equity is below our target, we can work back through this system of relations to pinpoint the source of the problem. We may find that the asset turnover is on target, so that we can turn our attention to the components of the profit margin. By working through these components we can isolate the source of difficulty—perhaps costs, or maybe our price is too low, or the number of units sold is off target.

Because such monitoring is important, it must be considered as an integral part of the financial modeling and planning process. Consequently, when the model is first designed, provision should be made for monitoring the future congruence of plan and reality. At the time of design, the variables that will be monitored should be specified, and the implementation of the plan should have the monitoring function provided for at every step along the way.

REFERENCES

ANTHONY, R. N., and G. A. WELSH. *Fundamentals of Management Accounting.* Homewood, Ill.: Richard D. Irwin, 1974.

BENSOUSSAN, A.; E. G. HURST; and B. NASLUND. *Management Applications of Modern Control Theory.* New York: Elsevier North-Holland, 1974.

BRANCH, B. "The Impact of Operating Decisions on ROI Dynamics." *Financial Management,* Winter 1978, pp. 54–60.

FRANKS, J. R; J. E. BROYLES; and W. T. CARLETON. *Corporate Finance: Concepts and Applications.* Boston: Kent Publishing Company, 1985.

INSELBAG, I. "Financing Decisions and the Theory of the Firm." *Journal of Financial and Quantitative Analysis,* December 1973, pp. 763–76.

JOHNSON, R. W., and R. MELICHER. *Financial Management.* 5th ed. Boston: Allyn & Bacon, 1982.

KAMIEN, M., and N. L. SCHWARTZ. *Dynamic Optimization: The Calculus of Variations and Optimal Control in Economics and Management.* New York: Elsevier North-Holland, 1981.

KROUSE, C. "Optimal Financing and Capital Structure Programs for the Firm." *Journal of Finance,* December 1972, pp. 1057–71.

WESTON, J. F., and T. COPELAND. *Managerial Finance.* 8th ed. Hinsdale, Ill.: Dryden Press, 1986.

INDEX

A

Account balances, aggregated, 86
Accounting module, 148–55
  account balances, 154–55
  aggregative expression, 155
  cash flows, 154
  equations in, 148–50
  equilibrium, making of, 155
  flow between periods, 155
  functional equations, 153
  income statement generation, 150, 153–54
  periods in planning horizon, 152
  receivables, 155
  sectors, connections between, 151–52
  securities, treatment of, 154
  sequential solution, 152
  simultaneity, avoidance of, 152
  sources and uses of funds, 152, 155
  variables, treatment of, 149–50
Accounts payable, 222–24
Accounts receivable
  aggregative equation, 182
  credit collection, 183
  distributed lag relationship, 183
  forecasts, 183–85
  formula, 197
  loans, 184
  as percent of sales, 183–84
  and sales, 182–83
Accrual accounting, and investment evaluation
  accrued revenue, reconciliation of with cash receipts, 218
  cash expenses formula, 217–18
  and cash flows, 215
  cash from sales, 216
  cash receipts formula, 216
  credit sales, 216
Accrual accounting, and investment evaluation—*Cont.*
  and EBDIT, 215–16
  operating cash flow formula, 219
  operating costs, investment project, 217
  prepaid expenses, 217–18
  receivables increase, 216
Assets, valuation of
  cash flow available to pay dividends, 16
  equity securities, 16
  present value of cash flow, risk-adjusted, 16
  risk, adjustment for, 16–17
  stock value maximization, 16–17

B

Balance sheets, 18, 60, 69, 242, 249
Banks
  accounts receivable modeling, 184–85
  cost studies, commercial, 166–67
  reserve requirements on commercial, 11–12
Borrowing
  cash flow, 318–19
  constraint, 250, 319–20
  decision variables, 318, 334
  discount rates, 319
  net present values, 319
  terms added for, 320
  variables in objective function, 319
Breakeven analysis
  cash breakeven sales formula, 46
  contribution margin, 44
  dollar volume of sales breakeven formula, 47
  earnings and sales levels, diagram, 49
  EBDIT formula, 48

Breakeven analysis—*Cont.*
and EBIT, 46
equity capital return, 47–48
and net income, 47–48
operating income, EBDIT, 46
revenue compared to costs, 43
total costs, 43
total costs, 43–44
uses, 42

C

Capital asset pricing model, 254–61
debt financing, 255–56
equity capital costs, 256
equity value, formula, 257
mixed financing, 256
net income, 257
required ROI, 254–55
simultaneity problem, 256–57
stock value as function of financing choice, 257–59
unleveraged financing, 255
Capital rationing, 305–14
acceptance criteria, 306
budget constraint, 309–10
cash flows, 309–10
decision variables, 311
expenses in period, 310
general form of problem, 311
integer programming, 311–13
net present value, writing of, 308–9
portfolio, choice of, 308
summary data, 306–7
Cash balance module, 174–79
cash as balancing account, 176
cash balance, end of period, 175
cash balances adjustment, 178–79
decision rules, 176–77
desired cash, 177–78
flow balancing model, 176
inventory theory, 178
liquid assets, 175
long planning horizon, 175
net cash inflow, 176
stock balancing model, 175–76
total assets, 175
Cash, *See* Cash balance module
Cash flows
accounting, 154
accrual accounting, 215
balance equation, 156

Cash flows—*Cont.*
between periods, 155
borrowing, 318–19
capital rationing, 309–10
cash balance, 176
constraints, 339, 359–61
debt financing, 325–26
equilibrium, 159
equity, 197
financing decisions, 248
future discounts, 321
investment evaluation, 192
lending, 317–18
long-range planning, 331
Monte Carlo simulation, 283–84, 288–90
net present value, 317
over many periods, 289–90
risk adjustment, 288–90
seasonal and monthly, 34
step function, 332–33
time trend, 108–9
unleveraged value of, 322
weighted average cost of capital, 194
working capital, 200
Computers, 5–7
and FORTRAN, 5–6
IFPS, 5–6
mathematical optimization, 6
specialization, 6–7
spreadsheets, software for, 5
statistical packages, 6
Constraints
balancing, 337–38
borrowing, 325, 334
cash flow, 339
dividends, 339–40
industry-specific, 19–20
insolvency risk, 325–26
later periods, 337–38
legal, 22–23
net earnings, 338
period linkings, 337
step function, 331, 333
target financial ratio, 339
technological, 18–19
Contingency plans, 268–69
Current assets and liabilities, linear programming model for management
borrowing variables, 357–59

Current assets and liabilities, linear programming model for management—*Cont.*
cash balance constraint, 353–54
cash flow constraint, 359–61
coefficients, 363–65
decision variables, 349–51
goals, link to decisions, 352–53
model, complete, 361–63
objective, 351–52
planning horizon, 348–49
Cyclic financing needs, *See* Seasonal and monthly financing needs, anticipation of

D

Debt, length of, 169, 225
Debt financing
borrowing decision variables, 322–23
borrowing rate, 323
breakeven, 250
cash flows, 250, 325–26
debt/asset ratio as limit, 324
external needs, 71, 74–75
and investment choice, 322–23
linear programming, 321
weighted average capital cost, 323
Debt financing and sales-driven accounting module
decision parameters, 227
discretionary sources of funds, 228
external financing, 226–27
financing module sector, 226
inputs, 225
interest expenses, 225
length of planning horizon, 228
Decomposition of trends
centered 12-month on one month, 124
chart, 123
cyclic components, isolation of, 127–28
and growth in sales, 125–26
monthly sales, 125–26
seasonal adjustment factors, 123–24, 127
Decision alternatives, 156
Decision, compared to goal, 16–17
Delphi technique, 145
Demand, forecasts of, 20
Depreciation, 169, 212
Discount rates
future, 321
lending, 317
risk-adjusted, 287–88
Discretionary sources of financing, 224–25
Dividends and equity financing
internal financing, net of dividends, 239
maintenance of, 238
payout ratio, 237
as residues from asset investments, 239
retained earnings, 237–38
total spontaneous financing, 237
Du Pont framework for financial analysis, 328–83
Dual variables, 344–46

E

Earnings, elasticity of, 49–50
Earnings per share, 248, 253
EBDIT
accrual accounting, 215–16
breakeven, 48
equity, 197
investment evaluation, 207
spontaneous financing, 220
weighted average cost of capital, 195
working capital, 200
EBIT
breakeven, formula, 46, 48, 54
financing decision, 252
leverage, 50–51
Econometric forecasting models, structural
data for, 131
hypothesis testing, 129–30
least squares linear regression, 130, 132
sales, 129–30
t-statistics, 132
Economy, constraints from, 21–22
Equilibrium in simulation model
cash balance, check on, 159
cash flows for balance of system, flowchart, 159
financing, need for network of, 157
flow, balance equation, 156
investment and financing, simulation flowchart, 158

Equilibrium in simulation model
  cash balance, check on—*Cont.*
  plug variables, 156–57
  short-term working capital operations, 158–59
  stock balancing, 156, 160
Equity approach to investment evaluation
  cash flow, 197
  and EBDIT, 197
  financing, 235
  and net present value, 196
  present value of equity, 197
  return on, 252–54
Equity financing
  equations for, 232
  issue costs, 231
  issue price per share, 231
  risk, 321–23
  stock issue, 230–31

F

Financing decision, case study
  all-debt financing, 249–50
  all-equity financing, 246–47
  asset turnover, 242
  balance sheets, combined debt and equity financing, 249
  cash balance adjustment sector, 245
  combined debt and equity financing, 247
  earnings per share, 253
  EBIT, 252
  financial leverage, degree of, 252–53
  highest present value alternative, 254
  leverage, 249, 251
  net income compared to revenues, 251–52
  objective, 241
  operating costs, 243
  price/earnings ratios, 242, 245–46
  return on equity compared to financing plans, 252, 254
  revenue levels compared to earnings per share, 253
  total revenue, 243
  trial cash flow sheet, 248
Financing decisions, goals of
  management, responsibility of, 14
  and resources of firm, 15
  stockholders' reactions, 14–15
Financing module, 219–20
Financing, planning for
  alternative routes, 12–14
  assets, 11
  constraints, 13–14
  destination choice, 12–14
  detail, 13–14
  long-range planning, 12
  route feasibility, 13–14
  strategic analysis, 12
  time range, 11
Financing, spontaneous, 220–24
  accounts payable, 222–24
  and cash flows, 220–21
  credit purchases, 223
  depreciation, 222
  EBDIT, 220
  lagged variables, 223–24
  long periods, 222
  net profit margin, 222
  payments on account, 223
  percent of sales ratios, 224
  spontaneous income, 223
Fixed assets
  accounting model, 191
  definition of output, 190
  fixed assets, 189
  new investments, 190
  output increase, 188–89
  as resource, 18
  sales decline, 189
  technology of production, 189–90
  unit industry sales, 190
Forecasting accuracy assessment
  confidence compared to length of time, 136
  confidence intervals, 134–35, 137–38
  dependent variable forecast, 136
  random disturbance term, 135
  standard error of forecast, 137
  variables, relationships between, 135
Forecasting, defined, 8
Forecasting methods, quantitative, 105–6
Forecasting, sources of data for, 129

Forecasts
  cost, 165–66
  factors in, 20
  five-year, 162
  general, 21
  receivables, 185
  regional, 21
  sales, 20
  task in, 161–62
Future cash flow discounts, 321

G

Growth, financing needs
  dividend forecasts, 76–77
  external needs, 74–75
  financial ratios, 61
  growth rate, 65–66
  internal equity financing, 63–64
  liability accounts, 63
  pro forma statements, assumptions for, 67
  required external financing, 64
  required investment, 62
  retained earnings, 63
  share price formula, 76–77
  spontaneous financing, 63
  stock price, realism in, 77–78
  total assets required for period sales support, 62
  tradeoffs, 64–65

I

Income generation
  asset categories, 169
  average interest rate method, 170
  cost generation, 163
  costs, forecast for, 167
  depreciation, 169
  fixed cost component, 164
  first-difference regression model, 164–65
  individual debt issues, 170–71
  interest expense, 169–70
  lag, regression equation for, 168
  least squares regression, 164–65
  linear regression model, 164
  price per unit, 161–62
  production costs, 163–69
  production forecast, 167–69
  sales, cyclic, 164–65
  sales model, equations, 161
  short detailed model, 167
Income generation—*Cont.*
  total variable costs compared to number of units, 166
  unit production forecast, 166
  units sold, 161–62
  variables, 161–63, 166
Income statements, 45, 60, 68, 194, 221, 242, 246
  modified, 194
  pro forma, 68
Income stream, expected, 253–54
Industry, structure of, 21
Information from model, 89–90
Inventories, 185–88
  economic order quantity policy, 188
  optimization models, 188
  production, 187
  stock requirement, 186
  variables, tracking of, 186–87
Investment evaluation, example
  accounting policy, 209
  asset sale proceeds, 211
  debt financing, effect on net present value, 214
  depreciation schedule, 210
  EBDIT, 208–9
  economic constraints, 203
  equipment stock, 206
  fixed asset investment, 206
  incremental operating cash flow, 212
  net present value, expressions for, 202, 204–5, 214
  objective, 202
  operating cash flows, 208, 212, 214
  operating costs, 208
  outlays, chart, 207
  planning horizon, 203
  project investment, 206
  technological constraints, 203
  trade payables, 207
  weighted average capital cost, debt, 212
  working capital, 206–8
Investment evaluation, direct
  cash flow, 192
  cost, 192
  decision criteria, 192
  net present value method, 192
  rate of return, 192
Investment module, 172–74

Investment module—*Cont.*
  adjustment to sales approach, 172–75
  asset category, required stock of, 173
  assets compared to sales, time series linear regression, 173
  investment as driving force, 172
  lagged relationships, 173–74
  long planning horizon, 174
  passive response, 172
  percent of sales model, 173
  required assets, change of between periods, 173
Investment as perpetuity, 327
Investment schedule, generalized
  decreased ROR, expressions for, 328
  investment decision variables, 327
  marginal return, stepwise decline of, 327–28
  and net present value, 327
  return compared to amount invested, 326–27

L

Labor as constraint, 19
Lags
  accounts receivable, 183
  distributed relationship, 97, 183
  financing decision, 249, 251–53
  investment module, 123–24
  regression equation, 168
  spontaneous financing, 223–24
Least squares
  income generation, 164–65
  linear regression, 130, 132
  time trend, 109–10
Legal environment, problems with, 22–23
Lenders, flows to, 193
Lending and linear programming
  borrowing rate, 317
  cash outflows, 317–18
  constraints, 317
  decision variables for, 316–17
  discount rate, 317
  fund transfer in time, 316
  and net present value of cash flow, 317
  noninteger values, 318
  and objective function, 317
Leverage
  and EBIT, 50–51
  elasticity of earnings compared to sales, 49
  interest payment, 50
  leveraged cash flow values, 322
  operating, 50
  present value of income stream, 52
  variable-cost method, 50
Leverage, corporate example
  developmental costs, 53
  EBIT breakeven, 54
  loss, chance of, 56–57
  manufacturing phases, 53
  and net present value, 57
  profit forecast, 55–56
  recurring costs, 53–54
  revenues, 53
  revenues and costs diagram, 55
  sales probability, 56–57
  time value of money, 57–58
  total cost of production, 54
  total variable costs, 54
Liabilities, constraint, 18
Limited budget, *See* Capital rationing
Linear programming
  borrowing, 300
  on computer, 302
  constraint equations, 300
  decision variables, 299–300
  general form, 301–2
  investment problem, 302
  linearity, 302–3
  objective function, 300
  problem in mathematical form, 301
  simplex algorithm, 301
  subscripts, 301
Linear programming models for financial planning
  constraints, 304
  investment projects, 304
  net cost minimization over year, 303–4
Liquid asset as resource, 18
Long-range planning model
  after-tax debt cost, 329
  cash flows, 331
  equity variable in objective function, 335
  flotation cost, 335

Long-range planning model—*Cont.*
  funds for dividends, 336
  investment decision variables, 33
  net present value, 331
  objective, 330–31
  optimal values, 341
  perpetual annual cash flow, 331
  planning horizon, 329–30
  raising equity capital, 335–36
  sources and uses of funds, 343
  table of coefficients, 342
  transaction costs, 335
  two-year model, 329
  valuation expression, 336

M

Management as constraint, 19
Mean forecast error, 134
Mean square error, 133–34
Model, development of
  congruence between model and data, 96
  constraints, 92–93
  data input, 95
  decision alternatives, 91
  decisions, linkages to goals, 94
  detail needed, 90
  distributed lag relationship, 97
  evaluation of information, 89–90
  external data, 96–97
  future forecasts, 97–98
  goal choice, 94
  importance of problem, 89
  problem definition, 88
  structure input, 90–91
  system, current state of, 95–96
  time horizon of problem, 88–89
  time path of firm, 96
  variables, relationships between, 97
  who uses information, 90
Model, nature of
  decision variable, 82
  demand function, 82
  individual operating decisions, 85
  managerial benefits of, 86
  objective maximization, 82
  parameters, 82–83
  periods in planning horizon, 84
  revenue as function of unit price, 83
  tasks in making, 83
Model, nature of—*Cont.*
  total revenue, 82
Model, optimization of
  constraints, 103
  decision variables, 102–3
  objective function, 102
Model, simulation, 98–102
  decision set, 99
  excess output problem, 101
  financial statement comparisons, 101
  input, 99–100
  as link to results, 99
  number of choices compared to numbers of values and variables, 102
  and objective function, 101
Monte Carlo simulation
  cash proportion as normal distributed variable, 276–77
  collection variables, 279–80
  credit sales, 279
  expected collections, 282
  random drawings, 277, 280
  random variables, assessment of, 279
  receivable collection, 278
Monte Carlo simulation and net present value
  cash flow scenarios, 283–84
  draws from distributions, 284–85
  frequency histograms, 286
  net present value, range, 285
Monthly needs, *See* Seasonal and monthly financing needs, anticipation of

N

Net present value
  borrowing, 319
  capital rationing, 308–9
  of cash flow, 317
  equity, 196
  expressions, 202, 204–5, 214
  investment evaluation, 192
  investment schedule, 327
  leverage, 57
  long-range planning, 335
Nonlinear programming, 298
Nonlinearity, conditions for, 303

O

Opinion surveys, 145
Optimization
  bulk of data, 294–95
  calculus techniques, 296
  constrained, 298
  of decision variable, 295
  derivatives, 296
  objective function, 298
  pricing problem, 298
  search procedure, 295–96
  total revenue as function of unit price, 297

P

Plan, monitoring of
  abandonment of project, 379–80
  capital investment decision, input for, 376
  continuance of project, 378–79
  returns, 376–78
Planning
  alternative routes, 9
  benefits of, 26–27
  certainty, 9
  constraints, 9
  decision, compared to objective, 10–11
  destination, choice of, 10
  establishment of entity as, 8
  and forecasting, 8
  greater will for, 4
  market value maximization criteria, 10
  progress criteria evaluation, 10
Planning horizon
  cross-sectional detail, 25
  detail, control of amount, 25
  detail in final plan, 24–25
  excess detail, 24
  extension method of finding limit, 26
  growth trends, 25–26
  and problem, nature of, 23–24
  proper length of, 24
  reasonable choice, 25
  subperiods, 24–25
  time series detail, 25
Political constraints, 22–23
Present value
  of equity, 197
Present value—*Cont.*
  of income stream, 52
  of risk-adjusted discount rate, comparison to, 290
  of risky amount, 290
Production technology as constraint, 18–19
Products mix, 19
Project
  contingent, and linear programming, 315–16
  costs of, 195, 378–79
  mutually exclusive, and linear programming, 314–15
  persistence with, 378–79

R

Rate of return (ROR)
  decreased, 32
  investment evaluation, 192
Regression
  assessment of results, 114–16
  coefficient of variation, 114
  mean square error, 114
  root mean square error, 114–15
Resources, types of, 17–18
Risk adjustment and Monte Carlo simulation
  capital asset pricing model, 291
  cash flow distribution, 288–90
  discount rate, setting of, 290–91
  present value compared to risk-adjusted discount rate, 290
  present value of risky amount, 289
  required return on investment, formula, 291
  risk premium, formula, 291
  risk-adjusted discount, 287–88
  risk-adjusted present value of cash flow, formula, 289
Risk, nature of, 3–4

S

Sales driven accounting module, 148–49
Sales
  cyclic, 164–65
  equations, 161
  elasticity of, 149
  forecasts of, 132–33
Scenario simulation, 269–75

Scenario simulation—*Cont.*
cash receipts and disbursements, 271, 273–74
financing needs, range of, 272
receivables collection, 270, 272
Seasonal and monthly financing needs, anticipation of
assumptions for budget development, 31
bad debt, omission of, 34
cumulative cash item, 34
cumulative required financing, 34–35
financing costs, 34
forecasting, 37
interest on borrowed funds, 39
month-by-month funding needs, 35
month-end cash balance, 34
net cash flow, 34
noncash expenses, absence of, 34
planning horizon choice, 36–37
receipts and disbursements, example, 32–33
receivables collection speedup, 39–41
repayment of loans, 35
required funding time profile, 36
revised cash budget, 38
value maximization, 37
Securities
accounting about, 154
classes of holders of, 192–93
decision variables about, 354–57
equity, 16
issue price, 231
Securities, marketable
face values, 181
market values, 181–82
model, 180
percent of assets, 180
percent of sales, 180
short-term equations, 181
Shadow prices, *See* Dual variables
Software, financial, 110, 139, 312
Stock, common, 231, 257, 290
Stock value, dividend method
constant-growth model, 234
finite horizon evaluation, 234
net income, 235
number of shares outstanding, division by, 235
Stock value, dividend method—*Cont.*
present value of dividends, 234
Stock value, formula, 336
Stock value, price/earnings model
issue price, 231
simultaneity problem, 233
simultaneous variables, use of, 233
Subjective forecasting, 144
Supply sources, 19

T

Taxation, 171–72, 194, 322
Time series models
analysis, 139
autoregressive procedures, 140–41
autoregressive-moving average procedures, 142
combined model, 143
lags, choice of length, 142–43
moving average procedures, 141
procedures isolated in, 139–40
sales forecasts, 142–43
turning points, 143
Time trend, exponential smoothing, 120–22
sales forecast, 120
Time trend, extrapolation, 106–8
arithmetical growth rate, 106–7
geometrical growth rate, 107
percent change, 106–7
short-term forecasts, 108
Time trend with linear extrapolation, 108–15
actual vs. predicted sales, 112
cash flows, 108–9
constant-change model, 108–12
constant-growth model, 112–13
continuous-growth model, 113
deviations from line, 109–10
deviations term, 108–9
future forecasting, 110–12
least squares, 109–10
logarithmic formula, 113
regression line, 110–11
sales, formula, 108–9
Time trend, smoothing of
errors, 118
mean square forecast error, 118
moving averages, 115–19
number of periods for calculation, 119

Time trend, smoothing of—*Cont.*
 root mean square forecast error, 118–19
 sales forecast, 116
 simple type, 115
 smoothing effect, 117
 variable without trend, 119

U–V

Uncertainty, dealing with, 267–69
Unexpected events, preparation for, 22
Valuation, 16

W

Weighted average cost of capital
 by alternatives, 261
 cash flow for, 194
 debt, 212
 evaluation of investment, 192–96
 formula, 260
 and net present value, 195–96
Working capital in investment evaluation
 cash flow, 200–1
 and EBDIT, 200–1
 factors in investment project, 200
 inventory changes, 200–1
 inventory, purchases and sales in, 201